Some White Folks

Chicago Studies in American Politics

A SERIES EDITED BY SUSAN HERBST, LAWRENCE R. JACOBS, ADAM J. BERINSKY, AND FRANCES LEE;

BENJAMIN I. PAGE, EDITOR EMERITUS

Additional series titles follow index

Some White Folks

The Interracial Politics of
Sympathy, Suffering, and Solidarity

JENNIFER CHUDY

THE UNIVERSITY OF CHICAGO PRESS   CHICAGO AND LONDON

The University of Chicago Press, Chicago 60637
The University of Chicago Press, Ltd., London
© 2024 by The University of Chicago
Published 2024
Printed in the United States of America

33 32 31 30 29 28 27 26 25 24   1 2 3 4 5

ISBN-13: 978-0-226-83441-2 (cloth)
ISBN-13: 978-0-226-83443-6 (paper)
ISBN-13: 978-0-226-83442-9 (e-book)
DOI: https://doi.org/10.7208/chicago/9780226834429.001.0001

Library of Congress Cataloging-in-Publication Data

Names: Chudy, Jennifer, author.
Title: Some white folks : the interracial politics of sympathy, suffering,
    and solidarity / Jennifer Chudy.
Other titles: Interracial politics of sympathy, suffering, and solidarity |
    Chicago studies in American politics.
Description: Chicago : The University of Chicago Press, 2024. | Series: Chicago studies in
    American politics | Includes bibliographical references and index.
Identifiers: LCCN 2023056421 | ISBN 9780226834412 (cloth) | ISBN 9780226834436 (paperback) |
    ISBN 9780226834429 (ebook)
Subjects: LCSH: Racial justice—United States. | White people—United States—Attitudes. |
    United States—Race relations.
Classification: LCC E185 .C526 2024 | DDC 305.800973—dc23/eng/20231214
LC record available at https://lccn.loc.gov/2023056421

♾ This paper meets the requirements of ANSI/NISO Z39.48-1992 (Permanence of Paper).

TO SOME LITTLE MULTIRACIAL FOLKS, YUNA
AND MINA, AND THEIR FATHER, NITIN.

There's no doubt that there's some folks who just really dislike me because they don't like the idea of a black President. Now, the flip side of it is there are some black folks and maybe some white folks who really like me and give me the benefit of the doubt precisely because I'm a black President.

PRESIDENT BARACK OBAMA, 2014

Contents

CHAPTER ONE

Introduction

An Underexplored Force in American Racial Politics

There is racial inequality in America, and some people are distressed over it, while others are not. This is a book about the white Americans who are. More specifically, this book focuses on white racial sympathy over Black Americans' suffering and its consequences for modern American politics. Reversing course from a long tradition of studying the powerful and pernicious effect of prejudice, this book considers the other side of the coin: the possibility that some white people are distressed over Black suffering and that this racial sympathy carries important political consequences.[1]

The experience of Black people in America is not reducible to a single characterization; the full range of Black humanity includes joy, pain, humor, resilience, longing, and more.[2] Yet this is a book about American politics, and within this specific domain, Black Americans' suffering is a salient feature. This is because the country's political institutions and actors have built a political system in which Black Americans consistently fare worse than white Americans, sometimes with fatal consequences. This racial gap has been designated the "divide without peer" (Kinder and Sanders 1996). Black children attend worse schools. They come from families who live in worse neighborhoods and have fewer opportunities to leave. They access worse-quality health care, which contributes to higher mortality rates, and so on. Black Americans experience unique disadvantages in American society.[3]

Such inequality is not limited to the present day; it has been institutionalized and has been pervasive since the start of the American experiment

(Dahl 2003). Even Alexis de Tocqueville, who believed Americans' "passion for equality is ardent, insatiable, eternal and invincible," acknowledged the country's deeply entrenched racial inequality (Stokes 1990). Slavery was, according to Tocqueville, an "odious institution" impressing a "fatal influence" on the young country. He made a bleak projection: "I do not think that the white race and the black race will come to live on a footing of equality" (2000, 341), a prescient observation that has, for the most part, borne out.

Black suffering is, therefore, present and historical. It exists in plain view even in a country where "apartheid" levels of housing segregation shield white Americans from daily exposure to it (Massey 1990). Therefore, even if suffering represents only one dimension of Black Americans' experience, it is an important one. Its durability and ubiquity have attracted the attention of many, including scholars like myself. And for years, scholars have sought to identify the multiple causes of this suffering, including white people's racial prejudice. Social science researchers dedicate considerable effort to understanding white Americans' racial attitudes because these attitudes can generate and sustain inequality.

This work has produced an impressive and deep canon on racial prejudice. Its lineage can be traced to the aftermath of World War II, when groundbreaking work in social psychology sought to understand the destructive forces behind Nazism. Prejudice arises out of conditions of inequality (Kinder 2013) and often comes with devasting consequences, starting with, according to Gordon Allport (1954), "antilocution" and ending with extermination.[4] Given its prevalence and power, it seems sensible to reduce the study of out-group attitudes to this one: prejudice.

However sensible, scholars' focus on prejudice has rendered an incomplete understanding of white racial attitudes. Consider the following examples. In 2020, white residents of a small Colorado town gathered for a racial justice candlelight vigil timed with the majesty of a desert sunset (Muller 2020). The vigil was in honor of George Floyd, a Black man killed by a white Minneapolis police officer in May of that year. Around the same time, a radio show based out of Fargo, North Dakota, featured an interview with a white man who noted that Floyd's death made people "extremely frustrated. 'Kid like me from South Dakota could never imagine otherwise. We're gonna see more people speak up and that's what we gotta have, period'" (Cramer 2021, 23).

When Barack Hussein Obama ran for president, many white Americans supported him with exuberance, with some even going so far as adopting his middle name as their own in a show of solidarity (Kantor 2008). Although he lost the white vote, pictures from his election night show white people responding to his victory with euphoric celebration and tears of joy.[5] In local politics, the city of Seattle voluntarily adopted a decades-long experiment with mandatory busing to integrate its schools in the 1970s. This policy was promoted by a coalition of city leaders, including the majority white school board. In Los Angeles, white Americans were crucial in spearheading Tom Bradley's campaign to become the city's first Black mayor (Sonenshein 1993).

And if we go back further, we find traces of attitudes akin to racial sympathy. Since this country's establishment as a republic, white people have lined up both in opposition and in support of the many policies that affect Black Americans. In the early 1830s, for example, abolitionist ideas became increasingly prominent among whites in Northern churches and politics, contributing to a regional animosity between North and South in the lead-up to the Civil War (Castiglia 2002). Following the Civil War, the Populist Party started an agrarian movement on a platform that merged poor African Americans' and white farmers' common economic interests against those of the white Democratic Party elite in the South (Woodward 1938). Decades later, white clergy leaders Orloff Miller, Clark Olsen, and James Reeb traveled to Selma, Alabama, to support civil rights campaigns. Once there, they were met by a violent mob of white men opposed to their work. Reeb later died from injuries related to the attack.[6]

What do we make of these outcomes? We do not know why white people would behave this way or what would compel them to support a range of policies or political outcomes that bring no obvious material benefit to their group. We do not know the emotions and origins of this concept, nor do we have the tools to study it. We do not know who these white Americans are. We do not understand the nature of their racial sympathy or its political effects. This book attempts to fill this void.

Racial Sympathy and American Politics

In a country that has been "scarred from the beginning by a largely impermeable Black-White color line" (Sears 2008, 133) and where "the burden of slavery and discrimination that blacks have borne in America is a uniquely oppressive burden" (Sniderman and Piazza 1993, 80), when some white people think about Black Americans, racial sympathy surfaces in an

enduring and meaningful way. The most sympathetic white people are se-
verely distressed about Black suffering, which they perceive as widespread
and serious, and the least sympathetic are indifferent to Black suffering,
which they perceive as negligible. Between these two extremes lie most
white Americans.

Racial sympathy could impact many areas of a white person's life: the
people they befriend, the careers they pursue, the neighborhoods they in-
habit, and the charities they sponsor could all, in principle, be shaped by
this unique racial attitude. In *Some White Folks*, I argue that racial sympathy also influences white Americans' politics. Indeed, most white Americans do not interact with Black people on a day-to-day basis, and when
they do, these interactions are often brief and superficial (Sigelman et al.
1996). Politics is, therefore, one of the few venues in which white people
can express and exercise racial sympathy.

And they do. In this book, I argue that racial sympathy, defined as
white Americans' distress over Black Americans' suffering, has important
political consequences. Racial sympathy, which I occasionally abbreviate
to *sympathy*, can shape white Americans' political opinions on an impressive range of public policies, from the social welfare state to the criminal
justice system. Under certain circumstances, racial sympathy can influence
their political behaviors, too. It is a genuine and distinct racial attitude
with broad implications. This book shows that racial sympathy matters in
American politics.

This book reveals the range of racial sympathy's influence and illustrates how this attitude differs from others. A long line of scholarship has
established the political importance of group-based attitudes. Some of this
work has considered the possibility of an attitude akin to sympathy, exploring topics like empathy and guilt. Much of it is oriented toward studying the political consequences of a quite different attitude: prejudice. I
reference these psychological concepts throughout this book to highlight
the similarities and differences between this and the existing racial attitudes literature.

This context is valuable, but this book is centered on racial sympathy.
Accordingly, I develop an account of the origins of racial sympathy and
explain how white Americans' emotional reactions to Black suffering become lodged in their political attitudes. I create a new measure specifically
designed to reflect this distinct attitude. I demonstrate the consistent and
robust relationship between racial sympathy and various political outcomes
using this new measure. I also show how sympathy differs from other con-

cepts, such as low prejudice, theoretically and empirically. *Some White Folks* challenges conventional wisdom on the nature, measurement, and role of racial attitudes. It also provides a framework for thinking about important political outcomes, such as white support for Black Lives Matter (BLM).

The surveys I consult in this book offer a broad—in some cases nationally representative—snapshot of sympathy. The analyses we can conduct on big samples, such as those collected by national surveys, help us grasp how racial sympathy could impact historic large-scale political phenomena, like presidential elections or protest activity. I complement these analyses with survey experiments, which permit us to assess questions related to cause and effect. Through these exercises, we understand what conditions turn sympathy on and off.

Sympathy can be observed outside of surveys, too, and in some parts of the book, I draw on insights I learned by listening to and speaking with white people about their racial sympathy. Through their stories, I discovered sides of sympathy I had not anticipated, enriching my understanding of this complicated and important topic. If the quantitative studies permit me to understand the prevalence of sympathy, the qualitative work reveals the microlevel thought processes and emotions behind the attitude. I occasionally alternate between qualitative and quantitative evidence to probe racial sympathy across different levels of generalizability and depth.

I embark on this inquiry equipped with studies spanning diverse periods and requiring distinct methodological tools; despite this variety, the findings largely converge in the following ways. First, racial sympathy is not simply the opposite or absence of prejudice or a catchall sympathy for any marginalized group; instead, it is a concept uniquely centered on Black misfortune. Second, racial sympathy matters for public opinion. It is consistently associated with white Americans' opinions on a wide range of issues that expand the government, in the case of redistributive policies. But on other occasions, it leads white people to support efforts to reign in the government's reach, as in the case of policies related to the criminal legal system. Finally, racial sympathy can also shape political behaviors, such as protesting. However, transmitting sympathy from attitude to behavior often requires other conditions. I explore two pathways to action in this book—efficacy and mobilization. These forces can help launch sympathy into politics, but they are likely not the only ones. In the conclusion, I discuss other key conditions and offer suggestions for future research.

Some White Folks is a study of American politics. And for several reasons, when I use the term *racial sympathy*, I am referring specifically to white Americans' distress over Black Americans' suffering. A racially sympathetic white American could also hold sympathetic feelings for Latino, Asian, multiracial, and Indigenous Americans, and these attitudes could influence opinion on immigration or access to the Dakota Access Pipeline, for example. This is plausible; however, since the Black/white divide represents the United States' most salient racial cleavage, this iteration of racial sympathy is the focus of this book (Hutchings and Valentino 2004).

Given the breadth of Black suffering, non-white groups could also be distressed over it and carry this attitude into their politics. In the case of the Black Lives Matter movement, for example, research on Latino Americans' opinions has found that once group members are informed about BLM, they exhibit a generally supportive stance toward the movement (Corral 2020). Other work has found that Asian Americans who acknowledge anti-Black racism are more likely to support BLM (Merseth 2020; Yellow Horse et al. 2021). Relatedly, journalists have documented intergroup support in their coverage of protests following Floyd's murder.[7] For example, an article covering Native solidarity with BLM describes how "many Indigenous-led organizations are expressing solidarity and committing to the movement, citing the ways in which 'Indigenous Sovereignty and Black Liberation go hand in hand.' "[8] As a group, multiracial people have diverse racial backgrounds, presenting challenges for detecting generalizable trends. Despite this, research has found that multiracials tend to carry liberal social attitudes (Davenport 2018; Davenport, Franco, and Iyengar 2022; Masuoka 2008). Some multiracial people may exhibit attitudes akin to sympathy, which could impact their politics.

The foregoing suggests that attitudes like sympathy could exist in these populations. These groups could be compelled to participate in protest activity or support policy efforts to mitigate racial inequality because they are distressed over Black suffering and want to do something about it. However, they may be inclined to do so for reasons quite distinct from why white people pursue these efforts. For example, self-identification with many of the groups listed earlier does not preclude Black self-identification. Approximately 12 percent of Latinos identify as Afro-Latinos, according to a May 2022 Pew Report on the group.[9] Many people identify as Black- or Afro-Indigenous.[10] The 2020 census found that approximately four million multiracial Americans identify part of their racial background as Black.[11] To the extent that these individuals are distressed over Black suffering, it could be related to their group attachment or lived experiences that might include suffering. As I discuss in the book, this is quite different from how white Americans come to form out-group attitudes such as racial sympathy.

Of course, many other people of color do not identify as Black. They may learn about Black suffering the same way white Americans encounter it—perhaps at home, or in their neighborhoods or schools, or from the news. But similar exposure does not guarantee a similar psychological reaction. After all, as members of non-white racial groups, many people of color have experienced discrimination firsthand to varying degrees. To take just one example, one of the articles covering the summer 2020 protests described how Asian Americans' support of BLM was related, in part, to reactions to the string of anti-Asian hate crimes. One interviewee commented on this cross-racial coalition building, noting, "Obviously both communities have similar issues, particularly in confronting white supremacy."[12]

White Americans' experiences and opportunities vary a great deal; I do not mean to suggest that everyone in the group lives a carefree life or has never encountered a setback.[13] For the most part, however, white people, as a group, are not disproportionately impacted by racially motivated hate crimes or fatal mistreatment at the hands of the police (Zhang, Zhang, and Benton 2022).[14] The same racial status that insulates them from these nefarious forces also supplies them with important political power and influence. Most people of color do not occupy this uniquely privileged position. Thus, even if they are distressed over Black suffering, they also carry with it their own experience with or proximity to racial disadvantage. This empathetic dimension makes the nature of their sympathy different from that of white Americans'. This important topic warrants scholars' attention as the country becomes more racially diverse, and I return to it in the conclusion. For now, it should be clear that white distress over Black suffering is distinct, defined in part by the "peculiar institution" of slavery and also the axes of racial power in the United States (Kim 2000, 9).

Why Does It Matter?

Books and articles about white racial attitudes are usually about a specific one: white racial prejudice. Indeed, scholars often use the term *racial attitudes* as a synonym for racial prejudice.[15] This attention is reasonable; the pernicious attitude is widespread and influential. For this reason, authors, artists, journalists, and ordinary people have sought to make sense of America's "scar of race" for centuries (Sniderman and Piazza 1993).

The stakes of prejudice are high. Why, then, embark on a study of sympathy? This book began with the proclamation that racial inequality exists in the United States. Isn't this evidence that racial sympathy must not matter very much?

These are important questions. However, the stakes of sympathy could also be high. The research in this book demonstrates that sympathy can be activated under certain circumstances. My experimental results show that when racially sympathetic white Americans encounter Black suffering, their sympathy is turned on and spills into their political judgments and opinions. They produce this reaction not because they lack prejudice but because *they possess* sympathy. This suggests that in addition to our many commendable efforts to reduce the effects of prejudice (see Paluck et al. 2021), we might also consider ways to increase the influence of sympathy.

Racial sympathy can flow not only into white people's opinions but also into their political behaviors. Under some circumstances, higher levels of racial sympathy correspond with an increased likelihood to protest, for example. And if white people take their sympathy to the streets, participating in demonstrations like those we witnessed in the summer of 2020, elites may pay attention. In some cases, they may also be responsive to these demands.[16] Outside of protest, racial sympathy can also map onto more conventional political behaviors, such as volunteering in a campaign or contributing to a candidate. Another reason to study sympathy is to understand the sources of this citizen engagement, which could lead to cross-racial coalition building.

The country's demographics are changing. The 2020 electorate was the most diverse in American history.[17] Projections suggest that white Americans will eventually be displaced as the majority racial group. With these trends afoot, why study this racial group? First, white Americans still constitute the country's largest racial group, so for the moment, their attitudes and opinions play a considerable role in democratic processes; this is unlikely to change soon, even with the transformation of the electorate. Relative to other racial groups, white Americans will likely enjoy positions of economic and political power into the foreseeable future, exercising considerable influence in American politics (Fraga 2018; Jardina 2019). Even as other groups rightfully deserve our attention, it is for this reason that political researchers continue to study white people. Expanding our knowledge of this group strengthens our understanding of future political outcomes.

Further, at various moments in American history, many white people have perpetuated—or, at a minimum, benefited from—a system that privileges their group while disadvantaging Black Americans. Some white people have worked assiduously to dismantle this system. Others register their disapproval in no uncertain terms, and I discuss these people in more detail in the next chapter. However, others do not take this course, and many vehemently rebuff any culpability. A sense of responsibility is not a requirement of racial sympathy, and I explore this when I contrast sympathy with guilt. In all cases, however, studying white Americans shows us how higher-status groups understand their position vis-à-vis other groups and if there are circumstances that lead to reparation.

For all of these reasons, white racial sympathy for Black Americans' suffering warrants inquiry. *Some White Folks* challenges our understanding of racial attitudes, an important topic with a venerable intellectual history. But the book also provides insight into the psychology of advancing racial equality. As long as the "divide without peer" shows no signs of abating, it is important to learn about racial sympathy and its political consequences.

Looking Ahead

Reversing course from a long tradition of studying prejudice, this book illustrates that nontrivial proportions of white Americans are distressed over Black suffering and that this racial sympathy has important political consequences. Racial sympathy is not interchangeable with low prejudice or equivalent to a broader social sympathy for any marginalized group. Instead, racial sympathy is a powerful *racial* attitude centered around the unique history of Black-white race relations. As such, it is not captured by existing research and is worthy of its own examination. In *Some White Folks*, I bring together a range of disciplines and methods to do just this. The breadth of the enterprise is to ensure that the relationship between sympathy and American politics is durable across datasets, specifications, methods, and time. Before proceeding, I offer some guideposts for where we are headed.

The next chapter introduces racial sympathy. In the first section, I locate the project historically and intellectually. I start by discussing past occasions in which white Americans have professed support for Black Americans in politics. I then summarize racial attitudes literature and highlight the few occasions this scholarship has acknowledged the possibility of racial sympathy. Much of this work is based on the foundational scholarship that established group-based attitudes' central role in American public opinion. I define racial sympathy and speculate on its origins. I discuss sympathy's relationship to politics, considering why sympathy might map onto opinion and when we might observe its effects on white people's behaviors.

Most research on white racial attitudes revolves around prejudice. One of the main contributions of this book is to demonstrate that racial sympathy is distinct from its more famous sibling. I attend to this throughout the book but identify the conceptual similarities and differences between racial animus and racial sympathy in this chapter. This theorizing leads to several expectations for the book's empirical chapters, which are identified at the end of chapter 2.

Chapter 3 takes up the measurement of racial sympathy. Here, I consider previous efforts to measure the concept and evaluate their strengths and weaknesses. I pay special attention to the possibility that racial sympathy may be substantively and functionally equivalent to low prejudice. I also detail the qualitative research I conducted to understand the concept better, beginning with a series of participant observation sessions. These sessions, of which I provide excerpts, inspired the creation of a survey measure—a four-item index presenting vignettes of Black people suffering across different scenarios. I present this racial sympathy index and summarize its descriptive properties. In their seminal work on construct validation, Donald Campbell and Donald Fiske instruct scholars that "before one can test the relationships between a specific trait and other traits, one must have some confidence in one's measure of that trait. Such confidence can be supported by evidence of convergent and discriminant validation" (1959, 100). Accordingly, I enlist a series of validation exercises to improve our confidence that the racial sympathy index actually captures white distress over Black suffering.

In this chapter, I also present the book's sources of evidence. We gain greater confidence in our findings when we observe convergent results across several independent studies. For this reason, I track the relationship between sympathy and politics across multiple studies conducted over a period of almost thirty years. Each study is distinct, but the results are similar; together, they demonstrate racial sympathy's consistently significant and substantively meaningful role in American politics.

Who are racially sympathetic white people? Chapter 4 employs the racial sympathy index to answer this question. Although this group is occasionally caricatured as highly educated and affluent, these analyses reveal that the attitude is present throughout the white electorate. The second part of the chapter considers whether their sympathy is rooted in Black suffering specifically or represents a more general sympathy for any marginalized group. I conduct additional analyses that distinguish sympathy from related concepts, such as guilt. I also explore the relationship between sympathy and self-monitoring, or a "chronic concern" that some people have to "regulate self-presentation with regard to social norms" (Berinsky and Lavine 2012, 28). Previous research has found that these concepts can shape white Americans' political outcomes (Agadjanian et al. 2023; Chudy, Piston, and Shipper 2019; Terkildsen 1993; Weber et al. 2014). I do not dispute this, but I do find that white Americans' guilt and social desirability concerns are quite distinct from their levels of racial sympathy. These discriminant validity exercises suggest that my original measure adequately captures the concept of white Americans' distress over Black suffering.

The preceding chapters provide the tools to measure racial sympathy. Equipped with these tools, the next chapters assess the relationship between sympathy and public opinion. Using multiple surveys and experiments, I explore the association between racial sympathy and support for racialized policies that implicitly or explicitly reference race.

Chapter 5 examines racial sympathy and support for redistributive public policies. With gaping inequality between white and Black America, policymakers have introduced several interventions to mitigate these racial disparities, such as affirmative action, welfare, and business subsidies. White people's opinions on these issues are impacted, in part, by their racial sympathy, and I examine the conditions under which racial sympathy becomes activated through survey experiments.

The policies described in chapter 5 represent the "first face" of the state: those that bestow benefits to individuals and groups. Government efforts to exercise "social control by means of coercion, containment, repression, surveillance, regulation, predation, discipline, and violence" (Soss and Weaver 2017, 560) represent the state's "second face." In chapter 6, I trace the relationship between racial sympathy and criminal legal institutions, such as the police, and affiliated entities, like Black Lives Matter, an organization and phrase associated with "the movement against police brutality in Black communities in the United States" (Bonilla and Tillery 2020, 947). I find that white distress over Black suffering influences whites'

opinion toward both the first and the second face of the state. In chapter 6, I also demonstrate that racial sympathy can be made more salient
under certain conditions.

Sympathy's influence may be characterized by its breadth. But how far
does it go? Chapter 7 considers this question. After consulting long-form
interviews and survey data, I find that racial sympathy's effect on political behavior is less consistent and, in some cases, much weaker than it
is on opinion. One explanation for this disconnect is that racially sympathetic whites' attitudes may not be genuine. This is plausible, but for
the most part, racial sympathy appears to retain a strong connection with
white Americans' attitudes, even when we account for these concerns.
That said, the attitude is more strongly connected with individual-level
behaviors, such as educating oneself about racism and listening to people of color, instead of social or political behaviors, such as voting or
campaigning.

Chapter 8 considers how racial sympathy *could* translate to political
behavior. Here, I consider two possibilities: political efficacy and social
movement mobilization. Political efficacy is "the feeling that political and
social change is possible and that the individual citizen can play a part in
bringing about this change" (Campbell, Gurin, and Miller 1954, 187).
White Americans may carry high levels of racial sympathy, as chapter 4
suggests they do, and they may hold these attitudes genuinely, as confirmed
by chapter 7. However, if they do not feel efficacious, it is possible that
they will not act on their sympathy, no matter how deeply they experience
it. Social movements such as BLM can provide racially sympathetic white
Americans with direction and prompt concrete behaviors that facilitate political action directly targeted at reducing Black suffering. My results suggest
that, in both cases, racial sympathy can be mobilized, ultimately contributing to important political outcomes.

In chapter 9, I recapitulate each chapter's main points and attempt to
bring them into dialogue with each other. I also raise questions that I hope
will inform future research. Why would the country's most privileged racial group feel low efficacy? Could sympathy give rise to backlash? How
will demographic change impact racial sympathy? What role will technology play? Are levels of sympathy rising? If so, why? What can leaders and
elites do to channel sympathy into political behavior? What does this book
foretell for the future of the Democratic Party? What can we expect for
American politics more generally?

To these important questions, I can only offer initial speculation. I hope

others will explore them and, in doing so, consider the full tapestry of attitudes informing our politics. Although this book documents the importance
of racial sympathy in particular, its broader takeaway is that race influences
American public opinion and political behavior for many reasons. If racial problems are as intractable as Tocqueville cautioned, our politics will
continue to grapple with questions about inequality and suffering into the
foreseeable future. We will be better positioned to address them if we understand American politics with racial sympathy.

CHAPTER TWO

What Is Racial Sympathy?

A s we start our journey together, allow me to introduce you to Gunnar Myrdal. Myrdal was an economist on an important mission: completing a comprehensive study of the "Negro problem" in the United States. He was an outsider, a young Swede, which gave him, some argue, objectivity; he was a modern "Tocquevillian" (Smith 1993). The Carnegie Corporation of New York commissioned Myrdal to undertake this endeavor in 1938. By 1944, he presented the foundation and the world with his results: *An American Dilemma: The Negro Problem and Modern Democracy*. This "masterwork" of social science has shaped policy and scholarship for decades (Kinder and Drake 2009). Supreme Court justices consulted Myrdal when they ruled in the *Brown v. Board of Education of Topeka* decision (Henderson 2004). Generations of researchers studying race in America have turned to Myrdal to assess the country's progress toward achieving "modern democracy" (Kinder 1986; Smith 1993; Sniderman 2008). Like other responsible social scientists, Myrdal began the second chapter of his book by assessing the state of research. He noted: "Wandering around the stacks of a good American library, one is amazed at the huge amount of printed material on the Negro problem. A really complete bibliography would run up to several hundred thousand titles" (1944, 27).

Years later, the bibliography grows longer still. In the study of American politics alone, scholars have considered white prejudice against African Americans, one of the primary sources of the Negro problem, across numerous dimensions, including how to measure it (Kinder and Sanders 1996; see also Davis and Wilson 2022; DeSante and Smith 2020; Huddy and Feldman 2009; Tesler and Sears 2010) and how it relates to support for public policies (Hutchings 2009) and for Black politicians like Obama (Stephens-Davidowitz 2014; Stephens-Dougan 2020; Tesler 2016), Colin

Powell (Kinder and McConnaughy 2006), and Kamala Harris (Ma, Hohl, and Kantner 2021). Scholars have considered how prejudice affects white opinion of controversial objects like the Confederate flag (Hutchings, Walton, and Benjamin 2010) but also seemingly uncontroversial objects, like a Portuguese water dog named Bo (Tesler 2016). There are cues that activate it (Mendelberg 2001; Stephens-Dougan 2016; Valentino, Hutchings, and White 2002) and emotions that stir it (Banks 2014).

And yet, even with this exhaustive list, we have developed only a partial understanding of white racial attitudes in American politics. Otherwise put, although our bibliography might present a "huge amount" of material, this knowledge is somewhat narrowly confined to prejudice. We know very little about other white racial attitudes that might play a role in the "Negro problem and modern democracy."

This chapter has three aims. The first is to situate the project in the broader American politics and public opinion literature. Although the lion's share of work on white racial attitudes focuses on racial prejudice, it has occasionally acknowledged sympathy. Some of this work is historical; it demonstrates that a force like racial sympathy has existed for centuries. Much of it was produced around Obama's election, so I devote special attention here. This background information helps us position the current enterprise within its broader context. The chapter's second aim is to offer a conceptualization of racial sympathy. Informed by research in psychology, political science, and political theory, I introduce racial sympathy and describe its properties. I consider sympathy's origins and its role in public life. In the final section of the chapter, I lay out my empirical expectations for the following chapters.

One of the main contributions of this project will be to demonstrate, with each chapter, that racial sympathy is distinct from prejudice or low prejudice. Since I engage in this exercise throughout the manuscript, chapter 2 also scrutinizes the relationship between racial animus and racial sympathy. This chapter supplies the theoretical foundations necessary to understand this important but neglected racial attitude.

American Racial Sympathy Over Time

This book is set in the twenty-first century in the United States. Most of my evidence comes from between 2008 and 2021, a period aligning with Obama's ascension, Trump's victory, and, eventually, Biden's election.

Obama's arrival on the political scene ignited political scientists' interest in racial sympathy. We begin there partially for that reason but also for practical reasons: most data that measures sympathy was collected after 2008.[1]

Yet, as I suggest in chapter 1, racial sympathy has existed throughout American history. And as thorough as I hope to be in this book, I offer a detailed portrait of only its latest manifestation. Before doing so, I provide a glimpse of other historical moments in which white Americans have expressed distress over Black suffering. I do not offer an overarching narrative of these separate instances, which, as you will soon see, involve distinct actors, motives, and political circumstances. Nor is this account comprehensive. Instead, I present this background to document traces of American racial sympathy's long and complex presence. This context can help us understand and assess racial sympathy in its contemporary form.

In the previous chapter, I highlighted some well-known occasions of racial sympathy, such as the abolitionist movement and violence related to Bloody Sunday. These are important events involving well-known historical figures such as Harriet Beecher Stowe or James Reeb.[2] Yet there are traces of racial sympathy in other, less famous, moments, too. One example of this can be found in *Lanterns on the Levee*, an autobiography by William Alexander Percy (1885–1942). Percy, the son of a US senator from Mississippi, grew up with admiration for his family's Black servants. This admiration spilled into his politics. When his father mounted a campaign against an anti-Black candidate, Percy defended his father's pro-Black political platform, writing, "This fight to protect the Negro is merely part of our fight for decency in politics" (Percy 2006, 228).

His commitment to this fight was ultimately fleeting. He later delivered scathing critiques of the Black residents of the Delta. As he reflected on racial relations in the South in the conclusion to his autobiography, he observed that "the whole atmosphere of America is such as to mislead and endanger the Negro" (Percy 2006, 306) and chided Black people, urging them to "learn to be a white man morally and intellectually" (2006, 309).

Following the Civil War, Tom Watson (1856–1922) was on the vanguard of the Southern Populist movement. A lively orator and savvy politician, Watson courted newly enfranchised Black people as potential members of the Populist Party. Together, they were "united by resentment of the crushing opposition of capitalist and industrialism" (Woodward 1938, 187), which exploited both white farmers and Black people. After a string of electoral defeats, Watson retreated into solitude for years. During this period, he became maniacally obsessed with deprecating Catholic, Jewish, and Black Americans. His biographer, C. Vann Woodward, observed, "there was a peculiar malignity that pervaded his tirades against the Negro. A friend betrayed is the enemy most despised" (1938, 375).

Percy and Watson's distress over Black suffering was ultimately fickle. This volatility contrasts with the steadfast commitment to racial justice characteristic of many white participants in Freedom Summer, a 1964 voter registration drive to increase the number of registered Black voters in Mississippi. Over seven hundred mostly white volunteers joined African Americans during this period to fight against voter intimidation and discrimination at the polls. This experience had a profound impact on the participants. Years later, many pursued careers related to social justice and progressive causes. These white volunteers "resisted the general drift of political and cultural change . . . even those who are not presently active seem still to be attuned to a political vision and way of life glimpsed in Mississippi and nurtured in succeeding years" (McAdam 1990, 219).

The 1960s were a watershed moment for race in the United States, so I will return to this period throughout the book. When thinking about white Americans' sympathetic attitudes during this time, it is tempting to recall the Freedom Summer volunteers or those white people who participated in the March on Washington. Many of these people, especially in the case of Freedom Summer, were drawn from an elite class of Northern college students, a deliberate recruiting strategy pursued by the Student Nonviolent Coordinating Committee (McAdam 2003).

However, racial sympathy could be found in other quarters, too. In his book on Southern white attitudes during the Civil Rights Movement, historian Jason Sokol observed that "instances of sympathy for the plight of blacks were isolated, and it often took horrific displays of violence like the Monroe lynchings to install even fleeting compassion" (2008, 31). Yet, even with this backdrop, some white Southerners came to carry an attitude akin to sympathy. Interestingly, they did so less out of a sense of conviction than of resignation. One of Sokol's interviewees, a white Mississippi planter, noted: "Most of us don't want it to begin with, but it's a matter of facing reality. . . . I'm not a very good moralist or a strong religious thinker, but it seems to me that if there's one sin above others it is to deprive a man of human dignity" (2008, 117). White students at the University of Georgia opposed integration, "but when it became clear that desegregation could not be stopped, they made an about-face and agreed to adapt" (Sokol 2008, 155). In both cases, pragmatism was central to the attitude. There were some white Southerners who enthusiastically supported racial integration throughout the 1960s, but many others "arrived accidentally at pro-integration positions" (Sokol 2008, 341). And there were those like Joseph

Cumming, a journalist from Decatur, Georgia, who supported Black Americans' plight and authored numerous articles in which he depicted the Civil Rights Movement in a positive light. He also marched alongside Civil Rights activists during a hospital worker's strike in Charleston, South Carolina. He and other white journalists who covered the movement earned the nickname "sympathetic referees" from John Lewis (Sokol 2008, 442).

As these examples indicate, white Americans have expressed distress over Black suffering for centuries and have done so for varied reasons. This history also suggests that racial sympathy can coexist with racial prejudice and can be found in unexpected places; this coexistence is a central focus of my research on contemporary racial sympathy. In all of these stories, racial sympathy finds a home in American politics. White Americans in starkly different political climates brought their sympathetic racial attitudes into their political opinions and behaviors. As I explain in the next section, this tendency reflects the significant role of social groups in shaping Americans' politics.

Group Centrism and Sympathy in American Politics

I began the chapter by introducing you to a famous economist. Now I will introduce you to a famous political scientist, perhaps the most influential in the study of American public opinion: Professor Philip Converse. Converse was, according to his *New York Times* obituary, the architect "of our understanding of public opinion."[3] He had many important publications, but the most renowned was his 1964 essay "The Nature of Belief Systems in Mass Publics." In this seminal work, Converse argued that the mass public often conceived of politics not in ideological terms—indeed, they could be characterized by their *lack* of ideological constraint—but rather in terms of salient social groups, such as those based on race and religion. Groups that were the most "visible," as delimited by physical characteristics or recognizable meeting spaces, were central to informing the psychology of the masses (Converse 1964, 237).

Converse's essay spawned a rich line of inquiry on the "group-centric" foundations of public opinion (e.g., Nelson and Kinder 1996). According to the theory of group centrism, when citizens evaluate government policies, they often do so through the prism of social groups. They think: Who does this policy impact? And what are my attitudes toward that group? Although it may seem surprising that individuals break society up into groups and issue opinions about them, decades of research in psychology, anthropology, and biology demonstrate that most people approach the world in this way (Allport 1954; Krebs and Miller 1985; Sherif 2012).

Within their research in this tradition, social scientists have mostly focused on examining out-group attitudes, with the preponderance of work focusing on negative attitudes. But the theory of group centrism is, in principle, broad. For example, Thomas Nelson and Donald R. Kinder observe: "Support for affirmative action among whites reflects sympathy for the plight of blacks . . . opposition to welfare programs derives from hostility to the poor" (1996, 1056). In each case, reactions to groups are *affective*, or emotional. Pamela Johnston Conover concurs, noting: "People have 'emotional' reactions to social groups . . . reactions differentiated beyond liking and disliking (e.g., sympathy, anger, pity, frustration)" (1988, 58). Indeed, this diversity of sentiment may have been anticipated by Converse when he proposed a hypothetical survey question to reveal both the negative and positive elements of white attitudes toward African Americans: "Are you sympathetic to Negroes as a group, are you indifferent to them, or do you dislike them?" (1964, 235). By including these three possibilities, Converse's question acknowledged that white attitudes toward Blacks could take several forms, including sympathy.

Outside the group-centric literature, other research has recognized the possibility of a political sympathy. General psychological orientations, such as humanitarianism and egalitarianism, may also lead white people to, for example, support redistributive efforts. People who subscribe to humanitarianism, defined as "a sense of responsibility for one's fellow human beings," tend to support social welfare policies (Feldman and Steenbergen 2001, 660). Humanitarians' commitment to assisting the disadvantaged leads them to "want the government to intervene and provide for those people" (2001, 661). Similarly, if someone possesses a "general commitment to equality," they may be more supportive of policies that attempt to level the playing field—for example, affirmative action or welfare. Stanley Feldman and others label this core belief "egalitarianism" (Bobo 1991; Feldman 1988; Feldman and Huddy 2005; Funk 2000).

Support for policies "hinge on the reputation of the group," according to the group-centric approach (Nelson and Kinder 1996, 1056). In contrast, the prosocial orientations of egalitarianism and humanitarianism extend, in principle, to any marginalized group. Egalitarians want an equal society for all disadvantaged groups, including immigrants, Black Americans, religious minorities, people with disabilities, the poor, women,

LGBTQ+ individuals, and so on. Similarly, a humanitarian's commitment to "fellow human beings" would be broadly applied to any policy area that sought to elevate others.

For years, researchers chiseled away at these topics. They considered the separate dimensions of prejudice, addressing its delicate measurement and, in many cases, its striking impact. They distinguished this, where possible, from the work on prosocial orientations like egalitarianism and humanitarianism. The result was a wide and thoughtful range of studies, some of which I detailed earlier. However, in 2007, researchers' attention began to shift as an African American senator from Illinois announced his candidacy for president. With his political ascendancy came renewed speculation about white Americans' racial attitudes. In the next section, I provide an overview of the scholarship on race in the 2008 election, which, like much of the work before it, centered on prejudice. There were, however, some inklings that white racial sympathy may have contributed to the election of the country's first Black president.

Enter Obama

What forces propelled Obama to victory in 2008? In particular, what role did race play in his astonishing election? When asked to reflect on how race influenced his candidacy, Obama himself observed: "There's no doubt that there's some folks who just really dislike me because they don't like the idea of a black President. Now, the flip side of it is there are some black folks and maybe some white folks who really like me and give me the benefit of the doubt precisely because I'm a black President."[4]

Previous research on Black candidates has come to similarly mixed conclusions (Citrin, Green, and Sears 1990; Highton 2004; Sass and Pittman 2000; Stephens-Dougan 2020). It has been challenging to establish overall patterns about the role of whites' racial attitudes here because there have been so few Black elected officials. The most informative and accurate observational research relies on observations, and lots of them. If we have only had one Black president, we cannot be sure that the "some white folks" who "really liked" Obama would carry these feelings toward any Black candidate or if they were drawn to Obama in particular.

The low number of Black elected officials is lamentable for many reasons.[5] But there is a work-around for scholars who want to study this phenomenon: they can create a fictitious world with Black candidates and track white people's reactions to them. There are costs to this experimental approach; the research subjects may not be very invested in a fictitious Black candidate that they encounter in a sterile college classroom or on-line survey. However, the experiment permits researchers to explore this question free from the idiosyncrasies of individual elections and candidates. Similarly, the experimental setting permits tighter insight into causality, a topic I explore in more depth in chapter 5.

With all these advantages, it has been depressing to researchers that the experimental results have been as mixed as the observational ones. For example, using a local sample in Tucson, Arizona, Carol K. Sigelman and colleagues conducted an experiment to examine white support of non-white candidates. They found that "positive prejudice" (or "reverse discrimination") caused some whites to "consistently bend over backwards to support minority candidates" over white candidates (1995, 250). On the other hand, other work finds that whites *do* discriminate against Black candidates under certain circumstances (Reeves 1997; Stephens-Dougan 2020; Terkildsen 1993).

For years, research on this topic seemed confined to the domain of state and local politics. However, with Obama's rise, scholars who study national elections began to take note, and many concluded—decisively—that the nontrivial population of whites who did not "like the idea of a black President" played an important role in the 2008 and 2012 elections (Hutchings 2009; Kinder and Dale-Riddle 2012; Piston 2010; Tesler and Sears 2010). Kinder and Allison Dale-Riddle estimate that Obama lost approximately 10 percent of votes he might have otherwise won from white voters had he been "a typical—that is, white—Democratic candidate" (2012, 104).

What about the "flip side" Obama referenced—those white folks who "really liked" Obama because of his race? Some research shows that Obama received support from a subgroup of white citizens who were especially enthused to elect Obama *because of* rather than despite his race. This counterintuitive outcome could have come about for a few reasons. Broad values systems, such as egalitarianism, may have influenced whites' vote choice in the 2008 and 2012 elections. The presidential election of a Black man with a multiracial heritage and a Muslim middle name was a step, perhaps, toward a more equal society in which any individual could be elected to the nation's highest political post. Obama also pledged to expand social programs, making him the egalitarian choice relative to his Republican opponents. It is plausible, therefore, that Obama captured some white Americans' support because some white people are egalitarians, and his candidacy appealed to their broad commitment to equality.

As plausible as this might be, research on the 2008 election has found that group-based attitudes were more powerful than values like egalitarianism (Kam and Kinder 2012; Piston 2010; Valentino and Brader 2011).[6] A commitment to equality may shape some important political outcomes (see Hutchings 2009), but it does not seem to be the main or even most important reason white Americans looked favorably on Obama.[7] Concepts such as "equality" or "responsibility for one's fellow human being" are hotly contested, making interpretation challenging (Feldman and Steenbergen 2001). Perhaps this is because, as Converse established, thinking about individual salient social groups is more psychologically accessible.

Accordingly, many scholars have studied how whites' group-specific attitudes drove their evaluations of Obama. Additionally, some scholars have argued that there are white Democrats who supported Obama *because* he rarely discussed race (Sides, Tesler, and Vavreck 2019).[8] Another related but distinct argument has been that Obama gained white support because he engaged in racial distancing, using negative stereotypes of African Americans to appeal to white voters' racial animus (Stephens-Dougan 2020). Both of these accounts suggest that Obama may have attracted white support because he embodied or conveyed a version of Blackness that did not disrupt the status quo.

Quite separate from these accounts, some scholars argue that white Americans may have carried positive attitudes about Black people and Obama's election drew them out. For example, in a 2009 article, Paul M. Sniderman and Edward Stiglitz uncovered an association between responses to whites' positive stereotypes about Blacks (which they call "esteem for blacks") and vote choice for Obama. They argue that this relationship is different from the relationship between negative stereotypes and vote choice. Furthermore, two books by symbolic racism scholars, written independently (Kinder and Dale-Riddle 2012; Tesler and Sears 2010), also suggest that pro-Black attitudes led some whites to vote for the country's first Black president. These scholars find that in both the 2008 Democratic presidential primary and the 2008 general election, those on the low end of the racial resentment scale, a commonly used measure of prejudice, were especially likely to support Obama. Michael Tesler and David O. Sears argue that Obama's support from "racial liberals" is one of the "keys to understanding how Obama won the White House" (2010,

37). Based on these findings, both books conclude that some white people favored Obama due to his race.

Research on these "pro-Black" attitudes is still in its infancy. Despite the valuable contributions of this scholarship, however, substantial questions remain. Sniderman and Stiglitz define *esteem* as white Americans' "wish [for] life to go well" for Blacks (2009, 1). It is not clear, however, if this attitude represents "a wish for life to go well" for Blacks *in particular* or a more general positive orientation toward all racial groups akin to egalitarianism or humanitarianism. This ambiguity has consequences for our interpretation; if esteem is a broader orientation, then it may extend to any non-white candidate, including politicians such as, for example, Andrew Yang, Alexandria Ocasio-Cortez, or Ted Cruz. Would a white Obama supporter who wishes "life to go well" for Black Americans endorse these other candidates based on similar grounds? Or is there something distinct about white attitudes toward Black people in particular?

The authors also argue that whites with "esteem" for Blacks favor a Black candidate over a white one. However, the theoretical basis for this expectation is somewhat puzzling. Indeed, the argument that esteem for an out-group leads to favoritism for a member of that out-group seems inconsistent with predominant theories of intergroup attitudes in social psychological research, which emphasize in-group favoritism—the widespread, pervasive tendency for people to privilege groups to which they belong over groups to which they do not belong (Hogg and Abrams 1988; Kinder and Kam 2009; Tajfel and Turner 1986; Turner, Brown, and Tajfel 1979). This line of scholarship has also demonstrated that it is not necessary for one to derogate an out-group in order to favor one's in-group; indeed, liking an out-group often coexists with in-group favoritism (Brewer 1999). It is one thing to "wish life to go well" for members of an out-group, like Black Americans; it is quite another to elevate a member of that group at the expense of one's in-group. In sum, Sniderman and Stiglitz's research does not make clear why or under what conditions "esteem for blacks" should lead whites to favor Black candidates.

In regard to the research of racial resentment scholars, one difficulty presented by their conceptualization of symbolic racism is that the concept itself has typically been defined as an anti-Black attitude. For example, Kinder and Sears describe symbolic racism as "a blend of anti-black affect and the kind of traditional American moral values embodied in the Protestant Ethic" (Kinder and Sears 1981, 415; see also Kinder and Dale-Riddle 2012, 52; Tesler and Sears 2010, 18).[9] Since symbolic racism was initially "born out of a need to explain widespread white opposition to black candidates and race-targeted policies in the post–civil rights era," this conceptualization is reasonable (Tesler and Sears 2010, 62; see also Kinder and Sanders 1996, 92–93). However, there is not much within this definition suggesting that symbolic racism, even at its "low" end, could be a pro-Black attitude.

That said, symbolic racism scholars occasionally consider those whites who score low on their index to be "generally sympathetic toward blacks" (Kinder and Sanders 1996, 106; Tesler and Sears 2010, 19). However, scant attention has been paid to clarifying what the "sympathetic" or "racially liberal" part of the scale captures or understanding the types of behavior that may emanate from there. For example, on page 114 of *Divided by Color*, Kinder and Lynn M. Sanders find that "white Americans who express racial sympathy on the racial resentment scale (a perfect score of 0) show up almost precisely at the color-blind 0.5 neutral point on all three stereotype measures: they say whites and blacks are indistinguishable." But if those scoring low on the symbolic racism index view whites and Blacks as indistinguishable, it is unclear why they might engage in behavior like favoring a Black candidate because of his race.

In short, the work on Obama should be commended because it drew attention to the multiple dimensions of racial attitudes. However, since so much research is engrossed in examining prejudice, scholars lacked the appropriate theoretical and methodological tools to fully understand why white Americans might support a Black candidate like Obama or, more generally, endorse a political outcome that brings no obvious benefit to their own group. It is particularly worthwhile to consider whether the tools we developed to measure racial prejudice should be imported to understand something quite different. These measures were born from a need to understand white people's *opposition* to racialized public policies. To understand their *support*, a different theoretical and empirical approach is necessary. The one I propose in this book is called *racial sympathy*.

Racial Sympathy

Why would a white person carry sympathy toward a Black individual or Black people as a group? After all, much of the research on intergroup relations has confirmed the widespread presence of ethnocentrism, a "predisposition to divide human society into in-groups and out-groups"

(Kinder and Kam 2009, 31) that entails "favoritism toward in-groups and animosity toward out-groups" (2009, 85).

Animosity toward the out-group (or lack thereof) is not the primary attribute of racial sympathy; rather, racially sympathetic individuals can be characterized by the distress they experience in response to Black Americans' suffering. Racial sympathy is both cognitive and emotional—it is cognitive insofar as it relies on the recognition of either past or present suffering and emotional in that it conjures an affective reaction to these circumstances. Note that this definition of racial sympathy does not refer to the presence or absence of prejudice. Instead, racial sympathy captures its own unique dimension of intergroup attitudes.

Like any label, the term *racial sympathy* is not perfect. Each word is simultaneously precise and broad. *Sympathy* was widely used by eighteenth-century British philosophers such as Lord Shaftesbury (1671–1713), Francis Hutcheson (1694–1746), David Hume (1711–1776), and Adam Smith (1723–1790) to refer both to "the mechanisms of emotional transmission or acquisition and to various feelings and benevolent motives which those mechanisms can produce" (Sander and Scherer 2014, 153). Some psychologists might be alarmed by the non-specificity of "various feelings."[10] Lauren Wispé, for example, defines sympathy as an "increased sensibility to another person's suffering as something to be alleviated" (1986, 68). According to this definition, sympathy could arise when a friend has health problems or a coworker is mistreated in the office.

For these occasions, sympathy is likely fleeting; in this book, when I write about racial sympathy, I am referring to a *stable* attitude or durable "psychological tendency" (Eagly and Chaiken 1993). Like other racial attitudes, the stability rests on a "stored affective reaction" white people have to Black Americans (Conover 1988). Attitudes toward social groups have strong emotional components. For example, Antoine J. Banks and Nicholas A. Valentino (2012) suggest that white racial prejudice contains the "emotional substrates" of anger and disgust. Racial sympathy, on the other hand, taps into the stored affective reaction of distress. It is likely accrued through preadult experiences, some of which I discuss shortly, and persists into later stages of life. This stored sympathetic reaction may be challenged under some circumstances, but it probably persists, likely because it crystalizes across one's life span (Henry and Sears 2009). In chapter 3, I discuss why I decided on the term *sympathy* in particular. For now, it should be clear that I am using the word to reference a stable attitude.

Racial sympathy's first word—*racial*—should also be clarified. Race and racial categories are not based on biological reality but instead on powerful social inventions. This does not mean, however, that they are inconsequential. Even if racial classifications have shifted over time, they are "inscribed in law, entrenched in social experience, imprinted on economic life, and influential, still today" (Kinder 2013, 814). For all these reasons, race remains "central" to understanding American society and thus American politics (Hutchings and Valentino 2004).

Race is not a synonym for *Black*, so why do I use the term *racial sympathy* to refer to white distress over Black suffering in particular? In the United States, the concept and origins of "race" have often been tied to Black Americans. The country's first census in 1790 classified people into two civil-status distinctions: free or slave, taxed or untaxed. Applying these distinctions "generated a count of three ancestry groups (European, African, and [untaxed] Native American), which set the foundation for all racial classifications to come" (Prewitt 2005, 6). Thus, the category of race in the United States was created with Black people in mind.

From there, it has been ascribed with special force to Black Americans with the "one-drop rule," which "categorized individuals with any degree of black heritage as singularly black" (Davenport 2020, 222). Perhaps because of this, Black people have been by far the largest racial minority group in the country until recently (Sears and Savalei 2006). Further, major historical domestic events related to race—such as the Civil War and the Civil Rights Movement—centered on abolishing slavery and striking down legal barriers for Black people. Centuries of discriminatory treatment, due in part to the government's initial categorization of this group, have made the racial divide between white and Black Americans especially pronounced.

In the contemporary United States, phrases like *race targeted*, *racial justice*, or even *racial disparities* are often understood as referencing Black Americans even though they do not single out a racial group. Perhaps for all of these reasons, many people who study the United States, myself included, employ the word *racial* on phenomena that impact Black Americans specifically, as concepts such as racial resentment (Kinder and Sanders 1996), racial distancing (Stephens-Dougan 2020), racial cues (White 2007), and racial priming (Mendelberg 2001) illustrate.[11] There are shortcomings to this approach, and as I discuss in the conclusion, the country's demographic landscape is changing such that the racial sympathy of the twenty-second century could look quite different than it does at present. Nevertheless, I proceed with the broad term *racial* here in part to join dialogue with other research on the topic but more importantly to reflect the country's political history and "original sin" of slavery.

Some have argued that individuals support policies out of a sense of self-interest. Put plainly, "an action or policy is in a man's interests if it increases his opportunities to get what he wants" (Barry 2010, 124). And what "he wants" is often material. According to this reasoning, white Americans may adopt racially sympathetic attitudes for instrumental purposes; like Tom Watson, they think they will get something out of it. However, most white people are not politicians building coalitions and angling for office. Still, ordinary citizens might see Black Americans' advancement as somehow contributing to the advancement of the country as a whole, or perhaps they support "pro-Black" political efforts because they think it makes them look good and assume that these efforts have a low likelihood of transpiring; perhaps they perceive it as costless.

However, as with other racial attitudes, the political effects of whites' sympathy tend not to be rooted in white citizens' self-interest but instead in more symbolic concerns. Although a white person with racial sympathy may not experience the tangible consequences of her actions, since "one's relevant personal 'stake' in the issue is an emotional, symbolic one" (Sears, Hensler, and Speer 1979, 371), racial sympathy can still shape opinion on a range of political objects.

We might also expect for racial sympathy to contribute to white Americans' political behaviors, as well. Insofar as behavior might be considered an extension of opinion, white Americans who are distressed over Black suffering may engage in behaviors to rectify it. That said, scholarship has found that the link between attitude and behavior may not be as straightforward. Rather, the expression of attitude might depend on other psychological and environmental factors. Accordingly, Russell H. Fazio and Mark Zanna suggest that "rather than asking whether attitudes relate to behavior, we have to ask 'Under what conditions do what kinds of attitudes held by what kinds of individuals predict what kinds of behavior?'" (1981, 165).

Indeed, work on white racial prejudice has demonstrated that prejudice's influence on behavior depends on other factors (Cepuran and Berry 2022; Krupnikov and Piston 2015; Petrow 2010)—that is, prejudice is most impactful under certain "key conditions." Research on prosocial emotions offers some clues as to what these key conditions might be for sympathy. "Motivations" and "goals" are crucial components of altruism, defined as "a motivational state with the ultimate goal of increasing another's welfare" (Batson 2011, 15). Thus, a white person's sense of efficacy, or ability to achieve a given outcome, may be especially important in the transformation from sympathy to action. Externally, certain political environments could also mobilize racial sympathy. The surge of white people's activity during the Civil Rights Movement may reflect, in part, sympathy meeting a political and organizing climate that facilitated volunteer work or protest activity. Without this sort of climate, the transmission of sympathy into political behavior may be less likely.

That does not mean that sympathy is absent. Under the normal course of events, a person's level of sympathy is relatively consistent. Some commentators have suggested that the wave of protests following Floyd's murder in 2020 set in motion important changes to white racial attitudes. This has been characterized, in some quarters, as a "great racial reckoning" and as perhaps the "extraordinary event" for the twenty-first century.[12] The long-term impact of Floyd's death on racial sympathy remains to be seen. Racial sympathy may have been drawn out into expression during the summer of 2020; however, it certainly existed before then, too. This is because, as a stable attitude, racial sympathy is present even when Black suffering is not making national headlines. In the next section, I expand on this point by exploring the concept's origins.

State versus Trait?

In this section, I offer some speculation on where racial sympathy might come from. Social and personality psychologists have typically pursued different approaches when examining the origins of out-group attitudes (see Reynolds et al. 2001). Personality psychologists consider individual-level factors that might influence out-group attitudes (Adorno et al. 1950; Altemeyer 1998; Sidanius and Pratto 1999). For example, some people may be resistant to change across all domains of their life. Such persistent stubbornness might be interpreted as a part of their personality.

In contrast, social psychologists examine how people's social circumstances impact their attitudes. Notable characteristics of an environment can be assessed with questions (e.g., How many people like me are around?

What is my status in this situation? Is it high or low? How do other people see me?). These types of questions are embodied in social psychological theories like social identity, threat, or social self-categorization (Tajfel and Turner 1986; Turner and Reynolds 2003). Though the first systematic explorations of out-group attitudes used personality-based accounts to explain the roots of prejudice, emphasizing, for example, the importance of an "authoritarian personality" (Adorno et al. 1950), scholars later came to emphasize the role of social and intergroup influences on attitude formation (e.g., Pettigrew 1959). For the most part, this social psychological approach has prevailed, particularly within political science, over the last decades.

Personality may still factor into out-group attitudes, however. One way we can detect this is by consulting the five-factor model of personality. This model was designed to systematize and clarify personality measurement (Goldberg 1999; John and Srivastava 1999; Sibley and Duckitt 2008). These "Big Five" factors are relatively independent, broad-bandwidth dimensions of personality, organized by five domains: Neuroticism, Extraversion, Openness, Agreeableness, and Conscientiousness. Scholars have examined the relationship between these personality traits and out-group attitudes and, of particular relevance to the present study, have identified the traits of Openness and Agreeableness as especially relevant to racial animus and sympathy, respectively.[13]

Variance in Agreeableness and Openness is determined by both genetic and environmental factors. Research has demonstrated that these traits are heritable at different levels. For example, in 1993, Cindy S. Bergeman and colleagues examined the genetic and environmental effects of Openness, Conscientiousness, and Agreeableness using a Swedish twin registry of monozygotic (identical) and dizygotic (fraternal) twins reared together and apart. The study found that genetic influences account for 40 percent, 12 percent, and 29 percent of the variance in Openness to Experience, Agreeableness, and Conscientiousness, respectively (Bergeman et al. 1993, 149). Estimates of shared rearing environments were modest for Openness to Experience (6%) and Conscientiousness (11%). Unlike Agreeableness, Openness is also understood to be more durable, which means that it is unlikely to fluctuate with age (McCrae and Costa 2003).[14]

Genetics, therefore, might contribute to individual differences in racial sympathy. This does not mean that individuals high on the traits of Openness and Agreeableness will always be racially sympathetic, nor does it mean that individuals low on Openness and Agreeableness will never carry racially sympathetic attitudes. Rather, it suggests that some individuals may be genetically predisposed to embrace racial sympathy from the outset.

In addition to the potential biological contribution, parenting or exposure to certain environments could encourage the development of racial sympathy. Developmental psychologists have demonstrated that white children learn racial attitudes from several sources, including their parents, caregivers, teachers, community members, and peers (see Allport 1954, 195; Bigler 1999; Clark and Clark 1939; Hraba and Grant 1970). In recent years, a burgeoning field of research has suggested that certain developmental techniques might not only reduce the impact of racism but also encourage the development of sympathy for marginalized groups (Eisenberg and Strayer 1990; Hamm 2001; Quintana et al. 2006).

Many white parents do not discuss race with their children (Apfelbaum et al. 2008; DeSante and Smith 2020).[15] A study by Jennifer A. Kofkin and colleagues found, for example, that approximately 25 percent of white parents never commented on race in any capacity. When probed to explain this behavior, the parents tended to remark that all people were the same or that their children had not asked (Kofkin, Katz, and Downey 1995). More recent research confirms that white parents routinely misjudge their child's ability to process race. They thus delay these important conversations, occasionally indefinitely (Sullivan, Wilton, and Apfelbaum 2021).

Schools offer another site for the transmission of racial attitudes. Some educators subscribe to a pedagogy focused on confronting "White racism in all its distinct manifestations . . . [it promotes] educational change to transform or oppose existing arrangements that are harming people of color" (Young and Laible 2000, 390). One common practice is for teachers to introduce white students to "the cultural ways of minority groups" (Aboud and Amato 2001, 79). Lessons that emphasize "typical cultural patterns, simplified for young schoolchildren," have the benefit of exposing students to the world beyond the classroom. Unfortunately, studies have found that this technique has no consistent effect on reducing prejudice or generating positive attitudes toward an out-group. Instead, by emphasizing difference, this approach reinforces an oversimplification of cultural patterns, leading to the development of negative stereotypes (Furoto and Furoto 1983; Pate 1988).

In contrast, research has found that when white students perceive *less* homogeneity within out-groups, they are more inclined to develop positive feelings toward out-group members. Although this research has not specifically examined the development of sympathy in particular, it suggests the potential of formal education as a venue for cultivating sympathy. For example, Frances E. Aboud and Virginia Fenwick (1999) evaluated an eleven-week curriculum program in which fifth-grade students used a textbook featuring profiles of thirty children from different racial and ethnic groups. Each profile included the child's name, photograph, likes and dislikes, personality traits, and preferences. The curriculum was centered on activities requiring cross-categorization and recalling the unique qualities of each of the children depicted in the profiles. After the class, white students who had taken part in this intervention curriculum assigned more positive attributes to non-whites than those white students in a control curriculum.

Outside of the formal curriculum, informal socialization practices may contribute to developing racial sympathy among children. For example, in a study of racial socialization, Jill V. Hamm found that many white parents lamented the limited contact their white children had with peers from different ethnic groups (2001, 81). Indeed, research has found that interracial interaction among children leads to improved acceptance of Black children by white children (Goldstein, Koopman, and Goldstein 1979), one of the justifications guiding the *Brown* verdict. Hamm noted that these parents were cognizant of the barriers facing interracial contact, such as social segregation, yet "rarely assumed responsibility for broadening contact, preferring to defer socialization to other agents such as school" (2001, 83).

School communities can be powerful in this respect. Students who attend racially diverse schools are more likely to have interracial friends (Joyner and Kao 2000). The effects of racially diverse schools present during a student's school years but also follow into adulthood. Grace Kao and colleagues find that attending a diverse school and having an interracial friendship or romance as an adolescent increase the likelihood of having an interracial romantic relationship as an adult (2019). The authors also find that interracial relationships and friendships are most seldom among whites and Blacks, aligning with other research on the homophily of friendship networks (White and Laird 2021).

These studies were not designed to examine politics, so it is difficult to assess their applicability to the current enterprise. Nonetheless, it seems likely that a white person's parents, schooling, personality, and genetics may all predispose them to embrace racial sympathy. These factors do not guarantee racial sympathy, nor does the absence of these factors preclude it. Sources of sympathy may also vary from person to person, and several situational factors might matter, too, as I explore in subsequent chapters.

Nonetheless, previous research gives us some clues as to why some white Americans may be racially sympathetic while others are not.

Sympathy and Prejudice

In 1954, Allport defined prejudice as "antipathy based on a faulty and inflexible generalization." This antipathy "may be directed toward a group as a whole, or toward an individual because he is a member of that group" (1954, 9). Scholars have explored many varieties of prejudice and created an array of measures to capture the concept. From these efforts, we have learned much about what it means to score high on these measures. But we know very little about what it means to be low in prejudice. If one is free from prejudice, does another attitude lie in its place? As a final exercise in mapping sympathy theoretically, I consider its relationship to racial prejudice. In part, I do so out of recognition and respect for the important scholarship on racial prejudice, which has contributed much to our understanding of race and America.

However, I also do this because some scholars have equated low prejudice with sympathy. If sympathy is equivalent to low prejudice, why study it? Why not take everything we know about prejudice and invert it? There are several problems with this approach. Consider a white person who devotes his or her life to advancing Black interests. This person might score "low" on a measure of prejudice. But so too could a white person who does not have much, if any, reaction when he or she thinks about race. Tyrone A. Forman and Amanda E. Lewis call this "racial apathy" and, in their discussion of the devastation of Hurricane Katrina in predominantly Black New Orleans, note that many whites displayed an "indifference toward societal racial and ethnic inequality and lack of engagement with race-related social issues" (Forman and Lewis 2006, 177). Apathy, they argue, is an "increasingly central dimension in Whites' racial attitudes" (2006, 177). Insofar as emotions feed into prejudice, those individuals who score "low" on indices such as racial resentment or stereotype ratings may be more accurately characterized by "utter indifference" (Kinder 2013; Pettigrew 1982) toward Blacks rather than by their sympathy. Further complicating the matter, under conditions of an American "apartheid" (Kinder and Mendelberg 1995; Massey 1990), white detachment from Blacks' circumstances may amount to tacit approval of racial inequality. Otherwise stated, it is not clear whether the concept of racial sympathy is best represented on a bipolar dimension with racial animus as its opposite anchor.

Using measures of prejudice to approximate racial sympathy presents other complications. Of course, many who demonstrate hostility toward Blacks are less likely to feel sorry for that group; psychological research shows that disliking a person or group negatively correlates with the likelihood of feeling sympathy for them (Hareli and Weiner 2002). However, it is also possible that some white people carry racial animus and racial sympathy simultaneously. Psychologists Irwin Katz and R. Glen Hass argue that white Americans exhibit "racial ambivalence" in which "Blacks are perceived as deserving help, yet as not doing enough to help themselves . . . both attitudes may exist side by side within an individual" (1988, 894).

This possibility is present in political science research too. In their influential book, *Reaching Beyond Race*, for example, Sniderman and Edward G. Carmines argue that "declining to characterize black Americans in positive terms is one thing; publicly characterizing them in negative ones is quite another" (1997, 63). Even if white individuals do not attribute positive traits to Black people, they might not necessarily assign negative ones.[16] If withholding positive characterizations is not equivalent to assigning negative characterizations, as the authors argue, why would withholding negative characterizations be equivalent to assigning positive characterizations? That is, if a white American declines to characterize Black people as lazy, should we assume that he necessarily carries "sympathy and a positive regard to blacks" (77)? In short, there may be multiple dimensions to white people's racial attitudes. But as long as sympathy is equated with low prejudice, scholars forfeit an opportunity to investigate this possibility.

On the other hand, scholarship on Afro-pessimism has occasionally explored these themes.[17] Authors such as Frank B. Wilderson III, for example, have argued that white Americans' aspirations to be anti-racist and "pro-Black" are not possible because Blackness itself was developed to be synonymous with suffering and "social death" (Wilderson 2016). Saidiya Hartman's influential *Scenes of Subjection* explores this topic by arguing that slavery was foundational to the American project, specifically its notions of liberty (2022). Because anti-Blackness serves a central and functional role in American society, redemption for it is impossible, and thus, the promise of progress is an illusion. I pick up threads related to these perspectives throughout the book. For now, it is important to recognize that some scholars have thought seriously about white people's reactions and relationship to Black suffering.

The Political Consequences of Racial Sympathy:
Initial Expectations

The conceptualization of racial sympathy presented in this chapter leads to several expectations. The first expectation is that racial sympathy can be reliably measured. When psychologists introduce novel concepts or measures, they typically embark on a series of validation exercises. I take up this task with a new measure, the *racial sympathy index*, in chapter 3. In addition to exploring the measure's contents, I also attempt to distinguish it from broad values like egalitarianism and other group-specific attitudes, notably prejudice. These exercises allow us to better interpret the attitude's relationship with white public opinion.

Indeed, racial sympathy has the potential to shape public opinion because it is an attitude about a group, and, as this chapter makes abundantly clear, groups matter in politics (Nelson and Kinder 1996). Since racial sympathy reflects distress over Black suffering, I expect to observe a robust relationship between racial sympathy and support for public policies associated with Black Americans. Chapter 5 examines the effects of sympathy on policy efforts to eradicate economic inequality. Chapter 6 continues the enterprise by exploring white opinion on policies related to the criminal legal system. I expect sympathy to contribute to opinion in both of these distinct domains.

If racial sympathy exists and matters in politics, as I have argued, then I should be able to activate it. Chapters 5 and 6 demonstrate this point through a series of experiments that reveal the circumstances that increase the *salience* of racial sympathy on political outcomes. My theory of racial sympathy suggests that the attitude is based on perceptions of Black suffering. Accordingly, I expect racial sympathy will be activated when a policy's Black beneficiaries or victims are highlighted, affirming the concept's racial roots.

But sympathy may have its limits. The group-centrism literature predicts a powerful attachment between group attitude and policy opinion, not necessarily behavior. The work we *do* have on attitudes and behavior suggests that sympathy's impact may be inconsistent. Accordingly, I expect racial sympathy to convert into behavior in some, but not all, circumstances. In chapter 7, I begin to study this possibility. I do so by drawing on survey evidence and in-depth interviews with racial justice activists. These white Americans are unusually, deeply, and genuinely invested in

eradicating Black suffering. They also have financial and educational resources to underwrite their commitment. However, in examining this "extreme case," I find that such racial sympathy is not always successfully
channeled into political behavior.

In the final empirical chapter, I push further to investigate the circumstances under which sympathy *does* align with political participation. Specifically, I consider two instances in which sympathy has materialized into
action, building on work that has demonstrated the powerful role of efficacy and mobilization. These occasions offer some insight into the conditions that may translate attitude into behavior. As I describe in chapter 8,
however, they are likely not the only ones that matter, and I speculate
about others in the conclusion, chapter 9.

The foundational work in prejudice and politics introduced the powerful—and perhaps surprising—connection between animus and opinion,
stimulating subsequent research on its reach. This project's primary contribution is to draw our attention to an understudied but important racial attitude. The theory and expectations in this chapter represent my attempts to document racial sympathy. The empirical chapters enrich this
account and permit us to evaluate the relationship between sympathy
and a host of important political outcomes. In the next chapter, we begin
this enterprise with the crucial task of measurement.

CHAPTER THREE

Measuring Racial Sympathy

Sympathetic identification cannot be thought of as simply equivalent to what is usually measured under the term "prejudice." The two types of measures are clearly related, but not so much so as to consider one a close substitute for the other. Identification with the underdog appears to be a distinctive dimension, worth studying, if at all, in its own right. —Howard Schuman and John Harding, "Sympathetic Identification with the Underdog" (1963)

Is there racial sympathy in the United States? If so, how would we know it? How could we detect it? Assuming we find a tool to do just that, how could we be confident that it is a good one and that we are on the right track? How can we be sure that it captures what it ought to? These questions, though intimidating, are also familiar to those who set out to introduce psychological phenomena. The task is to construct a coherent, accessible, and precise instrument to track the presence of something often invisible. It is like tailoring a net and then casting it into the sea. Choosing the right mesh, weights, and drawstrings, planning its unique shape, and building it for the conditions it will encounter—keeping in mind the depths of the water, the strength of the current, the number of fishers—are all done in service of a goal: to bring back what we are looking for and nothing more. This is what we do when we set out to measure psychological concepts, and it is challenging. In fact, it is so challenging that Converse embarked on his influential study of ideology by referencing the maxim, "What is important to study cannot be measured and that what can be measured is not important to study" (1964, vi).

Converse ultimately made important strides in measuring that which cannot be measured, and in this chapter, I try to do the same. Here, I lay out the justification for a dedicated measure of racial sympathy and describe the development of an original instrument: the *racial sympathy index*.

Launching a new measure should be done with care. To return to the fishing analogy, the quality of our haul will be better if we construct our net by studying previous iterations and monitoring the current conditions. This chapter is divided into three parts. In the first part, I review other efforts to measure racial sympathy, mostly from the field of social psychology. I complement this valuable work, much of it conducted in labs or online, with fresh, firsthand observations of how white Americans make sense of Black suffering. To collect these observations, I listened. I listened for hours, in forums I will soon describe, to white Americans talk about Black suffering and describe their reactions to it. I read, too. I pored over hundreds of statements collected through open-ended questions on nationally representative surveys of white Americans. Through this process, I gathered valuable background information to develop the racial sympathy index.

The racial sympathy index is an original survey measure that tracks white distress over Black suffering. As an index, it is a compound measure aggregating answers across multiple survey questions. It was inspired by the many striking themes uncovered during my qualitative research, and I spend the second part of the chapter introducing it. When researchers debut a new measure, they often attempt to validate it—that is, to demonstrate that it measures what it intends to. This is a crucial task; assessing sympathy's prevalence and political power hinges on the measure that captures it. Fortunately, psychologists have developed tools for evaluating new concepts, and in this chapter and the next, I turn to them to conduct a series of validation exercises designed to improve our confidence in the racial sympathy index.

In the third part of this chapter, I attend to the convergent validity of racial sympathy. *Convergent validity* refers to how much a measure relates to other theoretically similar measures. If the racial sympathy index tracks white Americans' distress over Black suffering, it should be related to similar concepts, such as other racial attitudes. This would provide us with some initial assurance that our measurement method captures the concept it represents. There is another side to this, however. Although we want our measure to resemble related concepts, it should not be interchangeable with them. This notion is referred to as *discriminant validity*. In the next chapter, I examine racial sympathy's discriminant validity by demonstrating that racial sympathy—and the index representing it—is not equivalent to broader social sympathy. Rather, white Americans' racial sympathy is primarily concerned with Black suffering in particular.

These exercises may seem tiresome technicalities. If this book is about racial sympathy, why fret over other concepts? Why not bury the mundane measurement details in an appendix that no one will read? These are reasonable questions. However, as I hope to convey throughout this chapter, measurement can be tedious *and* thrilling. Measurement is a pivotal moment of transition and anticipation; here, we witness the theoretical forging with the empirical. We watch as personal stories are transformed into standard survey items to be viewed by thousands of Americans. And although any topic would benefit from careful attention to measurement, it is especially important for racial attitudes research, where disagreements over measures are, in the eyes of some scholars, "among the most contentious in all of public opinion research" (Hutchings and Valentino 2004, 390). In a subfield beset with arguments over measurement, this validation work provides an essential foundation for understanding and evaluating racial sympathy in American politics.

Previous Efforts to Measure Sympathy

Although I have called for a stand-alone measure of sympathy separate from prejudice, it should be noted that some measures of sympathy may already exist. Psychologists have made the most progress on this front. Reviewing their efforts will provide a baseline understanding of how sympathy has been measured in the past.

Psychologists' curiosity about sympathy extends into many domains, not just politics, and their research reflects this broader orientation. For example, some psychological scholarship conceptualizes sympathy as transitory. According to this line of research, difficult events such as unemployment and unjust treatment can and do temporarily elicit sympathy in everyday life (Clark 1997). Those engaged in this research often measure sympathy by first inducing it, with the induction taking various creative forms. For example, in one study, researchers showed participants animated clips of geometric shapes climbing a hill. Some shapes struggled while others ascended with ease. Participants were then asked to report whether watching the struggling shapes evoked sympathy, which the authors interpreted as a more general sympathy for the underdog (Kim et al. 2008).

In contrast, other psychological research considers sympathy as a more enduring *attitude*. Researchers in this tradition do not create sympathy but rather take readings of its existing level; here, sympathy is less about re-

sponding to a specific moment—sad news from a dear friend or the tragedy of the triangle who cannot climb every mountain—and is more of a
steady psychological tendency to be tapped. How could a person be consistently sympathetic? Wouldn't that get exhausting? In this formulation,
sympathy is not a general disposition but rather an affective reaction to
specific objects. When these objects come to mind, sympathy does, too.

Among the many objects that could stir emotion in politics, groups are
one of the most potent. Groups occupy a central role in most Americans'
political considerations, a topic covered at length in the preceding chapters (Nelson and Kinder 1996). And this centrality can be infused with
emotion. Indeed, Conover's cognitive-affective model argues that "people store affective 'tags' with group schemata. Thus, a particular group
evokes both a group schema and a stored affective reaction" (1988, 57).
Accordingly, researchers who study sympathy in this manner craft survey
questions to calibrate the attitude related to specific social groups.

Aarti Iyer, Colin Wayne Leach, and Faye J. Crosby use this approach
in their 2003 article "White Guilt and Racial Compensation: The Benefits
and Limits of Self-Focus." Surveying a sample of self-identified white
Americans, the authors asked respondents to complete the sentence:
"When I think about racial discrimination by white people toward blacks,
I feel. . . ." by selecting from a list of adjectives. If subjects chose the words
sympathetic, *compassionate*, or *empathetic*, their responses were grouped
into a single index to measure sympathy. The phrasing of the question stem
suggests that white people possess a consistent emotional reaction to
"Blacks" and "racial discrimination by whites," aligning with sympathy's
conceptualization as an attitude.

Some measures of prejudice, such as racial resentment, leave their "low
end" mostly undefined. However, others are operationalized such that their
low end could contain traces of an attitude resembling sympathy. For example, public opinion researchers occasionally examine whether their respondents assign negative stereotypes to different social groups, including Black Americans. These measures often allow subjects to rate groups
positively or negatively; in the case of Black Americans, respondents are
typically asked whether the words *lazy* or *hardworking* describe the group,
with the latter representing a positive trait. Similarly, feeling thermometers track how warm or cold one feels toward different groups and people; thus, they can reveal pleasant and negative attitudes.

Beyond these self-report survey measures, implicit measures, such as
the Implicit Association Test (IAT) and the Affect Misattribution Procedure

(AMP), are also, in principle, capable of capturing pro-Black attitudes like sympathy. These measures were designed to display the extent to which respondents associate African Americans with negative and positive stimuli (see Olson and Fazio 2004). Unlike explicit measures, implicit attitudes, as measured by the IAT and AMP, are intended to detect the attitude outside of the respondents' consciousnesses. However, like self-report measures, they rely on conjuring the "psychological tendencies" that surface when whites think about Black Americans.

This existing work demonstrates that an important concept—in this case, sympathy—*can* submit to measurement, despite Converse's warning. Based on the diversity of techniques, it also seems like there is no best practice; the measurement of sympathy could take various forms depending on how the author understands its components and function. In that vein, the current enterprise requires an instrument suitable for studying racial sympathy in American politics. I have argued that racial sympathy is an enduring phenomenon developed over the life span with diverse sources. Given this conceptualization, it would be inappropriate to induce and then measure the emotion of sympathy.[1] For this reason, many of the creative induction approaches psychologists pursue are unsuitable for my purposes.

The method of Iyer and colleagues (2003) is more consistent with this conceptualization of sympathy as an enduring trait. However, it also has some drawbacks, namely that their question and its answers collapse the emotions of sympathy, empathy, and compassion into a single concept, which they believe represents "sympathy." But is a mixture of sympathy, empathy, and compassion equivalent to sympathy? Do respondents know what these words mean? Even proponents of these measures acknowledge that these words may confuse respondents.[2]

Some psychologists argue that these are distinct emotions that should not be consolidated. On empathy and sympathy in particular, Lauren Wispé writes: "Although both have as their object the emotions of another person . . . they are different psychological processes. They have different implications for research, and the differences are important—enough so that the distinction between them should not be obfuscated" (1986, 320). Empathy is "the attempt by one self-aware self to comprehend unjudgmentally the positive and negative experiences of another self" (Wispé 1986, 318). One of empathy's primary characteristics is its vicarious nature; people high in empathy can "change places" (Smith 1976) with others, permitting them to "experience their emotional state" (Sirin et al. 2021, 40). Empathy may involve perspective taking and emotional contagion (Hatfield, Rapson, and Le 2009). Sympathy may require less—perhaps only the disapproval of others' suffering (Wispé 1986, 318). As I soon discuss, these distinctions affect the empirical analysis. For now, it seems prudent to keep the measurement of empathy and sympathy separate.

One benefit of the IAT and AMP is that, since these measures calibrate subconscious attitudes, they do not rely on subjects' cognitive or emotional capacities. Subjects do not need to know what *sympathy* means to score on the "pro-Black" end of these assessments. Instead, researchers can examine how long it takes respondents to associate positive images or words with phrases or pictures that reference Black people.

Research has found that white Americans' reaction times on these tests correlate with nonpolitical behaviors. For example, white Americans who are slower to make the Black-positive connection on the IAT display signs of anxiety when they interact with a Black, as compared to a white, experimenter: they make shorter visual contact with this person and tend to blink a lot while doing so (Dovidio et al. 1997). They also talk more and smile less in these situations (McConnell and Leibold 2001). These outcomes involve spontaneous judgments and behaviors. In contrast, the implicit measures have been less successful at predicting political outcomes (Ditonto, Lau, and Sears 2013; Huddy and Feldman 2009; Kalmoe and Piston 2013; Kinder and Ryan 2015).[3] This may be partly because political thinking is uniquely deliberate and effortful and, relatedly, because the "conditions of mass politics are special ones" (Sears 2001, 30). Implicit measures may approximate white sympathy for Black people but perhaps not in ways that organize political preferences.

Self-report measures are more likely to align with deliberate behaviors, such as answering survey questions or voting (Ditonto, Lau, and Sears 2013, 505), so why not proceed with inversions of the thermometers and stereotype measures? Throughout the remainder of the book, I demonstrate that racial sympathy is not interchangeable with the low end of various prejudice measures, nor is it equivalent to a broader sympathy toward any marginalized group; this is one of the main tasks of the discriminant validity exercises in chapter 4. Setting aside the empirical evidence, some white people may score on the "warm" end of these measures, which is predictive of political preference. Even if this is the case, we do not know why they registered this score and why it shapes their politics. Obtaining this knowledge requires studying sympathetic attitudes in their own right.

In sum, despite the valuable contributions of existing sympathy measures, important concerns remain. First, if some white Americans are sympathetic toward African Americans, they may not be able to articulate it. Implicit attitude measures are exempt from this critique but are not reliably associated with political outcomes. Since racial sympathy is not merely the opposite of prejudice, we cannot borrow from the library of prejudice measures. Instead, we must create a measure to capture white distress over Black suffering. In the next section, I detail my efforts to do just that.

Developing a New Measure

When I set out to design a new measure, my only prerequisite was that it ought to lend itself to a questionnaire format to allow for comparison with other racial attitudes research in the subfield, much of which is conducted through survey research. Survey measures are "the backbone of public opinion research" (Jardina 2019, 51), but it is a tall order to construct a closed-ended survey item representing the complexity of racial sympathy.

Not knowing quite where to start, I began thinking about sympathy's measurement by listening to how white Americans thought and talked about race. Talking about race may not come easily to many white Americans (Walsh 2007), and emotions may be difficult to articulate; even if we assume that individuals are aware of their emotions—and this is, perhaps, a generous assumption—they may be unable to express and categorize them using the precise jargon favored by academics (Barrett 2006; Boden and Thompson 2015). With these limitations, it may seem odd to turn to a qualitative technique like listening.

Respondents' imprecision might create a mess for survey researchers; however, in other respects, this very ambiguity provides an invaluable window into complex psychological processes such as sympathy. None of the white people I listened to used the term *racial sympathy* or identified distress over Black suffering as its nucleus. However, the scenarios they referenced revealed a great deal about how they thought about racial attitudes, as did how they talked—at times choking up, furrowing brows, releasing sighs of exasperation, all signs unveiling important clues I would have never encountered if I relied on existing measures, especially those of prejudice. As Allison J. Pugh notes, through listening, we can "situate the feelings people feel in an emotional landscape they themselves sometimes ascertain, and always convey" (2013, 47). For these reasons, listening was an ideal way to begin my measurement process.

Fortuitously, this period of exploratory research corresponded with a series of events on race hosted at my doctoral institution. In early 2013, the College of Literature, Science, and the Arts (LS&A) at the University of Michigan (U-M) planned a theme semester entitled "Understanding Race." Since 1980, the college has organized theme semesters by planning a variety of events on broad, interdisciplinary subjects, providing "intellectual and cultural immersion in a particular topic ... true to U-M's public mission, theme semester events are generally open to the public and are done frequently in collaboration with community organizations."[4]

Programming for the "Understanding Race" semester included museum exhibitions, plays, performances, documentaries, and lectures on the topic of race. These events often included a participatory element. For example, there were "talk-back" sessions after theater performances that offered opportunities for audience members to discuss the production with the director and actors. I would attend these performances, stationing myself in the back of the auditorium, watching the show, and observing the talk-back session, scribbling notes throughout.

The U-M Museum of Natural History featured different programming through its exhibition on "Understanding Race," with guided tours on Saturday mornings. The tours flowed into optional open-dialogue sessions on race guided by trained facilitators. The exhibit's curators used a compelling mix of light, sound, and image to transport visitors to different settings and periods. The dialogue sessions snapped people back to the present—they were held in bright classrooms, overhead fluorescent lights blasting, cold folding chairs forming a circle around the perimeter. I would sit with the attendees in one of these chairs and listen as they digested what they had just seen. Then I would go home and write up what I had observed. These events, and others like them, typically drew white people who wanted to share their reflections about race, so I went to them and listened. I paid close attention to the words attendees used and the salient images that they referenced.

I learned a lot from these sessions. Sometimes, however, I had follow-up questions for the people I listened to; they would mention something interesting, and I would want to know more—I wanted them to talk through an example or to provide further context. I did not ask these questions at the time, but I was inspired to complement the listening observation sessions with in-depth interviews conducted with white student leaders from the U-M Program on Intergroup Relations (IGR) throughout the spring and summer of 2013.[5] IGR is an on-campus social justice education program that "prepares students to live and work in a diverse world and educates them in making choices that advance equity, justice, and peace." Through these interviews, I had more opportunities to learn about how some white Americans thought about race generally and the circumstances of Black Americans specifically.

The white people I have described so far live in and around southeastern Michigan, which is a very specific (and cold) place. Although I would eventually turn to high-quality nationally representative surveys to examine racial sympathy in the electorate, I decided that I needed some more geographic diversity even at this exploratory stage. Therefore, I supplemented the listening sessions and in-person interviews with a series of national qualitative surveys about race hosted on Amazon's Mechanical Turk (MTurk) platform in the fall of 2013. I also reviewed open-ended responses from the 2008 American National Election Studies (ANES), which provided a few opportunities for respondents to share their perspectives on race, specifically as related to Obama's election. I provide more information about these data sources shortly.

For now, I present some initial impressions gleaned from these sources, as I reviewed them guided by the "logic of discovery" rather than the logic of verification. This former approach focuses on theory generation rather than theory testing (Luker 2008, 175). During this process, and throughout these four distinct data sources, a few themes consistently emerged. First, many white Americans regularly expressed distress over Black Americans' circumstances. Rarely did they indicate that they were able to relate to the experience of Black people, which is to say that they did not articulate their attitudes as expressions of empathy; rather, their tone was often one of sadness, coupled with remorse, frustration, and regret. For example, during one semi-structured discussion after the museum tour, a moderator asked the group why racial prejudice persisted. A white woman observed: "If you look at Detroit, and you know, you're saying the schools are bad and everyone there is a certain race, then you're putting a bunch of people who, you know, have been socially downgraded, and giving them the worst of things, and then blaming it on the color of their skin . . . people don't understand that Blacks' skin color doesn't cause the bad schools. It's really distressing."

Here, the participant notes that Black people in Detroit have experienced misfortune as "downgraded" individuals and that "people" have misidentified the causes of this suffering. She concludes by observing that this is "distressing" to her. Throughout this particular discussion, guided by trained facilitators, white people voiced similar comments in which they noted their sadness about the unequal conditions Black Americans faced.

At another "Understanding Race" event, a white man commented: "I have friends who are African American and I have talked to them about what it's like to be Black. They told me about times they've been treated differently—followed around stores, or people assumed they weren't smart—and I feel really sad for them—it's also terrible knowing that some people can be so horrible."

This insight revealed that white sympathy for Blacks is often rooted in specific episodes—in the first case, the situation of schools in Detroit, and in the second, a conversation with Black friends. More generally, these two observations seemed to be part of a broader trend: participants did not articulate their distress in terms of broader ideology or values but instead referenced specific instances of Black hardship.

This observation was confirmed during my interviews with the white leaders of the Intergroup Relations program. When I asked what compelled them to take on leadership roles in the group, they often referenced a salient incident as motivating their participation or, at the very least, awakening them to the hardships faced by Black Americans. One white female leader of IGR told me that she joined the group after hearing white dorm mates say negative things about the only Black student in her residence hall. Another student said he enrolled because he had recently visited a predominantly Black neighborhood in Detroit and was disturbed by the visible poverty.

The two national surveys complemented the data from Ann Arbor. In the first survey, conducted on the MTurk convenience sample in 2013, respondents were offered an opportunity to input their opinions through open-ended responses. In perusing the comments of white respondents in this anonymous setting, I recognized themes that had also appeared during the research in Michigan. For example, one person said: "I have friends who are African American, and I have talked to them and heard them relate instances of prejudice and racism that makes me feel terrible knowing that is how our society treats other individuals."

Another noted: "A kid could try his hardest, be the smartest kid in school, and he STILL would have less of a chance of making it if he was from a poor Black neighborhood than your average white kid."

A third person wrote: "I frequently read news reports about Black people being harassed or persecuted. They are discriminated against like crazy."

In all cases, the respondents are focused on specific episodes and peo-ple—friends, a hypothetical student, news reports. The open-ended an-swers do not reveal an engagement with broader themes such as justice, equality, or humanity but rather a focus on how Black Americans experi-ence inequality.

Similar comments were found in the open-ended responses from the 2008 ANES. Most ANES questions are multiple-choice, and subjects re-cord their attitudes using discrete response options. However, in 2008, respondents were invited to explain, in their own words, why they liked Obama, the Democratic candidate. One white female respondent said she liked Obama because "he seems to be very sincere about what he's doing and . . . he has struggled being a minority." Other white respondents indi-cated that Obama's race was part of the motivation for liking him and that the historical significance of his election and the notion that it was now "time for a Black president" made him a desirable candidate. Some linked Obama's election to the speeches of Martin Luther King Jr., thereby con-necting Obama to a history of Black suffering.

The quality and depth of the responses differed substantially, which is expected with open-ended answers (Converse and Presser 1986). It may be especially challenging for some subjects to identify emotions based on differences in emotional expressiveness (Salovey and Mayer 1990). None-theless, the responses seemed to converge around sorrow or regret about Black people's circumstances. Rarely did white respondents explain that they liked Obama because they could relate to his experience specifically or the experiences of African Americans more generally.

Indeed, in many cases, subjects went out of their way to emphasize that they *could not* imagine what it was like to be Black. For example, one theme semester participant recalled witnessing a recent microaggression. He de-scribed watching a white person confuse the names of two Black men, noting

> I was disappointed and uncomfortable watching it. And I can understand why it would have made the guys . . . uneasy.
>
> It's so hard to gauge how often these things happen because I'm rarely put in their situation; I don't know what it's like. But white people should be less ignorant and just learn people's names.

I found similar comments in the 2013 MTurk study. Of the ninety-five white people who completed the study, only five subjects expressed their attitudes empathetically, such as: "I have been the target of social injustice, and it doesn't feel good." Most responses did not contain elements of vicarious thinking or feeling, aligning with the concept of "social alexithymia." This concept was developed from psychiatric theory by Joe R. Feagin and is defined as "the sustained inability to relate to and understand the suffering of those who are oppressed" (2013, 27–28). Based on these observations, while racial sympathy might have multiple emotional components, sympathy seems to be the most central and often-expressed emotion.

After months of reading and listening to white Americans' views on race, I began to see the outlines of racial sympathy. Their emotional reactions to episodic instances of Black suffering seemed to form a "psychological tendency" directed toward "a particular entity," aligning with Alice H. Eagly and Shelly Chaiken's definition of an attitude (1993). Across the exploratory research, I found that the white people I heard from did not claim to know what it was like to face racial discrimination; indeed, many acknowledged that they could never understand what it was like to be Black. Instead, the comments they offered in person (through group discussions and interviews) and anonymously (through national surveys) centered on the sadness and distress that occurred when they thought about tangible instances of Black suffering. These observations guided the development of the racial sympathy index.

The Racial Sympathy Index

Using the language and themes I observed in my preliminary research, I formed an original measure of racial sympathy. I did so by adapting an approach pursued by Howard Schuman and John Harding in their article "Sympathetic Identification with the Underdog." In this piece, the authors composed a series of fictional vignettes, each featuring a member of an ethnic out-group meant to elicit sympathy. For example: "A colored man born in New England goes South for the first time and sees in Mississippi bus station waiting rooms, one for colored and one for whites" (1963, 231).

After reading each vignette, the authors asked subjects whether they experienced "sympathetic identification" with the out-group member depicted in the vignette. They found this sympathetic identification was associated with support for African Americans who challenged Jim Crow segregation, such as the Black students who participated in Woolworth's lunch counter sit-ins.

The benefit of these vignettes is that they enable subjects to react directly to specific stimuli rather than abstract notions of discrimination and inequality, concepts that citizens, especially white citizens in my exploratory research, seemed unlikely to invoke.[6] Instead, the vignettes allow subjects to "easily identify the broader set of issues to which this particular one apparently belongs . . . they can use their general attitude toward the broader set of issues to determine their attitude toward this particular one" (Schwarz 1994, 135). W. Russell Neuman, George E. Marcus, and Michael MacKuen employed a similar approach in their 2018 study of the news. Rather than ask whether current events made their subjects feel enthusiastic, angry, or anxious, they had them review summaries of five news stories. They then queried how the specific story made them feel.

There is reason to believe this approach is well suited for measuring racial attitudes and racial sympathy specifically. A National Research Council panel on measuring racial discrimination suggested that vignettes offered one way to overcome subject errors related to limited memory, interpretation, and telescoping, observing: "One fruitful avenue for improvement might be greater use of the factorial vignette method, in which stories are presented to respondents about people being questioned by the police, applying for a job, running for political office, and the like" (Blank, Citro, and Dabady 2004, 171).[7]

I updated Schuman and Harding's measures by composing a series of new vignettes that depicted instances of prejudice or discrimination, like the originals. Unlike the original measures, my vignettes featured only Black people and provided response reactions designed to measure sympathy, not sympathetic identification. After reading each vignette, subjects were asked to report how much sympathy they felt for the Black character(s), with answer choices ranging from "I do not feel any sympathy" to "A great deal."[8] I initially created approximately twenty vignettes depicting Black suffering and pretested them through a series of cognitive interviews on convenience samples. The vignettes that were ultimately selected for the four-item index were chosen because they were successful during the pretests—that is, they produced meaningful variation, were easy for subjects to understand, and cumulatively presented a range of scenarios and iterations of Black suffering.

I could have designated a single vignette to collect sympathy. After all, many important concepts in political science, such as age or income, are measured with just one item. Relying on a single item could be risky

TABLE 3.1 **The Racial Sympathy Index**

Vignette 1: Mrs. Lewis, a white woman with young children, posts advertisements for a nanny on community bulletin boards. She receives many inquiries and decides to interview all applicants over the phone. Mrs. Lewis is most impressed with a woman named Laurette, who has relevant experience, is an excellent cook, and comes enthusiastically recommended. Mrs. Lewis invites Laurette over for what she expects will be the final step of the hiring process. When Laurette arrives, Mrs. Lewis is surprised to see that Laurette is Black. After Laurette's visit, which goes very well, Mrs. Lewis thanks her for her time but says that she will not be offered the job. When Laurette asks why, Mrs. Lewis says that she doesn't think that her children would feel comfortable around her. Laurette is upset about Mrs. Lewis's actions.

Vignette 2: Tim is a white man who owns a hair salon. His business is growing rapidly and so he decides to place an advertisement to hire new stylists. In the advertisement, he writes that interested applicants should come for an interview first thing next Monday. When he arrives at the salon on Monday, he sees a line of seven or eight people waiting outside the door, all of whom appear to be Black. He approaches the line and tells the applicants that he's sorry, but the positions have been filled. The applicants are upset; they feel they have been turned away because of their race.

Vignette 3: Milford is a mid-sized city in the Northeast. The main bus depot for the city is located in the Whittier section of Milford, a primarily Black neighborhood. Whittier community leaders argue that the concentration of buses produces serious health risks for residents; they point to the high asthma rates in Whittier as evidence of the bus depot's harmful effects. The Milford Department of Transportation officials, who are mostly white, state that Whittier is the best location for the depot because it is centrally located and many Whittier residents take the bus. Furthermore, it would be expensive to relocate the bus depot to a new location. Whittier community leaders are very upset by the department's inaction.

Vignette 4: Michael is a young Black man who lives in a midwestern city. One day Michael is crossing the street and jaywalks in front of cars. Some local police officers see Michael jaywalk and stop and question him. Michael argues that he was just jaywalking and is otherwise a law-abiding citizen. The police officers feel that Michael is being uncooperative and so they give him a pat down to see if he is carrying any concealed weapons. Michael is very upset by this treatment.

here, however. One vignette's characters, setting, and circumstances may elicit sympathy from some white Americans but not from others. Thus, we could not tell whether people were responding to the characteristics of the specific vignette or expressing a more general attitude. Another way of putting this is that any survey question is likely to contain, despite our best efforts, some amount of random error caused by natural variability in the measurement process. Scholars will often aggregate answers to related questions to diminish this possibility (Kinder and Sanders 1996). Accordingly, I consult multiple vignettes—in this case, four—to form the racial sympathy index. This additive index captures the extent to which whites carry distress over Black Americans' suffering across a range of contemporary contexts. The racial sympathy index is presented in table 3.1.

The index does not rest on the subject's ability to parse differences between related but distinct concepts such as sympathy, empathy, or compassion. Further, the scenarios provide tangible instances of discrimination, similar to those offered by my interviewees and survey respondents. These characteristics reflect how white Americans spoke and wrote about this topic in my qualitative research.

The vignettes are all distinct. Some feature individuals, while others have groups. Some are set in employment settings, others in neighborhoods and streets. In some cases, the reader knows that the Black character feels they have been discriminated against. In other instances, this information is omitted. This variety is intentional and presents Black Americans' suffering in various formats. If I am picking up on a racial attitude that endures across contexts, I should find that white Americans' distress over Black people's suffering is more or less consistent across these different scenarios. I explore this point empirically, but first, I introduce the sources of evidence.

Sources of Evidence

Just as random error is mitigated by consulting multiple survey items, evaluating racial sympathy across multiple sources helps ensure the results are robust over time and not sensitive to idiosyncrasies of a single data collection. In total, I consult ten quantitative national surveys spanning almost thirty years to examine the role of racial sympathy in American politics. Most of my results come from five national surveys containing the original racial sympathy index. Since these studies are fundamental to the project, I introduce them here. Cumulatively, they supply multiple opportunities to explore racial sympathy and its political consequences.

Occasionally, I had a more narrow, targeted question about racial sympathy: "What if racial sympathy is in fact something else?," or "Is this the same thing as guilt?," "Or maybe this is empathy?" All questions circle around the issue of discriminant validity, which I address shortly. When haunted by these questions, I fielded other surveys on convenience samples. I describe those here too, but since I regularly consulted the comprehensive surveys, I discuss them in greater detail.

Almost all chapters employ data from the 2013 Cooperative Congressional Election Study (CCES), which contains the original measure of racial sympathy presented in table 3.1. The 2013 CCES was a national stratified sample administered by YouGov/Polimetrix in November 2013; half of the questionnaire consisted of "Common Content," sixty questions covering a wide range of political attitudes and politician evaluations, and the other half contained "Team Content," in which individual researchers submitted their own questions to ask a subset of a thousand individuals. The racial sympathy vignettes were submitted through "Team Content" and, as such, were distributed to approximately 1,000 respondents, 751 of whom identified as white.

To approximate national representativeness, the CCES uses a two-stage selection and weighting scheme, based off of census estimates and propensity-score weighting. Studies have found that the CCES sample performs similarly to the ANES on important variables, like vote choice (Ansolabehere and Rivers 2013; Vavrek and Rivers 2008). In one article, Stephen Ansolabehere and Douglas Rivers compare the demographic composition of Obama and John McCain supporters across the 2008 ANES, the 2008 CCES, and exit polls. They find the distribution of the vote to be "remarkably similar to the exit polls for both the ANES and the CCES" (2013, 320). In this spirit, appendix table 3.1 displays some key demographic attributes of the CCES white respondents, with appropriate weights applied, compared to other nationally representative surveys.

The 2013 CCES sample resembles recent samples collected by reputable academic surveys, such as the ANES and the General Social Survey (GSS), with respect to gender, education, and age. Organizers of the CCES have acknowledged that they cannot strictly classify the sample as nationally representative (Ansolabehere and Rivers 2013), and others have criticized opt-in surveys more generally, arguing that the survey mode may produce distinct results because respondents who self-select into the sample are unique (Malhotra and Krosnick 2007). Nonetheless, the distributions presented suggest that the white sample in the 2013 CCES shares important characteristics of the white samples collected in other reputable academic surveys.

Two years later, in the summer of 2015, I contracted with Survey Sampling International (SSI) to field a two-wave national internet study. SSI is a sampling firm that matches its sample to the census on such key demographics as gender, age, income, and education. Additionally, SSI targets certain subpopulations through its selection procedure; accordingly, an all-white sample was used for the experiment. The first wave of the SSI study was administered in August 2015, and the second wave one month later, in September 2015. The racial attitudes questions were administered in Wave 1, while the experimental stimulus appeared in Wave 2, making it unlikely that the former contaminated responses to the latter.

The 2016 YouGov sampling frame was constructed using estimates from

the 2010 American Community Survey (ACS), the 2010 Current Population Survey, and the 2007 Pew Religious Life Survey on criteria of gender,
age, race, education, ideology, party identification, and political interest.[9]
The study was limited to those respondents who self-identified as white
and went into the field in August 2016. It was also a two-wave study, and
the second wave appeared in mid-September of that year.

The 2020 YouGov study was administered on either side of the contentious 2020 presidential election—the first wave in late October 2020 ($n =$
884) and the second wave in February 2021 ($n = 613$), representing approximately 30 percent attrition. I refer to these separate administrations
as Wave 1 and Wave 2, respectively. YouGov included weights derived from
2018 ACS and vote choice to match the sample to the white voting population. Like the SSI study, the 2020 YouGov study also has the attractive
feature of panel design: the same participants were surveyed at two different points in time. For this study alone, I included the racial sympathy
index on both waves, allowing me to assess the stability of the measure.

The most recent survey hosting the racial sympathy index is the 2020
Collaborative Multiracial Post-election Survey (CMPS). Despite the survey's title, it was fielded in 2021 from April to August; nonetheless, I refer
to it as the 2020 CMPS throughout the text.[10] In contrast to the other
studies, the CMPS recruits a diverse sample; of the 14,988 respondents,
3,002 (~20%) identified as white, and I restrict my analysis to this subpop-
ulation. The data are weighted, like the YouGov studies, through a post-
stratification raking algorithm to fall within the margin of error of the adult
population in the 2019 census ACS one-year data file for age, gender, education, nativity, and ancestry. The sample included respondents sourced
from a list of registered and nonregistered voters. Reflecting the multiracial
composition of the sample, the self-administered questionnaire survey itself
was made available in ten languages (Frasure, Wong, and Vargas 2021).

I supplement these comprehensive national studies with several other
sources. First, where possible, I attempt to examine the relationship between sympathy and public opinion using the ANES and the GSS. As I
discuss later in this chapter, these surveys all contain a serviceable measure of racial sympathy and a rich assortment of relevant independent variables. To approximate national representativeness, all ANES analyses
in this book use probability weights. I also use weights for analyses conducted with the 2013 CCES, 2016 YouGov, 2020 YouGov, and 2020 CMPS
studies.

In addition to these surveys, I also used the MTurk platform to conduct convenience studies in 2013, 2015, and 2017. The 2015 study included

several open-ended questions and also a section that served as a pilot for the experiments discussed in later chapters, and the 2013 MTurk survey is referenced earlier in this chapter. Specific to the current enterprise, the 2017 MTurk study was specifically designed to explore the relationship between racial sympathy and other related concepts. Because the MTurk platform is "extremely inexpensive both in terms of the cost of subjects and the time required to implement studies" (Berinsky, Huber, and Lenz 2012, 351), it is well suited for these purposes. MTurk studies are, unlike the preceding surveys, strictly convenience samples. They are, however, more demographically diverse than a typical convenience sample, such as those I collected in person in Michigan. All analyses in this book are limited to self-identified white Americans, who tend to be adequately represented on MTurk and elsewhere.

In chapters 7 and 8, I return to qualitative data to explore the relationship between racial sympathy and political behavior by drawing on long-form interviews with racial justice activists. Since the sampling and methodology are unique to those later chapters, I will reserve further discussion of that data until then. For now, we have a sense of the multiple data sources, spanning distinct methodologies and periods, that I will use to assess racial sympathy and its role in American politics.[11] Table 3.2 lays out the key measures that appear in the ten surveys consulted throughout the book.[12]

Every survey also included prejudice measures. The racial resentment index appeared in each study listed in table 3.2.[13] In six surveys, respondents were also queried about the negative stereotypes they harbored against African Americans. These items offer an opportunity to examine whether racial sympathy is equivalent to low prejudice, so I reference them consistently throughout the text. This is a crucial point. If racial sympathy is interchangeable with the low end of these existing measures, then there would be no need to invest in dedicated measurement or analysis of the concept. Fortunately, I find that sympathy is unique in several ways I will soon detail. But let's not get ahead of ourselves. First, we should consider sympathy on its own terms.

How Widespread Is Racial Sympathy?

To start, how much racial sympathy is there? When we began the chapter, we did not know how to answer this question. However, with the racial sympathy index, we now have a tool deliberately crafted to capture white

TABLE 3.2 **Racial Sympathy and Related Measures across Data Sources**

	1994 GSS	2008 ANES	2012 ANES	2013 CCES	2015 SSI	2016 YouGov	2017 MTurk	2020 YouGov Wave 1	2020 YouGov Wave 2	2020 CMPS
Racial Sympathy Index				*	*	*	*	*	*	*
Single-Item Racial Sympathy Question	*	*	*				*			
Egalitarianism	*	*	*		*		*			
Humanitarianism					*					
Implicit Attitudes		*								
Feeling Thermometer		*	*							
Guilt						*				
Empathy							*			

Americans' views on Black suffering. We also have multiple surveys fielded during diverse political moments—election years and off years, times when racial topics were in the national spotlight and other times where they were not, the Obama years and the Trump years. This range supplies a diverse political landscape to study sympathy, ensuring that the findings are not tethered to a specific political moment. I leverage the multiple studies by analyzing the average scores of the racial sympathy index items in table 3.1. I use the YouGov studies for this analysis because they share the same platform, facilitating easier cross-study comparison.[14] The distribution of the answer choice for each item appears in table 3.3, with the two waves of the 2020 YouGov study presented separately.

The distributions reported in table 3.3 suggest that substantial proportions of white respondents reported feeling sympathetic toward the Black individual(s) described in the vignettes. In most cases, approximately 20 to 50 percent of white Americans reported feeling either "a lot of" or a "great deal of" sympathy. There are some patterns to note across surveys. First, aligning with the qualitative research that focused on the saliency of episodes, the vignettes that focused on stories of specific Black individuals (vignettes 1, 2, and 4) attracted more sympathy than the bus depot vignette, which described a struggling Black neighborhood. This is consistent with "person-positivity bias," which occurs when "attitudes toward groups are cognitively compartmentalized from attitudes towards individual group members" (Sears 1983, 223). Even though the Black neighborhood aggregates Black people, it attracts less sympathy than the other scenarios.

By design, each vignette provides a distinct version of Black disadvantage, thus attracting different levels of sympathy. Looking down the rows of table 3.3, we see that they did. We also observe that some white Americans have no qualms indicating that they lack sympathy under certain circumstances. In 2016, for example, almost a third of the respondents indicated that they had "no sympathy" for a Black man being patted down by the police for jaywalking. A similar percentage reported feeling no sympathy for a Black neighborhood plagued by bus fumes.

Racial sympathy could be a manifestation of social desirability pressures—that is, white people reporting the "right" attitudes because they are concerned with self-presentation, not because they are genuinely distressed over Black suffering. I discuss this important topic in later chapters. For now, it is sufficient to observe that, in certain instances, nontrivial percentages of white Americans indicate that they have no sympathy for the Black Americans described in the vignettes. This aligns with existing

TABLE 3.3 **Distribution of the Racial Sympathy Index Items**

	2013 CCES	2016 YouGov	2020 YouGov Wave 1	2020 YouGov Wave 2
		Vignette 1: Mrs. Lewis		
A great deal of sympathy	43.6	30	57.42	48.5
A lot of sympathy	29.4	32.37	23.06	26.8
Some sympathy	16.7	23.85	11.38	16.7
A little sympathy	4.54	2.82	5.39	3.99
I do not feel any sympathy	5.81	10.96	2.75	4.4
		Vignette 2: Hair Salon Applicants		
A great deal of sympathy	37	35.6	53.74	44.62
A lot of sympathy	27.3	27.23	22.02	29.01
Some sympathy	22.45	20.34	13.83	15.28
A little sympathy	8.34	4.5	7.16	6.02
I do not feel any sympathy	5.01	12.34	3.25	5.08
		Vignette 3: Bus Depot		
A great deal of sympathy	11.08	14.47	17.85	21.27
A lot of sympathy	18.91	21.61	24.59	19.63
Some sympathy	37.34	28.84	32.55	31.09
A little sympathy	18.28	8.08	12.66	13.49
I do not feel any sympathy	14.4	27	12.35	14.53
		Vignette 4: Michael, Police		
A great deal of sympathy	19.83	21.94	35.88	30.51
A lot of sympathy	19.99	22.78	20.25	24.52
Some sympathy	24.48	17.73	21.92	16.14
A little sympathy	15.05	7.25	10.69	13.31
I do not feel any sympathy	20.66	30.31	11.26	15.52

Sources: 2013 CCES, 2016 YouGov, 2020 YouGov
Weighted responses.

work that has demonstrated that the influence of social desirability pressures on racial attitudes questions, similar to the ones I examine here, may be overstated (Axt 2018; Sears 2004).

Table 3.3 displays another interesting pattern: rising sympathy over time. This mirrors trends in other racial attitudes, such as decreasing racial resentment (Engelhardt 2019; Hopkins and Washington 2020). Andrew M. Engelhardt has argued that since 2000, there has been a "genuine attitude change" among white Democrats driven by "learning, and often, the contribution of external forces" (2021b, 2). Among whites in the 2013 CCES sample (n = 751), the average level of racial sympathy was .63. For whites in the 2016 YouGov sample (n = 600), the average level of racial sympathy was .58. By the 2020 sample, the average level was .7 in Wave 1 and .69 in Wave 2 (n = 612). Elsewhere in the manuscript, I discuss why racial sympathy might respond to external events and change over time. This is an important point, especially given discussion about the nature and durability of white Americans' "racial reckoning" in the summer of 2020 (Davis and Wilson 2021; Jardina and Ollerenshaw 2022). I return to this point later, but for now, it is important to note that any differences observed among surveys may also reflect the underlying characteristics of the sample. In this case, there is a significantly higher percentage of highly educated respondents in the 2020 YouGov study compared to the 2013 and 2016 studies (appendix table 3.1).

Further, the increasing levels of sympathy depicted in table 3.3 reflect aggregate readings of the attitude; however, they may not be equivalent to stability at the individual level. Converse's research offers some guidance here, for he found that mass attitudes could appear stable over time, while individual preferences fluctuated wildly, "as though random" (1964). Otherwise put, aggregate and individual-level change may function in distinct and independent ways (Erikson, MacKuen, and Stimson 2002).

Although Converse and others have considered mass stability and micro fluctuation, the opposite is possible: mass fluctuation and individual-level stability.[15] One could imagine, for example, a scenario in which most individuals express stable attitudes but the overall mean shifts because a few people are responsive to external stimuli or "extraordinary events" (Sears and Funk 1999, 23). A comprehensive study of the GSS found, for example, some evidence of "persistent change" in public behaviors and beliefs about high-profile issues. Still, this broad effect was driven by a subset of individuals, specifically younger people (Kiley and Vaisey 2020). Therefore, although the means convey interesting evidence of growing sympathy in the macro polity, it is necessary to look at the distribution of individual responses to assess the psychology of individual sympathy.

Correlations provide one tool for assessing stability. A correlation coefficient is a statistical measure of the strength of the relationship between the relative movement of two variables. The values of the coefficient range between −1.0 and 1.0. A correlation of −1 represents a perfect negative correlation; as one variable x increases by z units, y decreases by exactly z units, and vice versa. A correlation of 1 represents a perfect positive correlation; when x increases by z units, y does too.

Using correlations, we turn to the 2020 YouGov Panel, which fielded the racial sympathy index at two times, thus permitting me to evaluate changes in individual-level sympathy. The two-wave survey was intentionally designed with a lengthy intermission of nearly three months.[16] I anticipated that during this period, Americans would encounter vivid political stimuli that could impact levels of racial sympathy. Of course, I could not have anticipated the truly unusual nature of this time period, which included an election night without a declared winner, President Trump pressuring the Georgia secretary of state to change the state's vote totals, the January 6 insurrection, and an impeachment effort. The insurrection in particular, during which symbols like the Confederate flag, hung nooses, and other white supremacist images were flaunted by rioters, had the potential to evoke higher levels of sympathy for Black people.[17] If this was case, we would not expect to observe a high correlation between white subjects' racial sympathy scores in Wave 1 and Wave 2.

Did these tumultuous months alter white individuals' levels of racial sympathy? On balance, the answer to this question appears to be no. Figure 3.1 compares the distribution of the racial sympathy index across Wave 1 and Wave 2 of the 2020 YouGov study. The correlation between the two waves was quite high: 0.78.[18] In general, those white Americans who did not feel sympathetic toward Black Americans did not register more sympathy after these events. However, most white Americans who were sympathetic in late October 2020 were still sympathetic in February 2021.

For those accustomed to scales of resentment or prejudice, the distributions of racial sympathy presented in figure 3.1 may come as a surprise. Indeed, they seem to run counter to previous research on racial attitudes. Kinder and Sanders find, for example, that "substantial majorities" of white Americans exhibit racial resentment (1996, 108).[19] Does figure 3.1 contradict this finding?

To address this question, it is important first to reiterate that racial animus and sympathy are independent concepts. It is, therefore, appropriate that they yield distinct distributions. The out-group orientation of sympathy, as focused on Black people's suffering, may make it a more palatable racial attitude and thus more attainable for most white people. It is also possible that a white person could simultaneously exhibit high levels of sympathy and resentment, a possibility raised in the preceding chapter. For racial resentment in particular, a white person could believe both that Black people do not adhere to the Protestant work ethic and that, on other occasions, they are discriminated against and that this discrimination is distressing.

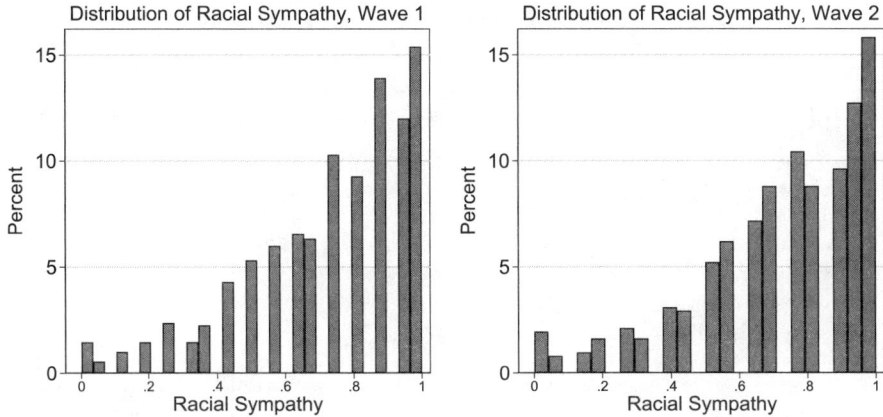

FIGURE 3.1. Distribution of the Racial Sympathy Index
Source: 2020 YouGov
n = 613 by Wave 2

Correlations provide an opportunity to examine this point empirically. Across the studies consulted in this book, I find that the correlations between the racial resentment and the racial sympathy indices range from −0.45 to −0.59. Since racial sympathy, like resentment, is a racial attitude that some whites harbor about Black Americans, we would expect them to be related. However, the magnitude of this correlation suggests that the concepts might not be interchangeable.

The racial sympathy index is coded from 0 to 1, with a score of 0 indicating that across all scenarios, the subject reports no sympathy for Black people. A score of 1 indicates that the subject reports "a great deal of sympathy" for the Black subject across four vignettes. The targets of discrimination were men and women, individuals and groups, personable and abstract, young and middle-aged. Yet, across the vignettes, respondents expressed relatively consistent levels of sympathy. This is reflected in a relatively high Cronbach's alpha.[20] In 2013 CCES, α is .74 for the four-item index, and in the 2016 YouGov study, α is 0.76. In the first and second waves of the 2020 YouGov study, α is 0.83 for both waves. Respondents are responding to each instance of Black suffering similarly, suggesting that the index is tapping into attitudes toward Black Americans generally, and not just the individuals and groups named in the vignettes.

We can examine response convergence in other ways. The items' item-rest correlations—that is, the correlation between an item and the scale

TABLE 3.4 **Principal Factor Analyses of Responses to Racial Sympathy and Racial Resentment Indices**

	2013 CCES		2016 YouGov		2020 YouGov	
Variable	Factor 1	Factor 2	Factor 1	Factor 2	Factor 1	Factor 2
PFA Results Eigenvalues	3.43	2.8	3.56	3.12	4.28	3.64
(% of variance explained)	43	35	44	39	54	46
Vignette 1: Mrs. Lewis	0.1	0.88	0.08	0.89	0.09	0.93
Vignette 2: Hair Salon Applicants	0.05	0.86	0.06	0.91	0.01	0.91
Vignette 3: Bus Depot	−0.06	0.63	−0.05	0.65	−0.07	0.69
Vignette 4: Michael, Police	−0.23	0.58	−0.29	0.47	−0.35	0.54
Racial Resentment, Irish	0.93	0.11	0.94	0.14	0.95	0.06
Racial Resentment, Generations	0.88	0.01	0.81	−0.07	0.9	−0.01
Racial Resentment, Try Harder	0.79	−0.07	0.88	0.07	0.89	0.01
Racial Resentment, Deserve	0.84	−0.02	0.72	−0.19	0.85	−0.08

Sources: 2013 CCES, 2016 YouGov, and 2020 YouGov, Wave 1

formed by all other items—provide another opportunity to evaluate the association between the scale items (Nunnally and Bernstein 1994). Indeed, I find the responses are highly correlated with each other. Factor analysis confirms this point. Responses to the four vignettes load heavily and roughly equally on a single factor in all studies. This means that there is a single factor that can explain the interrelationships among the collection of questions that constitute the racial sympathy index. These results are presented in appendix table 3.2.

In addition to the factor analysis among the racial sympathy items, I conducted a factor analysis in which I combined the racial sympathy index questions with the questions from the racial resentment scale. Since scholars have argued that the racial resentment scale can capture sympathy, and two of the scale's questions draw attention to African American suffering, this analysis permits me to examine whether the two concepts lie on a single dimension or are instead independent.

The results of this analysis, which are, like appendix table 3.2, principal factor analyses with promax oblique rotation, are presented in table 3.4. Although the aggregate distributions of sympathy and resentment may fluctuate across surveys, table 3.4 demonstrates that the individual items remain related in similar ways. In all three surveys, factor analysis retains two factors (those with eigenvalues greater than 1); these factors explain a large proportion of the variance in responses. Consistently, the racial sympathy index loads well onto one dimension, and the racial resentment index loads well onto another. Notably, in no case do the "sympathetic" items of the racial resentment scale load heavily onto factor 2, suggesting that if these components capture a form of racial sympathy, it is substantively distinct from the type of sympathy represented in the racial sympathy index. As confirmation of this point, when I combine the two "sympathetic" items of the racial resentment scale into an abridged two-item index and calculate the correlation of this index with the racial sympathy index, I find that these two indices are only moderately correlated, ranging from 0.44 to 0.59.

In the final empirical section of this chapter, I continue to explore the characteristics of racial sympathy with a series of validation exercises examining the relationship between sympathy and other related measures. In each instance, I am looking to answer the basic question of convergent validity: Is the measure related to other theoretically relevant measures? If so, this would provide initial evidence that we got the instrumentation of racial sympathy right and that these measures approximate white people's distress over Black suffering.

Racial Sympathy, Political Predispositions, and Other Racial Attitudes

To expand the scope of the validation exercises, we set aside the YouGov studies for the moment and turn to the other data sources. Fielding original surveys, made possible through research firms like YouGov and collaborative studies like the CMPS, provides scholars a terrific opportunity to test their own measures and examine new research topics. However, these surveys are often expensive, and pricing schemes and space considerations prohibit most scholars from asking too many questions.

In contrast, large academic studies, such as the ANES, routinely field hundreds of questions on various topics, including race. The ANES has other attractive features that contribute to its reputation as the "gold standard among public opinion surveys" (Aldrich and McGraw 2011, 3). It provides a nationally representative sample, thus alleviating concerns about any distinctiveness of opt-in respondents. The ANES does not, of course, include the racial sympathy index. It does, however, ask respondents a question related to racial sympathy: "How often do you have sympathy for blacks?" In shorthand, I refer to this as the "ANES question," because it has appeared on two iterations of the ANES—the 2008 and 2012 Time Series.

This label is somewhat of a misnomer because the item was first used on the GSS. Like the ANES, the GSS is a large-scale nationally representative survey. It is an omnibus survey covering many topics "in order to monitor and explain trends in opinions, attitudes and behaviors" in the United States (NORC n.d.). It has been conducted since 1972, and in 1994, it also featured the "How often do you have sympathy for blacks?" item as an approximation of prejudice (Pettigrew 1997). I interpret this question as capturing the extent to which a respondent regularly feels sadness when he or she thinks about African Americans and thus believe it is closely related to my own conceptualization of racial sympathy. The sample compositions of the 1994 GSS, 2008 ANES, and 2012 ANES are presented in appendix table 3.1.

The ANES question asks respondents to reflect on the frequency of their sympathy, and questions about frequency are often challenging to interpret. Most people have difficulty recalling the frequency of routine, tangible tasks, such as watching television (Converse and Presser 1986). It is a tall order to expect that respondents would be able to calibrate frequency for feeling an emotion; respondents may differ in their interpretation of what it means to "always" have sympathy.

Further, the question is stripped of context. One white person may "always" have sympathy when he thinks about police brutality against Black Americans but not when he hears about their economic disadvantage. In this case, what does he think about when encountering the ANES question? In short, it is hard to interpret what white people mean when they say they "always" have sympathy toward Blacks. For these reasons, the racial sympathy index is preferable because it standardizes the nature of the sympathetic reaction. It also, by design, aligns with how white Americans think about Black suffering, according to my qualitative research.

Nonetheless, the excellent quality of the ANES and GSS samples and their wealth of important theoretical controls make these surveys a valuable resource. In a MTurk convenience study fielded in 2017, I found that the correlation between the racial sympathy index and the ANES question was 0.69, suggesting that the ANES question is adequately correlated with the racial sympathy index and can serve as a serviceable approximation of racial sympathy. Thus, using the ANES measure, which I scale from 0 to 1, I extend the validation exercises beyond racial resentment to evaluate the relationship between racial sympathy and other related measures.

I do this because I want to assess the *validity* of racial sympathy. Validity is observed when scholars find "agreement between . . . efforts to

TABLE 3.5 **Correlations between Racial Sympathy and Political Predispositions**

Variables	1994 GSS	2008 ANES	2012 ANES	2015 SSI	2016 YouGov	2017 MTurk	2020 CMPS
Party Identification	−.07*	−.19*	−.11*	−.23*	−.33*	−.1*	−.33*
(1 = Republican)	(1147)	(1273)	(853)	(541)	(587)	(87)	(4067)
Ideological Identification	−.12*	−.21*	−.13*		−.28*		−.36*
(1 = Conservative)	(1144)	(1000)	(740)		(573)		(4336)
Egalitarianism	−.05	.30*	.19*	.41*		.39*	
	(1046)	(1288)	(862)	(551)		(87)	
Limited Government		−.12*	−.15*	−.23*	−.27*	−.22*	
		(1286)	(858)	(551)	(600)	(87)	
Humanitarianism				.26*		.23*	
				(549)		(87)	

Sources: 1994 GSS, 2008 ANES, 2012 ANES, 2015 SSI, 2016 YouGov, 2017 MTurk, 2020 CMPS

* $p \leq 0.05$. Table entries are the Pearson correlation coefficients. The number of observations appears in parentheses. Analyses are weighted where possible. For the 2012 ANES, only face-to-face respondents are evaluated.

measure the same trait through maximally similar methods" (Campbell and Fiske 1959, 83). Based on the theory of racial sympathy presented in the preceding chapter, we would expect racial sympathy to be correlated with other related variables; after all, many tap into the sources of white public opinion on racial matters. It would be odd to find, for example, that racial sympathy did not correspond at all with partisanship when so much research has demonstrated the racial foundations of the contemporary American parties (Carmines and Stimson 1989; Kinder and Sanders 1996; Tesler 2016).

Similarly, we expect positive correlations with racial sympathy and other measures that could, in principle, track *positive* attitudes toward Black people, such as the prosocial orientations of humanitarianism and egalitarianism, concepts explained in more detail in the preceding chapter. Insofar as these measures approximate orientations that might relate to the country's racial landscape, we should find evidence of "convergence" (Campbell and Fiske 1959, 83) through a positive and significant correlation with the sympathy measures.

Correlations are presented, by survey, in tables 3.5 and 3.6, with the general predispositions appearing in table 3.5 and the racial attitudes measures in table 3.6. Although not every study contains each measure, the tables provide an opportunity to detect general patterns. In doing so, we find that racial sympathy corresponds with the factors we expect it to. Partisanship, ideology, and preferences for limited government are all

TABLE 3.6 **Correlations between Racial Sympathy and Racial Attitudes Measures**

	1994 GSS	2008 ANES	2012 ANES	2015 SSI	2016 YouGov	2017 MTurk	2020 CMPS
Racial Resentment	−.25*	−.40*	−.28*	−.44*	−.55*	−.37*	−.44*
	(1177)	(1286)	(861)	(552)	(600)	(87)	(4627)
Stereotypes	−.13*	−.18*	−.18*	−.24*	−.31*	−.45*	.3*
	(1139)	(1245)	(856)	(551)	(600)	(87)	(4627)
Interracial Contact	0.09*						
	(796)						
Black Feeling Thermometer		.27*	.3*				
		(1265)	(848)				
White Feeling Thermometer		.15*	.3*				
		(1271)	(848)				
White Linked Fate							.12*
							(4627)
White Identity							−0.04*
							(4627)
Implicit Attitudes		−.15*					
		(1176)					
Guilt					*.42		
					(600)		
Empathy						.26*	
						(87)	

Sources: 1994 GSS, 2008 ANES, 2012 ANES, 2015 SSI, 2016 YouGov, 2017 MTurk, 2020 CMPS
* $p \leq 0.05$. Table entries are the Pearson correlation coefficients. The number of observations appears in parentheses. Analyses are weighted where possible. For the 2012 ANES, only face-to-face respondents are evaluated.

significantly negatively correlated with the sympathy measures, whether specified using the ANES item or the racial sympathy index. Table 3.5 reveals that egalitarianism and humanitarianism are positively correlated with racial sympathy; those white Americans who are generally committed to equality or feel a sense of responsibility for their fellow human beings are also more likely to carry distress over Black suffering. Given that sympathy relies on perceptions of disadvantage and suffering over the conditions of one's fellow human beings, these positive and significant correlations corroborate the operationalization of sympathy in both the ANES and index formats.

Table 3.6 expands this analysis by evaluating the correlations between racial sympathy and existing racial attitudes measures. Again, this analysis investigates whether racial sympathy measures relate to theoretically similar concepts and their measures. Such evidence would give us confidence that the measures designated to capture sympathy function appropriately. As with table 3.5, the correlations are displayed by survey, with the measures of racial attitudes appearing across the table's rows. By and large, the coefficients confirm the racial dimension of this attitude, demonstrating that the racial sympathy index relates to other measures designed to reflect white people's racial attitudes.

Racial sympathy is negatively correlated with racial resentment items, corresponding with the analysis presented earlier in the chapter. From table 3.6, we also observe a negative relationship between racial sympathy and an index of negative stereotypes often used to approximate racial prejudice (Hutchings 2009; Piston 2010; Sniderman and Carmines 1997). Sympathy is correlated with implicit negative racial attitudes collected by measures such as the AMP. And while the correlations in the table suggest that racial sympathy is not interchangeable with these items, we can see that sympathy corresponds with them, as it should. These validated measures are, like racial sympathy, meant to capture white people's attitudes about Black people.

In addition to evaluating the prejudice measures, we can also study the correlations between racial sympathy and existing measures that conceivably capture positive or "pro-Black" variables (Craemer 2008). Friendship or contact with African Americans (1994 GSS) positively correlates with sympathy. A correlation coefficient cannot determine whether sympathetic attitudes precede friendship or if friendship generates sympathy, as might be expected by the contact hypothesis (Allport 1954). Feeling thermometers permit respondents to indicate how "warm" or "cold" they feel toward different groups, including Black Americans (2008 and 2012 ANES). Those white people who feel warm toward Black Americans also exhibit higher levels of sympathy. As with the contact variable, the causal direction here is unclear. Whether warmth toward Black people causes or is the product of sympathy cannot be parsed out from the correlational data. However, the strong and positive relationship between sympathy and this commonly consulted racial attitude is clear.

I next examine the relationship between racial sympathy and other white racial attitudes that come closer to approximating distress over Black suffering: white collective guilt and empathy. White Americans who are empathetic, who can "put themselves in the mind" (Baron-Cohen et al. 2001, 241) of Black Americans, are also more likely to feel distressed over their suffering. This may be because, as a vicarious attitude, they also feel, or come close to feeling, the experience of suffering. It is also possible that they possess "empathic ability," defined as "perspective taking—the cognitive recognition of another's emotional state that occurs rapidly, and perhaps automatically"—and can "possess the potential" to react to someone in need (Feldman et al. 2020, 345). Empathy has been characterized as both an affective state and an ability, with more recent research by philosophers and psychologists focusing on the latter conceptualization (Sander and Scherer 2014). In both cases, sympathy requires less; it represents only sad feelings toward another.

I did not field empathy measures in any national studies. However, I included questions measuring racial sympathy and empathy in the 2017 MTurk study. For the former, I used my racial sympathy index, and for the latter, I consulted the "Reading the Mind in the Eyes" (MIE) index, used as a measure of empathic ability by Feldman and colleagues (2020). The MIE requires respondents to correctly categorize the emotional expressions depicted in eighteen pictures of faces—specifically the eyes, hence its name. Political scientists have used this measure to study empathy in politics (Feldman et al. 2020; Loewen, Cochrane, and Arsenault 2017), as have I. Here, I find my respondents' scores on this measure were indeed positively correlated with the racial sympathy index.

In a related concept, collective guilt is rooted in white Americans' reactions to their in-group's role in perpetuating Black suffering (Chudy, Piston, and Shipper 2019). Since both guilt and sympathy involve a recognition of Black suffering, the positive and significant correlation between the two attitudes is expected. In the next chapter, I discuss how guilt's emphasis on the in-group transgressions makes it substantively distinct and also rarer than sympathy. The correlation coefficients on the empathy and guilt items suggest that these concepts are certainly related but may also contain some distinct elements.

Like guilt, there are other concepts that touch on white people's assessments of their own group, and I present them in table 3.6. White Americans distressed over Black suffering are less likely to score high on measures of the white identity examined in Ashley Jardina's influential book (2019). Substantively, this means they do not have a strong sense of commonality, attachment, and solidarity with their racial group (Jardina 2019, 3). However, they also do not completely disassociate from the group. As the table indicates, racial sympathy positively correlates with warm feelings about white people. It is also the case that higher levels of racial sympathy correspond with higher levels of white linked fate, or the notion that one's fate is bound up with the group's. In-group distancing is not part of the conceptualization or operationalization of racial sympathy, so these positive correlations are not worrisome. In fact, they reveal an important aspect of racial sympathy: it does not require de-identifying with whiteness. Instead, some racially sympathetic white Americans can simultaneously carry positive attachments to their group while also feeling distressed over Black suffering.

Convergent validity is the extent to which a measure relates to theoretically similar concepts. By this definition, racial sympathy passes multiple tests of convergent validity. The correlations in tables 3.5 and 3.6 are in the expected range and direction. Further, these results are robust across survey and measure of sympathy. Whether racial sympathy is represented by the vignette index or the single ANES question, the measure corresponds with other well-established political and psychological measures. Therefore, we have compelling initial evidence that we have what appears to be a valid and reliable measure to capture sympathy.

Conclusion

In this chapter, I demonstrate that racial sympathy *can* be measured. The racial sympathy index was inspired by listening to white people talk about their racial attitudes. The result is an original instrument that taps into a unique and coherent dimension of white racial attitude. It is not merely an inversion of prejudice or a substitute for other existing measures. I support this claim through a wide range of validation exercises, drawing on multiple sources and methods of evidence, both qualitative and quantitative.

Like congressional bills, social science measures are often introduced but rarely adopted. For many psychological measures, longevity relies on replication. If the previous trajectories of racial attitudes measures are any guide, these replication efforts could both increase and complicate our understanding of racial sympathy. Initial efforts to replicate my validation exercises provide some assurance, however. In a 2021 article, a team of criminologists examined the reliability and validity of the racial sympathy index (Hannan et al. 2021). They found that sympathy and resentment were different dimensions of white racial attitudes, aligning with my results. Kellie R. Hannan and colleagues conclude their article by recommending that "criminological studies of race-related policies, whether in punishment or policing, should incorporate Chudy's racial sympathy scale as a standard measure in the analysis" (2021, 29). I hope that the analyses presented in this chapter provide researchers with the confidence to include the racial sympathy measures generally and the index measure in particular in future analyses. Doing so will supply even more insight on how to measure this understudied but important attitude.

In their seminal work on construct validation, Campbell and Fiske argue that "for the justification of novel trait measures, for the validation of test interpretation, or for the establishment of construct validity, *discriminant* validation, as well as convergent validation, is required. Tests can be invalidated by too high correlations with other tests from which they were intended to differ" (1959, 81). Racial sympathy is related to existing survey items, and this is a good sign. I have theorized that sympathy is a politically relevant racial attitude, and the analysis in this chapter provide us with some proof that it is. But what sort of racial attitude measure is it, exactly? And who carries it? I address these crucial questions in the next chapter.

CHAPTER FOUR

Who Are Racially Sympathetic White People?

In 2021, the political journalism website Politico published a profile about a "certain type of young person" who "probably majored, or are majoring, in political science or public policy" (Ward 2021). The horror! Depicted as privileged and highly educated, these young people are, according to the article, almost always Democrats and yet also a potential liability for the party, as this archetype values "atypical" issues "that matter to college-educated liberals but not to the multiracial bloc of moderate voters that the party needs." The cartoon accompanying the article, drawn by Michelle Kondrich, featured a bearded white man wearing an unpretentious gingham shirt and simple work boots. However, his everyman outfit is accessorized with expensive details: an upscale Swedish backpack and a chrome laptop adorned with stickers. One of these stickers displays his support for BLM.

The *New Yorker*'s Daily Shouts serves up a weekly column of "humor, satire and funny observations" for its readers. In June 2020, it featured "A Day at the Church of White Guilt," depicting a fictitious church in which congregants took part in a communion of "His blood (the mimosa) and His body (the avocado toast) in a holy eucharist of brunch" (Otis and Johnson 2020). Written by comedians Randall Otis and Josh Johnson, the piece references books (*White Fragility* by Robin DiAngelo) and movies (*The Blind Side* and *The Help*) that are especially sacred to this group.

And Thomas Edsall explores the "Democrats' Left Turn" in a series of online columns for the *New York Times*, focusing on white Democrats and, more specifically, those within this group who "call themselves liberal on social issues" (2018). Edsall has written on the topic on multiple occasions, weaving together quotes from scholars, party insiders, and pundits. In one instance, he invoked the term "racial sympathy," writing, "white liberal racial sympathy was, in turn, by far the strongest among the most affluent white liberals," who are, he noted, "well-educated, relatively upscale." He cited an analysis conducted using the racial resentment items. In a separate column, Edsall featured speculation, from William Galston, that this category of white people was "terrified of being caught behind a rapidly shifting social curve and of being charged with racism. As a result, they bend over backward to use the most up-to-date terminology and to lend public support to policies they may privately oppose. The fear of losing face within, or being expelled from, the community of their peers drives much of their behavior" (2021).

There's much fascination surrounding this "certain type" of white American. Although the preceding accounts differ in their terminology and objective—the New Yorker piece is, after all, satire—they are similarly captivated by the traits, preferences, and behavior of white people who sport BLM stickers on their laptops, watch movies featuring Black people triumphing in the face of adversity, or "call" themselves liberal on social issues. This flurry of attention may be a function of the recent news cycle. Many—though not all—of these articles were written after Floyd's murder in 2020 brought conversations about race into the national spotlight. It is unclear whether fascination with these topics will eventually fade. However, as I argue in chapter 2, this "type" of white person may have existed, in some iteration, at different moments in American history. It is worthwhile to understand the contemporary manifestation, especially if these individuals are responsible for the Democrats' "left turn," to use Edsall's projection. Familiarizing ourselves with the demographic profile of racial sympathy also provides a valuable foundation for subsequent chapters, which elaborate on the political preferences of the racially sympathetic.

In the preceding chapters, I argue that white distress over Black suffering, which I term racial sympathy, is a unique racial attitude with consequences for American politics. I have also suggested that since racial sympathy is not the inverse of racial prejudice, we cannot use existing measures of racial attitudes to approximate it. Chapter 3 introduces a measure of racial sympathy and demonstrates that it passes multiple tests of convergent validity.

In this chapter, I employ this tool to identify the racially sympathetic. Who, exactly, are they? I start by describing the relationship between sympathy and basic demographic categories such as age, education, and party. Contrary to the media accounts that have depicted racial sympathy as a feature of the especially affluent or well-educated, my analysis suggests that highly sympathetic white Americans are diverse with respect to age, educational status, income, region of residence, and religiosity. They are, however, significantly more likely to identify as Democrats and liberal, a trend that I observe across multiple independent surveys.

The consistency of this pattern begs a question: What, if anything, is distinct about racial sympathy? Democrats and liberals tend to champion causes benefiting various marginalized groups, and they may do so for reasons distinct from distress over Black suffering. I address these important considerations with a series of discriminant validity analyses. Here, I consider whether racial sympathy is equivalent to sympathy for any marginalized group, as we might expect for those white people with a strong Democratic identity. I also consider the relationship between racial sympathy and concepts commonly invoked with it: self-monitoring and guilt. Self-monitoring refers to the tendency to carefully regulate one's presentation according to social norms, similar to the behavior described in Edsall's article. As discussed in the preceding chapter, guilt is a sense of responsibility for negative actions. It can often result in repentance, which is perhaps why the congregants in Otis and Johnson's Daily Shouts piece end their "service" by solemnly declaring that they are sorry. When comedians roast white people who read *White Fragility* or contemplate white people's attempts to virtue signal or save face, are they referencing racial sympathy? I do not want to diminish the importance of these concepts; however, my work demonstrates that sympathy is distinct from them and is measured uniquely and specifically to reflect white distress over Black suffering.

Placing racial sympathy relative to these established "ingredients" of public opinion helps illuminate its unique contribution. Although the main objective of this chapter is to develop a profile of racially sympathetic Americans, it also buttresses the preceding chapter's validation exercises. In particular, the analyses in the second part of the chapter provide further clarification as to what racial sympathy is *not*. Through these discriminant validity exercises, we gain a deeper understanding of what the racial sympathy measure does and does not capture. This better positions us to interpret sympathy's role in American politics.

Demographics

Perhaps through political cartoons, commentary, or other media, we have developed a notion of who racially sympathetic white people might be.

Equipped with the racial sympathy measure, we can now render a more precise portrait. Specifically, in the first part of the chapter, I examine the relationship between racial sympathy, as measured by the racial sympathy index, and a suite of important demographic variables.

There are many sources of white Americans' policy opinions. Previous research has demonstrated that education (Kam and Palmer 2008; Sears et al. 1997), age (Henry and Sears 2009; Schuman and Bobo 1988), gender (Hutchings et al. 2004), region (Valentino and Sears 2005), church attendance (Feldman and Steenbergen 2001), income (Gilens 1999),[1] and partisanship (Campbell et al. 1960; Carmines and Stimson 1989; Converse 1964; Mason 2018) can all influence public opinion to varying degrees. How do these pillars of opinion relate to racial sympathy?

To answer this question, I pool three national YouGov surveys featuring my racial sympathy index: the 2013 CCES, 2016 YouGov, and 2020 YouGov. These surveys were all internet studies conducted by YouGov; thus, they were administered and formatted similarly. Accordingly, I combine them into a single dataset, supplying a larger sample. This makes it less likely that a few outliers drive the associations I uncover.

Racial sympathy is an ordinal index, so deciding who is "low" and "high" in racial sympathy is a somewhat arbitrary exercise. For the analysis presented here, I look at those white respondents who issued the *most* sympathetic response to each of the four vignettes. For every vignette — from the Black nanny, Mrs. Lewis, to the polluted Black neighborhood — these white Americans expressed the maximum amount of sympathy, responding to each scenario with the answer "a great deal of sympathy." By this classification, approximately 10 percent (or 214 out of 2,235) of white survey respondents receive the label "highly racially sympathetic." This group is the subject of the first part of the chapter.[2] In the second part of the chapter, in which I consider the relationship between racial sympathy attitudes toward other marginalized groups, I return to studying white people at all levels of sympathy, as I did in the preceding chapter.

Age

A 2012 *Washington Post* article begins with the apparently well-established observation: "Everyone knows that one of the pillars of President Obama's 2008 victory was young people" (Cillizza and Blake 2012). Indeed, the majority (54%) of young white voters backed Obama in 2008, though this number dropped by 2012.[3] Scholars have explored whether young whites are more racially liberal than their older co-ethnics, generally finding that they are not (DeSante and Smith 2020; Engelhardt 2021a; Hutchings 2009).

However, it is still worth exploring whether young white adults might be especially sympathetic. As discussed in chapter 2, there are historic examples of young white people participating in the Freedom Summer campaign and trading the security of their leafy college campuses to register Black voters under occasionally dangerous conditions.

Evaluating racial sympathy over a life span requires longitudinal data that could track the same person's racial sympathy during different periods of their life. Unfortunately, this data does not, to my knowledge, exist. However, it is possible that age, even as measured at a single point in time, may still relate to racial sympathy and its attendant outcomes. For example, in a series of survey experiments conducted by Howard Schuman and Lawrence D. Bobo, the authors found that, among whites, age was the strongest predictor of support for open-housing laws that would conceivably benefit Black Americans (Schuman and Bobo 1988).

This could be for a few reasons. First, young white people may be especially influenced by liberal environments. In Theodore Newcomb's classic study of Bennington students, he found that many of his subjects, most of whom were white and from conservative households, often became more liberal during their time at the college (1943). It is also possible that young white people may have spent less time harboring the negative anti-Black attitudes that eventually "crystalize" or persist over a life span. Or, perhaps in the case of the Schuman and Bobo article, they may perceive, relative to older whites, that they have less to lose on housing laws; after all, it's unlikely they own a house. In any case, highly sympathetic white people may be young.

Gender

Some research indicates that women score higher on measures of sympathy than men (Eisenberg et al. 1989; Klein and Hodges 2001), a gap often attributed to differences in socialization. Girls are more likely to internalize a responsibility to care for others and to protect the vulnerable, whereas boys are more likely to emphasize individual justice (Gilligan and Attanucci 1988). This distinction can begin quite young and can be reinforced by gendered divisions of household labor (Doan and Quadlin 2019). Research has found that mothers and older siblings mention emotions more frequently to girls than boys by the time children are eighteen months old. By twenty-four months, the girls themselves referred to their feelings significantly more often than boys did (Dunn, Bretherton, and Munn 1987). These gaps persist throughout childhood (Kuebli, Butler, and Fivush 1995).

Moving to politics, political scientists have argued that the Democratic Party's advantage among women is shaped, in part, by the party's perceived advantage on race. Among a sample of Detroit-area citizens, Vincent Hutchings and colleagues (2004) found that frames that emphasized the importance of racial diversity improved evaluations of George Bush among white women but not white men. If white women's racial attitudes shape their political decisions and they have been socialized to sympathize with the most vulnerable, we have reason to expect that women, relative to men, may be more likely to score high on racial sympathy.

Education and Income

Education influences white Americans' experiences with poverty, employment, health, marriage, and more (Goldin 2006; Ladd 2012; Ross and Wu 1995; Torr 2011); it is no surprise that education also shapes politics. People with higher levels of education are more likely to participate in politics (Berinsky and Lenz 2011; Kam and Palmer 2008; Verba, Schlozman, and Brady 1995). They are also more likely to carry tolerant attitudes (Bobo and Licari 1989; Sullivan et al. 1981). John L. Sullivan and colleagues (1981, 94) go so far as to suggest that among the many factors that influence voters' tolerance, education is "foremost" among them.

Why is education so powerful? Highly educated environments could "encourage greater racial tolerance" (Oliver and Mendelberg 2000, 575), which corresponds with Newcomb's Bennington study. Campus norms, student politics, and course syllabi could contribute to white students' perceptions of Black suffering. Other work argues that the *type* of person who elects to pursue more education may be distinct. This research has found that education is a proxy for preadult experiences that simultaneously predispose some people to pursue higher education and participate more in politics (Berinsky and Lenz 2011; Kam and Palmer 2008). Similar forces may influence some white people, even before they take a single class, to be more racially sympathetic than others who do not select this route. For all these reasons, racially sympathetic whites may be especially highly educated; this is implied by the Politico article described earlier in the chapter.

TABLE 4.1 **Racial Sympathy, Age, Gender, Education, and Income**

	Highly Racially Sympathetic Whites	All Whites
Mean Age	45.19	50
Male	32.24	45.86
Female	67.76	54.14
College Graduate	37.41	35.17
Income > 70k	35.18	35.67

Source: Pooled YouGov File (2013 CCES, 2016 YouGov, 2020 YouGov)
n = 2235

Education is related to income, with more highly educated individuals typically earning more money than those who are not. Accordingly, highly racially sympathetic whites may also be richer than the average white American. The relationship between white Americans' material status and racial attitudes has been explored elsewhere, often through the group position and threat paradigm.[4] If low-income whites think they are competing with African Americans for finite rights and resources, they may be less inclined to view them with sympathy (Blumer 1958; Bobo and Hutchings 1996). In this view, high-income whites can afford to be sympathetic because it is relatively costless; perched securely atop the racial hierarchy, they perceive scant personal trade-offs to supporting politicians and policies that could elevate Black Americans. On the other hand, perhaps their higher incomes insulate them from thinking too much about others' suffering.

Age, gender, education, and income are four important dimensions of white public opinion. How do they relate to racial sympathy? Are highly racially sympathetic whites overwhelmingly young, female, highly educated, and wealthy? To explore the answer to this question, I present the relationship between these variables and the racial sympathy index in table 4.1.

Table 4.1 has two columns of data. In the left column, I display the percentage of "highly racially sympathetic whites" by demographic category labeled in the row title. So, for example, if we were to look at all highly racially sympathetic whites across my three samples, we would find that approximately 37 percent of them graduated from college (and 63% did not), 35 percent of them made more than $70,000 (and 65% of them did not), and so on. In the right column, as a reference, I display the distribution of this attribute among all whites in my pooled sample. I replicate the setup of table 4.1 in the following pages; it is intended to illustrate how highly racially sympathetic whites may be distinct within their own racial group.[5]

Compared to the full sample of white Americans, those white people who are highly racially sympathetic are significantly younger and more likely to be female. They are also, on average, younger than those whites low on racial sympathy. A significant negative correlation exists between age and racial sympathy (Pearson $r = -0.09$ in the pooled data).[6] This is a relatively modest coefficient. Looking at the average ages, displayed in the first row of table 4.1, we can see that the highly racially sympathetic white person is middle-aged, not especially young. Since age tends to correspond with other important attributes, such as Democratic partisanship, it is important to evaluate whether the relationship between age and racial sympathy remains when other factors are taken into consideration.

Generally, racially sympathetic white Americans are also more likely to have graduated college than whites with lower levels of racial sympathy ($p < 0.05$, two sample t-test). The correlation between education and racial sympathy is positive and significant (Pearson $r = .18$, pooled data). But we cannot determine whether higher education fosters higher levels of racial sympathy or, instead, if highly sympathetic white people are more likely to pursue higher levels of education. Otherwise put, correlation is not causation. In either case, racial sympathy tends to increase as education increases. However, as with the preceding factors, the difference is modest; just like the general population, most highly racially sympathetic white Americans do *not* possess a bachelor's degree.

Given the relationship between education and income, it is not surprising that white Americans high in racial sympathy tend to have higher levels of income than those low in racial sympathy. In contrast to the other demographics outlined earlier, this difference is not statistically significant. Although this group may be described as "upscale"—eating avocado toast and toting $80 Scandinavian backpacks—white people with the highest levels of racial sympathy do not have distinctly high incomes.

Finally, we come to gender. Racially sympathetic whites are much more likely to self-identify as women than men, lending some initial support to the power of gender socialization. The correlation between gender and racial sympathy is significant and positive, rivaling education (Pearson $r = .17$). As with the preceding categories, confounding variables potentially cloud our interpretation of this relationship. Among white people, there is a big gender gap with respect to college completion: 39 percent of white men do not have a college degree compared to 27 percent of white women. White women are, therefore, more likely to be highly educated than white men.[7] We might reasonably wonder whether white women's higher levels of sympathy are driven by their gendered socialization or their education. I return to this question shortly. For now, the initial analysis suggests that gender plays some role in white people's sympathy.

This analysis begins our sketch of racial sympathy in the electorate. In the next section, I consider partisanship—generally acknowledged to be *the most* influential component of Americans' political psychology—and ideology.

Partisanship

Among the many psychological forces that shape white Americans' politics, "none is more important than Americans' abiding loyalty to a political party" (Sides, Tesler, and Vavreck 2019, 22). For this reason, scholars have studied partisanship across multiple dimensions, including its origins and persistence over time (Campbell et al. 1960; Green, Palmquist, and Schickler 2004).

Throughout the twentieth century, the Republican and Democratic parties became increasingly divided on race. During this period, the Democratic Party gained a reputation as more liberal on racial matters (Carmines and Stimson 1989; Kinder and Sanders 1996; Schickler 2016), in part because they supported the pro–Civil Rights position (Kuziemko and Washington 2018). Preceding this legislation, the party had been courting Black voters for some time, especially as the Great Migration opened up the franchise to the millions of Black Americans who relocated to large cities in the urban Northeast, Midwest, and West (Grant 2020). The party also changed its electoral rules and procedures. In the late 1960s and early 1970s, the Democratic Party adopted several reforms, in areas like delegate selection, which had the effect of increasing the influence of its Black members (McAdam 1999; Shafer 1983).

Since then, the party's association with Black Americans has continued and, in some ways, deepened. The nomination of Obama "racialized" almost everything he touched, including his party. According to Tesler, throughout Obama's candidacy and presidency, "white racial liberals became increasingly Democratic while white racial conservatives became increasingly Republican" (2016, 163). Simultaneously, salient social divisions, such as religion, class, race, and geography, are now projected onto partisan identities. Many of these identities are immutable, making bipartisanship or compromise an especially formidable task (Mason 2018).

Partisanship is now strongly connected to voters' racial identities and attitudes. White partisans denigrate the opposing party for racial reasons; among white Democrats, those who recognize racism's role in holding Black Americans back are more likely to vilify Republicans than those white Democrats who do not carry this belief (Kalmoe and Mason 2022). The relationship between race and partisanship has become so fused that these two factors are now, to quote a 2020 article, "inseparable" (Westwood and Peterson 2020). There is no indication that these trends will abate.

There is, therefore, ample reason to expect that highly racially sympathetic white people are more likely to be Democrats. Political parties are sometimes described as having three "faces"—as organizations, "on the ground" or among the electorate, and in the government. These functions organize and reinforce each other. In each case, the three faces of the Democratic Party likely promote racially sympathetic views among its white members.

Ideology

Ideology is related to but distinct from partisanship. Partisanship is tethered to parties, which derive strength from the three faces described earlier. The party is an identifiable and highly visible group and is one to which many Americans carry an attachment (Green, Palmquist, and Schickler 2004). On the other hand, liberalism and conservativism do not have this organizational feature, making them "fair game for intellectual historians and political theorists but rather less helpful to ordinary people trying to follow, not all that determinedly, what is going on in political life" (Kinder and Kalmoe 2017, 133). Decades ago, Converse (1964) characterized most Americans as "ideologically innocent," meaning they lack a consistent, structured configuration of beliefs, a description that has been reaffirmed with more recent analysis (Kinder and Kalmoe 2017, 41).

Insofar as efforts to mitigate Black suffering involve or require the expansion of government, it is reasonable to expect that white people who feel distressed over Black suffering would also support a state that is more liberal in its provision of resources. One way to approximate ideol-

TABLE 4.2 **Racial Sympathy, Partisanship, and Political Ideology**

	Highly Racially Sympathetic Whites	All Whites
% Democrat	57.48	31
% Independent	11.68	17.58
% Republican	12.15	31.2
Ideology (0 = Very Liberal)	0.22	0.41

Source: Pooled YouGov File (2013 CCES, 2016 YouGov, 2020 YouGov)
n = 2235

ogy is to gauge citizens' taste for a limited government, and another way is to ask them where they might place themselves on a scale ranging from "Extremely Liberal" to "Extremely Conservative." In table 4.2, I use the self-identification measure, but in other studies, if available, I use the limited government measure instead. The latter is preferable because it is a multi-item measure, which reduces measurement error. While acknowledging the limitations of ideology as an explanatory variable, it is nonetheless fruitful to consider the relationship between ideology and racial sympathy, and I do so in table 4.2.

Approximately 31 percent of whites in my pooled sample identified as Democrats; this number was almost double when I restrict the analysis to those who score at the top of the racial sympathy scale. White Republicans are especially likely to exhibit low levels of sympathy; in the 2020 YouGov studies, roughly half of Republicans fall in the bottom quartile of racial sympathy. These results affirm the powerful relationship between race and partisan attachment. Many, though certainly not all, white Democrats are highly racially sympathetic, and many, though certainly not all, white Republicans are not.[8]

The results for ideology are similar. In the last row of table 4.2, a score of 0 could be interpreted as evidence that everyone in that column identifies as very liberal. A score of 1 would mean that all individuals in that column identify as very conservative. The mean of .22 at the bottom of the "Highly Racially Sympathetic Whites" column suggests that this group is especially likely to identify as liberal or prefer a more active role for government. Although we should practice caution when interpreting ideological identification, table 4.2 provides evidence that many highly racially sympathetic white Americans are drawn to the "liberal" label, whether out of a sense of loyalty or for symbolic reasons (Conover and Feldman 1981). Overall, among white people, Democrats and liberals are more likely to score high on the racial sympathy measures. These strong relationships corroborate the argument that white Americans' racial attitudes are prominently represented in their political identities.

Religiosity

As testament to the power of the partisan divide, research has found that it routinely spills out of politics and into many other areas of American life. Although there are many domains I could consider, ranging from family dynamics (Iyengar, Konitzer, and Tedin 2018) to coffee preferences (DellaPosta, Shi, and Macy 2015; Hiaeshutter-Rice, Neuner, and Soroka 2023), I take up two especially important to the current enterprise: religion and region. Partisanship, religion, and region have become so intertwined that it can sometimes be difficult to establish distinctions among them.

Consider religion. During the 1960s and 1970s, a subset of Americans became preoccupied with "morality politics," fixating on topics such as legal protections for gays and lesbians, abortion access, church-state separation, and the legalization of marijuana. These issues provided a "new and substantively different political dimension on which the parties could differentiate themselves" (Margolis 2018, 29). Since, then, the "religion gap," or the "tendency of most religious Americans to espouse conservative political beliefs and prefer Republican candidates" (Olson and Green 2006, 455), has persisted.

Scholars often refer to the three *B*s of religion—belonging, behaving, and believing—as ways to think about this multidimensional topic (Olson and Warber 2008). Among these, the "behaving" dimension, which captures the frequency of religious behavior, such as attendance at worship services, could be especially influential in politics. Frequent church attendance not only signifies an individual's commitment to religion but also could reinforce the effects of the "beliefs" or denomination, which might have consequences on attendant political opinions and preferences. This could be because clergy preach certain messages from the pulpit or because congregants reinforce these messages by increasing the interactions with like-minded members of the denomination (Wilcox 1990). In his study of "the social roots of antifeminism," Jerome L. Himmelstein (1986) found, for example, that church attendance was the most important factor in differentiating antifeminists from feminists.

Other research has examined the "nones"—those characterized by the "absence" of practicing religion.[9] Among white people, this group is more likely to be young, liberal, and highly educated (Baker and Smith 2009). Their disengagement with religion may stem from an aversion to conservative institutions and traditional power structures. If this is the case, they may also sympathize with Black Americans who have been typically oppressed by hierarchical institutions. Further, David E. Campbell and colleagues argue that some Americans adopt the "none" label to disassociate themselves from the new Christian right. In a set of experiments, they demonstrate that religious disaffiliation "is due at least in part to a backlash to the mixture of religion and conservative politics, especially the Religious Right" (2021, 137).[10]

Religion, then, may align with racial sympathy in meaningful ways.[11] Indeed, at other moments in American history, religion generally—and churches specifically—played an important role in efforts to eradicate Black suffering. In 1837, for example, fewer than one in four adult Americans belonged to any church; however, it was estimated that seven-eighths of the membership of predominantly white antislavery societies were members of Protestant churches (McPherson 1995). Perhaps because of this, Massachusetts abolitionist Charles K. Whipple observed that "the Anti-Slavery movement . . . was at its commencement, and has ever since been, thoroughly and emphatically a religious enterprise" (McKivigan 1984, 18).[12] Hundreds of years later, some white religious leaders continue to use their pulpits to espouse racially liberal messages.[13] Despite this, I expect a negative relationship between racial sympathy and religious engagement in contemporary politics because of the strong relationship between the Republican Party and racial attitudes. Accordingly, highly racially sympathetic whites might be less religious, perhaps to the point where they opt out of religion, or at least religious services, entirely.

Region

Geography or region may also factor into white Americans' racial attitudes. The unique political and cultural environment of the eleven states constituting the former Confederacy, or what I will refer to as "the South," create a distinct and politically meaningful subnational identity for all racial groups (Williams 2021).[14] Research has found that Southern whites are remarkably homogeneous across multiple dimensions, including their high levels of racial animus. In the South, white racial prejudice is strongly related to political outcomes, such as presidential voting and

TABLE 4.3 **Racial Sympathy, Church Attendance, and Living in the South**

	Highly Racially Sympathetic Whites	All Whites
% Attend Church Never	50.94	38
Attend Church Once a Week or More	12.74	21.36
% Southern	20	28.28

Source: Pooled YouGov File (2013 CCES, 2016 YouGov, 2020 YouGov)
n = 2235

party identification, a relationship that has strengthened over time (Valentino and Sears 2005). If environments matter for shaping whites' racial attitudes—and the evidence suggests they do (Oliver and Mendelberg 2000; Walsh 2007)—it seems reasonable to expect that highly racially sympathetic white Americans are unlikely to live in the South. Table 4.3 presents the relationship between church attendance, geography, and racial sympathy.

There are some noteworthy patterns. Most racially sympathetic whites do not live in the South, but then again, most white Americans also do not live there. That said, a sizable percentage of highly sympathetic white Americans in the United States—approximately one in five—are Southerners. Highly racially sympathetic whites are not especially religious, as defined by a survey question that asks respondents how often they attend religious services. Interestingly, over half never attend church, though about one in eight attend services once a week or more. Although this measure only captures the "behaving" element of religion, it nonetheless suggests that on this politically important dimension, highly racially sympathetic white Americans are distinct.

All Together Now

So far, this chapter treats these important categories as separate or independent factors. This makes for a tidy survey analysis, but forces like partisanship and education do not operate in a vacuum in the real world; instead, they influence each other in meaningful ways. We know, for example, that young voters also tend to be Democratic. If young white people are more likely to be racially sympathetic, can we attribute this to their age or partisanship? Or, to take another example, the earlier analysis explores the relationship between region and sympathy. However, the South is a religious region of the country and contains the Bible Belt;

what appears to be the influence of region could be the influence of religion and so on.

Regression offers one way to consider the contributions of each of these factors. Specifically, multiple regression is a statistical technique that permits the researcher to account for the many factors (independent variables) related to an interesting outcome, the dependent variable. The procedure measures the separate effects of each independent variable on the dependent variable, thus permitting us to gauge the relative contribution of each independent variable. For this reason, regression is an ideal tool for this analysis and many that follow. Since regressions constitute such an important source of my evidence, I now take some time to walk the reader through the interpretation of an ordinary least squares (OLS) regression table.[15] Those who remember their statistics course from when they "probably majored, or are majoring, in political science or public policy" can skip ahead to table 4.4.

The summary statistics presented in the previous pages are artificially suspended from reality and reflect a world in which, for example, partisanship can be partitioned from education and age does not shape one's religiosity. A properly specified regression model permits us to approximate the complexity of our social world. Its accuracy and interpretation depend, in part, on the identification of the many factors that could account for important political outcomes and the statistical "control" of them. I expand on this logic in the next section, where I conduct a series of regressions to understand the components contributing to a white person's score on the racial sympathy index. The variables introduced in the first part of chapter 4 serve as my regressors or the independent variables. I include them in my regression to understand the variation of the outcome variable: racial sympathy. Since many of these independent variables have already revealed themselves as meaningful to sympathy, I suspect some will remain influential here.

To capitalize on the racial sympathy scale's full 0–1 variation, I return to analyzing all respondents in the YouGov surveys. This approach permits me to examine a larger sample, leveraging the responses from thousands of white Americans. We can be more confident about the accuracy of our findings when we observe consistently similar results across independent studies. As with the preceding chapter, the results in table 4.4 are presented by survey.

Table 4.4 depicts the results of four separate regressions. Each model contains the same independent variables (displayed in the rows) and the same dependent variable (the racial sympathy index). The column

TABLE 4.4 **Antecedents of the Racial Sympathy Index**

Variables	2013 CCES	2016 YouGov	2020 YouGov Wave 1	2020 YouGov Wave2
Age	−0.04	−0.08	0.03	−0.04
	(0.042)	(0.051)	(0.050)	(0.051)
Gender (1 = Female)	0.02	0.11***	0.10***	0.06***
	(0.021)	(0.026)	(0.023)	(0.023)
Education	0.06	0.16***	0.04	0.04
	(0.037)	(0.049)	(0.043)	(0.044)
Income	−0.02	−0.12*	0.02	0.06
	(0.052)	(0.064)	(0.055)	(0.055)
Region (1 = South)	−0.01	−0.06**	−0.02	−0.05**
	(0.023)	(0.028)	(0.025)	(0.026)
Party ID (1 = GOP)	−0.16***	−0.21***	−0.19***	−0.25***
	(0.035)	(0.040)	(0.051)	(0.050)
Limited Government	−0.08**	−0.05	−0.17**	−0.18***
	(0.032)	(0.034)	(0.068)	(0.059)
Church Attendance	0.00	−0.00	0.05	0.08**
	(0.029)	(0.037)	(0.039)	(0.037)
Constant	0.74***	0.67***	0.69***	0.77***
	(0.047)	(0.055)	(0.067)	(0.055)
Observations	751	533	503	503
R-squared	0.143	0.214	0.280	0.345

Sources: 2013 CCES, 2016 YouGov, 2020 YouGov
*** $p < 0.01$; ** $p < 0.05$; * $p < 0.10$
Cell entries are ordinary least squares regression coefficients (standard errors in parentheses). In the 2020 YouGov study, ideology is measured by self-reported ideology. In all other studies, it is measured using the limited government index. Data are weighted for national representativeness. All variables are coded from 0 to 1.

headings signal that this model was run through the data of four different surveys: the 2013 CCES, the 2016 YouGov, and the two waves of the 2020 YouGov study. Further, comparing results across multiple independent surveys can help us detect patterns. Table 4.4 displays that partisanship and ideology have the strongest association with a white person's level of racial sympathy. How do we know this? We learn this by looking at the titles of the rows and then examining the number that appears to their right; these are called regression coefficients. The coefficients in this regression table display the association of each independent variable with the dependent variable of racial sympathy. We find, for example, that a one-unit increase in education is associated with a 6 percent increase in the racial sympathy index in the 2013 CCES. In this same survey, a one-unit increase in age is associated with a 4 percent reduction in racial sympathy.

What is "one unit" of age? In this table and almost all others in the book, unless explicitly noted, I have recoded the variables from 0 to 1. Advancing "one unit" means we are traveling the full range of the scale.

Thus, going from the lowest level of education (did not complete high school, coded "0") to the highest (postgraduate degree, coded "1") is associated with an increase of 0.06 on the racial sympathy index (out of 1, because, like the independent variables, I have coded the dependent variables from 0 to 1, as well).

Earlier, it seemed like higher levels of education defined highly racially sympathetic whites; they were much more likely to have a BA relative to other members of their racial group. They were characterized as highly educated in the Politico piece. What happened? Regression happened. When conducting the multiple regression, I accounted for the simultaneous contributions of multiple social and demographic factors. Was this a fluke? Is education significantly related to racial sympathy even while accounting for other factors? Maybe, but since we observe this pattern in three out of four surveys consulted, it seems more likely that education's contribution to sympathy is perhaps more modest than previously understood.

In table 4.4, party identification and ideology roar through as the largest coefficients. How strong are they? To answer this question, we can consult the magnitude of the coefficient. Remember, all variables, including the dependent variable, are coded from 0 to 1; thus, a decimal point can be interpreted as a percentage. Depending on the survey, differences in partisanship and ideology account for 5 to 25 percentage points on the racial sympathy scale. Is this large? It is hard to assess the magnitude in the abstract. But with the uniform 0–1 coding scheme, we can try to answer this question by sizing up the coefficients in relation to each other. When we do, we see that partisanship and ideology are often the largest in the models. The other coefficients do not display a consistent relationship with sympathy, though in most cases, they are in the expected direction. Racially sympathetic whites do tend to be more educated than nonsympathetic whites. However, net of other factors, education is not related to sympathy and partisanship *is* related to sympathy. Partisanship can affect many areas of white Americans' lives; here, we find it can make a big difference in their level of racial sympathy too.

So too can gender. In three out of four cases, gender is significantly associated with higher scores on the racial sympathy index. The variable of gender is coded the highest value, 1, if the respondent identifies as female. Thus, the positive and significant coefficient for gender can be interpreted as showing that white people who identify as women are more likely to express higher levels of racial sympathy than white people who do not identify with this group. As previously discussed, this may have something to do with how women are socialized, which is related to their positions in the country's social structure (Lizotte 2016). Eagly and colleagues explain the relationship between these two factors: "For example, the general expectation that women are and should be sensitive, warm, soft-hearted, and peaceable . . . likely arises from their disproportionate occupancy of caring roles" (2004, 796). That said, since the result is not consistent across all studies and the magnitude is, in some cases, more modest, we should not overemphasize this relationship.

The regressions displayed in the preceding table demonstrate that party and ideology are reliable components of racial sympathy; after all, the coefficients on these variables are significant in every case for partisanship and in three out of four surveys for ideology. In other ways, the roots of the attitude are diverse. This exercise does not establish a narrow archetype of the racially sympathetic person; racial sympathy can be found in many corners of the white electorate, but especially among liberals and Democrats.

A General Liberalism?

The preceding results bring us to a reasonable question: Is what I refer to as *racial sympathy* actually general liberalism? If *racial* sympathy extends to any socially marginalized group aligned with the Democratic Party, then we need not invest further effort in studying racial sympathy specifically. Instead, we could simply study very liberal white people or white people who are strongly identified with the Democratic Party. In either case, we would not, I'm afraid, require the rest of this book.

Discriminant validity is demonstrated by evidence that measures that are theoretically unrelated are, in fact, empirically unrelated. The preceding part of the chapter establishes the broad parameters of racial sympathy; the remaining sections bring them into focus. By helping us see what sympathy is not, the discriminant validity exercises identify the boundaries between sympathy and other psychological concepts. If racial sympathy represents distress over *racial* suffering in particular, it should not be highly correlated with suffering based on other attributes. Further, if sympathy is primarily based on out-group attitudes, it should not primarily be oriented toward the in-group. In all cases, these demonstrations would provide evidence of racial sympathy's discriminant validity.

I'll begin with the possibility that racial sympathy is equivalent to a broad social sympathy. Many white Americans feel sympathy toward multiple marginalized groups (and, of course, many feel none). The concept of racial sympathy ought to capture white Americans' views toward marginalized racial groups in particular. I test this by examining the relationship between gender sympathy, or one's distress over women's suffering, and racial sympathy. If racial sympathy is distinct from a broader social sympathy, it ought to exhibit only a modest relationship with gender attitudes and policies.

Of course, there are many women within the category of "Black Americans." I do not mean to suggest that Black women are excluded from a measure capturing gender sympathy. However, work by Corrine M. McConnaughy and Ismail K. White (2011) suggests that when white respondents reflect on the category of "women," they may not be thinking about Black women unless a qualifier, the racial group, is named (4).

Relatedly, in a survey experiment, Jim Sidanius and colleagues described an affirmative action policy. Subjects were randomly assigned to conditions that identified the beneficiaries of these programs as either women, Blacks, or "the poor." Non-Black respondents evaluated affirmative action differently depending on the category referenced in the experimental stimulus. Specifically, they were least opposed to the program when the beneficiaries were women and most opposed when the beneficiaries were Black (Sidanius et al. 2000, 218). Elsewhere in the book I further probe the distinction racially sympathetic white people might make between "poor" and Black. For now, based on the foregoing and the fact that only 14 percent of women in the United States are Black, I expect that when many white respondents view the category "gender," they, for the most part, will not be thinking of Black women in particular.

Following the approach of the racial sympathy vignettes, I included two measures of gender sympathy in the 2013 CCES and 2020 YouGov study. In these vignettes, a woman is described as facing a discriminatory situation. Subjects were asked to indicate their sympathy for the woman described, mirroring the format of the racial sympathy vignettes.[16] As with the racial sympathy index, I combine respondents' reactions to the vignettes into an additive index representing gender sympathy (2013 CCES α = .74, 2020 YouGov α = .75).

Table 4.5 presents the results displayed in the now familiar OLS regression table. Rather than evaluating the correlates of racial sympathy in isolation, as I did in table 4.4, here I present the antecedents of racial

TABLE 4.5 **Correlates of Racial Sympathy, Gender Sympathy, and Racial Resentment**

Variables	2013 CCES			2020 YouGov		
	Racial Sympathy	Gender Sympathy	Racial Resentment	Racial Sympathy	Gender Sympathy	Racial Resentment
Age	−0.04	0.07	0.13***	0.02	0.09**	0.14***
	(0.041)	(0.044)	(0.044)	(0.040)	(0.043)	(0.040)
Gender	0.03*	0.02	0.03	0.09***	0.09***	−0.02
	(0.018)	(0.020)	(0.019)	(0.018)	(0.020)	(0.020)
Education	0.04	0.02	−0.12***	0.07*	0.07	−0.17***
	(0.032)	(0.041)	(0.037)	(0.036)	(0.043)	(0.040)
Income	0.05	−0.01	−0.02	−0.02	−0.06	−0.02
	(0.045)	(0.054)	(0.047)	(0.045)	(0.053)	(0.053)
Region (1 = South)	0.00	−0.00	−0.00	−0.02	0.00	0.01
	(0.020)	(0.024)	(0.022)	(0.021)	(0.025)	(0.020)
Party ID (1 = GOP)	−0.14***	−0.12***	0.26***	−0.17***	−0.11***	0.27***
	(0.035)	(0.040)	(0.032)	(0.038)	(0.041)	(0.050)
Ideology				−0.18***	−0.17***	0.37***
				(0.052)	(0.050)	(0.069)
Limited Government	−0.09***	−0.10***	0.19***			
	(0.029)	(0.030)	(0.029)			
Church Attendance	−0.02	−0.03	0.02	0.06*	0.02	0.01
	(0.029)	(0.033)	(0.028)	(0.032)	(0.034)	(0.029)
Constant	0.73***	0.77***	0.38***	0.79***	0.80***	0.18***
	(0.030)	(0.033)	(0.035)	(0.038)	(0.039)	(0.039)
Observations	751	751	751	503	503	503
R-squared	0.139	0.099	0.354	0.279	0.177	0.580

Sources: 2013 CCES, 2020 YouGov

*** $p < 0.01$; ** $p < 0.05$; * $p < 0.10$

Cell entries are ordinary least squares regression coefficients (standard errors in parentheses). In the 2020 YouGov study, ideology is measured by self-reported ideology. In all other studies, it is measured using the limited government index. Data are weighted for national representativeness. All variables are coded from 0 to 1.

sympathy, gender sympathy, and racial resentment side by side. Like the preceding table, the results from multiple surveys are displayed to help us detect patterns. The 2013 CCES results appear on the left side of the table, and the results from the 2020 YouGov study are depicted on the right. Although these surveys were administered on independent samples seven years apart, the relationships between demographics and attitudes remain remarkably similar, specifically with respect to the distinctions between the attitudes. Across both surveys, education and age seem to be strongly related to racial resentment and less consistently with racial and gender sympathy, for example.

Based on this evidence, it seems that white liberals and Democrats are more likely to sympathize with women *and* Black Americans. Few other categories consistently predict these attitudes; white Americans high on racial sympathy and gender sympathy can be found across different ages, levels of education, regions, and income categories.

Sympathy for the Underdog

Thus, a broader social sympathy may be afoot. Liberal and Democratic identification both factor into a white person's level of racial sympathy *and* gender sympathy. So how can we know if racial sympathy is uniquely racial? If racial sympathy represents a broader social sympathy, then we would expect to observe its effects not only on matters of race but also on policies that impact other groups, too. This is because, unlike racial sympathy, being liberal and being Democrat likely translate into support for a range of socially marginalized groups.

In chapter 2, I theorized that racial sympathy is specifically based on white distress over Black suffering. Reflecting this conceptualization, the racial vignettes all feature Black people suffering. By evaluating racial sympathy's relationship to other marginalized groups, we gain insight into whether the measure has appropriately operationalized as racial sympathy, providing evidence of its validity.

To evaluate whether racial sympathy reflects a broader "sympathy for the underdog," I conduct a series of regressions to examine the influence of racial and gender sympathy on support for so-called women's issues (Burns et al. 2016). These include, for example, support for abortion, requiring companies to allow up to six months of unpaid leave for parents to spend time with their newborn or newly adopted children, and preferential treatment for women when applying for jobs or promotions.[17] All questions appeared on the 2013 CCES, and the third question was administered in the 2020 YouGov study. The regression results are presented in table 4.6.

In the chapter's preceding regression tables, racial sympathy was the dependent variable, representing the outcome we were trying to understand or the variable that depends on the levels of the other (independent) variables. Here, and for the remainder of the book, I present tables with different dependent variables—in most cases, political opinions or, later, reported political behavior. With this setup, I am trying to understand the roots of these opinions or behaviors among white Americans. There are many forces that factor into these important political outcomes; is racial sympathy one of them? I begin to evaluate this question in table 4.6, where I take up the possibility that racial sympathy may impact white Americans' views of women's issues policies. Within each policy area, I analyze three different model specifications. In the far-left column of table 4.6, labeled Model A, I examine the relationship between racial sympathy and policy opinion. In Model B, I consider the relationship between gender sympathy and opinion. Finally, in Model C, I include both gender and racial sympathy and examine the association of both of these attitudes with policy opinion.

The gender sympathy index, representing distress over women's suffering, leads some white people to support policies that conceivably benefit women. The substantive effect is large; in the case of women's affirmative action, the magnitude of the coefficient represents between one-sixth to almost one-fourth of the scale. In contrast, the racial sympathy index is not generally associated with these gendered public policies.[18] Indeed, when the racial sympathy index and gender sympathy index are included in the same model—Model C—the racial sympathy index is significantly associated with *opposition* to affirmative action for women. On the other hand, this pattern is not observed in the 2020 YouGov data. Here, the coefficient on racial sympathy is initially statistically significant; however, once the gender sympathy variable is added, it loses its significant relationship with women's affirmative action. Although these inconsistent results complicate our understanding of support for women's affirmative action, they also demonstrate that racial sympathy is independent from sympathy for other marginalized groups.

Racial resentment is significantly associated with opinion on women's issues policies. On some occasions, the coefficient on racial resentment is

TABLE 4.6 **Racial Sympathy, Gender Sympathy, and Support for Gendered Public Policies**

| | 2013 CCES | | | | | | | | | 2020 YouGov | | |
| | Abortion | | | Women's Leave | | | Women's Affirmative Action | | | Women's Affirmative Action | | |
Model	A	B	C	A	B	C	A	B	C	A	B	C
Racial Sympathy	0.04		-0.10	0.26***		0.17	0.07		-0.12**	0.13**		0.06
	(0.068)		(0.085)	(0.082)		(0.109)	(0.053)		(0.063)	(0.062)		(0.071)
Gender Sympathy		0.12**	0.18**		0.22***	0.12		0.17***	0.25***		0.14***	0.12**
		(0.060)	(0.078)		(0.070)	(0.092)		(0.044)	(0.053)		(0.052)	(0.060)
Racial Resentment	-0.11*	-0.11*	-0.13**	-0.19**	-0.24***	-0.21**	-0.32***	-0.32***	-0.35***	-0.36***	-0.38***	-0.36***
	(0.062)	(0.059)	(0.062)	(0.088)	(0.084)	(0.088)	(0.049)	(0.046)	(0.048)	(0.067)	(0.062)	(0.066)
Party ID (1 = GOP)	-0.15***	-0.14***	-0.14***	-0.27***	-0.27***	-0.26***	-0.12***	-0.11***	-0.11***	0.04	0.03	0.04
	(0.052)	(0.051)	(0.051)	(0.068)	(0.069)	(0.069)	(0.042)	(0.041)	(0.041)	(0.061)	(0.060)	(0.060)
Ideology	-0.08*	-0.07*	-0.07*	-0.14***	-0.14**	-0.14**	-0.06**	-0.05*	-0.05*	-0.18***	-0.16**	-0.17***
	(0.040)	(0.040)	(0.040)	(0.055)	(0.056)	(0.055)	(0.028)	(0.028)	(0.028)	(0.066)	(0.065)	(0.065)
Constant	0.42***	0.35***	0.39***	0.60***	0.64***	0.58***	0.74***	0.66***	0.70***	0.59***	0.58***	0.55***
	(0.092)	(0.084)	(0.092)	(0.119)	(0.113)	(0.120)	(0.061)	(0.061)	(0.063)	(0.073)	(0.069)	(0.077)
Observations	833	833	833	830	830	830	836	836	836	503	503	503
R-squared	0.292	0.298	0.299	0.246	0.245	0.248	0.308	0.327	0.332	0.378	0.384	0.385

Sources: 2013 CCES, 2020 YouGov

*** $p < 0.01$; ** $p < 0.05$; * $p < 0.10$

Cell entries are ordinary least squares regression coefficients (standard errors in parentheses). The column headings display the dependent variables, which are questions about policy opinion. Coefficients on additional control variables included in the models here are not shown for space considerations; the following variables were included in the models: income, age, education, gender, region (South), and church attendance. In the 2020 YouGov study, ideology is measured by self-reported ideology. In the 2013 CCES, it is measured using the limited government index. Data are weighted for national representativeness. All variables are coded from 0 to 1.

the largest in the model. The policies related to women in the workplace are especially striking; going from the lowest to highest level of racial resentment is associated with an almost 40 percent point drop in support for women's affirmative action—the equivalent of moving from "Neither in favor nor against" to "Strongly against" among the question's answer options in the 2020 YouGov study. To the extent that women's policies may serve disadvantaged women, thereby prompting racial considerations, we might expect racial resentment to have the strongest effect on abortion (see Griffin 1992). However, that is not the case. Instead, racial resentment is most strongly related to those policies shaping women's workplace experiences. The relative precision of the racial sympathy item should provide us with increased confidence that the measure represents distress over Black suffering in particular and not a broader social sympathy.[19]

An In-Group Attitude?

Self-Monitoring

Getting clear about what sympathy is and is not will put us in the best position to examine sympathy's role in American politics. So far, we know that sympathy measures relate to other politically important attitudes and dispositions; this was demonstrated in the preceding chapter. This chapter has clarified the contents of sympathy and shown that white Democrats and liberals are likely to score at the highest levels of sympathy. And yet, the preceding gender sympathy analysis revealed that racial sympathy probably is not a catchall for any social sympathy.

There is more to this important point, and I return to it later in the book. For now, we should note that white Americans' sympathy for Black Americans and their sympathy toward other non-white groups, such, for example, immigrants from Asia and Latin America, has not always been entwined. However, as elite rhetoric on immigration has made the topic more salient and politicized by voters, the norms of racial politics have changed in ways that may have heightened racial sympathy's applicability to other racial groups (Abrajano and Hajnal 2015; Reny, Valenzuela, and Collingwood 2020). The increasing racialization of American politics may have important consequences for sympathy.

I set aside these dynamics for a moment to attend to another feature of sympathy that warrants further clarification: the extent to which racial

sympathy reflects concerns about one's self or in-group. I have conceptualized sympathy as a primarily out-group-focused attitude, but is it possible that, for some white people, racial sympathy contains an evaluation
of *us* or *me* even as it also invokes attitudes about *them*? In the preceding chapter, I found that racial sympathy was positively correlated with
warmth toward white Americans and linked fate with the group (table 3.6). Racially sympathetic white Americans exhibit attachment to
their group, even if they may not carry a strong sense of white racial identity (Jardina 2019).

Still, these individuals might weigh other considerations related to
their individual esteem or self-concept in ways that shape their sympathy.
One possibility is that white Americans' sympathy toward Black people
may not be genuine but instead be a force akin to virtue signaling. There
is some basis for this concern. Tali Mendelberg (2001) argues that there
are "powerful egalitarian norms about race" in the United States. These
norms create an environment where "almost all whites genuinely disavow
the sentiments that have come to be most closely associated with the
ideology of white supremacy . . . nearly every white person today has a
genuine commitment to basic racial equality in the public sphere" (2001,
19). She suggests that the norm of equality has important consequences
for American politics; namely, it requires politicians to resort to subtle
racial cues to win elections. Mendelberg offered these observations over
twenty years ago. Subsequent work has questioned whether these norms
remain relevant or if new norms have emerged (Arora 2019; Newman
et al. 2021; Stephens-Dougan 2020). On the right, one new norm is captured by "overtly hostile" racial rhetoric (Valentino, Neuner, and Vandenbroek 2018, 757), which has become an accepted practice among Republican elites, like Trump.

New norms may also be emerging on the left. Specifically, among some
white Democrats, a commitment to "basic racial equality" may no longer be sufficient. Instead, white Americans may now feel that they must
express support and sympathy for Black Americans above and beyond
egalitarianism. Scholars are only beginning to examine this possibility
(Engelhardt 2021c). However, some white Americans may already be
adjusting their survey behavior accordingly, and if this is the case, they
may log high scores on racial sympathy despite not carrying distress over
Black suffering.

To evaluate this possibility, I consult the self-monitoring scale, a survey
item designed to reflect an enduring predisposition in which individuals

are "chronically concerned with the appropriateness of their interpersonal behavior. They carefully regulate their self-presentation with regard to social norms and contexts, and thus are highly responsive to social and interpersonal cues" (Berinsky and Lavine 2012, 28). If racial sympathy is driven by a desire to conform to norms rather than genuine distress over Black suffering, we should be able to observe this by evaluating responses to the self-monitoring scale.

This scale has been used in hundreds of studies across different disciplines and has been validated specifically for use in political science research (Berinsky and Lavine 2012; Gangestad and Snyder 2000). In the 2020 YouGov study, I included these three questions, which I used to form an additive index, transforming responses to these items onto a 0–1 scale, where higher values indicate a greater propensity to self-monitor.[20] In later chapters, I see whether my results, which document the link between sympathy and political opinion and behavior, differ based on levels of self-monitoring. For now, I focus on the general relationship between self-monitoring and sympathy: Are those who are racially sympathetic also those who are likely to self-monitor?

To examine this question, I compute the correlation between the self-monitoring scale and the racial sympathy index; it is .09. Although this correlation coefficient is positive, it is quite low. If we were to include it in table 3.6, which presents the correlations between racial sympathy and other racial attitudes, it would be among the smallest in the table. The average self-monitoring score for those respondents at the highest level of racial sympathy, as defined earlier in the chapter, is .32. The score is .29 for the entire sample and .28 for the 85 percent of the sample that did not indicate the most sympathetic reaction to every vignette. In neither case are these averages significantly different from the highest sympathy group.

The diligent reader will recall that correlations computed between two variables cannot account for the contribution of multiple factors. For example, self-monitoring and racial sympathy may be significantly correlated, but this outcome may reflect the possibility that both variables are related to higher levels of education. If that is the case, then the positive correlation may actually be reflecting the shared contribution of education, not necessarily the relationship between distress over Black suffering and chronic concern about the appropriateness of personal behavior. Multiple regression permits us to evaluate the contribution of multiple simultaneous factors. In appendix table 4.3, I show that the components or ingredients of sympathy and self-monitoring are quite distinct. To be

more precise, the variables that have consistently exhibited the strongest association with sympathy—partisanship and ideology—are not
significantly associated with self-monitoring. Age is not significantly associated with sympathy in the multivariate models presented here. In contrast, the relationship between age and self-monitoring is significant ($p <$
0.05). Older white Americans are significantly less likely to self-monitor
than younger white people.

The development of implicit measures, like the AMP, was born of
these concerns. However, research that has examined social desirability's influence on the measurement of racial attitudes has come to more
qualified conclusions. In a study comparing implicit and explicit attitude
measures, Jordan R. Axt (2018) found that direct self-report racial attitudes were more likely to correspond to the constructs they represent,
making them superior to implicit measures. This is not to deny that some
political science has detected social desirability bias, such as race-of-
interviewer effects, whereby white survey takers give more racially liberal
responses to Black interviewers than white ones. However, it is less clear
whether the frequency of these outcomes occurs "in sufficient magnitude
to threaten the main findings of survey research" (Sears 2004, 296).

In sum, racial sympathy is not equivalent to high self-monitoring. Self-
monitoring may play a role in certain domains and under specific circumstances, which is not to be denied (Berinsky and Lavine 2011; Terkildsen
1993; Weber et al. 2014).[21] And my analyses do reveal traces of social
desirability's presence; sympathy and self-monitoring are positively correlated, and the most racially sympathetic Americans have higher self-
monitoring scores than those lower on sympathy do. In both cases, however, the magnitude of the effect is quite small. In chapter 7, I revisit the
self-monitoring index and use this valuable tool to investigate whether
accounting for self-monitoring eliminates the relationship between sympathy and political outcomes. For now, we have evidence that white distress over Black suffering seems not to be, at its core, a guise for monitoring one's behavior.

Guilt

Self-presentation and adhering to social norms are the primary attributes
of self-monitoring. In contrast, collective guilt, or what I refer to as simply *guilt*, is experienced in an intergroup context when an individual, in
their capacity as a group member, feels responsible for "specific negative

actions" exercised by their in-group toward out-groups (Doosje et al. 1998; Iyer, Leach, and Crosby 2003; Iyer, Schmader, and Lickel 2007). As with sympathy, there may be multiple routes to guilt. Assessments of past and present fictitious and actual events may contribute to higher levels of collective guilt. Parents may raise their children to be attentive to these dynamics, or they could originate in schools or among peer groups. In these ways, sympathy and guilt may share similar sources. There is, however, a distinct component to guilt. Whereas sympathy does not require self-awareness of one's whiteness, guilt requires the extra acknowledgment of one's group membership. Guilt focuses inward. In the case of white Americans, collective guilt is remorse a white person experiences because of "a fraternal association with in-group members who committed deplorable acts against Black people" (Chudy, Piston, and Shipper 2019, 969; Harvey and Oswald 2000, 1793).

This differs from sympathy's focus on the out-group. Sympathy does not require assessments about the in-group or its culpability. Thus, a white person may feel sympathy for Black people because she believes the group to be disproportionately poor, without feeling guilty if she does not believe that white people are responsible for Black poverty. As suggestive evidence of this possibility, the results in table 3.6 depict the positive relationship between a white "feeling thermometer," representing how "warm" the respondent feels toward white people, and racial sympathy. Sympathetic whites can retain positive attitudes toward their own group even while carrying distress over Black people's circumstances.

At this point, we know that we need a good measure to come to these conclusions about the empirical manifestations of guilt. Elsewhere, my colleagues and I have introduced and validated a collective guilt measure based on social psychological research (Chudy, Piston, and Shipper 2019; Iyer, Leach, and Crosby 2003). As with the self-monitoring scale, the questions for these items appear in the appendix. The 2016 YouGov study hosts both racial sympathy and guilt, thus permitting us to evaluate the relationship between these two variables.

Guilt is far less common than sympathy. Indeed, more than half of white Americans in the 2016 YouGov study report feeling zero collective guilt for their group-based advantage. This distribution, presented in figure 4.1, is comparable to estimates from other studies, such as the 2016 ANES Pilot (Chudy, Piston, and Shipper 2019). Viewing the distributions of guilt and sympathy side by side provides some initial indication that these attitudes are distinct. Indeed, guilt and sympathy load onto two

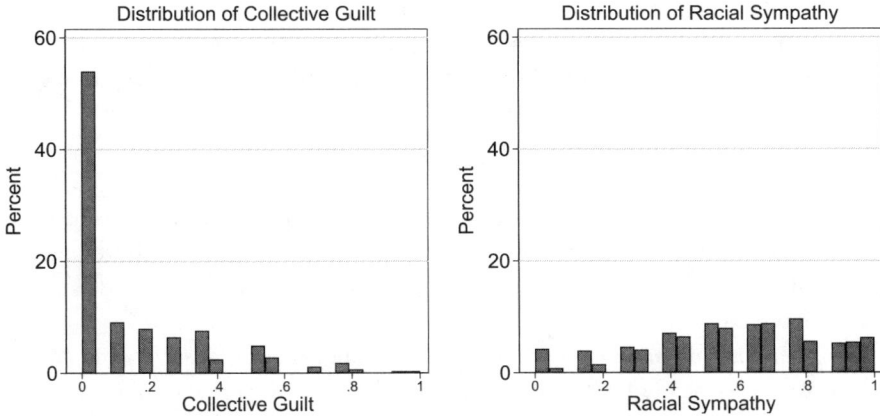

FIGURE 4.1. Distribution of Collective Guilt and Racial Sympathy
Source: 2016 YouGov

separate factors on factor analysis. They also have different antecedents; notably, being older is significantly associated with lower levels of guilt. On the other hand, there is no significant relationship between age and sympathy. These analyses appear in the appendix and suggest that sympathy and guilt are distinct, a topic I have explored in detail elsewhere.[22]

As with the self-monitoring analysis, I consider this point in further detail in subsequent chapters. For now, we proceed with a sense of the demographic profile of the highly racially sympathetic. These white Americans are liberal and more likely to identify as strong Democrats. This analysis shows that racial sympathy does not equate with sympathy for any marginalized social group. Self-monitoring and guilt are also related but are ultimately distinct from sympathy. Instead, the discriminant validity analyses undertaken in this chapter suggest that racial sympathy represents a substantively unique racial attitude.

Conclusion

Racially sympathetic white Americans are often cast as young, highly educated people focused on "broader inequality," to take a headline from a 2020 *FiveThirtyEight* article.[23] Elsewhere, they have been depicted as feeling guilt or shifting their behavior to impress others. It has been difficult to assess the accuracy of this description or to identify the composition of this group generally. Does white distress over Black suffering fit a certain profile of white person? And is this person more broadly sympathetic to any discrimination or inequality?

The analyses in this chapter shed light on these questions. Racial sympathy exists in the young, old, rich, and poor. Some white Americans who have lots of education are racially sympathetic, but some white Americans without lots of education are racially sympathetic, too. Church attendance and region, though powerful forces in American politics, do not seem to meaningfully shape racial sympathy.

Partisanship and ideology, on the other hand, are significantly and consistently associated with racial sympathy. White people who identify as Democrats and liberals are more likely to carry distress over Black suffering than white Republicans and conservatives. The impact of these identities on racial sympathy is quite strong. Given the robustness of the finding, it is reasonable to wonder whether having racial sympathy is merely equivalent to being a white liberal. After all, partisanship, in particular, has long been intertwined with race in American politics, a trend that seems to have only intensified after the election of Obama (Tesler 2016).

However, the discriminant validity analyses find that racial sympathy is specifically rooted in white distress over Black suffering. Although it shares common roots with gender sympathy, racial sympathy is not significantly associated with policies designed to address gender inequality, nor is it interchangeable with Democratic positions on various other issues, from the environment to gun control.

In sum, racial sympathy is carried by a wide range of white Americans who experience distress over Black suffering. This chapter cleared up important misconceptions about racial sympathy, but, by the end of it, we learned a lot about what racial sympathy does *not* do. In the next chapter, I reveal the concept's power as I begin to demonstrate the many ways in which white distress over Black suffering shapes white public opinion. I do so by examining the relationship between racial sympathy and policy areas that, unlike the policies described in table 4.6, implicitly or explicitly impact Black Americans. I start with redistributive policies in chapter 5. In chapter 6, I take up the important relationship between racial sympathy and opinions of the criminal legal system.

CHAPTER FIVE

Public Opinion on Redistributive Policies

S ince the 1970s, income inequality has grown in the United States. The share of income accrued by the top 1 percent more than doubled between 1978 and 2007 (Ashok, Kuziemko, and Washington 2015). The 2020 coronavirus pandemic compounded this trend. The global health crisis cemented long-standing economic inequalities, "exposing and exacerbating" economic disparities between the haves and the have-nots (Perry, Aronson, and Pescosolido 2021). As one example, Black Americans, who have long been economically disadvantaged in comparison to whites, faced a sharp rise in unemployment and wage loss due to the pandemic, which impacted their savings.[1]

Prejudice is both a source and consequence of this persistent inequality (Kinder 2013). Accordingly, political science research has documented that white Americans' prejudice contributes to their opposition to various policies that may address economic inequality, which could conceivably close racial gaps. It is why white people, to quote a seminal book on the topic, "hate welfare" (Gilens 1999).

Yet, many surveys that display white opposition to these programs also unearth white support for these same policy areas. For example, in the 2020 ANES Time Series, approximately 22 percent of white Americans indicated that federal welfare should be increased. More than 30 percent thought the government should help improve the social and economic conditions of Black people.

The purpose of this chapter is to examine the influence of racial sympathy on American public opinion, specifically as it relates to redistributive public policies. Chapter 3 provides the tools to measure racial sympathy.

Chapter 4 introduces us to racially sympathetic white Americans. This chapter builds on that analysis by evaluating the relationship between racial sympathy and white public opinion. I do this by conducting a series of analyses exploring the association between racial sympathy and support for redistributive policies, especially those that are racialized—that is, those policies that implicitly or explicitly reference race—using the 2013 CCES. I replicate these results with two other national surveys conducted by YouGov, one in 2016 and one in 2020. Across these diverse, independent samples and measures, a consistent pattern becomes clear: racial sympathy is significantly associated with racialized redistributive public policies across time and survey.

I approach this by visiting different areas of redistributive policy, each addressing a different facet of racial economic inequality. Collectively, they are all policies that could conceivably reduce the economic suffering of Black Americans and accordingly would be attractive to racially sympathetic white Americans. I begin with policies focused on providing financial assistance. I then consider policies intended to increase Black Americans' educational opportunities. Given the well-documented relationship between education and income, policies that expand access to education could also, in principle, position Black Americans for higher-paying jobs.[2]

The last policy area I consider is one of the most contentious: reparations. H.R. 40, a bill establishing a federal commission to study the legacy of slavery and develop proposals for redress and repair, including reparations, has been introduced and mostly ignored in every session of Congress since 1989. However, the policy has received renewed attention in recent years. As just one example, the city of Evanston, Illinois, launched a program to provide reparations payouts in 2021. Evanston is unusual, and most white Americans object to this policy. But not all do. I will examine whether distress over Black suffering contributes to white Americans' support of these payments.

These policies seek to redistribute resources from the haves to the have-nots. For my final analysis, I examine the conditions under which racial sympathy is most meaningful in politics. Even though social and economic inequality abound, racially sympathetic whites are especially supportive of public policies that explicitly rectify *racial* inequality. I demonstrate this through a national survey experiment.

Not all who rely on government antipoverty assistance are Black. Some programs, such as the Supplemental Nutrition Assistance Program (SNAP), or food stamps, are mostly used by white people, for example.[3]

Nonetheless, because many white Americans tend to overestimate the percentage of welfare recipients that are Black and accordingly bring their negative stereotypes to bear, they "hate" the policy area (Akesson et al. 2022; Gilens 1999). But racial sympathy is one reason why others do not. This chapter illustrates that white distress over Black suffering is connected to whites' opinions on important redistributive policies.

Government Aid to Black Americans

I begin by considering a broad policy area: government aid to Black people. Should the government redistribute resources to African Americans? Although the government may choose to redistribute resources using the criteria of economic need, this policy area specifies race as the basis for resource redistribution. It provides an excellent venue to investigate the political power of racial sympathy. If white distress over Black suffering shapes policy preferences, we should expect to observe its effects in this arena.

More specifically, the survey question that represents this item asks respondents to place themselves on a seven-point scale ranging from "Blacks should help themselves" to "Government should help Blacks." Previous research on this question has found that racial animus, across different forms, leads some whites to oppose government aid to African Americans (Hutchings 2009; Kinder and Sanders 1996; Piston 2014; Sears and Henry 2003). This analysis reexamines the relationship between racial attitudes and support, featuring racial sympathy as the measure of racial attitudes. I do so by conducting an ordinary least squares regression (OLS) in which I regress the policy area—in this case, government aid to Black people—on the racial sympathy index. The results of this analysis appear in table 5.1.[4]

As the first column of table 5.1, labeled "Model 1," displays, partisanship, education, and gender are all factors that make a white person more or less likely to embrace government aid to Black people—a result that is expected, given previous research. What is perhaps unexpected, however, is that in addition to these factors, racial sympathy is also an influential source of white opinion in this policy area. The coefficient has a substantively meaningful magnitude, representing over one-third of the scale.

One might reasonably observe, however, that Model 1 does not account for principles or values on government intervention. Since

TABLE 5.1 **Racial Sympathy and Government Aid to Black People**

Variables	Government Aid to Black People		
	Model 1	Model 2	Model 3
Racial Sympathy	0.35***	0.32***	0.11**
	(0.050)	(0.051)	(0.045)
Party ID (1 = GOP)	−0.23***	−0.14***	−0.01
	(0.032)	(0.036)	(0.029)
Income	−0.06	−0.05	−0.05
	(0.055)	(0.052)	(0.044)
Age	−0.00	0.01	0.07**
	(0.042)	(0.041)	(0.033)
Education	0.08**	0.06*	0.00
	(0.033)	(0.032)	(0.027)
Gender (1 = Female)	−0.05**	−0.06***	−0.02
	(0.020)	(0.020)	(0.016)
Region (1 = South)	−0.04*	−0.03	−0.00
	(0.023)	(0.022)	(0.017)
Church Attendance	0.01	0.03	0.02
	(0.030)	(0.029)	(0.024)
Limited Government		−0.15***	−0.05**
		(0.029)	(0.022)
Racial Resentment			−0.60***
			(0.034)
Constant	0.24***	0.29***	0.67***
	(0.051)	(0.053)	(0.045)
Observations	750	750	750
R-squared	0.306	0.346	0.589

Source: 2013 CCES
*** $p < 0.01$; ** $p < 0.05$; * $p < 0.10$
Cell entries are ordinary least squares regression coefficients (standard errors in parentheses). Data are weighted for national representativeness. All variables are coded from 0 to 1.

"government aid to Black people" is fundamentally and unambiguously a policy about government spending, it is possible that support for this policy area more accurately rests in principles about the size of government than it does attitudes about African Americans specifically.[5] Indeed, some scholars have argued that opinions on racial policies reflect a taste for government intervention more so than prejudice toward Black Americans (Sniderman and Carmines 1997). By this logic, whites who favor a smaller government would oppose any redistributive policy, regardless of the beneficiary, simply because it expands the size of the state. Model 2 considers this possibility by including the limited government index, represented by a three-item index, with a score of 1 corresponding to a strong preference for smaller government.

As the analysis indicates, principles of limited government are significantly associated with opinion in this policy area. The results in the second column of table 5.1 suggest that those individuals who are less inclined to support an active government are also less likely to endorse government aid to Black people. However, even with the contribution of ideology, I find that sympathy targeted toward African Americans matters. Indeed, including a preference for limited government in the model only slightly erodes the contribution of sympathy.[6]

Thus far, the analyses reveal that racial sympathy is significantly associated with opinion on government aid to Black people and that it is not reducible to preferences for limited government or partisanship, among other factors. In some respects, these results correspond with previous research, which has demonstrated the powerful influence of racial attitudes on opinion in this domain. Yet there is one crucial difference: the majority of previous work has considered the consequences of *prejudice*. Is the association between sympathy and opinion distinct from the association between prejudice and opinion? If the answer to this question is no, this suggests that a single measure of prejudice can capture the full range of racial attitudes leading whites to support or oppose government aid to Black people.

Yet, as I have conceptualized it, racial sympathy is not merely the absence of prejudice or resentment but is instead a distinct and politically powerful dimension of racial attitudes. To further examine the relationship between sympathy, resentment, and opinion, I conduct an additional analysis displayed in the far-right column of table 5.1, labeled "Model 3." In this model, I allow for the possibility that low animus in the form of racial resentment drives some white people to embrace government aid to Black people. And indeed, the analysis confirms that resentment is powerful, exhibiting the largest coefficient among many influential regressors. Since previous research has demonstrated that racial resentment is significantly associated with opinion in this policy area, this strong effect is expected (see Kinder and Sanders 1996, 117).

But does prejudice, as measured here by racial resentment, capture the full extent of racial attitudes that shape public opinion in this domain? Based on the racial sympathy coefficient, displayed across the first row of table 5.1, the answer to this question is no. Even considering the powerful effect of racial resentment, racial sympathy continues to be significantly associated with opinion about government aid to Black people. Although the effect of racial sympathy is diminished, its consistent association with policy opinion suggests that the racial sympathy index is capturing unique dimensions of racial attitudes that low animus cannot.

It is worth noting that the racial resentment coefficient is larger in magnitude than sympathy's. Why might this be the case? Some scholars have argued that racial resentment contains nonracial elements (Huddy and Feldman 2009), and certainly the analyses presented in the preceding chapter demonstrate that racial resentment is significantly associated with a host of political variables, including partisanship, preferences for limited government, education, and age.[7] In contrast, although the racial sympathy index is related to ideology and partisanship, it is, relative to resentment, less politicized. The format of the measure, which probes subjects' sympathetic reactions to scenarios seemingly distant from political life, may contribute to this. For this reason, racial sympathy may have less political impact than resentment. That said, racial sympathy matters beyond resentment's impressive contribution.[8]

Based on the results in table 5.1, it seems clear that racial sympathy is significantly associated with support for government aid to Black people. In the next table, I expand this analysis. Table 5.2 includes results from four surveys—the 1994 GSS, 2008 ANES, 2012 ANES, and 2020 YouGov—in which I replicate the model presented in table 5.1.[9] In each case, I find that racial sympathy is significantly associated with government aid to Black people. The magnitude is consistently strong. In the case of the 1994 GSS and 2020 YouGov studies, going from the lowest to highest level of racial sympathy is associated with an increase representing almost one-fourth of the scale. In chapter 4, I outline the importance of partisanship; many political scientists consider it to be one of the most—if not the most—important dimensions of white Americans' political psychology (Sides, Tesler, and Vavreck 2019; Converse 1964). Not only is the magnitude of racial sympathy larger than that of partisanship, it is also more consistently significant. Across five national surveys, the association between sympathy and policy support is strong and substantial.

"Government aid to Black people" is a somewhat general policy intervention. Do the effects of racial sympathy hold when we look at more specific redistributive policies? I consider this possibility by examining two policy areas that designate defined funding interventions. The questions for these items begin with the preamble, "Here are several things that the government in Washington might do to deal with the problems

TABLE 5.2 **Racial Sympathy and Support for Government Redistributive Policies**

Variables	Government Aid to Black People				Support for Black Businesses	Support for Black Schools
	1994 GSS	2008 ANES	2012 ANES	2020 YouGov	2013 CCES	2013 CCES
Racial Sympathy	0.22*** (0.060)	0.17*** (0.037)	0.12*** (0.027)	0.22*** (0.074)	0.24*** (0.070)	0.17** (0.084)
Racial Resentment	−0.98*** (0.088)	−0.49*** (0.038)	−0.53*** (0.024)	−0.42*** (0.060)	−0.44*** (0.063)	−0.37*** (0.074)
Party ID (1 = GOP)	−0.03 (0.049)	−0.09*** (0.030)	−0.08*** (0.017)	−0.07 (0.049)	−0.09* (0.048)	−0.16*** (0.061)
Limited Government	0.05 (0.072)	−0.06*** (0.022)	−0.08*** (0.014)	−0.21*** (0.063)	0.05 (0.041)	−0.08 (0.048)
Constant	1.17*** (0.090)	0.69*** (0.049)	0.73*** (0.027)	0.93*** (0.071)	0.57*** (0.078)	0.80*** (0.094)
Observations	414	1,003	2,820	505	288	289
R-squared	0.336	0.378	0.442	0.576	0.413	0.389

Sources: 1994 GSS, 2008 ANES, 2012 ANES, 2013 CCES, 2020 YouGov
*** $p < 0.01$; ** $p < 0.05$; * $p < 0.10$
Note: Cell entries are ordinary least squares regression coefficients (standard errors in parentheses). Full model is specified in table 5.1. Here, for space considerations, I show the most relevant and powerful controls. For the 2012 ANES, only face-to-face respondents are evaluated. For the 1994 GSS and 2020 YouGov studies, I use a measure of ideology in place of the limited government index. For the 2020 YouGov study, racial sympathy is measured in Wave 1 and opinion toward the dependent variable is measured in Wave 2. Data are weighted for national representativeness. All variables are coded from 0 to 1.

of poverty and unemployment. I would like you to tell me if you favor or oppose them." After each policy area, respondents are presented with a scale ranging from "Strongly favor" to "Strongly oppose." The two policy areas I consider here are whether the "government in Washington" should give "business and industry special tax breaks for locating in black areas" and "spending more money on the schools in black neighborhoods, especially for preschool and early education programs." My expectation is that white people who are distressed about Black suffering will support these policies more than whites who are not.

These results appear in the far-right columns of table 5.2. Cumulatively, the table's six columns span different periods, surveys, and question formats; however, the pattern is remarkably consistent. Whether government aid to Black people is described in general terms or as a specific policy, whether in 1994 or 2020, whether represented as a single question or a four-item index, racial sympathy is associated with white support for these measures.

Welfare

The word *welfare* has a fairly clear "center" but rather fuzzy "borders" (Gilens 1999, 12). Some of the fuzziness may come from its name. What is often referred to as welfare is a specific assistance program: the Temporary Assistance for Needy Families (TANF), which replaced Aid to Families with Dependent Children (AFDC) in 1996. It is a national program distributed through grants to the states. Making things fuzzier still, this federal arrangement means that there is drastic variation in the distribution of the program, depending on where someone lives (Allard 2008).

Although many like the welfare *state*, large percentages of white Americans "hate" welfare as a policy (Gilens 1999). Martin Gilens argues that welfare attracts this opposition because it is "a 'race-coded' topic that evokes racial imagery and attitudes even when racial minorities are not explicitly mentioned" (1999, 67). In other words, it is implicitly racialized. White Americans who subscribe to the negative stereotype that Black people lack a strong work ethic want to slash spending on welfare programs. They also carry negative feelings toward welfare recipients. Spencer Piston (2018) builds on this line of work, arguing that sympathy for the poor and resentment of the rich may also undergird Americans' opinions toward a wide range of redistributive programs.

Government aid to Black Americans is not the only way the government can offer financial assistance to African Americans. Welfare provides similar resources but, because of its somewhat ambiguous name, does so without an explicitly identified beneficiary. Even still, racially sympathetic white Americans might support it because of its implicit association with African Americans.

Accordingly, I expect racial sympathy to shape opinion on welfare. I examine this possibility by again regressing policy opinion, in this case on welfare, on racial sympathy (table 5.3). And as with the preceding analyses, I once again find that higher levels of racial sympathy are associated with more support for the policy. The coefficient on racial sympathy is significant in four out of six cases. The effect appears to be smaller than government aid, a result to which I return later in the chapter. Nevertheless, it is clear that white distress over Black suffering is strongly and positively associated with white opinion on this central tool of antipoverty policy. Racial sympathy, then, matters for both explicitly and implicitly redistributive policies.

TABLE 5.3 **Racial Sympathy and Welfare**

Variables	1994 GSS	2008 ANES	2012 ANES	2013 CCES	2016 YouGov	2020 CMPS
Racial Sympathy	0.06 (0.057)	0.05 (0.032)	0.07** (0.026)	0.15** (0.062)	0.17*** (0.065)	0.14*** (0.023)
Racial Resentment	−0.28*** (0.081)	−0.25*** (0.039)	−0.26*** (0.025)	−0.28*** (0.052)	−0.19*** (0.063)	−0.26*** (0.022)
Party ID (1 = GOP)	−0.18*** (0.049)	−0.07*** (0.027)	−0.11*** (0.018)	−0.12*** (0.045)	−0.09** (0.045)	−0.06*** (0.020)
Limited Government	−0.05 (0.072)	−0.10*** (0.022)	−0.15*** (0.015)	−0.17*** (0.034)	−0.17*** (0.038)	−0.01 (0.025)
Constant	0.62*** (0.093)	0.87*** (0.042)	0.71*** (0.025)	0.80*** (0.061)	0.69*** (0.082)	0.57*** (0.027)
Observations	508	1,159	3,092	628	564	3,914
R-squared	0.113	0.220	0.302	0.432	0.273	0.192

Sources: 1994 GSS, 2008 ANES, 2012 ANES, 2013 CCES, 2016 YouGov, 2020 CMPS
*** $p < 0.01$; ** $p < 0.05$; * $p < 0.10$
Note: Cell entries are ordinary least squares regression coefficients (standard errors in parentheses). Full model is specified in table 5.1. Here, for space considerations, I show the most relevant and powerful controls. For the 2012 ANES, only face-to-face respondents are evaluated. For the 1994 GSS, I use a measure of ideology in place of the limited government index. For the 2020 YouGov study, racial sympathy is measured in Wave 1 and opinion toward the dependent variable is measured in Wave 2. Data are weighted for national representativeness. All variables are coded from 0 to 1.

Affirmative Action

Affirmative action programs were introduced by President Lyndon B. Johnson in 1965. Through executive order, Johnson required all federal contractors to take "affirmative action" in hiring decisions, including recruitment, selection for training, and pay (Gamson and Modigliani 1987). Subsequently, the policy area has remained "controversial" (Kinder and Sanders 1990), especially as courts have handed down opinions about what, exactly, the policy does and does not include. Proponents of affirmative action, especially race-based affirmative action, have typically defended the program on the grounds of "remedial action"—that is, an attempt to remedy past and present racial inequalities.

The opposition to the program has centered on whether or not those groups served by affirmative action are receiving an unfair advantage. As Kinder and Sanders note, over time, this has morphed into a cry against reverse discrimination, where opponents fixate on "whether the rights of whites must be sacrificed to advance the interests of blacks" (1990, 76). Although we have learned a lot about what motivates the opponents of affirmative action, we know comparatively little about the white Americans who support it. The preceding chapter demonstrates that Americans who carried gender sympathy, or distress over women's suffering, were more likely to approve affirmative action programs for women. In this chapter, I consider whether *racial* sympathy affects support of affirmative action programs for Black Americans.

The results, presented in table 5.4, demonstrate that, just as it is with the government aid to Black people policy, racial sympathy is significantly associated with support in this area. Racially sympathetic whites are more likely to support affirmative action across surveys. And they do so across many forms. The 2012 ANES results suggest that affirmative action in higher education, at work, and through hiring is more likely to be supported by whites who are high in racial sympathy compared to those who are not.

In general, I observe the largest and most consistent effect of racial sympathy on those policies that explicitly name Black people as beneficiaries. This is likely because these policies have explicit information about *who* is relevant, thus facilitating "interstitial linkage" between the policy area and group attitude (Converse 1964; Nelson and Kinder 1996). The association between racial sympathy and support for government aid to Black people, a policy area that explicitly references African Americans, is uniformly significant, regardless of model specification.

Affirmative action may be a little different. In table 5.4, the one racial sympathy coefficient that is not significant comes from the 2013 CCES. This is notable because the CCES affirmative action question asks subjects to report their opinion on programs that "give preference to racial minorities" in employment and college admissions. The affirmative action questions that appear on the other surveys refer to Black people specifically rather than all "racial minorities," thus more easily linking distress over Black suffering to opinion. Additionally, the relationship between welfare and racial sympathy is somewhat inconsistent, perhaps because welfare is only implicitly racialized and citizens might not always connect the policy to the relevant group (see Converse 1964, 236).

Nevertheless, the preceding results reveal notable consistency: the relationship between racial sympathy and support for redistributive policies is robust across survey, specification, measure, and year, and these results are not limited to this conceptualization of prejudice. In the appendix, I demonstrate that the relationship between sympathy and policy opinion on government aid to Black people, welfare, and affirmative action is robust to models that consider the impact of many other alternative

TABLE 5.4 **Racial Sympathy and Affirmative Action**

Variables	1994 GSS	2008 ANES	2012 ANES			2013 CCES	
	Affirmative Action	Affirmative Action	Universities	Work	Hiring	Black Scholarships	Affirmative Action
Racial Sympathy	0.09**	0.15***	0.10***	0.09***	0.14***	0.25***	0.01
	(0.04)	(0.039)	(0.031)	(0.030)	(0.033)	(0.085)	(0.068)
Racial Resentment	−0.32***	−0.40***	−0.40***	−0.40***	−0.49***	−0.42***	−0.57***
	(0.057)	(0.044)	(0.030)	(0.030)	(0.032)	(0.071)	(0.067)
Party ID (1 = GOP)	−0.05	−0.06*	−0.08***	−0.05***	−0.02	−0.09*	−0.07
	(0.033)	(0.03)	(0.021)	(0.020)	(0.023)	(0.056)	(0.052)
Limited Government	0	−0.04*	−0.10***	−0.10***	−0.07***	−0.05	−0.14***
	(0.047)	(0.023)	(0.016)	(0.016)	(0.018)	(0.047)	(0.037)
Constant	0.46***	0.58***	0.67***	0.62***	0.61***	0.64***	0.84***
	(0.06)	(0.05)	(0.029)	(0.031)	(0.036)	(0.091)	(0.074)
Observations	628	1099	3,085	3,092	3,041	289	570
R-squared	0.108	0.236	0.274	0.258	0.287	0.390	0.445

Sources: 1994 GSS, 2008 ANES, 2012 ANES, 2013 CCES

*** $p < 0.01$; ** $p < 0.05$; * $p < 0.10$

Note: Cell entries are ordinary least squares regression coefficients (standard errors in parentheses). Full model is specified in table 5.1. Here, for space considerations, I show the most relevant and powerful controls. For the 2012 ANES, only face-to-face respondents are evaluated. For the 1994 GSS and 2020 YouGov studies, I use a measure of ideology in place of the limited government index. Data are weighted for national representativeness. All variables are coded from 0 to 1.

explanations for white support in these areas, including feeling close to Black Americans, implicit positive racial attitudes, rejecting negative stereotypes, holding egalitarian values, carrying personality traits like agreeableness and openness, guilt, empathy, and having interpersonal contact with Black people. In reviewing these results, conducted on independent, nationally representative datasets, a consistent pattern emerges: racial sympathy influences racialized public policies across time and sample. That it does so regardless of the influence of these other related theoretical concepts suggests that racial sympathy is a distinct and powerful dimension of opinion in American politics.

Reparations

In summarizing the racial divide in public opinion, Kinder and Sanders observed: "Of all the various policies we consider, affirmative action is the least popular, among blacks and whites alike" (1996, 27). The authors did not consider reparations in their book, perhaps because in 1996, the prospect of reparations seemed so far-fetched that there was no reason to devote precious survey time to this topic. The issue now receives more mainstream attention. In the 2020 Democratic primary, some presidential candidates spoke directly about their support for the policy area, with three candidates calling for restitution—Kamala Harris, Elizabeth Warren, and Julián Castro. In 2021, California's slavery reparations task force began working on a report to the state Legislature documenting the state's role in perpetuating discrimination against its Black residents and suggesting policies for reparations. They submitted it for consideration in 2023. The State of New Jersey launched a similar task force that year.

Even with this flurry of interest, most white Americans are unenthusiastic about the possibility of reparations. The major academic surveys omit this topic—neither the GSS nor the ANES ask reparations questions. My own surveys find that reparations are indeed an *un*popular policy area among whites, with levels of opposition rivaling those found with affirmative action. Consider figure 5.1, which depicts white support for the four policy areas discussed in this chapter using the 2020 YouGov study.[10]

There are several reasons why white people might oppose reparations. Many white Americans do not feel responsible for what they perceive to be past transgressions (Iyer, Leach, and Crosby 2003). Michael Daw-

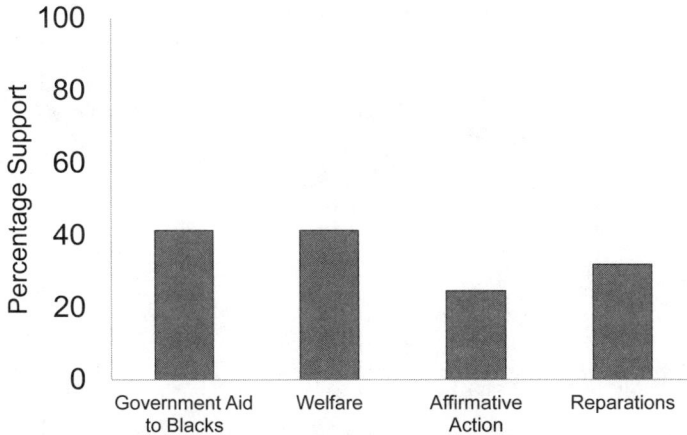

FIGURE 5.1. White Americans' Support for Redistributive Policies.
Source: 2020 YouGov

son and Rovana Popoff (2004) find that whites who discredit accounts of Black voter disenfranchisement are especially likely to oppose reparations policies. More recently, Ashley V. Reichelmann and Matthew O. Hunt (2021a) demonstrate that white Americans who are older, more conservative, and do not consider race relations to be important are especially inclined to oppose reparations.[11] Despite this resistance, it is important to remember that there are instances in which reparations legislation *has* succeeded in the United States, including reparations for Indigenous tribes and Japanese American World War II internees (Craemer 2009). Reparations were also awarded to slave owners after the Civil War (Ray and Perry 2020).[12]

Of course, this important insight helps us understand widespread resistance to the policy. But what about white Americans who support reparations? Drawing on survey items from the 2020 YouGov study and the 2020 CMPS, I consider the role of racial sympathy in shaping opinion toward this controversial topic. These results appear in table 5.5.

Resembling the preceding tables, table 5.5 displays a positive and consistently statistically significant relationship between racial sympathy and redistributive policy opinion. White Americans who score high on my racial sympathy index are more likely to support reparations than those who do not. In the case of the 2020 YouGov study, the magnitude of this effect is sizable—representing nearly one-quarter of the scale.

TABLE 5.5 **Racial Sympathy and Support for Reparations**

Variables	2020 YouGov	2020 CMPS	
	Reparations	Reparations Due to "Generations of Racism"	Reparations Due to "Role in Slavery"
Racial Sympathy	0.23***	0.14***	0.15***
	(0.063)	(0.030)	(0.031)
Racial Resentment	−0.58***	−0.50***	−0.55***
	(0.069)	(0.030)	(0.033)
Party ID (1 = GOP)	−0.02	−0.03	−0.10***
	(0.013)	(0.025)	(0.029)
Ideology	−0.09	−0.25***	−0.12***
	(0.080)	(0.034)	(0.036)
Constant	0.78***	1.00***	0.93***
	(0.066)	(0.041)	(0.038)
Observations	503	1,827	1,833
R-squared	0.672	0.513	0.514

Sources: 2020 YouGov, 2020 CMPS
*** $p < 0.01$; ** $p < 0.05$; * $p < 0.10$
Note: Cell entries are ordinary least squares regression coefficients (standard errors in parentheses). Full model is specified in table 5.1. Here, for space considerations, I show the most relevant and powerful controls. For the 2020 YouGov study, racial sympathy is measured in Wave 1 and opinion toward the dependent variable is measured in Wave 2. Data are weighted for national representativeness. All variables are coded from 0 to 1.

Reparations policies may attract "robust opposition" (Hunt and Reichelmann 2021a) from whites high in racial prejudice. Table 5.5 confirms this possibility, but it also shows us that the minority of whites who *do* support reparations, whether described as "cash reparations to Black people in our country who are the descendants of slaves" (which was the phrasing of the 2020 YouGov question) or an effort "to address inequities caused by generations of racism" or "to address America's role in slavery" (as the items were phrased in the CMPS), do so, in part, because of their racial sympathy. Distress over contemporary instances of Black suffering aligns with support for a policy that would acknowledge and atone for historic atrocities. Support for this policy area, however anemic, would be even weaker without racial sympathy.

Activating Racial Sympathy

This chapter describes policies designed to mitigate the economic gap between white and Black Americans. We now have ample proof of sympathy's political relevance. However, under what conditions is racial sympathy *most* impactful? In reconsidering the range of policies described in this chapter, I conduct survey experiments to investigate the circumstances under which racial sympathy is especially salient or most likely to influence white Americans' opinions in these policy areas.

To this point, my primary source of evidence has come from surveys. As you will recall, national public opinion surveys have many attractive features. If sampled properly, a cross-sectional survey can provide an informative and representative snapshot of a population at a point in time. Reputable academic surveys like the ANES and GSS carry this trait; they are conducted on nationally representative probability samples, which is one important reason why I include these studies to complement my own.

However, even the best surveys can only provide insight about relationships, or correlations, between variables. The preceding results tell us a lot about the associations between racial sympathy and policy support, but they do not definitively illustrate that racial sympathy *causes* white people to endorse these public policies. What causes these outcomes we observe? To answer this question, we turn to another method: experimentation.

Experiments differ from surveys in at least two important ways. First, the experimenter *creates* the conditions to be observed. In observational studies, we, as the name suggests, observe the complex and occasionally confusing preferences of our subjects. In experiments, we intervene by manipulating an independent variable of interest. This relates to the second unique attribute of an experiment: control. An experimenter can systematically vary a study's conditions, permitting us to "study the same general situation with and without the crucial element" (Aronson and Ellsworth 1990, 11).

In this book, the "crucial element" is race. After all, racial sympathy is a reaction to Black suffering. By randomly assigning subjects to treatment and control conditions, the former mentioning Black people and the latter not, I can isolate whether thinking about Black people *causes* shifts in white opinion. Racial sympathy should be "activated," or more salient, when the policies reference Black—but not poor—Americans based on this logic. These experiments demonstrate the causal nature of sympathy and also help us interpret the preceding results: Are sympathetic whites thinking about race when they support these redistributive economic policies?

To answer this important question, I conduct three survey wording experiments on the 2013 CCES, which I refer to as *Social Policy Experiments*. In each, subjects are asked to provide their opinion on a policy area.

For half of the sample, the policy is described to benefit "the poor," and for the other half of the sample, the policy is described to benefit "blacks."[13] By changing the beneficiary in this way, I am systematically varying "the crucial element" while holding other aspects of the policy constant. This is one of the assets of the experimental approach. The question wording appears here with the manipulation presented in brackets:

> Here are several things that the government in Washington might do to deal with the problems of poverty and unemployment among [black/poor] Americans. Please indicate whether you favor or oppose each.
>
> Government giving business and industry special tax breaks for locating in [black/poor] neighborhoods (Strongly favor / Strongly oppose)
>
> Spending more money on [black/poor] schools (Strongly favor / Strongly oppose)
>
> Providing scholarships for [black/poor] students who maintain good grades (Strongly favor / Strongly oppose)

Does racial sympathy's impact vary based on a policy's beneficiary? Are Black beneficiaries more likely to elicit racial sympathy than poor beneficiaries? To provide some context for this analysis, political science research has demonstrated that aid to the poor is routinely and significantly popular among whites, while aid to Black people is substantially less so (Gilens 1999; Piston 2018). However, this difference in support may be diminished among those white people who are sympathetic to Black Americans, just as it is exacerbated among those who are resentful (Kinder and Sanders 1996). By specifying an interactive relationship, I am suggesting that the impact of racial sympathy on policy support will depend on another variable—in this case, whether subjects receive either the "Black" or "poor" experimental treatment. I will provide more information on interactions later in the book. For now, I present the interactive influence of sympathy and experimental condition (policy beneficiary) on policy support in table 5.6.

Individuals low in racial sympathy are especially *unlikely* to support the policies when they are described to benefit Black people. The magnitude of this penalty is substantial; relative to antipoverty policies, linking these policies to African Americans causes whites with low racial sympathy to withdraw support consistently—the coefficients across table 5.6's first row are significant and negative.

TABLE 5.6 **Social Policy Experiments: The Conditional Effect of Racial Sympathy on Public Policy**

Variables	Business Subsidies	Scholarships	Schools
Black Condition = 1	−0.40***	−0.40***	−0.11
	(0.075)	(0.071)	(0.076)
Racial Sympathy	−0.04	0.02	0.21**
	(0.094)	(0.081)	(0.089)
Black Beneficiary × Racial Sympathy	0.35***	0.29***	−0.01
	(0.109)	(0.107)	(0.110)
Racial Resentment	−0.21***	−0.32***	−0.29***
	(0.061)	(0.058)	(0.056)
Party	−0.09**	−0.07	−0.15***
	(0.044)	(0.045)	(0.049)
Limited Government	−0.02	−0.08**	−0.12***
	(0.037)	(0.034)	(0.035)
Constant	0.86***	0.99***	0.86***
	(0.097)	(0.087)	(0.095)
Observations	569	570	571
R-squared	0.261	0.365	0.355

Source: 2013 CCES
*** $p < 0.01$; ** $p < 0.05$; * $p < 0.10$
Note: Cell entries are ordinary least squares regression coefficients (standard errors in parentheses). Full model is specified in table 5.1. Here, for space considerations, I show the most relevant and powerful controls. Data are weighted for national representativeness. All variables are coded from 0 to 1.

For those whites high in racial sympathy, we observe a different pattern. In two out of three cases, the positive and significant coefficient on the interaction of experimental condition and sympathy suggests that racial sympathy is uniquely triggered when the policy beneficiary is African American. This is to say that racially sympathetic whites tend to bring their sympathy to bear when they learn that a policy influences African Americans.

Interaction analyses, such as those presented in table 5.6, are sometimes more intuitive when presented visually. I depict the information supplied in table 5.6 graphically in figure 5.2. In these figures, the level of racial sympathy is measured on the X-axis and the level of support for the policy on the Y-axis. For example, figure 5.2a displays the conditional influence of racial sympathy on support for the business subsidy policy by experimental condition. Each condition is shown in different lines; a solid line represents the poor condition, and a dashed line represents the Black condition. On the left-hand side of the chart, the distance between the solid and dashed lines suggests that low sympathizers reject the business subsidy policy when it is described to serve Black beneficiaries.

As we move from the lowest to highest levels of racial sympathy, we see there is a corresponding increase in support for the policy in the Black condition, as displayed by the diagonal dashed line. This ascending

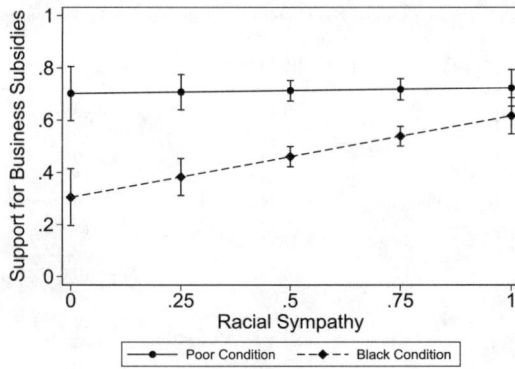

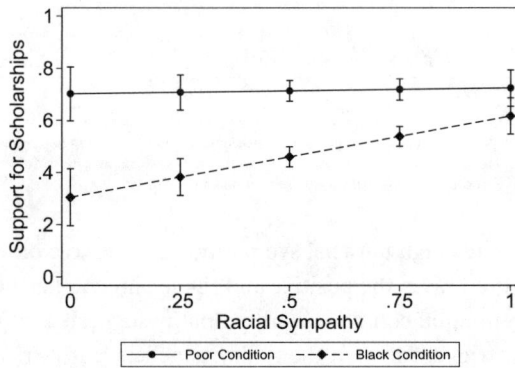

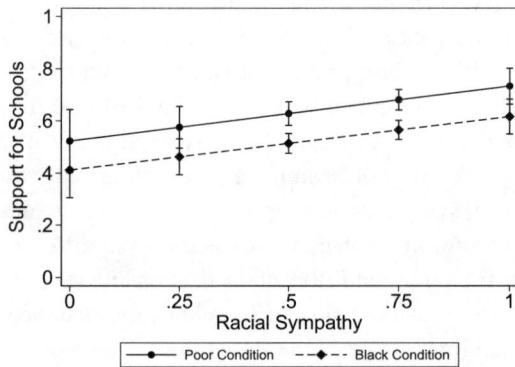

FIGURE 5.2. Social Policy Experiments, 2013 CCES (a) Business Subsidies, (b) Scholarships, (c) Schools
Source: 2013 CCES

level of support is not apparent in the poor condition, where the policy receives high approval across levels of racial sympathy. At the highest level of racial sympathy, the Black condition is supported at similar levels to the poor condition. As figures 5.2a and 5.2b display, this pattern is observed among the racially sympathetic for both the business subsidy and scholarship policies, though not for the school policies. Nonetheless, based on the results displayed in table 5.6 and figure 5.2, it seems that if all whites were sympathetic to Black suffering, aid to Black people could be just as popular as aid to the poor.

The goal of the Social Policy Experiments was to examine whether emphasizing a policy's racial dimensions—that is, drawing attention to the Black population it serves—could activate racial sympathy. The results suggest that by cueing race, elites can increase the salience of racial sympathy on white opinion. Whereas previous studies have found that emphasizing a policy's racial dimension may cause some whites to retreat, the results of the Social Policy Experiments suggest that sympathetic whites have no qualms about supporting a policy linked to Black beneficiaries. Thus the experiments identify one avenue for sympathy's activation and also confirm that the concept is firmly rooted in race, not economic status.

I found that racial sympathy was not activated for the "school" policy like it was for the business subsidy and scholarship policies. One possible interpretation of this puzzling result is that supporting "schools in black neighborhoods," as the question reads, may sound like an endorsement of segregated schools. Indeed, "separate but equal" schools were the catalyst to the *Brown v. Board of Education* case that ruled de jure segregation was a violation of the US Constitution's Equal Protection Clause. As such, policies described as supporting schools in Black neighborhoods may raise concerns about perpetuating racial separation. Thus, the unique history of this policy area may introduce additional considerations that were not intended as part of the experimental manipulation.

Although the Social Policy Experiments provided some valuable insight on sympathy's activation, they also prompted some important questions. First, to the extent that the American poor are often racialized (Gilens 1999), some respondents may associate the "poor" condition with African Americans. Since this control condition may have unintentionally activated racial sympathy, the Social Policy Experiments provide a conservative test of the priming of racial sympathy. Additionally, though racial sympathy demonstrated impressive predictive strength, so too did racial resentment. I conducted a subsequent set of analyses of the Social Policy Experiments in which I included a variable representing the interaction of racial resentment with the experimental condition and found that the low end of racial resentment strongly influenced support in the Black condition relative to the poor condition.[14] I return to the question of resentment's activation in the next chapter; for now, though, it seems as if some of the stimuli that activate sympathy may also activate resentment.

In the CCES, the independent variable of racial sympathy and the experimental manipulation appeared in the same single-wave survey. It is possible, therefore, that the effect of sympathy on policy support is overstated as subjects may have been thinking about racial sympathy when they encountered the experiment. For this reason, it will be important to ensure that subjects' responses to the experiment are not contaminated by their responses to the racial sympathy index, a concern I attend to in the next chapter.

Conclusion

In 1996, the State of California passed Proposition 209, a ballot initiative banning affirmative action at California public universities. By 2006, only ninety-six African Americans were admitted to UCLA's incoming class of five thousand students.[15] In 2020, Californians again voted against a measure that would have repealed the state's ban. According to longitudinal research by Zachary Bleemer, voters' decisions in 1996 set in motion a process whereby underrepresented students "cascaded into lower-quality colleges," resulting in lower degree attainment and, eventually, lower average wages (2022, 115). The absence of government intervention, through programs such as affirmative action, can have grave consequences for racial and ethnic minorities.

I do not mean to suggest that these programs are without defects. In some cases, they require serious improvement to truly better the lives of marginalized Americans.[16] Social programs like those described here can also carry important negative consequences. Joe Soss and Vesla Weaver (2017) demonstrate the dark side of welfare services. Even if they provide material support, many of these programs police citizens' behaviors through social regulation and intense monitoring. Jamila Michener (2018) demonstrates that highly federalized and fragmented social programs, such as welfare, generate inequality and can depress political participation.

What I hope to convey, however, is that racially sympathetic white Americans support a more expansive government because the primary alternative possibility—neglect—has often led to damaging outcomes for African Americans, as the California affirmative action example makes clear. Indeed, the measures of policy support in chapter 5 are often framed with respect to redistributive funding: Should there be more or less? By indicating "more," racially sympathetic whites are assigning the state at least some responsibility in addressing racial economic inequality. How the state administers these policies is an important but separate question.

The redistributive policies in this chapter are not universally popular; in some cases, the majority of white Americans oppose them. But I have demonstrated that to the extent white Americans *do* support government aid, or affirmative action, or welfare, or reparations, they do so, in part, out of sympathy for Black people.

In contrast, there are policy areas where the state's involvement is more unambiguously associated with negative outcomes for Black Americans. Here, the state and its agents are tools for entrenching or exacerbating suffering; accordingly, racially sympathetic Americans want to curtail its influence. In the next chapter, I turn my attention in this direction by examining public opinion toward criminal justice policies.

CHAPTER SIX

Public Opinion on the Criminal Legal System

As the preceding chapter demonstrates, racial sympathy is associated with support for a wide range of social policies. Not all white Americans experience distress over Black suffering, and the degree of sympathy varies. Nonetheless, some white Americans who carry sympathy bring it into their politics. They support long-established, well-known social policies, such as affirmative action. Racially sympathetic white Americans also endorse smaller programs designed to improve conditions for African Americans, such as subsidies to Black businesses. There are a variety of policy efforts designed to mitigate the economic divide between white and Black Americans; in general, racially sympathetic white Americans favor them. And they favor them partly *because* they are racially specific— that is, they target African Americans as a racial group (Sniderman et al. 1996). The policies described in chapter 5 use government as a tool to alleviate Black suffering.

Yet Black suffering takes many forms in the United States. In recent years, many politicians, journalists, and academics have turned their attention to the criminal legal system as a particularly conspicuous site of Black suffering. The criminal legal system refers to "all of the institutions responsible for policing and punishing crime throughout the country" (Harris, Walker, and Eckhouse 2020, 428). These include local entities (e.g., municipal police and sheriff's departments) and national agencies (e.g., federal crime investigation and immigration enforcement).

The association between the criminal legal system and Black suffering is long-standing. Indeed, Samuel Walker (1980) argues that the early eighteenth-century Southern slave patrols were direct precursors to the modern police. Prisons and jails are so prevalent in the United States that the term *mass incarceration* is often used synonymously with the American penal system. The American imprisonment rate is estimated to be between six and twelve times the rate of other Western countries (Garland 2001). And, like policing, it has been racialized since its inception (Alexander 2020; though see Forman 2012).

Not all Americans are critical of these institutions. For example, according to a 2020 Gallup Poll, most white Americans (56%) express confidence in the police (Jones 2020). This Gallup Poll was conducted less than a month after the murder of Floyd, a Black man, at the hands of white Minneapolis police officer Derek Chauvin. The case brought nationwide attention to the fatal consequences of police misconduct. Even under these circumstances, many white Americans expressed "a great deal" or "quite a lot" of confidence in the police.

Yet, the summer of "racial reckoning" following Floyd's death also made clear that white people were grappling with the idea and reality of Black suffering. Demonstrations erupted in major American cities, the suburbs, and, somewhat surprisingly, small white towns throughout June 2020. This was not the first time Americans protested against police brutality. Since 2014, there has been heightened attention to the numerous unarmed Black civilians killed by police officers. Many of those deaths also drew Americans of all races to the streets in protest.

If Black Americans' economic suffering, as described in chapter 5, comes from a state that is negligent, the Black suffering brought about by the criminal legal system comes from a state that is inescapable — a state whose surveillance and enforcement regularly trespass into the private lives of many Black Americans with damaging and sometimes fatal consequences. Under these circumstances, some white Americans may support curtailing the size and scope of the government. They may, for example, be critical of the police and support reducing their funding. They may also back efforts like BLM, an organization and phrase associated with "the movement against police brutality in Black communities in the United States" (Bonilla and Tillery 2020, 947), even when activists engage in contentious tactics. Finally, they may prefer less punitive punishments for Black Americans. This chapter explores these possibilities by examining the relationship between racial sympathy and opinion on the criminal legal system.

For this, I rely on four independent sources of evidence; chronologically, they are the 2015 SSI study, the 2016 YouGov study, the 2020 YouGov study, and the 2020 CMPS. These surveys were fielded during a time period marked by high-profile cases of police brutality against African Americans.[1] The police killings of Eric Garner, Michael Brown, Tamir Rice, Freddie Gray, Breonna Taylor, Floyd, and others made the racial dimensions of the criminal legal system especially salient. These deaths were also highly episodic in nature—that is, they are "event-oriented" (Iyengar 1990). In this respect, the analyses in this chapter differ from those in chapter 5. The policies described in the preceding chapter attend to more thematic trends in American society—poverty, education, and opportunity. One goal of this chapter will be to see whether these episodic issues also attract sympathy. This will give us more insight into the circumstances under which sympathy matters.

I build on these survey results with two national experiments. In the first, I find that racial sympathy is primed when a Black American, but not a white American, interacts with the police. This demonstrates that negative evaluations of criminal legal institutions, such as the police, are shaped by reactions to *racial* suffering. In the second experiment, I consider the limits of racial sympathy. Can racial sympathy be extinguished if a Black person is seen as culpable for a crime? My results suggest that highly sympathetic white people endorse more lenient punishments even when a Black individual is responsible for a crime. They arrive at this outcome not because they lack prejudice but because *they possess* racial sympathy. The consistent results across the survey, time, and domain provide more evidence of racial sympathy's significant role in American politics.

The State's Second Face: The Criminal Legal System

Although there are many configurations of the criminal legal system, they all have a common effect: the subjugation of racially and economically marginalized populations (Weaver and Lerman 2010). For example, according to a report from the US Department of Justice, in 2018, the Black imprisonment rate (1,501 for every 100,000 Black adults) was nearly twice the rate among Hispanics (797 per 100,000) and more than five times the rate among whites (268 per 100,000).[2]

There are also racial differences in arrests. In the last thirty years, even against a backdrop of falling crime rates, the racial disparity in arrests increased substantially (Redbird and Albrecht 2020). In 1999, the average police agency arrested 5.48 Black people for every white person. By 2015, the average had increased to 9.25 arrests. These outcomes can hollow out neighborhoods, leaving residents in a cycle of deprivation and poverty (Fagan, West, and Holland 2004).

Political science research has often overlooked the racial inequalities of the criminal legal system. In describing political scientists' reactions to the death of Brown and the unrest in Ferguson, Missouri, Soss and Weaver observed: "Scholars in political science appeared to be caught off guard as if events had pushed them onto unfamiliar empirical and conceptual terrain" (2017, 566). Specifically, the authors argue that political scientists tend to emphasize the "first face" of the state—those policies that bestow benefits to individuals and groups, such as those discussed in chapter 5. At the same time, they tend to neglect the state's "second face,"—those policies in which the government seeks to "exercise social control by means of coercion, containment, repression, surveillance, regulation, predation, discipline, and violence" (Soss and Weaver 2017, 567). The criminal legal system is the state's second face.

Much of the existing political science research on the criminal legal system has focused, perhaps unsurprisingly, on white Americans' racial prejudice. This is partly because the media often covers crime according to a specific formula; "crime" is something that is violent and perpetuated by non-white males. Thus, watching crime stories on the local news heightens negative stereotypes white people may hold and increases their support for punitive measures (Gilliam and Iyengar 2000). The effects of this association are wide-ranging and consequential. For example, white jurors are more likely to assign harsh punishments, including the death penalty, to Black defendants (Dovidio et al. 1997; Sommers and Ellsworth 2003). Jessica J. Sim and colleagues found that reading a newspaper article about Black—but not white—criminals led to racial bias in a first-person-shooter task, a lab activity that simulates shooting a gun at an unarmed target (Sim, Correll, and Sadler 2013).[3]

We know that "first face" state policies attract both whites' racial prejudice and sympathy. Is that the case for "second face" policies, too? Criminologists have already begun to explore this possibility. Using the racial sympathy index I developed, Hannan and colleagues find that those white Americans at the highest levels of racial sympathy view capital punishment as racially discriminatory. Further, they are more likely to view rehabilitation as the main goal of prison (Hannan et al. 2021). But what about other aspects of "social control"? In this chapter, I analyze white opinion on the criminal legal system and its critics and assess whether racial sympathy extends to both "faces" of the state.

Evaluations of the Police

I begin by analyzing white Americans' attitudes toward the most familiar "second face" of the state: the police. In some predominantly Black communities, police are the main form of government that citizens encounter; they serve as "the central representative of the state" (Forman 2004, 2). Soss and Weaver make this point emphatically with the title of their 2017 article: "Police Are Our Government."

Black Americans are generally quite aware of repression and harassment by police. (Brunson 2007; Weaver, Prowse, and Piston 2020). Historically, in contrast, many white Americans hold the police in high esteem. On the other hand, public reaction to recent high-profile instances of brutality also suggests that some white Americans are critical of police for their mistreatment of Black Americans. In this case, it is possible that whites' distress over Black suffering may contribute to their negative impressions of the police.

I begin to explore this possibility by looking at white opinion on police performance. American policing is an expansive enterprise, and there are many dimensions to police performance, including response time, community relations, crime rates, and so on (Larsen and Blair 2009). However, given the string of high-profile police brutality cases, I focus on opinions related to police use of force.

I do so by consulting two questions. The first, which appeared in the 2016 YouGov study, asked: "How often do you think the police use more force than is necessary when dealing with Black people?" The answer options were "never," "rarely," "sometimes," "usually," and "always." The second was administered on the 2020 CMPS and asked subjects a more specific question: Should addressing police brutality be a priority for whites, as a racial group? Subjects chose among answer options ranging from "Very low priority" to "Very high priority." This question both acknowledges police brutality and implicates whites as at least partially responsible for dealing with it. In both cases, I expect racial sympathy to align with negative evaluations of police performance. White people who think that the police use force more than necessary likely think this way because they are distressed over Black suffering. This sympathy may also play into their perspectives on priorities and responsibilities. Consistent with the other analyses in the book, I isolate self-identified white respondents to explore the connection between sympathy and public opinion. The results appear in table 6.1.

TABLE 6.1 **Racial Sympathy and Evaluations of the Police**

| Variables | 2016 YouGov | 2020 CMPS |
	Police Use Force More Than Necessary	Whites Should Address Police Brutality
Racial Sympathy	0.18***	0.31***
	(0.053)	(0.025)
Racial Resentment	−0.25***	−0.34***
	(0.059)	(0.026)
Ideology (1 = Conservative)	−0.06	−0.09***
	(0.066)	(0.028)
Party ID (1 = GOP)	−0.05	−0.10***
	(0.039)	(0.021)
Constant	0.57***	0.71***
	(0.094)	(0.034)
Observations	512	3,660
R-squared	0.235	0.358

Source: 2016 YouGov, 2020 CMPS
*** $p < 0.01$; ** $p < 0.05$; * $p < 0.10$
Note: Cell entries are ordinary least squares regression coefficients (standard errors in parentheses). Full model is specified in table 5.1. Here, for space considerations, I show the most relevant and powerful controls. Data are weighted for national representativeness. All variables are coded from 0 to 1.

Table 6.1 illustrates that racial sympathy is significantly associated with evaluations of police performance. White Americans who are high on racial sympathy think that the police use unnecessary force. They also think that when this force takes the form of brutality, their racial group ought to address it. In both cases, the coefficients are substantively meaningful. To take one instance, going from the lowest to the highest level of racial sympathy is associated with over a 30 percentage point increase on the police brutality question. This represents the difference between a respondent assigning a "low priority" and a "high priority" to addressing police brutality, for example. The racial sympathy coefficient on the police use of force question is also significant, surpassing the contribution of party and ideology.[4]

Beyond these general perceptions of policing, racial sympathy may also impact opinion on police funding. Government spending on police departments has grown dramatically since 1965 (Weaver 2012). In 1951, American cities spent $82 per person on police. By 2016, this figure had ballooned to $286 in constant dollars (Epp, Maynard-Moody, and Haider-Markel 2016). Academics, community organizers, and Black nationalists have long called for reducing funding, defunding, and even abolishing the police in response to these escalating expenditures (Davenport 2021).

This position entered mainstream dialogue during the summer of 2020, when protesters invoked the phrase "defund the police" during demonstrations.[5] Subsequently, some municipalities attempted to downsize their police departments. Minneapolis, Minnesota, the site of Floyd's death, ran a ballot initiative to eliminate the city charter's minimum number of police officers.[6] Although these initiatives were not especially widespread, they are still part of the broad political discourse. For example, in the 2022 State of the Union address, President Biden drew bipartisan applause for his call to "fund the police." Does racial sympathy factor into opinions on this topic?

To consider this possibility, I examine two survey questions related to police funding using the 2020 CMPS. Some have equated defunding the police with police abolition. However, the phrase more accurately refers to efforts that would "reallocate or redirect funding away from the police department to other government agencies funded by the local municipality" (Ray 2020). The first CMPS question measures support for this topic as a matter of resource distribution. It asks whether respondents support "shifting some funds from local police departments to local social service agencies and urban community centers." Subjects indicate their response on a six-item scale ranging from "Strongly oppose" to "Strongly support." By emphasizing the reallocation of resources, rather than the elimination of police departments altogether, this question presents the policy in a less drastic, perhaps more palatable, form.

In contrast, a second CMPS question probes the limits of this support. Specifically, it asked whether "defunding the police" is "pushing things too far" or, on the other hand, if it is "not going far enough." Unlike the preceding CMPS question, this question does not reference resource allocation. A *USA Today*/Ipsos poll found the policy was significantly less popular when described without this qualification, presumably because respondents equate it with abolition (Elbeshbishi and Quarshie 2021).

Respondents who choose the highest value answer choice to this question are indicating that defunding "doesn't go far enough." This is a closed-form survey question, so we cannot be sure what going "far enough" entails. Still, it gives us a sense of degree; do white Americans want to reduce funding by a little or a lot? Since racially sympathetic white Americans associate the police with the mistreatment and suffering of Black Americans, I expect them to support curtailing police funding in both cases. This is precisely what I find in table 6.2.

White people who are higher in racial sympathy are more supportive

TABLE 6.2 **Racial Sympathy and Police Funding**

Variables	2020 CMPS	
	Shift Funding	Defunding Not Far Enough
Racial Sympathy	0.19***	0.05**
	(0.031)	(0.021)
Racial Resentment	−0.46***	−0.41***
	(0.032)	(0.022)
Ideology (1 = Conservative)	−0.25***	−0.19***
	(0.032)	(0.026)
Party ID (1 = GOP)	−0.10***	−0.05***
	(0.025)	(0.019)
Constant	0.93***	0.81***
	(0.040)	(0.028)
Observations	1,827	3,660
R-squared	0.536	0.406

Source: 2020 CMPS
*** $p < 0.01$; ** $p < 0.05$; * $p < 0.10$
Note: Cell entries are ordinary least squares regression coefficients (standard errors in parentheses). Full model is specified in table 5.1. Here, for space considerations, I show the most relevant and powerful controls. Data are weighted for national representativeness. All variables are coded from 0 to 1.

of efforts to reduce police funding when it is described as the reallocation of resources but even without this qualification. Moving from the lowest level of racial sympathy to the highest produces an almost twenty-point shift in support for reallocating funds away from the police to social service agencies and community centers. Although most white Americans, including leaders like President Biden, think defunding the police is too drastic, others think we should go even further. They think so partly because of their distress over Black suffering.

Black Lives Matter

In July 2013, Alicia Garza, a Black activist, logged onto Facebook to write a "love letter to black people." The post reflected on the acquittal of George Zimmerman, who shot seventeen-year-old Trayvon Martin in Sanford, Florida. Garza concluded her letter by writing: "I continue to be surprised at how little Black lives matter. . . . Black people. I love you. I love us. Our lives matter" (Jennings 2020, 15). Garza's friend, Patrisse Cullors, later abridged Garza's message into the hashtag #BlackLivesMatter.

The following summer, police officer Darren Wilson shot and killed Brown, who was, like Martin, an unarmed Black teenager, in Ferguson, Missouri. Organizers used Garza's phrase as they planned demonstrations, rallies, and freedom rides to protest Brown's death. Subsequently, BLM has become associated with a social movement that eschews hierarchy and centralized leadership structures as it advocates on behalf of Black communities (Cobb 2016). It has also been used as a more general rallying cry, animating "intense social and political activity, especially among younger people and others who have been less politically engaged" (Leach and Allen 2017, 543). In the summer of 2020, at the height of protests over police brutality following the death of Floyd, two-thirds of Americans said they strongly or somewhat supported BLM, according to a study conducted by the Pew Research Center.

The stated mission of BLM is to "eradicate white supremacy and build local power to intervene in violence inflicted on Black communities by the state and vigilantes" (Black Lives Matter n.d.). BLM combats and counters "acts of violence, creating space for Black imagination and innovation, and centering Black joy." Despite this broad platform, the organization has sometimes been associated with a single issue—police brutality—which "transformed into a movement through social media" (Cobb 2016).

The preceding section demonstrated the strong connection between racial sympathy and evaluations of the police. Accordingly, white distress over Black suffering likely contributes to views of BLM, too; racially sympathetic white people would likely endorse a movement that "intervenes in violence inflicted on Black communities." Support for BLM, however, may not be simply equivalent to being "anti-police." For one, as its mission statement suggests, its objectives are extensive. Eradicating white supremacy and building local power may involve the police, but it may involve a host of other institutions, too (Woodly 2021).

BLM opinions are therefore not a catchall for anti-police sentiment. Accordingly, in this section, I consider the relationship between racial sympathy and global evaluations of BLM as well as specific aspects of their mission and activities. Here again, I turn to the 2016 YouGov study and the 2020 CMPS. The first question I take up seeks to gauge the general level of support: "Based on everything you have heard or seen, how much do you support or oppose the Black Lives Matter movement?" Subjects selected answer options ranging from "Strongly support" to "Strongly oppose." This question appears on both the 2016 and 2020 studies.

TABLE 6.3 **Racial Sympathy and Black Lives Matter**

Variables	2016 YouGov Support for BLM	2020 CMPS Support for BLM	Black People Speaking Up Makes Country Better	BLM Protest about Unfair Conditions
Racial Sympathy	0.24***	0.22***	0.26***	0.11***
	(0.069)	(0.020)	(0.023)	(0.023)
Racial Resentment	−0.67***	−0.61***	−0.36***	−0.61***
	(0.075)	(0.021)	(0.024)	(0.022)
Ideology (1 = Conservative)	−0.17**	−0.22***	−0.10***	−0.06***
	(0.074)	(0.023)	(0.024)	(0.023)
Party ID (1 = GOP)	−0.09*	−0.17***	−0.06***	−0.12***
	(0.055)	(0.018)	(0.018)	(0.018)
Constant	0.75***	1.00***	0.65***	0.82***
	(.10)	(0.027)	(0.030)	(0.030)
Observations	511	3,660	3,660	3,660
R-squared	0.513	0.660	0.353	0.506

Source: 2016 YouGov, 2020 CMPS
*** $p < 0.01$; ** $p < 0.05$; * $p < 0.10$
Note: Cell entries are ordinary least squares regression coefficients (standard errors in parentheses). Full model is specified in table 5.1. Here, for space considerations, I show the most relevant and powerful controls. Data are weighted for national representativeness. All variables are coded from 0 to 1.

The second question, taken from the CMPS, draws explicit attention to Black Americans' protest activity and its benefits. It asks respondents to agree or disagree with the statement, "When Black Americans speak up and protest injustice in the U.S., it always makes the country better." Although the text does not make specific reference to BLM, it was immediately preceded by the question mentioned in the previous paragraph that gauged overall support for BLM. Therefore, it is reasonable to expect that respondents were thinking about BLM when they encountered this question. They could strongly agree, agree, neither agree nor disagree, somewhat disagree, or strongly disagree with the statement. I present the results of this analysis in the first three columns of table 6.3.

Previous work has found that white Americans low in prejudice support BLM, whether described in general terms or concerning Black protest (Reny and Newman 2021; Riley and Peterson 2020). Table 6.3 confirms this point; indeed, low-prejudiced whites tend to evaluate BLM favorably. The absence of prejudice certainly matters. But so too does the presence of sympathy. I find that distress over Black suffering contributes to whites' evaluations of BLM both in 2016 and 2020 with a magnitude equaling or surpassing ideology and partisanship.

But what do white people have in mind when they think about BLM and its protests? At times, discussion over BLM has centered less on its policy objectives and more on its strategies. In the 2014 protests that followed the death of Gray, critics cast the BLM protests as "unlawful 'riots,'" whereas others argued that these demonstrations were justified "uprisings" (Hooker 2016, 449). There were similar reactions to the demonstrations following Floyd's murder (Teixeira, Leach, and Spears 2022). Jonathan C. Reid and Miltonette O. Craig (2021) found that racial justice protests are often framed as threats to the public interest, even in relatively liberal outlets such as the *New York Times* and *Washington Post.*

This is not a new interpretation. In the early months of 1968, Angus Campbell set out to study the "long, hot summer of 1967," a moniker for the three months when outrage over racial injustice led to 150 demonstrations, riots, and protests throughout the country. In his examination of "white sympathy with the black protest," Campbell observed that "while most white residents of the cities accepted the right of the Negroes to protest in an orderly way against racial discrimination, they also believed that in the urban disturbances black people have gone too far" (1971, 17).

Could sympathy contribute to white Americans' views of BLM's protest tactics? If history is any indication, many white Americans turn their backs on Black demands when protest becomes confrontational (Kinder and Sanders 1996; Wasow 2020).[7] Some others may support any form of "the black protest." Indeed, if distress over Black suffering looms over other considerations, those white Americans who score at the highest levels of racial sympathy may view protests in a positive light.

To explore this possibility, I consult a question on the CMPS: "Some people say the Black Lives Matter protests were mainly a protest against unfair treatment of Black people. Others say they are mainly a way of vandalism and looting. Which of these statements seems more correct to you?" Respondents recorded their answers on a seven-item scale, with the lowest pole describing these events as "mainly a way of vandalism and looting" and the top end labeled as "protest against unfair treatment of Black people."

This question was inspired by Angus Campbell, and in his study of the Civil Rights protests, he found that 52 percent of his respondents "felt the riots were mainly or in part a way of looting rather than primarily a protest against unfair conditions" (1971, 17). Fifty years later, I find remarkably parallel results, with 55 percent of white CMPS respondents interpreting the protests in that vein.

But what about the white Americans who viewed the 2020 demonstrations as "against unfair treatment of Black people"? To what extent did their concern for Black suffering inform this view? As with the preceding analysis, I regress respondents' protest evaluations on their racial sympathy scores as captured by the racial sympathy index. I expect that white distress over Black suffering contributes to viewing the historical BLM protests in this light. The final column of table 6.3 displays these results.

When many white Americans saw the unrest of summer 2020 unfolding, they viewed it as "a way of vandalism and looting." There were others, though, who rejected this characterization. They did so, at least partially, because of their racial sympathy. As I demonstrate in the next section, it is because they possess sympathy that they resist negative narratives of Black Americans that may have been primed during this period. Support for BLM is rooted, in part, in white distress over Black suffering.[8]

Activating Racial Sympathy (Again)

The foregoing reveals the significant and consistent relationship between racial sympathy and white opinion of the criminal legal system. When this is taken together with chapter 5, we have evidence of sympathy's broad footprint in American politics.

In the preceding chapter, I describe a survey wording experiment in which I varied policy beneficiaries to be either "poor" or "Black." I found that racial sympathy was associated with support for public policies when they benefited Black people but not when these same policies were serving the poor. These results complement earlier work that has found that white Americans' support for a policy is sensitive to the group identity of the policy's beneficiaries (Kinder and Sanders 1996; Sniderman and Carmines 1997).

Do these findings extend to "second face" policies? I turn to two survey experiments to explore this question. The first survey, which I call the Victim Study, was administered on the internet by SSI in the summer of 2015. The second survey experiment, the Culprit Study, appeared in the 2016 YouGov study. Although there were some differences between the surveys (see chapter 3 for descriptions of each study), they are both two-wave studies. In each case, the racial attitude measures were administered

first, and then, after a one-month recess, respondents were invited to complete the second wave, which contained the experimental manipulation.
Given the time elapsed during the two waves, it is unlikely that subjects'
responses to the racial attitude questions influenced their reactions to the
stimulus. As a reminder, all analyses, including those presented here, are
limited to subjects who self-identify as white.[9]

Both studies also present subjects with scenarios they might encounter in the real world, contributing to their external validity. In the Victim
Study, subjects reviewed a fictitious newspaper article about an encounter between Jeffrey Young and the police. The article recounted how an
everyday citizen-police interaction escalated into violence toward Young.
The brutal nature of the episode is emphasized in a pull-out quote, reading: "According to Young, the police threw him on the ground and called
him lazy." Subjects were randomly assigned to read one of two conditions
of this story. In one condition, Young was white, and in the other condition, he was Black, as conveyed through photographs.

Following the stimulus, subjects were asked for their opinions on policing. Specifically, they were asked whether the American police do a good
job "using the right amount of force for each situation" and, separately,
"treating Black citizens with respect," selecting among the answer options "Very good," "Good," "Fair," "Poor," or "Very poor job." The distributions of each of these questions, for the total sample, are presented in
figure 6.1.

Most subjects evaluated the police as doing a "fair" or better job treating African Americans with respect (69%) or using the right amount of
force (57%).[10] The survey was administered soon after the high-profile
deaths of Gray and Alton Sterling, both resulting from police brutality.
Gray's death was particularly gruesome. He was dragged into a van by
six Baltimore police officers, who ignored his pleas for help as he suffered
fatal spinal injuries. In Baton Rouge, Louisiana, two police officers shot
Sterling at close range. Both encounters were recorded on video by bystanders. Despite these graphic episodes, the majority of the SSI subjects
continued to evaluate the police favorably.

But what about those who did not? As this chapter has made clear, policing is racialized; there is a long history of police mistreatment of Black
Americans. Racially sympathetic white Americans may be aware of this
history. If so, will they think more or less favorably of the police when the
victim's race is Black rather than white?

Indeed, in both cases, viewing the Black victim, relative to the white

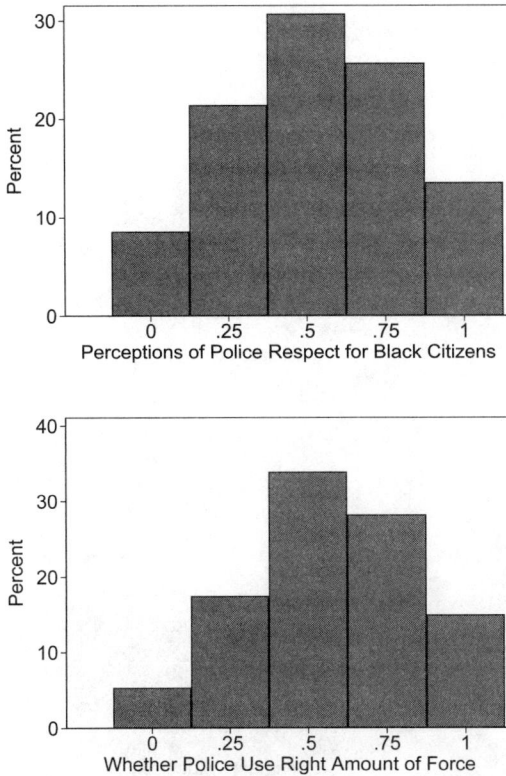

FIGURE 6.1. Distribution of Dependent Variables, Victim Study (a) Police Treat Black Citizens with Respect, (b) Police Use the Right Amount of Force
Source: 2015 SSI

victim, leads most white people to view the police in a more *positive* light, though the difference is not statistically significant. Consider figure 6.2, which depicts the main effects of the experimental manipulation. We see that the police are evaluated favorably whether the victim of their abuse is white or Black, perhaps reflecting white Americans' general support of the police. One interpretation of this result is that the episodes of police brutality against Black Americans do not, in the aggregate, shift white opinion.

However, those subjects who see a Black victim *and* are high in racial sympathy are significantly *less* likely to evaluate the police favorably, a pattern I observe across both dependent variables. This is displayed in table 6.4. Here, we find racial sympathy is only activated when the victim is Black.

Earlier in the chapter, I found that white people who carry high levels

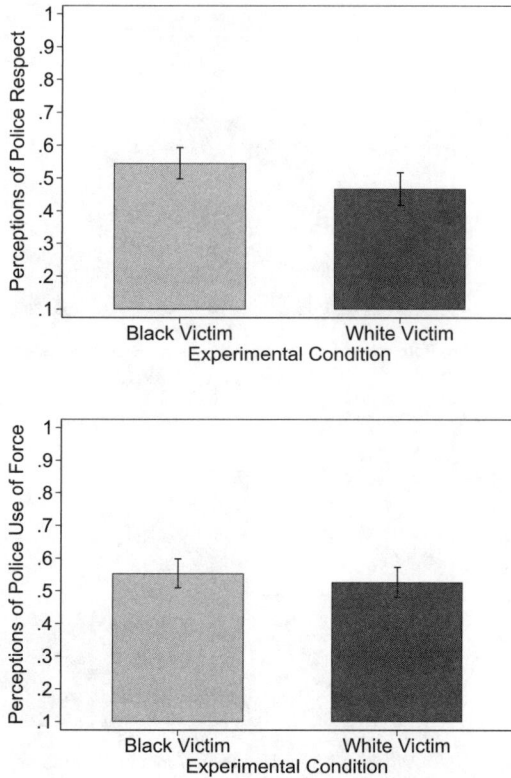

FIGURE 6.2. Main Effects, Victim Study (a) Police Treat Black Citizens with Respect, (b) Police Use the Right Amount of Force
Source: 2015 SSI

of sympathy are less likely to perceive the police as using the appropriate amount of force. The Victim Study shows us that reactions to police force are most influential when *Black* suffering is called to mind; otherwise put, white Americans' criticisms of policing may be attributable to the institution's racial transgressions. This result demonstrates that racial sympathy is foremost a racial attitude and is noteworthy because other studies find that white support for punitive policies actually *increases* when the victims are described as Black (Hetey and Eberhardt 2014; Peffley and Hurwitz 2002). In contrast, I identify a very different group of white Americans, whose endorsement *decreases* under these same circumstances.

In 2016, I fielded a follow-up study. By the time this second experiment, the Culprit Study, went into the field, Americans had learned about yet another high-profile fatal police encounter: Philando Castile, a Black man, was shot in his car by a police officer in Falcon Heights, a suburb of Saint Paul, Minnesota, on July 6, 2016. As with the deaths of Gray and Sterling, Castile's death was captured on camera, and the footage was widely distributed through social media and other outlets. It was filmed by his girlfriend, Diamond Reynolds, who was in the car with her four-year-old daughter. Three hours after the shooting, more than two hundred protesters gathered at the scene (Helsel, Walters, and Jamieson 2016). The protest over Castillo's murder continued for three weeks and was reignited in 2017, when the police officer, Jeronimo Yanez, was acquitted on all charges.

Rather than simply replicating the Victim Study, I explored an additional dimension of these episodes: perceived culpability. Victims of police brutality have occasionally been associated with illicit behavior. For

TABLE 6.4 **Victim Experiment**

Variables	Police Treat Black People with Respect		Police Do a Good Job Using the Right Amount of Force	
	Model 1	Model 2	Model 3	Model 4
Black Condition	0.12	0.10	0.18**	0.11
	(0.090)	(0.083)	(0.086)	(0.083)
Racial Sympathy	−0.12	0.05	0.13	0.20**
	(0.105)	(0.100)	(0.100)	(0.098)
Black Condition × Racial Sympathy	−0.35**	−0.28*	−0.40***	−0.26*
	(0.152)	(0.143)	(0.146)	(0.141)
Racial Resentment		0.58***		0.44***
		(0.101)		(0.100)
Limited Government		0.07		0.05
		(0.054)		(0.053)
Party ID (1 = GOP)		−0.05		−0.08
		(0.068)		(0.068)
Constant	0.60***	0.07	0.49***	0.10
	(0.060)	(0.108)	(0.057)	(0.107)
Observations	185	179	185	179
R-squared	0.110	0.313	0.045	0.175

Source: 2015 SSI
*** $p < 0.01$; ** $p < 0.05$; * $p < 0.10$
Cell entries are ordinary least squares regression coefficients (standard errors in parentheses). Full model is specified in table 5.1. Here, for space considerations, I show the most relevant and powerful controls. However, since not all scholars agree this is an optimal approach, I also present the bivariate results here (see Mutz 2015; and Morton and Williams 2010). All variables are coded from 0 to 1.

example, Staten Island police officers suspected Garner was illegally selling cigarettes, Brown was thought to have stolen a box of cigarillos, and so on. White Americans may fixate on these accusations to justify the officers' forceful response. Indeed, Republican Senator and one-time presidential candidate Rand Paul said that the NYPD police officers in the case of Garner were put in "a difficult situation" because they were trying to enforce a law that taxed cigarettes (McCalmont 2014). Accordingly, I was interested in whether adding an element of misbehavior, and thus a "culprit," to these scenarios prevents or prohibits the activation of racial sympathy on criminal justice matters.

In chapter 3, I described how white people can carry prejudice and sympathy simultaneously. These independent concepts may respond to similar stimuli in different ways. For prejudice, research has found that attaching negative stereotypes to Black people further depresses support for "pro-Black" political measures among whites high in racial animus. Mendelberg (2001) argues that implicit racial messages powerfully prime racial attitudes during campaigns, influencing white vote choice. Valentino and colleagues (2002) expand on this line of research, finding that resentment is cued when subtle racial stereotypes are paired with images of Black Americans. Do the negative racial cues that invoke prejudice influence sympathy, too?

To study this question, the stimulus of the Culprit Study featured a neighborhood "crime blotter,"[11] which recounted a recent instance of graffiti. In one condition, the crime blotter indicated that a white man had admitted to painting graffiti on a historic church. In the other, the blotter stated that a Black man had admitted to the same offense. According to Broken Windows Theory, having police crack down on low-level offenses, such as graffiti and fare evasion, is one way to prevent more serious crime (Wilson and Kelling 1982). Piston (2023) has argued that Broken Windows Theory functions less as a method of crime prevention and more as a tool to maintain order. In either case, Broken Windows is an influential concept in policing; Elizabeth Hinton has suggested that the premise of Broken Windows Theory operates as "the guiding principle of modern American law enforcement" (2021, 45). Thus, the stimulus captures an important dimension of the American criminal legal system.

The description of the graffiti incident was kept identical in the study's two conditions. The only difference between the two conditions was the race of the culprit, Gavin Tannis, as manipulated by a photograph. Subjects were randomly assigned to one of these conditions and were subsequently asked to provide their opinions on the appropriate punishment

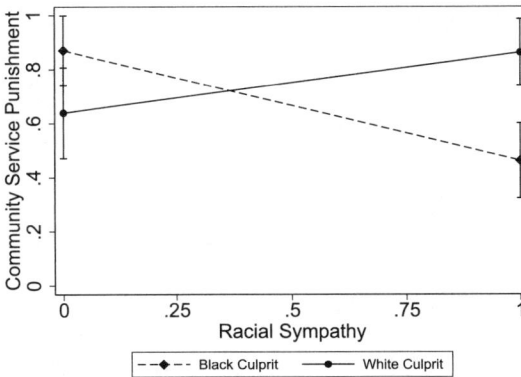

FIGURE 6.3. Racial Sympathy and Punishment, by Race of Culprit
Source: 2016 YouGov

for Tannis. In contrast to the SSI study, which features a Black victim, this study focuses on a Black culprit who is connected, as part of his description, with a negative cue. This addition makes the Culprit experiment distinct from the other experiments in this book and offers a distinct opportunity to consider the simultaneous activation of prejudice. It is potentially a harder test, then, for racial sympathy.

I begin my analysis by examining opinion related to the punishment of Tannis. Specifically, I consider responses to a question that asked subjects how many hours of community service Tannis ought to serve. I present the results in the form of a predicted probability plot, displayed in figure 6.3, with the full model appearing in table 6.5. The solid line represents those whites who viewed a photograph of Tannis as a white man ("White Culprit"), and the dashed line represents those whites who viewed a photograph depicting Tannis as a Black man ("Black Culprit").

Given the crime described in the stimulus, I expected almost all respondents to issue some form of punishment. After all, the culprit is identified as guilty of a crime, and research suggests that the public generally wants to punish people who break the rules (Tyler and Boeckmann 1997). Therefore, across both conditions, I anticipate that respondents will support harsh punishment for the culprit. That said, I am most interested in examining whether sympathetic whites are *less* inclined to punish Tannis when he is Black compared to when he is white.

Indeed, racially sympathetic whites issue different responses to the crime, depending on the race of the culprit. The predicted probability of

TABLE 6.5 **Culprit Experiment**

Variables	Model 1 Community Service Punishment	Model 2 Community Service Punishment
Black Culprit = 1	0.23**	0.26**
	(0.11)	(0.11)
Racial Sympathy	0.41***	0.24*
	(.13)	(.14)
Black Culprit × Racial Sympathy	−0.63***	−0.48**
	(.17)	(.20)
Racial Resentment (r coded)		−0.29*
		(.17)
Black Culprit × Racial Resentment		−0.26
		(0.22)
Constant	0.13***	0.09
	(.06)	(.07)
Observations	210	210

Source: YouGov 2016
*** $p < 0.01$; ** $p < 0.05$; * $p < 0.10$
Cell entries are ordinary least squares regression coefficients (standard errors in parentheses).
The dependent variable is coded such that 0 equals the "pro-Black" outcome (less punishment)
and 1 equals harsher punishment for the culprit. These results are robust to models with control
variables, including party identification, limited government, education, income, gender, region,
and church attendance. However, since not all scholars agree this is an optimal approach, I
present the bivariate results here (see Mutz 2015; and Morton and Williams 2010). Data are
weighted for national representativeness. All variables are coded from 0 to 1.

giving a harsh sentence for a Black criminal is .46 for those whites who
are high in racial sympathy and .87 for those who are low, a difference of
41 percentage points. Racial sympathy significantly attenuates the culprit's
punishment, but only when the culprit is Black. On the other hand, when
the criminal is *white*, the predicted probability of issuing a harsh sentence
is .86 for those who are high in racial sympathy and .64 for those who are
low. White people high in racial sympathy assign roughly half the amount
of community service to a Black culprit than they do to a white one for the
same offense. Racially sympathetic whites are not generally antipunitive;
however, they are significantly less likely to inflict harsh punishment on a
Black person who commits an offense. This provides insight into how racial
considerations may be motivating contemporary evaluations of policing.

Although the initial results suggest that racial sympathy can be activated, the experimental stimuli may also activate racial prejudice. After all,
previous research has shown that negative stereotypes of African Ameri-

cans can motivate some whites to endorse candidates or policies perceived to hurt African Americans (Valentino et al. 2002). In contrast, since sympathy is based primarily on white distress over Black suffering, negative stereotypes of Black Americans should not dampen the effect of sympathy.

To consider this possibility, I conduct an analysis in which I regress the interaction between racial sympathy and experimental condition *and* the interaction between racial resentment and experimental condition. The results are presented in the second column of table 6.5, labeled "Model 2." They suggest that once activated, racial sympathy retains a significant influence on policy opinion, even accounting for the activation of resentment. On the other hand, the effect of low prejudice is eliminated.

When racially sympathetic whites encounter narratives that associate Black Americans with crime, thus priming negative stereotypes, sympathy remains an important force in their political decision-making. Indeed, rather than merely lacking prejudice, because these whites *possess* sympathy, they can resist the cues that ordinarily activate animus.

Conclusion

In 1968, President Johnson charged the Kerner Commission with the task of identifying the origins of the "long, hot summer." Social scientists conducted in-depth studies of the affected cities and neighborhoods and concluded with a series of recommendations. Among the causes of the disorder, they singled out Black views of the police, writing, "to some Negroes, police have come to symbolize white power, white racism and white repression. And the fact is that many police do reflect and express these white attitudes. The atmosphere of hostility and cynicism is reinforced by a widespread belief among Negroes in the existence of police brutality" (Kerner Commission 1968, 5).

As Angus Campbell's work reveals, some white Americans were sympathetic to this interpretation. This group viewed African Americans' perspectives favorably, leading Campbell to observe that a "sympathetic attitude toward the black protest movement is intimately bound into a broader orientation toward the whole question of white-black relationships" (1971, 17).

Decades later, this orientation persists. In multiple national surveys, racially sympathetic white Americans are more supportive of efforts to reform the "second face" of the state: the criminal legal system. They favor various policing reforms, including defunding the police. They also support BLM and their protest methods. This is not because racial sympathy is equivalent to being antipunitive—there are circumstances in which white people high on racial sympathy support harsh punishments for criminal offenses; however, they become more critical of these systems when they punish Black actors.

The results in this chapter demonstrate yet another way in which racial sympathy is powerfully related to public opinion in the United States. When some white Americans evaluate the criminal legal system, they bring their racial attitudes to bear—not only prejudice, but sympathy, too. White people who are distressed over Black suffering are more likely to be skeptical toward the second face of the state, objecting to both its breadth and reach. Sympathetic white Americans carry these opinions, but what do they do to enact them? That is the topic for the final two empirical chapters.

CHAPTER SEVEN

Does Sympathy Lead to Action?

Racial sympathy is a distinct and consequential attitude in American politics. Whether applied to implicitly or explicitly racialized policies, racial sympathy's contribution is apparent across a range of domains. Sympathy's influence, then, may be characterized by its breadth. But how far does it go? This chapter takes up the question of whether racial sympathy extends to white political behavior. Here, I am interested in understanding whether the attitude of racial sympathy transcends policy opinions and materializes into political behaviors such as protesting and voting. Racial sympathy is consistently and robustly associated with opinion on many national, well-designed surveys; however, if the attitude is not channeled into intended or actual political behavior, its political impact may be only modest.

In some quarters, there has been much skepticism about white commitment to racial justice issues. For example, in an article for *Variety*, Caroline Framke (2020) observed: "Posting a black square on Instagram might make you feel better, but it doesn't help the cause you claim to support." Another article, written in May 2020, asks, as its headline, a provocative question: "White People Are Speaking Up at Protests. How Do We Know They Mean What They Say?" In the piece, the author observes, "Solidarity can be helpful, or it can be performative" (Patton 2020).

In the domain of survey research, scholars have considered the possibility that white respondents may not mean what they say. For example, Adam Berinsky and Howard Lavine (2012) find that social desirability concerns can drive white people's responses to racial survey items. Their research suggests that white people may misrepresent their views on studies because they do not want to appear racist. In contrast, other research shows that the impact of social desirability may be present but have only a modest impact on survey and experimental results (Sears 2004; Zizzo 2010). Although white people might try very hard to conceal racially insensitive attitudes in many circumstances, it is unclear whether the typical survey respondent would exhibit such effort in an anonymous, often online, survey setting. After all, as this book has already demonstrated, in these settings, most white people have no qualms about endorsing racially resentful attitudes or issuing positive endorsements of the police, even in the wake of violent instances of brutality against Black people. Nonetheless, social desirability bias is a powerful idea that is grounded in an academic literature. Thus, it is worthwhile to investigate its role for racial sympathy especially when it comes to political behavior.

Racial sympathy could be a sincere attitude, but it also could be one that does not consistently motivate political behavior. According to this line of thinking, a white person can express a rousing endorsement of affirmative action (well, at least as rousing as a closed-form survey question permits). It is also possible that this endorsement represents a true opinion, driven by genuine distress over Black suffering. However, if this endorsement ends once the survey is completed, the political impact of racial sympathy may expire.

To explore these possibilities, I draw on evidence from multiple sources of evidence. The first category of evidence comes from surveys. Here, I rely on the 2020 YouGov study, which has now been consulted multiple times throughout the book. The second source of data is qualitative; specifically, I conducted a series of long-form interviews with racial justice activists in the Boston metropolitan area. These interviews are not intended to replicate the survey results. Instead, they shed light on the motivations and objectives of a select group as an "extreme case" (Seawright and Gerring 2008, 301) of racial sympathy. If these highly sympathetic white Americans, all of whom voluntarily give their time to racial justice causes, are skeptical of undertaking political action, then it is unlikely that average citizens will.

Using data collected from these two different methods permits a more thorough analysis of the relationship between sympathy and behavior. In particular, the interviews allow me to evaluate whether the survey questions artificially prompt commitment to the public policies typically studied by political scientists. As I trace the relationship between sympathy and behavior, I consider both the surveys and the interviews. I find that in contrast to my earlier results, the impact of racial sympathy is more inconsistent. I then consider the reasons why this might be the case, including the possibility of social desirability bias. I conclude by discussing the limits of racial sympathy and prospects for change.

Interviews as a Method

In chapter 3, I referenced the various data sources for the project, including the YouGov surveys and the qualitative study on activists. Now that we have arrived at their chapter, I will offer more details on these activists and explain why I pursued interviewing as a method.

Survey analysis and experiments, the other methods I have used thus far, offer many attractive features. Surveys can be high in external validity; they help us make generalizations about the population. An experiment's strength lies in its internal validity. They shed light on cause and effect—does the independent variable influence the dependent variable? Through these two methods, it would seem like we have most of our bases covered.

However, interviews have several important features that distinguish them from surveys and experiments. When I identify a racially sympathetic white person in the spreadsheets of my quantitative data, I cannot ask him any questions, such as why he feels that way or what salient experiences contributed to his views. I cannot request that he describe the nature of this distress. I cannot probe a subject on what the vignette makes him think about. Such depth is a hallmark of interviewing. Qualitative methods can help us identify the essential microfoundations or roots of individual actions or attitudes (Mosley 2013, 2). In my interviews, I asked questions that invited open-ended responses, and from those, I followed up with more; the iterative nature of this method sharpened my understanding of racial sympathy.

This would have been impossible in an internet survey. It also would be unlikely in an experiment. To ensure that the manipulation is the only aspect that differs between a control and treatment condition, experimenters are expected to treat all subjects equally. If an experimenter asked different questions to each subject, she could inadvertently introduce error into her results.

The latitude—indeed expectation—to pose follow-up questions is a unique feature of interviews. And it was through this process that I encountered sympathy's potential limitations. Many of my interviewees supported the policies I explored in the book; none of them suggested that government services to African Americans ought to be curtailed or that police budgets should be expanded. But it was only through talking to the interviewees that I became attentive to how little they were thinking about the policies or politics I discuss elsewhere. The interview holds important *metadata* or *latent content*, defined as the "information we glean from an interview that is not directly articulated by the interviewee in response to our questions" (Lynch 2013, 36). Watching how an interviewee behaves, pauses, clears their throat, moves in their chair, or tears up would not have been possible in the sterile survey environment.

The participant observation sessions described earlier in chapter 3 were in public group settings, like museums and theaters. In contrast, the interviewees in this chapter were questioned individually, typically in homes or other private spaces, but sometimes in coffee shops or libraries. Some interviewees took us to meeting rooms at their offices, where we would chat after hours. Others reserved the community room at their senior center for our private conversation. We met some in the Newsfeed Café, a bright, modern, and airy public space in the Boston Public Library. One especially muggy and gray day in late July, we sat with an interviewee outside a Starbucks on the noisy Veterans of Foreign Wars Parkway. We had to speak up to hear each other over the sound of the traffic.

In group settings, the tone and content can be dominated by the views and personalities of individual participants. The participant shares his insights while navigating other social dynamics, including sanctioning or peer pressure (Hertel, Singer, and Cott 2009). By interviewing the activists one by one, with an assurance of confidentiality, I can be more confident that the views expressed represented interviewees' genuine attitudes and opinions. That said, interviewer effects, or the influence of an interviewer's individual traits on the interview process, mean that respondents may still be reacting to social dynamics during the course of an interview. In later sections, I speculate as to how my own identity may have been read by the activists.

That said, the interviews reported here are not the central source of data. I do not use them for hypothesis testing. The sample's composition is not representative, and so I caution the reader against generalizations. The interviews are just one component of my mixed methods research strategy. They provide an important seed for theory building and eventually generate valuable data interpretation insights. For all these reasons, the interview data in this chapter is a useful supplement to the evidence presented elsewhere in the book. Nonetheless, my intention was to collect the qualitative data in a thoughtful and rigorous way. I outline my process in the next section.

Interviewing the Racial Justice Activists

Beginning in August 2019, I conducted long-form interviews with white people who participate in racial justice causes. With the assistance of an undergraduate research assistant, Sasha Blachman, I interviewed these individuals over ten months. Finding this sample was challenging. As Marc Warren notes in his book on white racial justice activists, "There is no list of White racial justice activists from which I could randomly choose names" (Warren 2010, 10). Instead, I relied on a mixed recruiting strategy to locate my sample. The first step involved purposive sampling. My research team emailed several racial justice organizations in the Boston area, informing them that we were conducting a study related to "American politics and racial justice" and asking if they would send a study announcement to their membership. Some organizations obliged, others did not; some referred us to their Facebook page and instructed us to announce the study directly to their membership. This initial approach yielded a seed that we used to develop our snowball sample. Respondents referred us to their contacts after completing their interviews, and we eventually interviewed twenty-two respondents, a sample size in line with other mixed methods projects (Deterding and Waters 2018).[1]

All interviewees identified as white and resided in the Boston metropolitan area. We chose a limited geographic area because we initially conducted the interviews in person and wanted to build rapport, which can be important for discussing sensitive topics like race (Warren 2010). When the coronavirus arrived in the United States in March 2020, we moved the interviews online. This change in format did not impact the average interview time, which was approximately fifty-eight minutes in person and sixty-five minutes over Zoom, an internet video and communication platform. The interview schedule, or script, that we used throughout appears in the appendix. The interviews were recorded using a digital audio recorder and transcribed through Rev.com, an online transcription service. The data was analyzed with ATLAS.ti, a qualitative data analysis software often used by sociologists.

Our interviewees were uniformly happy to talk with us, and in many cases, it seemed they did not want the interviews to end. Many had personal connections to racial justice. Some mentioned Black spouses or children that made them have, in their eyes, an especially deep connection to issues related to Black suffering. Others came across the topic through academic or professional experiences. Some discussed how their college

TABLE 7.1 **Racial Sympathy Scores**

Item	2013 CCES	2020 CMPS	2020 YouGov	2019–2020 Activists Study
Racial Sympathy 1, mean	0.76	0.74	0.81	0.98
Racial Sympathy 2, mean	0.72	0.72	0.79	0.91
Racial Sympathy 3, mean	0.51	0.54	0.56	1
Racial Sympathy 4, mean	0.53	0.58	0.65	1
Average Level of Racial Sympathy	0.63	0.64	0.7	0.97

Sources: 2013 CCES, 2020 CMPS, 2020 YouGov, 2019–2020 Activists Study
Data weighted where possible.

experiences had been eye-opening in this respect—to be clear, it wasn't anything they learned in classes that caught their attention.[2] Instead, it was what they learned by observing racial politics play out on their campus. All subjects were emotional about the topic, but there was variation in how they expressed their feelings. Some respondents were warm and chatty; others proceeded with a sense of seriousness and urgency.

Each interviewee also completed a pre-interview survey with demographic and attitudinal questions, including the racial sympathy index. The pre-interview survey permits me to connect the interview data to the survey data more explicitly. Consistent with the other samples in this book, the respondents' answers to the racial sympathy index display high internal consistency ($\alpha = 0.83$).

Earlier, I described the activists as an "extreme" case or iteration of racial sympathy. The fourth column of table 7.1 reveals that the activists have significantly higher levels of racial sympathy than the general white population. They differ in other important ways, too. For example, they have, on average, higher levels of income and education. In the 2020 ANES, 14 percent of white Americans had an advanced degree, and 48 percent came from households with incomes over $80,000. In the Boston activists sample, these figures were 67 percent and 56 percent, respectively. Over 90 percent of the activists indicated that they were Democrats or leaned toward the Democratic Party.

Racial Sympathy and Political Participation

With this background information established, we can begin to evaluate the relationship between racial sympathy and white Americans' political behavior or participation. When I use the term *political participation*, I rely on the definition provided by Sidney Verba and colleagues: "Activities by private citizens that are more or less directly aimed at influencing the selection of governmental personnel and/or the actions they take" (Verba, Nie, and Kim 1978, 46). This is a flexible definition; the words "more or less" grant latitude in determining political relevance, though "government" anchors participation to a specific domain. "Activities" are a broad category but are decidedly different from the "opinions held by private persons," to quote a classic definition of public opinion (Key 1961).

Although racial sympathy has the potential to impact white people's actions across various activities—they could, for example buy products from Black businesses or read books by Black authors—as a venue, politics offers a few attractive features. Most importantly, perhaps, political engagement can have broad effects. The scale and scope of government equip it to shape outcomes for a larger group of people.[3]

But this is not the only category of action. I also include another category of behavior for consideration: "personal" behavior. Personal behaviors occur mostly at the individual level through interpersonal interactions and, unlike political behaviors, do not aim to influence government. For example, reading about race can be very informative and engaging for white people. It can spark a sustained commitment to eradicating Black suffering. Some of my racial justice interviewees were strongly moved by authors like Toni Morrison, for example. However, in and of itself, reading is an isolated activity that citizens choose to engage in on their own. I would classify it, therefore, as a personal activity. With both of these definitions in mind, let us begin to evaluate the relationship between racial sympathy and behavior.

I begin with the quantitative data sourced from the 2020 YouGov study. Respondents in this study were queried about a wide range of efforts that could promote racial equality and reduce Black suffering. Specifically, subjects were asked: "To address issues of race and racial inequality, how important is it for you personally to do the following activity?" A list of activities appeared below the question, and subjects rated each one on the seven-point scale ranging from 0 (Not at all important) to 1 (Extremely important). Personal (or more individual-level actions) activities included educating oneself about racism, confronting other people when they are being racist, opting to live in diverse communities, and listening to people of color. Political activities, including attending protests, voting in elections, and campaigning for candidates who prioritize Black issues, were also presented to subjects. These are, of course, just a few examples of "political" and "personal" behaviors; there are many others. Nonetheless, they present a sampling of common behaviors in both of these categories.

The analysis, presented in table 7.2, suggests that racial sympathy is only occasionally associated with political behaviors. On the one hand, for some behavioral outcomes, the relationship between sympathy and intended behavior is quite strong. For example, in the case of the second column, going from the lowest to highest levels of racial sympathy is associated with an increase of 40 percentage points in thinking it is important to confront other people who are being racist.

On the other hand, racial sympathy does not seem to significantly map onto behavior like voting or campaigning for candidates who prioritize Black issues. This suggests that even when white Americans possess high levels of racial sympathy, it may not consistently translate into their political behavior. The notable exception is protest; whites who are high in racial sympathy *do* consider protest to be an important method to address race and racial inequality. Perhaps this explains the large representation of white Americans participating in the protests following Floyd's murder in 2020 (Harmon and Tavernise 2020).

It is important to note that, as a survey measuring *intended* rather than observed behavior, these results likely overestimate the relationship between sympathy and action. Intentions, as expressed in surveys, do not always translate into actual political behavior (Achen and Blais 2010).[4] Indeed, there are many reasons why a respondent might claim certain behaviors on a survey but not actually execute them in real life. Moreover, the political behavior questions on the YouGov study ask respondents to rate the importance of various activities. Indicating that an activity is "important" is quite different than actually pursuing it. The true relationship between sympathy and behavioral outcomes may be even more limited than reported here.

That said, the preference for more personal-level behavior was also reflected in the interviews with the racial justice activists. In one question, subjects were asked how to facilitate racial change. Many responded by drawing attention to actions they were taking in their personal lives. Two examples appear below:

Example 1: And I was like okay, now that I realize how much I learned that was wrong, and how many biases I have that I now need to work so hard every

TABLE 7.2 **Personal and Political Behaviors**

	Individual Behaviors			Political Behaviors		
Variables	Educate Myself about Racism	Confront Other People When Being Racist	Listen to POC	Attend Protests	Vote in Elections	Campaign for Candidates Who Prioritize Black Issues
Racial Sympathy	0.36***	0.41***	0.32***	0.25***	0.09	-0.17
	(0.092)	(0.078)	(0.061)	(0.085)	(0.075)	(0.129)
Racial Resentment	-0.25***	-0.16*	-0.22***	-0.41***	0.00	-0.25**
	(0.083)	(0.090)	(0.083)	(0.091)	(0.073)	(0.128)
Party ID (1 = GOP)	-0.14***	-0.10	-0.07	-0.16*	-0.01	-0.00
	(0.053)	(0.061)	(0.047)	(0.082)	(0.055)	(0.098)
Observations	406	406	406	406	406	406
R-squared	0.401	0.395	0.358	0.498	0.246	0.072

Source: 2020 YouGov

*** $p < 0.01$; ** $p < 0.05$; * $p < 0.10$

Cell entries are ordinary least squares regression coefficients (standard errors in parentheses). The column headings display the dependent variables, which are questions about the importance of certain behavioral actions that could "address issues of race and racial inequality." Coefficients on additional control variables included in the models here are not shown for space considerations; the following variables were also included in the models: income, age, education, gender, region (South), ideology, and church attendance. Since research has found that political behavior, to a greater extent than opinion, is shaped by interest in politics, this model also includes a control variable for political interest. This question asks respondents how much they follow politics. The results are similar if the political interest variable is excluded. Data are weighted for national representativeness. All variables are coded from 0 to 1.

day to push against, what do I need to do to provide a different upbringing for them and try to give them some sort of inoculation from the biases and the stories? What choices are you making and if you expect them to do something different than you, they might rebel against you, probably will, but they're going to take what you do with your day as an example, whether it's one they want to push against or accept, but that's what they're observing. It's what do you spend your time with, who are your relationships with. So if you want to tell them don't be prejudiced and they see you only with white friends only watching white media, then what does that even mean, don't be prejudiced? Let's talk about what you learned in school and how did that play? And what was, let's have these folks over for dinner or go over to their house for dinner and talk about their lives and our lives and how they're different. Whatever you can think of.

Example 2: Young people are absolutely amazing, and so I am totally . . . anything you do, I support, I totally just want to follow your lead, and that's what I think we should do as old, white people . . . just listen to young people and just do what you tell us to do, because we've messed it up, we've really fucked it up. And we got our chance and we blew it, and so I know that's really not great, and I tell my . . . my kids are always like, "Thanks, thanks for leaving this for me. Thank you." I'm like, "I tried."

It is possible that these individuals responded in this manner because it simply did not occur to them to think about politics. Indeed, much of the work that examines political thinking among average citizens finds that political issues are typically "morselized" or separated from the broader context or significance (Lane 1962). Perhaps if subjects were guided to the topic of politics, they would be more attentive to the role government could play in reducing racial inequality.

However, even when explicitly prompted in this way, the activist interviewees continued to emphasize personal-level behavior. The following is a response to a question that asked whether government, policies, or laws should address racial inequality. The respondent observed: "So to be completely honest, change isn't going to come that way. So does the government need to be on board? Sure. But we need to . . . listen to indigenous people and we listen to Black and Brown people, we will understand what we need to do. And truly, in listening to those folks, this is going to happen when we work together and we move together and we make the changes that we want."

Another interviewee eschewed policy solutions, reasoning that since previous policies had failed, it was up to white Americans' hearts and minds: "I think it's laws but I also think that when you get to know some-one, and you [are] around people who are different from you, that changes hearts and minds. And I feel like there was a lot of talk in the sixties around busing, around housing, around all kinds of issues, and we are more seg-regated than ever. So people aren't getting to know each other on a per-sonal level."

In another effort to prompt respondents to think about politics, we asked respondents, "What is the number one issue that the federal or even state governments should do to mitigate racial inequality?" Here, too, re-spondents demonstrated an aversion to politics. In one case, a respondent identified voter suppression as the "number one" issue that must be ad-dressed by governments. She replied with a political response: "Voter sup-pression is super heterogeneous in terms of locales, I think. I think it's probably happening everywhere and gerrymandering to some degree is happening everywhere. But there do appear to be places where it is much worse than other places. And that affects all the other policy issues, and we're never going to get certain states to fuck off with their license re-quirements and their bullying and bullshit."

Later, this same respondent was asked to describe her political participation:

INTERVIEWEE: I don't even vote a lot. I vote sometimes when I think it's important or when I feel emotional about it. Like this is a landmark, I'm going to vote for it. But I don't, I'm not into voting as a regular . . . yeah, so I don't think that much about political parties and I don't know, it's not interesting.
INTERVIEWER: So would you say you don't like politics?
INTERVIEWEE: Sure, I see you gotta put a label on everything, I guess.

Among the twenty-two interviewees, nineteen indicated that pro-tests, organizing, and "taking it to the streets" were their preferred form of political engagement, aligning with the results of the YouGov survey (table 7.2). Activists are sometimes distrustful of existing political chan-nels, so it is not altogether surprising that they were skeptical of politics. What was surprising was how almost *any* discussion of government or policy seemed to be off the table.

In summary, white distress over Black suffering is significantly associ-ated with support for policies intended to rectify that suffering. However, this robust survey result is not consistently mirrored in white Americans' intended political behaviors. In both the survey and interview data, I find that even many white Americans with high levels of racial sympathy rebuff or ignore the prospect for political change via activities like voting and instead focus on individual-level behaviors like changing hearts and minds. The important exception to this pattern can be observed with protest; racially sympathetic white Americans *do* consider protest an important action. In the section that follows, I discuss two potential explanations for these results and present some initial evidence in support of each.

What We Want to Hear? Considering the Possibility of Self-Monitoring

In chapter 4, I discussed the concept of self-monitoring or the enduring predisposition in which individuals are "chronically concerned with the appropriateness of their interpersonal behavior" (Berinsky and Lavine 2012, 28). To gain the approval of those around them, those who self-monitor may misrepresent their true views on sensitive issues such as race. I found that although there were sympathetic white people who exhibited this type of concern, there were also sympathetic white people who did not. The correlates—or ingredients—of racial sympathy and self-monitoring were also quite different. Based on these analyses, it was clear that these were not interchangeable variables.

Still, even if racial sympathy is not the same as self-monitoring, it is important to consider whether racial sympathy is shaped or influenced by self-monitoring. More pointedly, I can observe whether the significant result between sympathy and political outcomes are in fact artifacts of dishonest self-reporting. To do so, I examine whether the results, especially the significant ones, hold among those respondents most likely to state genuine attitudes—that is, low self-monitors. These individuals are not easily swayed by various social norms and contexts. Instead, they are, according to Christopher R. Weber and colleagues, "guided by their inner dispositions" (2014, 66). Low self-monitors simply lack the desire—and may even lack the ability—to create and project false images of themselves (Gangestad and Snyder 2000). This is not to suggest that they are more racially sympathetic; rather, it is more likely that the racial sympathy scores of low self-monitors reflect their sincere racial attitudes, whether sympathetic or not. On the other hand, if the associations I present are limited to high self-monitors, this would undermine the argument that racial

TABLE 7.3 **Racial Sympathy, Opinion, Behavior, and Self-Monitoring**

Variables	Govt. Services	Affirmative Action	Educate Oneself about Racism	Confront Racist Others	Protest	Listen to POC
Racial Sympathy	0.19***	0.23***	0.38***	0.42***	0.27***	0.32***
	(0.052)	(0.071)	(0.091)	(0.079)	(0.086)	(0.063)
Racial Resentment	−0.61***	−0.47***	−0.23***	−0.17*	−0.43***	−0.22***
	(0.057)	(0.070)	(0.082)	(0.089)	(0.090)	(0.084)
Party ID (1 = GOP)	−0.07	−0.04	−0.14***	−0.11*	−0.17**	−0.07
	(0.064)	(0.069)	(0.051)	(0.061)	(0.081)	(0.046)
Self-Monitoring	0.01	0.07	0.10	0.15*	0.19**	−0.05
	(0.057)	(0.081)	(0.081)	(0.078)	(0.089)	(0.086)
Constant	0.69***	0.55***	0.56***	0.42***	0.42***	0.62***
	(0.066)	(0.092)	(0.102)	(0.095)	(0.104)	(0.076)

Source: 2020 YouGov
*** $p < 0.01$; ** $p < 0.05$; * $p < 0.10$
Cell entries are ordinary least squares regression coefficients (standard errors in parentheses). The column headings display the dependent variables, which are questions about policy opinion and the importance of certain behavioral actions that could "address issues of race and racial inequality." Coefficients on additional control variables included in the models here are not shown for space considerations; the following variables were also included in the models: income, age, education, gender, region (South), ideology, and church attendance. Since research has found that political behavior, to a greater extent than opinion, is shaped by interest in politics, the models in columns 4 to 6 also include a control variable for political interest. This question asks respondents how much they follow politics. The results are similar if the political interest variable is excluded. Data are weighted for national representativeness. All variables are coded from 0 to 1.

sympathy—rather than concerns about self-presentation—influences white policy opinion.

I find that the associations between racial sympathy and policy opinion are approximately equivalent across low and high self-monitors. I show this in three ways. First, I include self-monitoring as a control variable. These results appear in table 7.3 and demonstrate that the strong associations between racial sympathy, policy opinion, and some behavioral outcomes remain.[5] For space considerations, I present only the models that were previously significant in table 7.2, though the results are similar for the other variables, too. I also present results for two opinion variables to investigate whether the conclusions of the preceding chapter should be modified in light of self-monitoring. In all cases, I find that racial sympathy retains a significant relationship with the dependent variable. Self-monitoring *is* significantly associated with two behavioral outcomes—confronting others and protesting—but it does not seem to erode the contribution of sympathy.

Second, following the approach of previous research (Berinsky and Lavine 2012), I split the sample by low and high self-monitoring (median split). This analysis demonstrates that statistically significant, substantively meaningful associations can be found in most cases, even among low self-monitors. Third, I specify an interaction. I do so because the median split approach dichotomizes a continuous variable and may restrict meaningful variation. To address this concern, I conduct regressions interacting racial sympathy with the self-monitoring measure; once again, the results show approximately equivalent patterns across the self-monitoring scale. In other words, the slopes are not significantly different at low relative to high levels of self-monitoring. Both of these analyses appear in the appendix and suggest that white racial sympathy is not, for the most part, a matter of white people trying to present the "right" attitudes about race.[6] Instead, they suggest that distress over Black suffering may genuinely shape white Americans' policy opinions.[7]

Public Responsibility, Private Solutions?

Given the format of the interviews, which took place in person and were conducted by two multiracial individuals, it was difficult to evaluate respondents' sincerity. Most of the interviewees did seem to express a genuine commitment to racial inequality. A few people swore during their interviews, and some scholars interpret spontaneous swearing as a sign of close social distance between interviewer and interviewee (Fägersten 2012). In reviewing post-interview notes, our summaries regularly suggested that we had cultivated respondents' trust and they were comfortable showing their vulnerabilities. Of the twenty-two people we interviewed, five openly cried. These strong emotional reactions often came when interviewees were asked to reflect on the direction of the country. For example:

> When I think of the history, and the institutions that have maintained a system of inequality. In every department, from healthcare, to education, to criminal justice, I feel like I have to push myself toward hope. And optimism. . . . Our generation fucked up, you know? We did some good stuff, but . . . sorry. When I look at the youth, the Black kids I've taught who have been through so much . . . I want to be hopeful when they've been through so much. So much pain. [*Respondent cries*] I am struck that I started crying. Which, I know, speaks to my caring about it.

This quote reveals an interesting phenomenon: although respondents were adept at identifying institutional failures, many of the solutions they proposed were primarily individual. Most respondents were able to label racism as "structural, institutional, or systemic"—in fact, these words came up in almost every interview (twenty-one out of twenty-two). Although the interviewees acknowledged this dimension of racial suffering, few mentioned structures, institutions, or systems when asked to think about solutions. One interviewee noted:

> I think that the notion that we live in a white supremacy society and it's all around us, and then racism is baked into the institutions and even individuals aren't racist to change the institutions, that's a much more subtle, difficult concept to understand, and I think does require people to get some formal education just like I have to really understand the concept. It's not an easy concept to understand. It's easy for people to say, "You're a racist," or "You did a racist thing," that's easier to understand. That's why learning about it, educating yourself is so essential.

Another observed:

> The structure of white supremacy is so deeply embedded in everything, in every system, in every structure, in every human being, not every human being, because I know a lot of Indigenous and Black people who are very human. We need to get more people of humanity and more people who understand the systems and understand what is happening to be in those positions to influence government, but it's so much to understand what needs to happen, but certainly white people need to be educated, white people need to understand that the system is not working. And like I said before, until they realize what they're losing as a result of it, we're not going to get people involved.

In my interviews, I found that even the most racially sympathetic white Americans generated individual-level solutions to addressing racial inequality, which they characterized as fundamentally structural. I explored this further by consulting the open-ended questions in the YouGov study. Here, subjects were invited to respond at length to the following two questions: "In your opinion, what are the most important causes contributing to Black people suffering from inequality and/or discrimination in American society?" and "What can and should be done to reduce Black suffering?"

These questions appeared prior to any political variables. I ordered the questions in this way because I was concerned that the survey instrument itself, which later asked subjects to report their opinions on many policies, was artificially introducing political considerations into respondents' interpretations of racial inequality. Public opinion surveys require their respondents to think a lot about specific policies, an unusual situation for most citizens. By intentionally placing these open-ended questions first, I attempted to emulate a more realistic situation, as individuals, in their day-to-day lives, are not prompted to think about politics or specific policies.[8] Under these circumstances, do white Americans emphasize personal or structural solutions when they reflect on racial inequality?

Although these questions were optional, over 70 percent of respondents took the time to contribute their opinions. An undergraduate research assistant read through each response and developed a numeric coding system. Responses were coded "0" for answers that focused on individual level actions and "1" if the respondent focused more on the systemic and political. For example, responses to Question 1, which asked about the causes of Black suffering, included many answers that emphasized personal behavior, such as: "Because white people (especially in the South) think they are better than them. And anyone else for that matter that is not 'white' or of another race. Total discrimination still exists and it makes me sick." This and similar responses were coded 0. Responses that focused on structural reasons and were coded 1 included answers like: "Systemic racism in the laws and policies of the USA."

Question 2 asked about the solutions to Black suffering. Here, personal responses, coded 0, included, "Everyone should be more open and understanding of everyone else's feelings, history and be more open to having actual conversations with people with different backgrounds." Structural responses emphasized changing laws or policies, such as: "Reinstate the voting rights act; increase minimum wage; reform the police and stop the militarization of 'peace' officers; eliminate private prisons." These were coded 1.

Most white people thought of racism and its solution as primarily individual-level problems perpetuated by bad white people and addressed by the promise of education and young people. Many also suggested that Black Americans may be responsible for these circumstances and similarly placed the burden on their shoulders for repairing it.

Elsewhere, there was less consistency between the respondents' answers to the two questions. The second most common combination was

Problem (Political)

Political Problem, Individual Solution: 22%	*Political Problem, Political Solution: 18%*
Problem: • Systemic or historical racism • Unequal treatment: education, housing, police, job access • Specific policies: war on drugs, red-lining, Reconstruction Solution: • Listen to Black people • Educate ourselves/white people about racism • Treat everyone equally	Problem: • Systemic or historical racism • Unequal treatment: education, housing, police, job access • Specific policies: war on drugs, red-lining, Reconstruction Solution: • Explicitly racial policies: reparations, end policy brutality, voting rights act restoration, etc • Non-racial policies: drug decriminalization, increase minimum wage, universal healthcare, etc

Solution (Individual)   Solution (Political)

Individual Problem, Individual Solution: 53%	*Individual Problem, Political Solution: 7%*
Problem: • Individual racists, supremacists, hatred, prejudice, stereotyping, etc • Issues with "Black culture": Blacks not trying or working hard enough • Ignorance/lack of knowledge, education, or exposure Solution: • Listen to Black people • Educate ourselves/white people about racism • Treat everyone equally	Problem: • Individual racists, supremacists, hatred, prejudice, stereotyping, etc • Ignorance/lack of knowledge, education, or exposure Solution: • Explicitly racial policies: Voting Rights Act, anti-discrimination laws, police reform, reparations • Non-racial policies: education funding/policy changes

Problem (Individual)

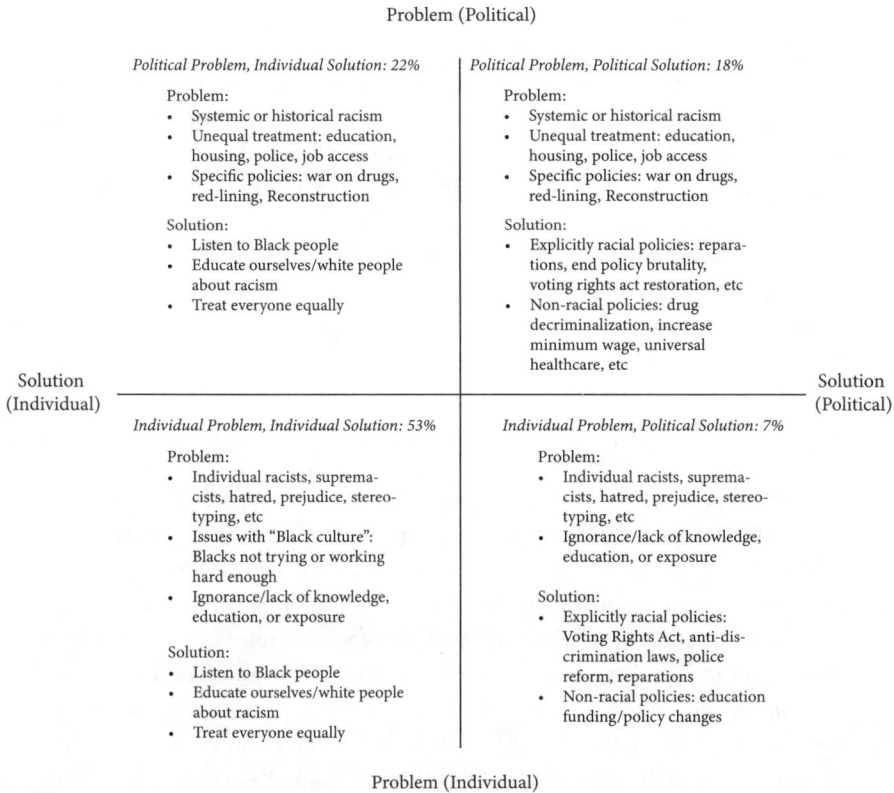

FIGURE 7.1. Racism and Its Solutions: Personal and Political
Source: 2020 YouGov

that subjects, in their answer to Question 1, were able to diagnose the "problem" as systemic but then paired this with individual-level solutions. For example, one respondent identified the "cause" of racial inequality as "systematic racism and white supremacy 'baked in' to almost every aspect of society, perhaps most typified by the practice of redlining in real estate that, although ostensibly banned, has created a persistent, structural state of inequality." This same respondent suggested that the remedy was "naming and drawing attention to the ways in which white supremacy contributes to Black suffering." Only 18 percent of those sampled identified systematic solutions to meet systematic problems.

The various configurations of the YouGov answers are presented in figure 7.1. On one axis, I present respondents' conceptualization of the problem as political or individual. On the other, I place their conceptualization of the solution, also political or individual. The chart also presents some of the common themes that emerged in each quadrant. Overall, it reveals the mixed assessments white Americans make about racism and its solutions. Whether or not they diagnose the problem as institutional or political, the majority of white people who responded to these items (75%) identified remedies that engage individuals, not political systems. Those white Americans with above-average levels of racial sympathy do fall in the "political problems" part of the diagram, but they are roughly equally distributed on the "solutions" axes. They do not favor political solutions over individual ones.

Conclusion

The results presented in this chapter enrich and complicate our understanding of racial attitudes in American politics. As the news articles cited earlier in the chapter suggest, in some quarters, white Americans' responses to Floyd's murder have been criticized as shallow or performative. Indeed, recent research has found that many white Americans who participated in the Floyd protests were motivated by grievances related to the coronavirus pandemic and dissatisfaction with the government and not by a desire to support BLM.[9] Although I do not have the racial sympathy scores of all Americans, the research in this chapter suggests that many white Americans who express sympathy over Black suffering, at least as depicted in the vignettes, do genuinely carry this attitude. As we know, many white Americans routinely have no issue airing prejudicial attitudes on anonymous surveys, such as the YouGov study discussed here. And even among the racial sympathy questions, on some items, hardly half of white Americans issue a sympathetic response. Skepticism may be warranted, but self-monitoring or social desirability concerns do not supplant the important role of racial sympathy.

What is not clear, however, is whether this attitude translates into meaningful political behavior. In the YouGov study, racial sympathy is significantly and consistently associated with behaviors that are primarily personal and individual. The relationship between racial sympathy and more overt political behaviors is less consistent; it is significantly related to protest but not to the other forms of political behavior I study here. Although I observe this trend in both the survey and interview data, it will be important to replicate this finding on other survey samples. Considering additional dependent variables will also provide insight into the phenomena. Could some candidates or elections be especially meaningful to racially sympathetic white Americans, inspiring their participation? This is a possibility I consider in more detail in the next chapter.

Racial sympathy is an important attitude that is robustly and reliably associated with public opinion. White public opinion would be significantly less supportive on matters such as government services to African Americans without it. And public opinion, or at least the perception of public opinion, can be an important consideration when political elites make decisions. Whether observing marches, studying polls, or consulting focus groups, politicians are often invested in responding to public opinion because, in many cases, their political careers depend on it (Stimson, MacKuen, and Erikson 1995).

When it comes to political behavior, however, racial sympathy may have a more modest impact. This is not for lack of sincerity; the survey and interview results suggest white people experience sympathy sincerely. But it is an attitude whose influence might be observed primarily outside of politics. Without a systematic strategy to address Black suffering, many white Americans instead endorse personal-level activities like reading books and listening to people of color. As long as this continues, their most passionate hopes for eradicating Black suffering may go unfulfilled.

CHAPTER EIGHT

Action and Perceptions of Efficacy

The preceding chapter paints a sobering picture: white people can sincerely experience distress over Black suffering, which broadly impacts their opinions toward public policies. Tempering this pattern, however, is the fact that racial sympathy has a modest—and at times, inconsistent—effect on their political behaviors. Many racially sympathetic white Americans favor private actions instead of political ones, a trend I observe through my interviews with racial justice activists and the 2020 YouGov survey. The exception is protest; higher levels of racial sympathy are significantly associated with an increased likelihood of intended protest, perhaps shedding light on why many white protesters took to the streets following Floyd's murder. Other forms of participation, such as campaigning for a candidate or voting, are less related to one's racial sympathy.

But are there certain conditions that could transform racial sympathy into behavior and expand its scope from private expressions of support into actions like donating, attending meetings, or participating in campaign activities? Sympathy's contribution to public opinion is consistent and strong; however, its impact on political behavior may not always be uniform. Instead, there may be key circumstances in which sympathy is more strongly brought out.

The activists I interviewed in the preceding chapter were highly sympathetic and were, by their own description, "activists." They engaged in time-consuming voluntary efforts to advance racial justice issues, sometimes with sustained and vigorous effort. For the most part, many of these efforts took place outside formal politics because, by their accounts, political change here was *not* possible. One interviewee made this argument pointedly. When asked what role the government should take in reducing racial inequality, she answered: "I definitely don't have a ton of faith in the federal government not fucking things up. So I'm not like, 'Yeah, let's get them in this.'" She later said: "Honestly, I feel like I keep learning about more fucked up things and we keep doubling down on it at the level of people in power . . . that's a function of just learning about existing systems and situations where Black suffering is mandated. Yeah, I guess [I feel] pessimistic."

To this respondent, the scale and breadth of Black suffering overpowered the possibility of reform. Another noted that although she saw herself as an "optimistic person," she ultimately felt pessimistic about the trajectory of change: "I'm an optimistic person . . . but it surprises me how pessimistic I'm feeling right now. . . . When I really think of the big picture, about race, on the one hand there's so much that we've raised up about this, which is good. But I think, who are we really impacting? Just people like me. We're not really impacting the rest of the country. So, I feel a little bit bummed out."

Comments like these were frequent and revealed, in my interpretation, elements of distrust, skepticism, blame, resignation, and exasperation, resembling some tenets of Afro-pessimism, as described in chapter 2. However, the respondents also devoted a lot of attention to assessing their own limited impact, which often resulted in aimless dejection. Although sympathy was present, the will for political action was in short supply.

In this final empirical chapter, I suggest that there are circumstances that can bring racial sympathy into the public sphere. And while many psychological and environmental factors might motivate sympathy, here I consider two possibilities in particular: efficacy and mobilization. In the first part of the chapter, I focus on efficacy and demonstrate that, during the Obama years, higher levels of efficacy may have boosted the impact of racial sympathy on political behaviors. Consequently, white Americans may have been more willing to undertake a range of political behaviors during this period. I also consider how sympathy may have shaped support for Obama more generally. Some white people viewed Obama through the lens of racial sympathy, but its impact is more visible on some outcomes and less visible on others.

In the second part of the chapter, I consider another possibility: social movement mobilization. I take up the specific case of BLM and explore how this movement may have directed white people to participate in political activities. Building on chapter 6, I show that not only did racial sympathy contribute to white Americans' views of the BLM movement, but it also may have spurred their participation in a range of activities by bringing visibility to them and offering ideas for how white people might participate. As with the preceding chapters, I organize the results by dependent variable; in the case of efficacy, I consider three categories of political participation: nonelectoral participation, turnout, and civic engagement. For the mobilization analyses, I distinguish among substantive issue areas, looking at the relationship between sympathy and participatory acts explicitly connected with BLM from those not.

This chapter offers two possibilities for channeling racial sympathy into political participation, but there are potentially others. Just as research on prejudice demonstrated that its influence on behavior is conditional on multiple other factors, I suspect sympathy may respond to many factors beyond those I consider here. It is not my intention to be deterministic, and the analyses here are offered in the spirit of informed speculation. In the conclusion, I suggest other fruitful avenues for future research.

Racial Sympathy and Efficacy

Efficacy presents one potential avenue for channeling sympathy into political action. Political efficacy is the "feeling that political and social change is possible and that the individual citizen can play a part in bringing about this change" (Campbell, Gurin, and Miller 1954, 187). Political behavior researchers often take up efficacy because it predicts participation and produces it (Abramson and Aldrich 1982; Finkel 1985). For this reason, political efficacy is "one of the most theoretically important and frequently used" concepts in political science (Niemi, Craig, and Mattei 1991, 1407). Efficacy matters for participation and may be especially influential in the case of sympathy.

In isolation, racial sympathy may only exhibit a modest relationship with participation. How could efficacy enable it? One way to think about this question is to consider how efficacy, in tandem with other concepts, generates participation. Emotions offer one pathway; efficacy and affect are a potent pair, for even if efficacy could involve cognitive considerations—like approximating the probability that your vote will impact an outcome—it is also infused with emotion. Efficacy's definition, after all, starts with the word *feeling*. Research has demonstrated that this component of efficacy can have consequences for citizens' participation. In the 1980 presidential campaign, for example, voters who were anxious and highly efficacious were more likely to be involved than voters who were anxious but not efficacious (Rudolph, Gangl, and Stevens 2000). Here, the effects of the emotion were conditional on individual differences in efficacy. High efficacy pushed anxious voters toward action, and low efficacy demobilized them.

Affect is a "central ingredient" of racial attitudes (Kinder 2013), and elsewhere in this book, I document the emotional roots of racial sympathy. Based on this, it seems plausible that feeling efficacious could lift sympathy into action. This conjecture is buttressed by research on prosocial behavior that has found, for example, that people may be more willing to pursue helping behaviors if they think they will be effective. As Shalom Schwartz explains, "When we learn that a person is suffering . . . we may be saddened, declare it a tragedy and with that, we could do something to help. But in the absence of any effective means of response, we do not experience a sense of obligation to relieve the victim's needs" (1975, 118). In this scenario, a perception of efficacy can transform sympathy from "sadness" into an "obligation to relieve."

Such a "transformation" can also be considered an *interaction*. In contrast to the linear-additive approach pursued in many of the preceding chapters, the interactive approach "adds an additional layer of complexity, asking not simply whether some relationship exists between an independent variable and a dependent variable, but under what conditions and in what manner such a relationship exists: for example, under what conditions is the relationship greater or lesser? Thus, this slightly more complex question posits that the effect of some variable X, on the dependent variable, Y, depends upon a third independent variable(s), Z" (Franzese and Kam 2009, 2).

This "slightly more complex question" has already been pursued in prejudice research. To take one example, studies of racial prejudice and the Obama elections argued that the activation of racial prejudice was conditional on the presence of "minimal cues" (Petrow 2010) or would only be observed among certain partisan populations (Krupnikov and Piston 2015) or when white Americans perceive relative discrimination (Cepuran and Berry 2022). This work has provided valuable insight into the interactive nature of racial attitudes, locating the "key conditions" in which the relationship between prejudice and behavior is strongest.

That said, it is also all piecemeal; it does not single out a specific condition most likely to launch a racial attitude into behavior. Further, like most other racial attitudes research, it is focused on the role of prejudice, which, I have argued, is distinct from sympathy. It offers suggestive but ultimately limited guidance on the conditions that might matter regarding sympathy and behavior. Thus, rather than replicate the approaches of these other scholars, I draw on the research related to efficacy and prosocial behavior. Based on it, I speculate that the effect of racial sympathy (X) on participation (Y) will depend on the third independent variable of efficacy (Z).

Racial Sympathy and Mobilization

Efficacy represents one pathway to spurring participation but is likely not the only one. The second possibility I consider is mobilization—in this case, as facilitated by the organization and social movement Black Lives Matter. In chapter 6, I provided background on BLM and demonstrated that higher levels of racial sympathy are associated with stronger support for the organization, even when it engages in contentious tactics. This analysis suggests that white racial sympathy was channeled into support for BLM. Could BLM have channeled racial sympathy into political behavior?

Social movements like BLM could facilitate this in many ways, but here I consider just one possibility: action mobilization. Mobilization is "a process of increasing the readiness to act collectively" (Gamson 1975, 15). Mobilization is less about transforming naysayers into supporters and more about shepherding latent interests into expression. As Hahrie Han explains, organizations "want to reach out to people who they know are sympathizers and activate their interests so that these previously quiescent sleeping giants will rise up and take action" (2014, 132). Such efforts could boost sympathy into political behavior.

Mobilization involves many steps, including framing an issue, targeting supporters, directing them to an activity, and ultimately compelling them to participate. In stages of "consensus mobilization," organizers parse out those who want to be affiliated from those who do not. As the name suggests, action mobilization is concerned with asking people to take different types of action (Klandermans and Oegema 1987). Multiple streams of influence contribute to this expression of participation, including networks or social embeddedness (Putnam, Leonardi, and Nanetti 1994) and politicized collective identity (Simon and Klandermans 2001). Emotions may stir involvement, too (van Zomeren et al. 2004).

Mobilization has several important components because it captures the exchange between individual psychology and the power of the environment. It has attracted scholarly attention and debate for decades across disciplines; thoughtful books and articles are filled with research documenting the mechanisms and effects of these movements.[1] Based on the volume of research on this topic, it is clear that social movements' role in society is multifaceted, vital, and broad. I cannot address its full impact. Instead, I suggest that political activities described in conjunction with BLM may be more likely to align with racial sympathy than activities without this designation. I examine these possibilities in the next section.

Efficacy and mobilization are, of course, related. Mobilization efforts attempt to lower the material and psychological barriers to participation, paving the way for broad engagement. They accomplish this, in part, by "enhancing citizens' belief in their own political efficacy" (Rosenstone and Hansen 1993, 174). Activists who attract a large following help ensure the viability and trajectory of the movement. In doing so, they avoid a disastrous outcome: a collective action movement lacking a collective. Bert Klandermans explains: "If many people think that few people will participate, many people will have doubts about the efficacy of their own participation. Thus a downward spiral ensues which is fatal to the willingness to participate" (1984, 588).

Mobilization and efficacy are deeply linked; I do not mean to suggest they are disconnected. I consider them separately here due to survey constraints—the 2008 and 2012 ANES studies predate the BLM movement, which began in 2013, and the CMPS did not carry the standard ANES efficacy items. These technicalities prevent me from conducting a full evaluation of these two variables and the relationship between them. However, and more importantly, the analyses in this chapter are conducted in the spirit of exploration. Thus, it is not my intention to pin down the precise behavioral mechanics of this process but instead to offer some possibilities.

Sympathy, Efficacy, and Participation in the Obama Years

I begin my analysis with efficacy. Here, I turn to two surveys that host both measures of sympathy and efficacy: the 2008 and 2012 American National Election Studies surveys. These surveys preceded the election and reelection of Obama, respectively. Although efficacy is a single concept, it has two dimensions: internal and external (Campbell and Converse 1972; Verba and Nie 1987). Internal efficacy refers to one's confidence in taking part in politics. People high in internal efficacy "are not intimidated by the challenges, conflicts or disagreements that occur in that arena" (Valentino, Gregorowicz, and Groenendyk 2009, 308). External efficacy refers to the perception that the government will be "satisfactorily responsive" to a citizen's input (Phoenix and Chan 2023).

Previous research suggests that internal efficacy may be especially responsive to emotions (Valentino, Gregorowicz, and Groenendyk 2009). Accordingly, I focus on the internal efficacy questions, which tap the "role of the citizen in political decision making" (Craig and Maggiotto 1982, 88) and are typically represented by two statements: "Sometimes, politics and government seem so complicated that a person like me can't really understand what's going on" and "I feel that I have a pretty good understanding of the important political issues facing our country." After each statement, subjects are presented with five answer options: "Disagree strongly," "Disagree somewhat," "Neither agree nor disagree," "Agree somewhat," and "Agree strongly." The responses to the first statement are reverse coded such that those individuals who "Disagree strongly" with it are scored as more efficacious.[2] Although these statements appear to reference assessments of individual competency, research has found that they also represent one's "psychological involvement" in political affairs more broadly (Niemi, Craig, and Mattei 1991, 1410).[3] Thus, these questions may approximate, for example, the connection that individuals feel to politics and their willingness to engage with it.

With these measures of efficacy, I explore the interactive influence of sympathy and efficacy on political participation. I will soon introduce three categories of political participation. In each case, I regress the political participation dependent variable on a variable that interacts white Americans' racial sympathy scores with their levels of efficacy.[4] The results are displayed in predicted probability plots, the same format readers encountered in the experimental analyses. This is because, like the experiments, the interactive analyses clarify when racial sympathy matters most.

The ANES participation variables provide a somewhat blunt instrumentation of political behavior. They do not indicate whether the participation was, for example, in service of Obama in particular or another candidate. In the next section, I address this concern by considering a suite of activities specifically tied to the BLM movement in particular. However, scholars have argued that white Americans' participation in elections with Black candidates represent their reactions to Black leadership specifically (Cepuran and Berry 2022; Hajnal 2007; Krupnikov and Piston 2015; Petrow 2010).[5] One of Obama's 2008 campaign slogans was "yes, we can"—an affirmation of efficacy that may have propelled sympathetic whites into various political behaviors. Thus, I consider white Americans' political behavior during these elections to reflect, at least partially, the extent to which they were willing to engage in activities related to the election of the first Black president.

During most American elections, including Obama's, academics, politicians, journalists, and citizens become routinely preoccupied with one aspect of political behavior: the vote. This is understandable, since voting, or what is sometimes referred to as "turnout," has important consequences on electoral outcomes and, ultimately, representation (Fraga 2018). However, voting is only one—and is a somewhat unusual—form of participation. Other forms of political participation are also foundational to the American democratic process. Activities such as giving donations or volunteering can lead to the ballot citizens evaluate on Election Day itself. Individual contributions are the "single largest source of campaign contributions" (Barber, Canes-Wrone, and Thrower 2017, 271) and can be used to fund many outputs, such as advertisements (Freedman, Franz, and Goldstein 2004; Morton and Cameron 1992) or canvassing efforts. Volunteering for a campaign can be a "transformative experience" that both registers prospective voters and energizes existing ones (McKenna and Han 2014). For these reasons and more, studying these types of behavior is informative. Verba and colleagues observe: "For the individual or for particular groups of citizens, the most important political activities may be those in the between-elections period" (1978, 47). Let us explore some of these important activities now by considering two categories of political participation: civic engagement activities and nonelectoral participation.[6]

Civic Engagement

I begin with civic engagement activities, a broad category capturing community involvement through behaviors such as participating in a demonstration, attending a municipal board meeting, signing a petition, donating to a religious organization, donating to other organizations, posting about politics, writing an op-ed, or contacting a politician. Although these activities vary with respect to their time and resource requirements, they

are similar in that they need not occur during an election. Rather, these
are the day-to-day volunteer activities that are, in the eyes of some scholars
and pundits, vital to a vibrant democracy (Putnam 2000). Indeed, engagement in voluntary associations were among the distinctive features of "democracy in America," according to Tocqueville (Skocpol and Fiorina 2004).

Racially sympathetic Americans might find civic engagement activities appealing. The behaviors in this category include many pathways to
reducing Black suffering; for example, speaking up in one's community
about racial inequality, protesting against unfair treatment of Black citizens, and donating to causes that advance Black interests would all fall
under the umbrella of "civic engagement." Based on the interactive relationship I suggested earlier, however, I expect that the relationship
between sympathy and civic engagement is conditional on one's level of
efficacy. If sympathetic white Americans feel confident that they can successfully navigate political issues or feel psychologically connected to politics, they will be more likely to participate in these activities. If they do
not feel this way, then sympathy may not extend into the public sphere.

To consider this possibility, I consult the ANES, which asks respondents whether they have participated in the previously mentioned civic
engagement activities. I coded the responses "1" if the subject reported
having done the activity and "0" otherwise. I then combine and rescale
these answers into an additive index, ranging from 0–1, which I refer to as
"civic engagement."[7] In the predicted probability plots, I regress the civic
engagement index on the interaction of racial sympathy and efficacy for
2008 and, separately, 2012.

Figure 8.1 presents two predicted probability plots, with each line representing a different level of efficacy. The solid line represents those individuals who report low levels of efficacy, and the dashed line represents
those who are highly efficacious. As the charts demonstrate, low efficacy
depresses the expression of racial sympathy across all levels. Even if a
white person carries strong sorrow over Black suffering, this sympathy
is unlikely to translate into civic engagement activities if he lacks the
skills or psychological involvement in politics. However, among the highly
efficacious, higher levels of sympathy *are* significantly associated with engagement in such civic activities as attending a meeting, signing a petition, or donating money. In this case—and others, as we shall soon find—
distress over Black suffering *can* find a meaningful outlet in politics.

Although this general trend is present in 2008 and 2012, it is only statistically significant in 2008. This result, in which sympathy is especially
salient in 2008, is one that I return to shortly. Nevertheless, the interaction

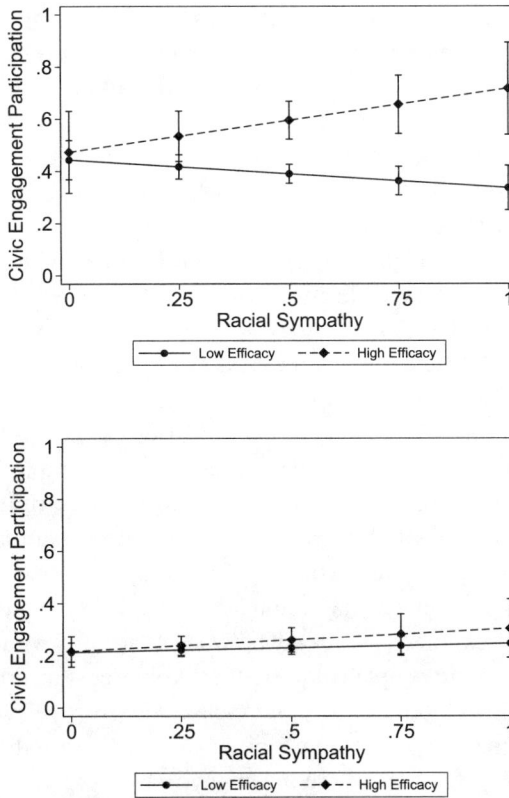

FIGURE 8.1. The Interactive Relationship Between Racial Sympathy and Efficacy: Civic Engagement (a) 2008 ANES, (b) 2012 ANES

between racial sympathy and efficacy is associated with an increased likelihood of civic engagement in both 2008 and 2012. On both occasions, racial sympathy is connected to participation in "uniquely American" civic activities (Verba, Schlozman, and Brady 1995, 7). These behaviors have the potential to "instill civic values, enhance political behavior, and improve democracy and society" (Theiss-Morse and Hibbing 2005, 230), and they may be linked, under some circumstances, to racial sympathy.

Non-voting Electoral Participation

Elections and campaigns require a lot of work, and not only for the exhausted candidates. By the time Election Day arrives, ordinary Americans have given hours of their time to activities like persuading others to vote, going to political meetings, and doing campaign work. They may have also committed material resources, such as donations, to campaigns, political parties, or other political organizations. They may sport campaign apparel—buttons, T-shirts, face masks—in support of their favorite candidates. I classify all of this behavior as "non-voting electoral participation"; unlike civic engagement, this is participation conducted in conjunction with a campaign, party, or election. These activities are part of a deliberate effort to shape electoral outcomes and representation. Unlike turnout, this includes many acts beyond voting; these can be multiplied in volume and, in some cases, communicate precise signals about citizens' preferences and concerns (Verba, Schlozman, and Brady 1995, 23).

The ANES queries respondents on a variety of non-voting electoral activities, including those listed in the preceding paragraph. Following the same procedure as the civic engagement variables, I group these items into additive indices of electoral "non-voting participation."[8] These activities could be appealing to racially sympathetic white Americans. For example, some candidates may, implicitly or explicitly, campaign on platforms that address racial inequality between Black and white Americans; racially sympathetic people could be their volunteers or donors. If a political party is considered to be more racially progressive, racially sympathetic whites may dispense their time or money to help them elect candidates to office. In short, there are many reasons why racial sympathy might shape this type of political behavior.

As with civic engagement, during the Obama years, I expect sympathy to be most strongly associated with behavior among those white people who feel high in efficacy. Under these circumstances, their sympathy corresponds with activity because highly efficacious people feel empowered and act on it. Without that confidence, sympathy may not inspire participation. I again regress an index of political behavior variables, coded and rescaled in a manner similar to the civic engagement variables, on the interaction of racial sympathy and efficacy. The results are presented in predicted probability plots in figure 8.2.

This duo of graphs suggests that when white Americans feel highly efficacious, racial sympathy can spill into the many political behaviors surrounding and sustaining American elections. As with the civic engagement results, the results appear to be the most pronounced in 2008, when Obama first ran for president. However, across both survey years, racial sympathy is associated with increased political behavior only under conditions

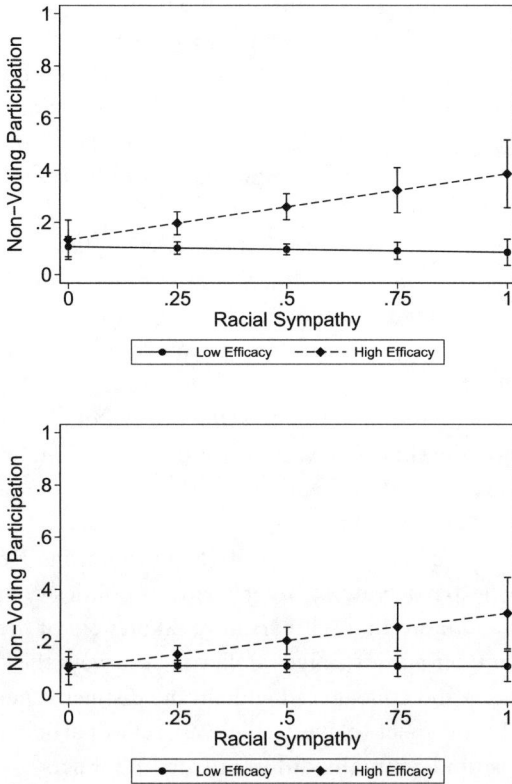

FIGURE 8.2. The Interactive Relationship Between Racial Sympathy and Efficacy: Non-Voting Participation (a) 2008 ANES, (b) 2012 ANES

of high efficacy. When a white person does not feel efficacious, sympathy takes on the inertia or "deactivation" characteristic of sadness. Building on the results presented in figure 8.1, we can detect a pattern: racial sympathy *does* seem to matter with political behavior during the Obama elections, but its impressive effects might only be observed among a subset of white Americans—those who feel high levels of efficacy.

Voting and Obama

We have arrived at turnout, or voting, the most famous form of political participation. Perhaps turnout is so renowned because of its relationship with electoral outcomes or because it is the most common form of political activity. In either case, scholars devote enormous amounts of energy to understanding turnout, predicting it, and identifying impediments to it (Fowler and Dawes 2008; Highton 2017; Krupnikov and Piston 2015; Leighley and Nagler 1992; Rolfe 2012; Teixeira 1987). I will not rehash this research here, but the sheer volume of attention to turnout speaks to its perceived importance.

The preceding analyses found that racial sympathy is associated with higher levels of civic engagement and non-voting electoral participation under conditions of high efficacy. Should we expect the same for turnout? Although we might hypothesize that turnout would behave similarly to the other dependent variables, there is some reason for hesitation. Citizens exercise less autonomy in voting than in the other forms of participation described earlier. For voting, the date, location, and format are often prescribed, with little flexibility. Further, the psychology of voting may be distinct. Voters report "a different mix of gratifications and a different bundle of issue concerns" (Verba, Schlozman, and Brady 1995, 24) than people who participate in other forms of politics do. It is for all of these reasons and more that scholars have taken note of the "uniqueness of the vote." In their authoritative book, which surveys the "world of participation," Verba and colleagues highlight the distinctiveness of the vote, explaining: "With respect to every single aspect of participation we scrutinize, voting is fundamentally different from other acts . . . to repeat, on every dimension along which we consider participatory acts, voting is *sui generis*" (1995, 23).

Indeed, in contrast to the other categories of participation variables, the impact of the sympathy and efficacy interaction does not seem to translate to turnout. I present these results in table 8.1. This table also displays the data used to generate figures 8.1 and 8.2 with more fine-grained detail, as "high" and "low" efficacy are somewhat arbitrary classifications.[9] Looking at the columns of the table, we observe the significant and positive effect of the racial sympathy and efficacy interaction in three out of four cases; higher levels of efficacy and sympathy correspond with increased non-voting participation and civic engagement, a finding replicated across two nationally representative samples during the Obama years. Note, however, the uniqueness of turnout. In this model, the interaction coefficient is negative in both cases. Also in both cases, the coefficients fail to meet the traditional threshold for statistical significance.

TABLE 8.1 **Racial Sympathy, Efficacy, and Political Participation in 2008 and 2012**

Variables	Civic Engagement		Non-Voting Electoral Participation		Turnout	
	2008 ANES	2012 ANES	2008 ANES	2012 ANES	2008 ANES	2012 ANES
Racial Sympathy	-0.37**	-0.01	-0.23**	-0.16*	2.06	1.84
	(0.156)	(0.090)	(0.100)	(0.091)	(1.494)	(2.470)
Efficacy	0.06	0.01	0.05	-0.02	2.84*	1.18
	(0.162)	(0.070)	(0.085)	(0.066)	(1.543)	(1.367)
Sympathy × Efficacy	0.70**	0.11	0.55***	0.43**	-3.15	-2.68
	(0.315)	(0.173)	(0.207)	(0.192)	(2.924)	(4.424)
Racial Resentment	-0.11	-0.11**	-0.00	-0.01	1.08	-1.29
	(0.080)	(0.048)	(0.045)	(0.040)	(0.875)	(0.849)
Party Identification	-0.00	0.02	0.02	0.03	1.31*	1.40**
	(0.062)	(0.030)	(0.030)	(0.034)	(0.685)	(0.625)
Limited Government	0.04	0.02	-0.02	0.01	-0.44	-0.49
	(0.051)	(0.024)	(0.025)	(0.023)	(0.522)	(0.543)
Political Interest	0.16**	0.12***	0.09***	0.16***	2.45***	1.05
	(0.063)	(0.036)	(0.033)	(0.034)	(0.750)	(0.872)
Party Contact	0.02	0.04*	0.01	0.06***	0.87**	0.49
	(0.037)	(0.020)	(0.022)	(0.019)	(0.435)	(0.429)
Close Election	-0.01	0.01	-0.00	-0.01	0.37	-0.48
	(0.039)	(0.027)	(0.022)	(0.019)	(0.421)	(0.488)
Constant	0.11	0.05	-0.02	-0.02	-5.35***	-1.39
	(0.112)	(0.062)	(0.070)	(0.044)	(1.282)	(1.142)
Observations	1,356	3,495	1,356	3,495	1,356	3,495
R-squared	0.316	0.239	0.250	0.245		

Sources: 2008 ANES, 2012 ANES

*** $p < 0.01$; ** $p < 0.05$; * $p < 0.10$

Cell entries are ordinary least squares regression coefficients (standard errors in parentheses). The turnout models display results from logistic regressions. The column headings display the dependent variables, which are different categories of political participation. Other control variables in the model include income, age, education, gender, region (South), and church attendance. For the 2012 ANES, only face-to-face respondents are evaluated. Data are weighted for national representativeness. All variables are coded from 0 to 1.

Voting is unique, as Verba and colleagues warned us. Not only do my results align with much of the previous scholarship on voting, but they also support those presented in the preceding chapter. There, too, racial sympathy was not associated with voting, for both the activists and the survey respondents. Nonetheless, it is still somewhat puzzling that in 2008, when the country was poised to elect its first Black president, higher levels of racial sympathy, even with the boost from efficacy, did not correspond with the turnout.

That is not to say that racial sympathy played no role in the Obama elections, however. The null turnout results may say more about the peculiarities of turnout than they do about sympathy. Voting is, after all, often undertaken for gratification for the act itself rather than for a tangible, expected outcome (Verba and Nie 1987).[10] Indeed, in other ways, white Americans' enthusiasm for Obama was present and important during these elections. This is especially the case in 2008, when the historic nature of Obama's presidency, and what it reflected for the state of Black suffering in the United States, may have made quite an impression on racially sympathetic white people. Indeed, in separate analyses that I present in the appendix, I find that in 2008, higher levels of racial sympathy are associated with significantly higher scores on a feeling thermometer tracking warm feelings toward Obama. Sympathy is also significantly associated with other positive endorsements; racially sympathetic whites are more likely to indicate that Obama makes them proud, that a Black president makes them pleased, and that they hope for a Black president. Due to question constraints, I cannot examine all of these variables in 2012. When I evaluate available ones, I find that, for the most part, the significant and strong relationship between sympathy and endorsement for Obama declined by the second time he sought office.

In chapter 2, I included a quote from an interview with Obama in which he shared his hunch that there were "some white folks" who "really" liked him.[11] My research affirms that characterization. But it also suggests that "liking" Obama manifests in different ways, depending on the election and the participatory outlet. Some white people may have joined Obama's legion of volunteers, donated to him, worn "Hope" T-shirts, and persuaded their friends and neighbors to vote for him out of a combination of sympathy and efficacy. The decision to vote itself may be more the by-product of other factors, some of which may interact with sympathy in meaningful ways.

Mobilization during Black Lives Matter

Based on the foregoing, it seems that certain circumstances, such as the first Black president being elected, may elevate sympathy's relevance to political behavior outcomes. This is because external conditions or events can help sympathetic white people identify tangible ways to act. Here, I consider the possibility that activities associated with BLM, the decentralized political and social movement that brought attention to anti-Black racism, may have provided similar clarity to white Americans. The 2008 and 2012 results predate the emergence of BLM in 2013. So, in that period, white Americans' motivation to participate may have had to come from internal factors such as efficacy. Once BLM brought visibility to Black suffering and identified outlets for its expression, the organization may have assumed or supplemented this function, thus mobilizing sympathy into behavior.

To examine this possibility, I consider the relationship between racial sympathy and participation in those activities specifically linked to BLM. By drawing attention to the banner of "Black Lives Matter" and identifying ways to act on its behalf, BLM may have mobilized sympathetic white people into action. I consider this possibility by examining the CMPS, which, unlike the ANES, features my original racial sympathy index. The survey also queries political behaviors specific to BLM. Whereas the ANES poses questions about protest participation in general, the CMPS queries respondents about whether protest activity was specifically in service of BLM. In that vein, I examine three outcomes related to participation: whether respondents participated in a BLM protest "or a protest against police brutality" in the last year; engaged on social media, Facebook, Twitter, Instagram, or other websites in support of BLM; or donated to BLM. These were all binary variables, coded "0" if the respondent indicated they did not participate in this activity and "1" if they did. Insofar as all these activities could be perceived as behaviors one could undertake to mitigate Black suffering, this specificity gives us further confidence in racial sympathy's relevance to political participation.

Whereas the preceding analyses considered the interactive effect of sympathy and efficacy, here I insert sympathy into the regression on its own, consistent with the models displayed elsewhere in the book. This is a more conservative test; we will recall that, in isolation, sympathy could depress or stall participation, partly because the attitude has demobilizing affective components. However, in an environment where Black suffering is being explicitly linked to a social movement activity, thus lowering boundaries to participation, I expect that higher levels of sympathy will be associated with an increased likelihood of participation. This increased participation should not be present across all domains but instead should be contained to activities related to BLM, reflecting its ability to mobilize behavior on its behalf.

I explore this possibility in table 8.2. Here, I present the results from a series of analyses in which I regress several political behaviors on the racial sympathy index and a number of theoretically relevant control variables. If higher levels of racial sympathy are associated with participation, this should be reflected in a positive and statistically significant coefficient across the first row of data.

Indeed, that is what we find. Higher levels of racial sympathy are associated with those activities related to BLM, including protesting, posting about it on social media, and even donating to it. Logistic regression coefficients, such as those presented in table 8.2, can be difficult to interpret substantively. We can receive assistance by calculating predicted probabilities. In doing so, I find that in the case of protest, for example, those white Americans at the seventy-fifth percentile of racial sympathy are over 30 percentage points more likely to engage in BLM protests than white people at the twenty-fifth percentile of the racial sympathy index. I find similar patterns for the other BLM-related dependent variables, as well.

What I do not find, however, is racial sympathy funneling into political activities broadly, mirroring results from chapter 4. Table 8.2 displays that racial sympathy is not significantly associated with protest participation on behalf of advancing economic equality. It is positively and significantly associated with protesting on behalf of women, but to a lesser degree than BLM protests. And although higher levels of racial sympathy correspond with an increased likelihood to donate to BLM, this trend does not extend to donations on behalf of political parties or candidates, at least in 2020. The precision of sympathy's application reflects, in my interpretation, the impact of the BLM social movement on mobilizing behavior targeted at reducing Black suffering. Altogether, the analyses reveal that social movements such as BLM may be able to mobilize participation among racially sympathetic Americans.

Mobilization is a complicated process; my analysis here is just a rough approximation of its impact. In thinking about the mechanics of mobilization, scholars parse out distinctions between direct and indirect

TABLE 8.2 **Racial Sympathy and Political Behavior Related to Black Lives Matter**

	BLM-Related Political Behavior			Other Types of Political Behavior		
Variables	Protest (BLM)	BLM Social Media Post	Donate to BLM	Protest (Women)	Protest (Economic Equality)	Donate to Candidates
Racial Sympathy	1.03***	1.07***	1.10*	1.98*	2.07	0.21
	(0.356)	(0.334)	(0.571)	(1.185)	(1.464)	(0.307)
Racial Resentment	−1.33***	−3.09***	−1.68***	−1.89***	0.73	−0.55*
	(0.319)	(0.297)	(0.505)	(0.731)	(0.840)	(0.280)
Party (1 = Republican)	−0.40	−0.91***	−1.10***	−0.45	−0.61	−0.14
	(0.265)	(0.229)	(0.365)	(0.643)	(0.712)	(0.229)
Ideology (1 = Conservative)	−1.09***	−1.17***	−0.51	0.77	−0.23	−0.20
	(0.337)	(0.283)	(0.477)	(0.824)	(1.006)	(0.309)
Political Interest	1.33***	1.08***	1.08***	3.61***	1.28	2.87***
	(0.290)	(0.232)	(0.399)	(0.866)	(1.189)	(0.307)
Party Contact	1.11***	0.78***	0.98***	1.96***	1.07**	1.04***
	(0.151)	(0.129)	(0.193)	(0.490)	(0.451)	(0.128)
Constant	−0.77	0.79*	−2.65***	−7.63***	−5.68***	−5.53***
	(0.505)	(0.435)	(0.681)	(1.282)	(1.950)	(0.507)
Observations	3,536	3,536	3,536	3,536	3,536	3,536

Source: 2020 CMPS

*** $p < 0.01$; ** $p < 0.05$; * $p < 0.10$

Cell entries are logistic regression coefficients (standard errors in parentheses). The column headings display the dependent variables, which are self-reported political behaviors. Coefficients on additional control variables included in the models here are not shown for space considerations; the following variables were included in the models: income, age, education, gender, region (South), church attendance, and years at current address. Data are weighted for national representativeness. All variables are coded from 0 to 1.

mobilization. In the former, political leaders personally court participation. With indirect mobilization, people are contacted through family, friends, neighbors, or others in their social networks (Rosenstone and Hansen 1993, 25). It is beyond the scope of my data to discern how exactly BLM succeeded in its mobilization efforts. Based on the Obama analyses, it seems likely that the movement may have boosted white people's sense of efficacy, which can spur changes in behavior, but this is speculation. I also cannot detect the duration and intensity of white Americans' commitment to this political participation. Eventually, the marches ended and the donations slowed.[12] What role did racial sympathy play in the pacing or intensity of white Americans' engagement, or disengagement, from these events? Unfortunately, I cannot answer these important questions. But based on the research presented here, it seems clear that racial sympathy can translate into behavior at certain key political moments.

Conclusion

White Americans who are low in efficacy tend not to participate in politics, and those who are high in sympathy are no exception. They may carry intense and genuine sympathy, but their overall orientation toward political effectiveness extinguishes its potential application. On the other hand, white Americans who are high in racial sympathy and have a sense of efficacy can be mobilized to act in some cases; so too can those who are mobilized by a social movement. The results in this chapter suggest that sympathy can have consequences for political behavior. The question is not, therefore, does sympathy matter for behavior, but instead, when?

I have offered two possible answers to this question, but there are potentially many others. Among individual-level attributes, interest, political knowledge, and one's sense of duty could also foster increased participation. Features of one's environment could matter, too. For example, if a white person's town or state began passing legislation especially harmful to Black Americans, this political climate could propel sympathy into action in distinct ways. If a white person's friends were highly engaged in participatory political activity, perhaps this person would dip their toes into politics, too. Steven J. Rosenstone and John Mark Hansen summarize the breadth of factors, some of them intangible, that shape participation: "People participate in politics because they get something out of it" (1993, 16).

This chapter reveals the dynamic nature of sympathy; it is a racial attitude that is likely to respond and adjust to the changing political landscape. In the book's conclusion, I consider this changing landscape and forecast what it might mean for racial sympathy. I offer suggestions on extensions for future research on this politically consequential attitude. I also reflect on what we have learned throughout this book and what questions remain.

CHAPTER NINE

Racial Sympathy in the Twenty-First Century

Certainly as a liberal, I believe that all laws and rules that discriminate against Negroes must be done away with, and I personally am optimistic enough to believe that within the next ten years all such laws and rules will in fact disappear. —Gunnar Myrdal, "Liberalism and the Negro: A Round-Table Discussion," 1964

There is no simple way to describe white attitudes toward black people. —Angus Campbell, *White Attitudes Toward Black People*, 1971

In 1950, social psychologists at Berkeley introduced scholars to two college students: Mack, "a man high on ethnocentrism," and Larry, "a man low on ethnocentrism." In their seminal work, *The Authoritarian Personality*, Theodor W. Adorno and his colleagues examined how Mack's negative views of the out-group led to a "prejudiced outlook of the world" (1950, 224). Since the publication of *The Authoritarian Personality* decades ago, there has been much social science research on people like Mack—that is, those who hold negative views of social out-groups.

But what about Larry? Although extensive literature explores the antecedents and consequences of out-group antipathy on political behavior (see Huddy and Feldman 2009 and Hutchings and Valentino 2004 for reviews), scholars have rarely considered the possibility that other group attitudes exist and have political consequences. This book addresses this omission by introducing racial sympathy and exploring the relationship between white distress over Black suffering and politics. *Some White Folks* enriches our understanding of whites' racial attitudes and provides, I hope, a launchpad for future research. To that end, I summarize where we have been and then provide suggestions for where we might go.

Summary of Findings

I define *racial sympathy* as white distress over Black suffering. White Americans carry racial sympathy as a response to the historical and contemporary suffering of African Americans, which they might learn about through parents, peers, and neighbors. Although racial sympathy has the potential to shape many areas of a white person's life, it has a special application in politics, where decisions about "who gets what" are sorted out (Lasswell 2018). When a white person is distressed over Black suffering, they may support political efforts to rectify this situation.

Political scientists have sometimes classified low-prejudice whites as "racially liberal." Racial sympathy is not the same as low prejudice, however. Instead, racial sympathy is a unique attitude requiring its own theory and measurement. In chapter 2, I provide an overview of the research on racial attitudes and highlight the conspicuous absence of this understudied attitude. Political science research has unearthed racially sympathetic outcomes on a few notable occasions. Yet, since the field has been so dedicated to studying prejudice, scholars have not had the conceptual tools to understand why some white folks might be motivated to support policies or politicians that could further Black interests. Most theories of "pro-Black" opinion emerge from bodies of research designed to understand prejudicial behavior and outcomes. Hence, I have found their accounts of racial sympathy, while heading in promising directions, to be limited at the outset by the purpose of their inquiry. Put another way, the conceptual framework they offer, the measures they test, and even the survey instruments they use are all informed by an effort to examine individuals like The Authoritarian Personality's Mack—those who are high in racial resentment, racial conservatism, or anti-Black affect. These tools, I argue, are not equipped to explain why white Americans might protest in support of BLM or support policies such as affirmative action. If a measure should be "anchored to appropriately fit the reality of respondents and theoretical foundations" (Davis and Wilson 2021, 241), racial sympathy requires its own dedicated conceptualization.

It also requires its own measurement. Chapter 3 takes up this task. In this chapter, I describe observations from a series of passive participant observation sessions in which I listened to white Americans talk about race. I observed that their reactions to Black suffering were primarily episodic and sympathetic. I constructed an original measure of racial sympathy to reflect these themes. Since measurement has been an important and controversial aspect of the racial attitudes literature, I investigate the racial sympathy index's convergent and discriminant validity and find that white Americans who experience racial sympathy do not necessarily subscribe to general social sympathy. Instead, racial sympathy matters most for policy areas that implicate African Americans. It is foremost a *racial* attitude.

We can use this measure to learn more about the racially sympathetic. Who are they? I explore this question in chapter 4. Although they may be depicted as especially well-off and educated, my results demonstrate that racial sympathy can be found throughout the white population. And while higher levels of the attitude tend to exist among Democrats and liberals, this does not mean the concept is equivalent to a broader sympathy, nor is it interchangeable with concepts like guilt or self-monitoring. Racial sympathy uniquely reflects white distress over Black Americans' suffering.

The heart of the book explores the relationship between racial sympathy and policies. In chapter 5, I consider social policies ranging from welfare assistance to reparations. Racially sympathetic white people are more likely to support government efforts to rectify racial inequality in these domains. Sympathy also carries into their opinions on the "second face" of the state; racially sympathetic white Americans want to curtail police influence and support the actions of social movements like BLM, as I explain in chapter 6. For both policy domains—redistributive and the criminal legal system—I demonstrate that racial sympathy is especially salient when the *racial* dimension of a policy is emphasized. This provides further insight into the conditions under which racial sympathy is accentuated in American politics.

Since Brown's death in 2014, white Americans have become increasingly attentive to the racial dimensions of the American criminal legal system. Some have rightfully asked, however, why nothing changes if white Americans truly care about Black suffering. The research presented in chapter 7, which draws on surveys and in-depth interviews with racial justice activists, begins to explore this question. I find that racial sympathy appears to be genuine but may align more with private actions than political ones. These actions can be personally meaningful and passionately pursued but may ultimately do little to disrupt laws and policies that sustain racial inequality. This does not mean that racial sympathy never materializes into political change. In chapter 8, I show that white Americans who carry high levels of efficacy *can* act on their sympathy; they are more likely to be civically engaged and participate in non-voting election behavior. They also can protest, donate, and spread information about race. But these outcomes are more likely if they feel efficacious or are presented with a specific opportunity that seems clearly linked to eradicating Black suffering. Overall, this book provides a wide range of evidence on racial sympathy in American politics, highlighting its limits and its power.

Previous work on racial attitudes has had difficulty accounting for the nature of racial sympathy, delineating its preconditions, identifying its subscribers, or fully understanding its political implications. This book addresses this omission by using multiple methods, datasets, and measures to trace the political influence of an understudied but influential racial attitude. This project provides additional evidence of race's role in American politics but also complicates our understanding of what this role might be. As Campbell's quote in the epigraph suggests, understanding white Americans' views on race is not simple. It is made more complicated by the changing landscape. How will racial sympathy evolve in the future? I consider some possibilities.

Technology

An hour after Brown was fatally shot by police in Ferguson, Missouri, a Twitter user posted, "I just saw someone die," along with a picture of Brown's lifeless body (Lurie 2014). Though police violence against African Americans is not new, technological innovations such as social media and phone cameras now provide vivid, often instant evidence of officer misconduct. This same technology can document related activism or protests that follow, using hashtags to publicize and organize the events. Once recorded, videos and photographs can reach a broad audience in minutes. During the initial week of protests in Ferguson, over 3.6 million posts appeared on Twitter related to Brown. According to Yarimar Bonilla and Jonathan Rosa, by the end of August 2014, "#Ferguson" had appeared more than eight million times on Twitter alone (2015). More recently, the video displaying the murder of Floyd has brought nationwide attention to police brutality.[1]

As of April 2021, 97 percent of Americans owned a cell phone of some kind and 85 percent had a smart phone.[2] These percentages have grown at a remarkable pace since 2011 and show no signs of reversing. As the

number of potential "citizen journalists" grows, it seems likely that we
will have more evidence for documenting "incidents of state-sanctioned
violence and contesting media representations of racialized bodies and
marginalized communities" (Bonilla and Rosa 2015, 5). Each instance
could ignite and activate racial sympathy.

In 1964, James Baldwin spoke about this kind of violence; to him, it
offered incontrovertible proof of Black suffering that white Americans
could not unsee. He observed: "I do think that one of the things that has
been almost crucial to American history can almost be summed up in the
metaphor of a black corpse . . . you can't now say, 'My neighbor can be
lynched and he's also innocent,' and still say that you're not responsible.
Do you see what I mean?" (quoted in Pineda 2021, 159). As technology
expands and improves, white Americans will have more documentation
of Black suffering, perhaps forcing them to reckon with their responsibility. Coverage that describes these instances as part of an overall pattern,
rather than as stand-alone incidents, may help extend sympathy from the
individual episode into broader political relevance (Iyengar 1990).

Although these visual displays of violence may be crucial to white
Americans' understanding, there are negative repercussions, too. Research demonstrates that these events have severe consequences for
Black people's emotional, mental, and physical health. Deion S. Hawkins
(2021) found that Black Americans were "traumatized" by viewing pictures or videos of police brutality. His Black interviewees "reported a
constant fear of dying, hyper alertness and lack of coping mechanisms"
(2021, 1). There are physiological burdens, too. The stressors of experi-
encing or even witnessing an instance of police brutality can trigger ac-
celerated heart and respiratory rates among African Americans. The
cumulative effect of seeing multiple events can be more damaging, caus-
ing "rapid wear and tear on body organs and elevated allostatic load"[3]
(Alang et al. 2017, 663). High allostatic load burden has been associated
with Black-white mortality disparities (Duru et al. 2012). In the view of
Afro-pessimism, this violence represents a continuation of slavery in new
forms (Ray et al. 2017). Future research could investigate the tension introduced by technology, which brings white awareness on one hand and
Black trauma on the other. Can the former exist without the latter?

This book demonstrates that many white Americans register sympathy for far less visual forms of Black suffering; sympathy was evoked
after reading fictitious vignettes with no pictures and even, in the case of
the experiments, upon seeing the word *Black*. In the cases of Brown and

Floyd, technology put Black suffering on vivid and indisputable display. Now that this evidence exists, what more can technology provide? Scholars might examine whether there is a saturation point whereby seeing Black suffering, as captured by technological advances, is no longer "crucial" to American history.

Sympathy Rising?

In light of the reaction to Brown and Floyd, some have speculated that white Americans' sympathy is rising. Throughout the book, I reference journalists' accounts of this "reckoning," but scholars have found evidence of it, too. Engelhardt demonstrates that, over time, white Americans, as a group, have moved toward the lower end of the racial resentment scale (2021c). This can translate into policy preferences, too, though perhaps only among subgroups. In their examination of white attitudes since 1986, Jardina and Trent Ollerenshaw (2022) find that white Democrats both carry increasingly liberal racial attitudes and support the types of racial policies I examine in this book. They find, for example, that in 2020, white Democrats support government aid to Black people and welfare at levels statistically indistinguishable from Black support in these areas.

Of course, rising "racial liberalism" can only be detected if there is an instrument that can accurately track it. Decreasing levels of racial resentment may reflect genuine attitude shifts away from resentment, or this finding could reflect that the measure no longer accurately reflects racial prejudice in its most prevalent form. Christopher D. DeSante and Candis Watts Smith (2020) explore this possibility in their book. In their study of millennial white Americans, they find that this group does indeed carry lower levels of racial resentment. However, they argue that because the current measures are "no longer sensitive to contemporary expressions of racism" (2020, 76), we cannot be confident that the shifts actually represent a decline in prejudice. Engelhardt (2021a) takes up this question for white Americans as a group, not just millennials.

The research presented in this book provides some insights into this shift. One important question is whether change at the aggregate level, as reported by many of the preceding studies, reflects change at the individual level. These are independent processes and need not happen simultaneously, as chapter 3 explains. It is difficult to parse out the difference because assessing individual change requires longitudinal surveys—studying the same individuals over repeated instances—which are in short supply, compared to cross-sectional surveys. The longitudinal data that does exist generally excludes measures of sympathy. My 2020 YouGov study found, at least over a four-month period, that there were minimal detected sympathy shifts at the individual level. If shifts in the aggregate are occurring, then it will be important to understand what exactly is prompting these shifts and how durable they may be.

Feeling Powerless?

From the first studies of political participation, researchers have consistently found that being better educated and older and having a higher income all influenced political participation (Verba and Nie 1987; Wolfinger and Rosenstone 1980). All of these demographics describe white Americans generally. Compared to people of color, whites also tend to report higher levels of efficacy (Cohen 2010; Phoenix and Chan 2023; Tate 1991). Given these resources, why would white Americans, such as those in this book, feel low levels of efficacy at all?

The interviews revealed themes of distrust, skepticism, blame, resignation, and exasperation. Some of the interviewees' comments caught me by surprise. Many of my interviewees occupied privileged societal positions, so I assumed they would feel emboldened to enact change. However, their discouragement and frustration were palpable. Their observations and emotions bore striking similarities to how Black opinion toward government is described by Davin L. Phoenix (2019). In his book, he describes Black sentiment toward politics as informed by "collective skepticism" (2019, 9) or a "racially distinct sense of resignation" (2019, 10); on the individual level, "one's modal disposition is one of *nothing will change. It's hopeless*" (2019, 9).

In learning about the scope of racial inequality and Black suffering, white Americans, even those with enviable resources, may begin to feel helpless and hopeless. Research has found that when people perceive extraordinary injustice, they may be *less* willing to engage in collective action than they would be when the injustice is smaller in scale. Specifically, Demis E. Glasford and Felicia Pratto found lower levels of bystander efficacy "in response to injustice perpetrated by a powerful perpetrator, relative to a less powerful perpetrator" (2014, 598). This may be a reasonable assessment: "Given less investment and stakes, bystanders may be especially responsive to cues regarding the likelihood that their action can be effective" (2014, 598). If high levels of racial sympathy correspond with a heightened understanding of the "powerful perpetrator" of racial suffering, then low levels of efficacy may result. This presents somewhat of a predicament; many racially sympathetic white Americans engage in efforts to learn more about Black suffering, but as they do, it is possible they increasingly disengage from political efforts that might rectify it.

This is a troubling paradox for a few reasons. One especially worrisome dimension is that, as sympathetic whites opt out of politics, they drift further away from Black preferences for action. In a recent Pew study, researchers asked Black adults which strategies were "most effective" for helping Black people move toward equality in the United States.[4] Of the five activities listed, Black adults were most likely to single out voting as especially important; almost two-thirds of Black people surveyed indicated voting was "extremely" or "very effective" in promoting equality. They ranked protesting, an activity endorsed by many sympathetic white Americans, as fourth out of the five strategies provided. Of course, it is possible that the respondents were evaluating these items in light of their own participation, not white Americans'. However, insofar as "listening to people of color" is an important goal of sympathetic white Americans, they may consider how Black opinion on behavior aligns with their own actions.

Backlash and Paternalism

My argument that racial sympathy can motivate whites to express support for African Americans does not imply that efforts to activate racial sympathy will always be successful. In an experiment conducted by Richard D. Harvey and Debra L. Oswald (2000), attempts to emphasize Black suffering backfired, instead increasing white *opposition* to programs intended to benefit African Americans. Similarly, in an experiment by Emanuele Castano and Roger Giner-Sorolla (2006), the authors emphasized subjects' awareness of their own in-group's culpability in mass killings of an out-group. When they did so, in-group members were more inclined to dehumanize the out-group. Perhaps this work helps us understand the trajectory of William Alexander Percy and Tom Watson, two white Americans described in chapter 2, who embraced, but later abandoned pro-Black political platforms. Future research could take up how sympathy over Black misfortune is affected in circumstances that threaten whites' positive group identity (Cole 2020; Lienesch 2023). These projects could consider the extent to which racial sympathy is rooted in whites' feelings about their own group members.

Relatedly, research in social psychology has found that stereotype threat, defined as the threat that "others' judgments or their own actions will negatively stereotype them in a given domain" (Steele 1997, 613), depresses the academic performance of women and African Americans. Although stereotype threat has often been studied in the context of marginalized groups, research by Jeff Stone and colleagues (1999) and Joshua Aronson and colleagues (1999) suggests that white men can be impacted by stereotype threat, inhibiting their performance in athletics and academics. Research on stereotype threat in politics is just beginning to emerge;[5] however, the results in chapter 7, which suggest that racially sympathetic whites were more inclined to punish their own group members than they were African Americans, suggest that some whites are especially likely to condemn discriminatory behavior of their fellow ingroup members. If that is the case, then, racial sympathy might be thought to implicate feelings about *us* just as it implicates those about *them*.

With respect to out-group attitudes, this project is an important first step toward broadening our understanding of attitudes toward marginalized groups more generally. Recent research in political science on empathy (Feldman et al. 2020), guilt (Chudy, Piston, and Shipper 2019), and stereotype content (Sides and Gross 2013) reveals a wide range of effects of group attitudes besides the unidimensional "like or dislike" account that dominates much of contemporary scholarship. Scholars could consider these distinctions more. We could design studies, for example, that parse out whether guilt is responsive to mobilization or if empathy is extended to some groups and not others. In addition to considering the role of sympathy, future work could take up the role of concepts like pride, disgust, or pity.

I have occasionally characterized sympathy as a "positive" racial attitude. I made this designation to contrast sympathy with the negative racial attitude of prejudice. However, it is possible that sympathetic whites may also offer support that might not be wholly benevolent toward African Americans. For example, Andy Baker writes about racial paternalism, which he defines as "a person's belief that, to be protected from its own lax moral discipline or inability to act, a particular race of people is in need of such interference from one's inherently superior ingroup" (2015,

97). Baker has argued that racial paternalism leads some white Americans to be especially supportive of foreign aid when it targets Africans.

Steven T. Moore has examined this phenomena in the United States, demonstrating that racial paternalism leads some white people to endorse restrictive policies affecting the out-group. They do so not out of animus but out of a belief that the out-group is "incapable of improving their own outcomes without interference" (Moore 2020, 5). This is not quite the same as sympathy; racial sympathy does not make adjudications on Black agency. Empirically, it is also linked with policies that provide resources to African Americans without the expectation of surveillance. Still, it is important to consider the relationship between paternalism and sympathy. Are there occasions in which focusing on Black suffering becomes paternal? Are some white Americans drawn to sympathy out of paternal tendencies?

Relatedly, work by scholars of gender has found that some men subscribe to "benevolent sexist" attitudes, defined as "a set of interrelated attitudes toward women that are sexist in terms of viewing women stereotypically and in restricted roles but that are subjectively positive in feeling tone (for the perceiver) and also tend to elicit behaviors typically categorized as prosocial (e.g., helping) or intimacy-seeking (e.g., self-disclosure)" (Glick and Fiske 1996, 491). Racially sympathetic whites are mixed with respect to negative stereotypes; they neither fully reject nor fully endorse them. Nonetheless, it is important to investigate the many roots of racial sympathy. Are sympathetic whites especially inclined to attach *positive* stereotypes, such as athleticism, to African Americans (Judd et al. 1995)? More generally, does African Americans' persistent economic and social disadvantage make it easier for whites to feel less threatened and therefore more sympathetic?

On the topic of gender, future work could also consider how these attitudes map onto intersectional identities. For example, work by McConnaughy and White suggests that white prejudice toward Black Americans is not monolithic; instead, the intersection of race and gender identities structures whites' stereotypes about African Americans such that white Americans view Black men in "uniquely pejorative terms" (2011, 4). Are certain subgroups of African Americans more likely to be viewed sympathetically? Are Black children or elderly Black people viewed with more sympathy than Black adults? What about Black members of the LGBTQ community? If sympathetic whites view distinctions among these groups, what are the political consequences?

Looking Elsewhere

What do the occasions in which sympathy has been especially potent have in common? What social and institutional forces encourage sympathy? The answers to these questions would provide additional insight on the broader social forces that shape racial sympathy. Exploring these questions could also provide clues about when we might expect sympathy for marginalized groups to emerge in other countries.

Indeed, work on reconciliation in post-Holocaust Germany (Olick and Levy 1997) and post-Apartheid South Africa (Gibson and Gouws 1999), for example, has found that in-groups can deliver restitution to mistreated out-groups, suggesting that legacies of suffering can map onto contemporary political preference. When, why, and how group-based sympathy will surface likely depends on several circumstances, such as the extent and nature of the out-group's oppression, whether other countries have reprimanded the in-group's actions, patterns of migration and geography, and other historical and country-specific factors. The subjugation of racial and ethnic minorities is not a uniquely American phenomenon. Future work could examine sympathetic attitudes in other countries. This research would also permit us to evaluate how American sympathy may be unique.

Changing Landscape

The American electorate is becoming more racially and ethnically diverse. When much of the canonical work on racial attitudes was produced, white and Black Americans represented the largest racial groups in the country. Subsequently, the share of Asian Americans and Latino Americans has increased, leading to new racial dynamics and political outcomes. As the United States becomes more demographically complex and diverse, how and when will whites support those with whom they do not share an ethnic background? The discriminant validity analysis in chapter 4 suggests that the racial sympathy index is firmly rooted in responses to Black suffering. This result is consistent with the theory of racial sympathy and the conceptualization of the measure, which was designed to reflect white sympathy over Black suffering in particular.

That said, the gender sympathy results suggest that other group-specific vignettes can predict support for group-specific policies—in this case, women. Examining sympathy toward other racial and ethnic groups, such as Latino and Asian Americans, requires theories and measurements that are specific to white perceptions of those groups, which may involve concepts like nativism and foreignness (see Aoki 1996). A study of Native Americans might include such aspects as references to displacement, insensitivity with respect to sports mascots, sovereignty, and forced cultural assimilation (see Doble and Yarrow 2007). Therefore, although the vignette approach could be used to study sympathy toward other racial groups, the vignettes themselves would need to present instances of discrimination applicable to those groups.

Further, whereas sympathy's relationship with "pro-Black" policies has been more or less consistently significant and positive over time, its application to policies serving other groups has shifted. For example, using the 1994 GSS, I find that racial sympathy is not associated with support for policies promoting work permits or citizenship for immigrants. In the surveys fielded during the Obama years, racial sympathy occasionally corresponds with support for "pro-immigrant" policies, but the results are inconsistent. In contrast, in the last national survey consulted, the 2020 CMPS, I find the relationship between racial sympathy and support for a host of immigration policies, such as citizenship for undocumented immigrants and making the visa process easier, is consistently significant and substantively meaningful, often surpassing the contribution of partisanship.

These outcomes may reflect several processes, including the increasing racialization of attitudes (Tesler 2012; Tesler 2016), intense partisan polarization (Mason 2018; Kalmoe and Mason 2022), and changing norms of racial politics, especially concerning immigrants (Reny, Valenzuela, and Collingwood 2020; Valentino, Neuner, and Vandenbroek 2018). In all cases, the changing political and demographic circumstances may be transforming the nature and applicability of sympathy. Chapter 8 demonstrates that the expression of sympathy is dynamic and responds to certain situational factors, perhaps including the presence and mistreatment of other non-white groups.

Future scholarship should also consider whether and how white racial sympathy might influence non-white opinion. First, do other non-white groups carry sympathy for Black people? How might this vary based on factors such as phenotype, experiences with discrimination, and Democratic partisanship? For immigrants, could their length of time in the United States or level of assimilation inform their distress over Black suffering?

Throughout the book, I have mentioned instances when white politicians highlighted racial inequality and called for reform. What are the consequences of these behaviors on Black opinion? Do Black citizens view these sympathetic racial appeals as genuine? As the Democratic Party becomes less white, white Democrats may be increasingly expected to address issues related to race and ethnicity. Assuming they do so, how will their efforts be received by non- whites?

What Can We Do with This Knowledge?

And now, we reach the finale. What do we do with this knowledge? When previous work took up prejudice, scholars could punt on the "what do we do?" question. They could note how it was important to diagnose a social illness and forecast gloomy days ahead.

I am thoroughly convinced by these findings and, perhaps because of them, often feel gloomy myself. Given my topic, however, we might reasonably expect a different answer to the "what do we do?" question. If accounts of prejudice conclude by identifying ways to extinguish its influence, should a book about sympathy include a growing guide? How can we make or spread more sympathy? And how can we get those white folks who *already carry* sympathy to work for structural change toward this goal?

There are now many popular takes on that question. What does the research in this book suggest? First, more racial sympathy is not a cure-all. It is true that without racial sympathy, white public opinion would be far less supportive of important public policies that would save or improve Black Americans' lives; the results in chapter 5 demonstrate this convincingly. However, the results in the preceding chapter suggest that even white Americans with high distress over Black suffering may only occasionally pursue political efforts to rectify it.

Racial sympathy and prejudice are not interchangeable, a theoretical and empirical theme throughout the project. Accordingly, even if racial sympathy were to become more widespread, we might not observe diminishing rates of prejudice. It seems, then, that my answer to the "what can we do?" question cannot be gloom-free. Prejudice and sympathy can continue to coexist and interact in interesting ways. And sympathy on its own may not guarantee political change.

But there are glimmers of hope. This book demonstrates that sympathy is more powerful under certain circumstances. For example, the preceding chapter suggested that if white Americans feel efficacious, they are more likely to channel racial sympathy into their political behaviors. In such a situation, sorrow can be transformed into political behavior. This sounds good, but also like a tall order against a backdrop of record levels of government dissatisfaction (Mettler 2018) accompanied by democratic backsliding (Mickey 2022). It may be an especially inauspicious moment for encouraging citizen efficacy.

And yet, this has been precisely the function of social movements and political leaders for decades. Leaders are often defined by their proximity to power. If cultivating relationships and fostering efficacy among membership is their "inside" power, then navigating the broad community and political climate constitutes their "outside" power. Effective leaders traverse both of these domains. They articulate the "inside" value to outsiders and "outside" value to insiders (Han, McKenna, and Oyakawa 2021).

Leaders could be especially instrumental in encouraging efficacy among followers. If people feel that leaders and institutions may be responsive to their demands, they may be more inclined to act. For example, in one experiment, white university students read a passage about the paltry number of Black faculty at their institution. They were then instructed to write a letter to the university's administration in support of hiring more Black faculty. Researchers then manipulated perceived efficacy by modifying an excerpt about the university's likelihood of responding to these letters. They found that students with higher perceived efficacy demonstrated "improved" intergroup attitudes and pursued antidiscrimination activities—in this case, distributing flyers about faculty representation across campus (Stewart et al. 2010). If leaders can stress that ordinary people's actions *will* make a difference in politics, heightening their sense of efficacy, this may encourage sympathetic white Americans to act.

From chapter 8, we already have suggestive evidence that the BLM movement may have done just this by hosting protests and offering opportunities to donate, giving white Americans with racial sympathy an outlet for their attitude. BLM was founded by Black people, and many of its active members identify as Black (Olteanu, Weber, and Gatica-Perez 2015). Thus, one interpretation of chapter 8's findings is that racially sympathetic white people's behavior depends on the vision and leadership of Black people. A charitable reading of this outcome is that rather than assuming that they know what is best, white Americans might be trying to respond to the demands and preferences of Black Americans. A less charitable reading is that white Americans do not know what to do and rely on Black Americans to shoulder this responsibility and shepherd their engagement. White political leaders rarely articulate action plans on racial justice, but their involvement could change these dynamics.

Institutions matter, and there may also be institutional arrangements or policies that could promote efficacy. Efficacy is rooted, to some degree, in early interactions between an individual and his environment (Bandura 1977). However, sociologists have also found that social structures, specifically class and education, significantly contribute to the development of self-efficacy. Civic education is one avenue for boosting political self-efficacy (Pasek et al. 2008). If citizens are better acquainted with the political system, they might feel less intimidated. Education in this regard could discuss racial inequality but also highlight the occasions in which change in this domain *has* occurred.

Across the world, different electoral systems have consequences for citizens' levels of self-efficacy. Systems of proportional representation are associated with enhanced efficacy and voter participation. However, the broad coalitions also associated with these systems can reduce efficacy, too (Karp and Banducci 2008). In general, this work suggests that leaders' influence extends beyond pep talks; if they want to boost efficacy, they can also consider policies that promote this effect.

Mobilization is a separate but essential question. Leadership here, strategically acting at opportune moments afforded by the political system, is essential. It enables disadvantaged groups to command more influence than their resources might otherwise allow (McAdam 1999). Much of the work on mobilizing Americans to advance racial justice has understandably focused on the role of Black political leaders (Adler 2001; Morrison 1987). This work has demonstrated that Black leaders can play a critical role in mobilizing protest and eventually shaping political outcomes. Can white leaders mobilize their own group in similar ways? To date, it is hard to say. LaFleur Stephens-Dougan's work finds that when politicians talk about race, voters evaluate Black and white politicians in different ways (Stephens-Dougan 2020). Her important scholarship has mostly considered the race of the messenger in the context of professing negative stereotypes about Black Americans.

What about white leaders who take the mantle—not as a side project, but as a core identity and agenda—of mitigating Black suffering? It is hard to evaluate how this type of person would be evaluated by all voters. Non-whites might be distrustful, at least initially, of such a figure. Other white people might derogate a "race traitor." The evidence in this book, however, suggests there would be some white Americans who would be responsive—and indeed, are craving—this type of leadership.

It seems unlikely that a single individual, no matter how enterprising and charismatic, could bring about these changes on their own. Still, leaders should not underestimate their potential here. Gabriel Lenz's work shows that citizens adopt the policy views of their preferred party or candidate (Lenz 2012). He summarizes, "Instead of politicians following the public will, the public appears to follow the wills of its politicians" (2012, 185). This means a politician could stake out support for "pro-Black" policy areas and expect some voters to follow.

Looking Ahead (Again)

So, there is some reason for hope. But now, in these final paragraphs, let us situate the project more broadly. This book does not dismiss the effect or prevalence of racial animus. This book does not suggest that white Americans are innocent or somehow not responsible for the country's painful racial history. Certainly, this book does *not* suggest that race no longer matters in American politics. In fact, what it suggests is quite the opposite; this book shows multiple ways that racial attitudes powerfully shape American politics—perhaps even more than we originally thought. It draws our attention to the complexity of intergroup attitudes that are often reduced, for understandable reason, to intergroup animosity.

Outside of politics, little is known about white people who elect to live in non-white neighborhoods or work on behalf of disadvantaged groups. What psychological and environmental factors lead to these outcomes? This book provides theoretical and empirical guidance for any work that seeks to uncover the complexity of intergroup relations across social settings. It presents encouraging evidence that these are fruitful inquiries worthy of exploration.

Overall, then, I build on a vast but ultimately narrow group attitudes literature. Indeed, by concentrating on animus, social scientists have developed only a partial account of how racial attitudes affect outcomes.. My work does not dismiss the influence of racial antipathy but rather adds an original dimension to our understanding of racial attitudes. Ultimately, this study of racial sympathy is a demonstration of the many and distinct ways that race influences American politics.

Acknowledgments

Everyone reads the acknowledgments, and everyone remembers the details. When I arrived at the doorstep of this much-anticipated section, a friend casually dropped this observation at my feet. For you, my dear reader, may hop around the measurement chapter, skim the chapter on redistributive policies, and altogether skip the final two chapters, but when you come here, you arrive ready to feast. I write these acknowledgments cognizant of this frightening reality, but also thankful that this moment of unusual attentiveness is also a moment in which I can convey my deep gratitude.

My foremost gratitude goes to Vincent Hutchings and Donald Kinder. I wrote a tribute to both of my doctoral advisers in my dissertation. Unfortunately, I cannot simply copy and paste it here, as their support and guidance have continued since then in new but no less important ways. Since I began publishing on this topic, scholars have critiqued this research. Vince has taught me how to critique those critiques, take their most important insights, and swiftly discard the rest. This book would not have been possible without Vince's incisive feedback, ability to anticipate problems (and then offer strategies for addressing them), and astute advice for navigating "this business." Don knows how to craft a rigorous and thoughtful book, and I'm grateful he shared that knowledge with me. With every conversation about this book, he pushed me to strengthen my theory and analysis above and beyond what I thought was possible. "When do books begin?" starts the acknowledgments section of *Divided by Color*, the book that, quite frankly, began this project. If this book resembles any of Don's work in any way, to any person, I will be overjoyed. Having both Vince and Don nurture this idea from inception to execution has been an indescribable privilege.

By reading the history books Rob Mickey recommended, I developed a sense of the complexity of racial sympathy. By running experimental designs by Phoebe Ellsworth, I developed a sense of the precision required to detect it. The unique historical-social-psychological combination supplied by this wing of my dissertation committee pushed me to delve more broadly and deeply into the topic. Although I did not know how to answer Rob's big questions or implement Phoebe's astute suggestions, I always enjoyed our time together. I remember one committee meeting when Texas Rob shuffled in wearing his cowboy boots and stone-washed jeans and delivered a self-deprecating one-liner, while Phoebe and I, Connecticut women that we are, sat there and watched silently, dressed identically in head-to-toe black.

As this last sentence suggests, the University of Michigan was a wonderful and, to my surprise and delight, quirky place to go to graduate school. I wish I could have packed my dissertation committee with the many talented faculty members in my department, but it was in my Michigan graduate training that I learned the dangers of having too many veto players and accordingly kept the committee small. Ted Brader and Pauline Jones deserve special recognition for their contributions to this project and my development as a scholar. Thank you also to Liz Gerber, Ken Kollman, Skip Lupia, Brian Min, Rocío Titiunik, Nick Valentino, and the late Hanes Walton Jr. for their support during my time in graduate school.

The Michigan graduate students were an inspiring group. They were also a lot of fun. Thank you to LaShonda Brenson, Logan Casey, Chinbo Chong, Eli Feiman, Vin Fusaro, LaGina Gause, Diana Greenwald, Portia Hemphill, Mike Hall, Bai Linh Hoang, Nathan Kalmoe, Kristyn Karl, Brad Kent, Elizabeth Mann Levesque, Fabian Neuner, Davin Phoenix, Molly Reynolds, Tim Ryan, Laura Seago, Josh Shipper, Josh Wondra, Nicole Yadon, and Alon Yakter. I want to convey a special gratitude to the ultimate Michigan alum, Ashley Jardina. Her book, *White Identity Politics* (2019), was a brilliant inspiration for this one in many ways. As I write all these names, I wish we could all be together again. Special thanks to my roommates over the years—among them, Hakeem Jefferson, Julia Kamin, Neil Lewis Jr., and Mike Prentice. As I write these names, I do not quite wish that we could all live together again, but I do reflect fondly on our time in the yellow house. Thank you to three Michigan alums who have gone above and beyond in their advocacy and investment in me: Hakeem Jefferson, Spencer Piston, and LaFleur Stephens-Dougan. I can't thank you enough for your consistent support and kindness.

Thank you to other scholars who have offered guidance and feedback over the years, including Antoine Banks, Andrea Benjamin, Francis Cullen, Lauren Davenport, Justin de Benedictis-Kessner, Pat Egan, Drew Engelhardt, Ryan Enos, Stanley Feldman, Hahrie Han, Hans Hassell, Eitan Hirsch, Leonie Huddy, Mayya Komisarchik, Tali Mendelberg, Jen Merolla, Susan Moffitt, Maya Sen, Debbie Schildkraut, Sandy Schram, Candis Watts Smith, Michael Tesler, and Paul Testa. Hakeem Jefferson first told Paul Sniderman about my work. Since then, Paul has been a wonderful cheerleader, supplying valuable advice and encouragement, especially when things got foggy at the end. Thank you to the participants and hosts of workshops at Boston University, Brown, Harvard, NYU, Florida State, Rochester, Stanford, and the University of Washington. Thank you also to the Boston area activists—I am deeply grateful for your insights and honesty.

Where was I at the end? Was it heaven or the Russell Sage Foundation? Sabbatical at RSF was a joyful time of research and community; it reminded me of graduate school in many respects. Thanks to my brilliant 2022–2023 cohort, especially Trevon Logan, Terry Maroney, and JT Thomas, who offered valuable substantive suggestions, and to Sheldon Danzinger, whom I suspect had something to do with RSF feeling a lot like Michigan (with apologies to Trevon). Thank you to the sociologists who adopted me for a year, especially Natasha Quadlin; whether we were going into the woods of power analysis or strolling through the trees of a large urban park with Nana and Gussie, spending the year in your company was a true joy.

Thank you to Wellesley College for supplying me with that magical sabbatical and also for its magical people who have encouraged this work for years, including my colleagues in the Department of Political Science—especially Maneesh Arora, Tom Burke, Danilo Contreras, Stacie Goddard, Laura Grattan, Igor Logvinenko, and Aditi Sahasrabuddhe. Thank you to the department's stellar administrators, especially Maura Cahn. Thank you also to the students who have dedicated many hours to support this book, especially Sasha Blachman, who co-conducted the interviews in chapter 7, and Addie New-Schmidt, who rescued countless parts of this project. Sancha Gonzalez, Lauren Kim, Jailene Lemus, Maureena Murphy, Claire Orriss, and Reyna Winter were terrific research assistants. As an undergrad, I served as Scott Allard's research assistant, and he put my name in his acknowledgments. That recognition propelled me to new heights. Sasha, Addie, Sancha, Jailene, Ree, Lauren, Reyna, and

Claire—I hope these acknowledgments have a similar effect on you (but also, no pressure—and I totally understand if you would rather not be a political scientist). Like Michigan, Wellesley was also generous with its funding of this project, for which I am very grateful.

I'm still in disbelief that my book will join the ranks of the other titles in the Chicago Series in American Politics. This is all possible thanks to Sara Doskow, who patiently worked with me for many years, even when the pandemic slowed my progress to a halt. Together with Erika Barrios, Michaela Luckey, Lindsy Rice, and Carol McGillivray, the team at Chicago offered expert guidance and support at every stage. Thank you also to my reviewers for their incisive and thoughtful comments. Adam Berinsky helped shepherd this to publication. His advice and guidance over the years have improved the project immeasurably. Parts of this work have appeared in published articles, including two in the *Journal of Politics*, a University of Chicago Press journal. These include the 2021 article "Racial Sympathy and its Political Consequences" (83, no. 1: 122–136) and the 2019 article "Guilt by Association: White Collective Guilt in American Politics" (81, no. 3: 968–981). Additionally, parts of chapters 7 and 8 appeared in a 2023 issue of *Polity* (55, no. 1: 168–194), coincidentally another University of Chicago journal.

At last, we near the final scene. Thank you to my dear friends. Steve Bow, Jen Chang, Jon Gagen, Jessica Gillooly, Ali Hassan, Gabe Heywood, Jessi Cardeña Hughes, Paolo Ikezoe, Cyprian Kibuka, Erin McNamara, Susan Nayowith, Andrew Orihuela, Drew Patterson, Julia Rocco, Nayeli Vivanco Romo, Chris Sommerfeld, Nicole Thie, Ezinne Uzo-Okoro, and Niambi Young—you're all great sports! Listening to me spiral about this over the last fourteen years must have been a lot. Special thanks to Anna Hidalgo—spiraling with you over sweet-potato stuffed pizza propelled me through the hardest parts of my revisions. My best friend, Rukesh Samarasekera, taught me how to be there for someone even if you can't understand everything they do or are going through. Thank you all for doing that for me.

And now for my family. Thank you to the Chudy, Kang, Walia, Lal, and Seth families. Thank you to my dad, Steph, and Nicola for letting me be kooky and relaxed. Thank you to my mom for letting me be proper and industrious. Thank you to Nitin for embodying both of these states perfectly. Nitin's jokes, advice, insight, feedback, notes, R lessons, wordsmithing, and encouragement kept me afloat throughout this long endeavor. It was made longer still by the arrival of Yuna and Mina. I initially worried

about all the writing time lost to parenting. However, wrangling boister-
ous and joyful toddlers with a dedicated and sympathetic partner was the
marvelous distraction I needed to get it all done.

Why do we study the acknowledgments? Perhaps to learn trade se-
crets, size up the author's network, and then judge their jokes. But if we
read the acknowledgments to verify that the author is a human being,
please know I am. Even now as I go through this book for the umpteenth
time, staring at years and years of hard work, I somehow have no recol-
lection of writing it. If there's a book that could help me understand *that*
unique psychological phenomenon, I would gladly read it. I suspect some
of my fogginess may be due to sheer exhaustion. More likely, I think that
the empowering sense of mission and confidence I received from my extraordinary supporters has cleared any recall of frustration or loneliness.
So yes, dear reader, I am a human being, a tired but grateful one, thankful
for having found this intriguing topic, a string of nurturing and stimulating workplaces, and the many happy memories I created along the way,
with the happiest of all shared with Yuna and Mina Walia.

Chapter 3

APPENDIX TABLE 3.1 **Demographic Attributes of National Surveys**

	Racial Sympathy Index					ANES Racial Sympathy Question		
	(1) 2013 CCES	(2) 2015 SSI	(3) 2016 YouGov	(4) 2020 YouGov	(5) 2020 CMPS	(6) 1994 GSS	(7) 2008 ANES	(8) 2012 ANES
% Male	49.26	51.18	48.74	48.85	51.56	43.86	44.82	48.86
% BA +	29.17	44.31	29.23	41.07	34.8	25.8	29.86	32.94
% Democrat	37.76	33.58	37.53	37.66	22.26	43.27	43.61	37.74
% Republican	42.19	28.78	36.98	44.71	43.62	44.02	44.67	48.68
Mean Age	49	45–54	49	50	50–69	46.67	47.53	45–54

Sources: 1994 GSS, 2008 ANES Time Series, 2012 ANES Time Series, 2013 CCES, 2015 SSI, 2016 YouGov, 2020 YouGov, 2020 CMPS Analyses are weighted where possible. For all 2012 ANES analyses in the Appendix, unless otherwise noted, the analysis is restricted to those respondents interviewed face-to-face.

APPENDIX TABLE 3.2 **Factor Analysis of Racial Sympathy Scale**
Principal Factor Analyses of Whites' Responses to Racial Sympathy Index

Variable	Factor 1
PFA Results	2.3
Eigenvalues (% of variance explained)	(58)
Vignette 1: Mrs. Lewis, Hiring	0.81
Vignette 2: Hair Salon Applicants	0.82
Vignette 3: Bus Depot	0.67
Vignette 4: Michael, Police	0.72

Source: 2013 CCES

(*continues*)

Variable	Factor 1
PFA Results	2.4
Eigenvalues (% of variance explained)	(59)
Vignette 1: Mrs. Lewis, Hiring	0.83
Vignette 2: Hair Salon Applicants	0.86
Vignette 3: Bus Depot	0.69
Vignette 4: Michael, Police	0.68

Source: 2016 YouGov

Variable	Factor 1
PFA Results	2.69
Eigenvalues (% of variance explained)	(67)
Vignette 1: Mrs. Lewis, Hiring	0.85
Vignette 2: Hair Salon Applicants	0.88
Vignette 3: Bus Depot	0.74
Vignette 4: Michael, Police	0.80

Source: 2020 YouGov Wave 1

Variable	Factor 1
PFA Results	2.73
Eigenvalues (% of variance explained)	(68)
Vignette 1: Mrs. Lewis, Hiring	0.85
Vignette 2: Hair Salon Applicants	0.90
Vignette 3: Bus Depot	0.76
Vignette 4: Michael, Police	0.78

Source: 2020 YouGov Wave 2

The Correlates of Racial Sympathy and Related Concepts

Variables	Racial Sympathy Index	Racial Resentment	Negative Stereotypes	Guilt	Gender Sympathy
Age	−0.07	0.09*	0.02	−0.14***	−0.03
	(0.051)	(0.049)	(0.023)	(0.048)	(0.063)
Gender	0.11***	−0.01	0.01	−0.01	0.10***
	(0.025)	(0.022)	(0.011)	(0.022)	(0.029)
Education	0.15***	−0.15***	−0.01	0.15***	0.07
	(0.049)	(0.038)	(0.018)	(0.042)	(0.056)
Income	−0.12*	0.08	−0.03	−0.08	0.04
	(0.063)	(0.053)	(0.028)	(0.053)	(0.078)
South	−0.05*	0.02	0.01	0.02	−0.02
	(0.027)	(0.024)	(0.012)	(0.022)	(0.031)
Party ID	−0.20***	0.19***	0.05***	−0.16***	−0.13***
	(0.040)	(0.034)	(0.017)	(0.039)	(0.047)
Limited Government	−0.07**	0.17***	0.00	−0.07**	−0.06
	(0.033)	(0.028)	(0.013)	(0.031)	(0.040)
Church Attendance	−0.01	0.02	0.00	−0.06	0.02
	(0.037)	(0.038)	(0.016)	(0.035)	(0.044)
Constant	0.68***	0.38***	0.49***	0.32***	0.67***
	(0.054)	(0.054)	(0.022)	(0.054)	(0.069)
Observations	566	566	566	566	566
R-squared	0.207	0.284	0.041	0.181	0.105

Source: 2016 YouGov

Cell entries are ordinary least squares regression coefficients (standard errors in parentheses). Data are weighted for national representativeness. All variables are coded from 0 to 1.

APPENDIX TABLE 3.4 **The Correlates of Racial Sympathy and Related Concepts**

Variables	Racial Sympathy Index	Racial Resentment	Negative Stereotypes	Egalitarianism	Humanitarianism
Age	−0.01	0.06**	0.00	0.05*	0.16***
	(0.035)	(0.029)	(0.019)	(0.030)	(0.036)
Gender	0.08***	−0.02	−0.01	0.03	0.03
	(0.021)	(0.018)	(0.012)	(0.018)	(0.022)
Education	0.03	−0.16***	−0.04*	0.01	0.04
	(0.042)	(0.034)	(0.023)	(0.035)	(0.042)
Income	0.03	0.01	0.03*	−0.01	0.05
	(0.038)	(0.031)	(0.021)	(0.032)	(0.038)
South	0.02	0.01	0.01	−0.00	0.02
	(0.022)	(0.018)	(0.012)	(0.019)	(0.022)
Party	−0.13***	0.17***	0.05**	−0.11***	0.03
	(0.035)	(0.029)	(0.019)	(0.030)	(0.036)
Limited Government	−0.09***	0.14***	−0.02	−0.19***	−0.16***
	(0.028)	(0.023)	(0.016)	(0.024)	(0.029)
Constant	0.58***	0.48***	0.54***	0.79***	0.75***
	(0.040)	(0.033)	(0.022)	(0.034)	(0.040)
Observations	534	534	533	533	531
R-squared	0.108	0.244	0.021	0.208	0.097

Source: 2015 SSI

Cell entries are ordinary least squares regression coefficients (standard errors in parentheses). Data are weighted for national representativeness. All variables are coded from 0 to 1.

Chapter 4

APPENDIX TABLE 4.1 **Correlation between ANES Question and Opinion on Other Policies**

Allowing children of immigrants to become permanent residents	Endorsing laws that protect homosexuals against job discrimination	Permitting gays and lesbians to serve in the army	Permitting gays and lesbians to marry	Permitting gays and lesbians to adopt children
0.092	**0.031**	**−0.017**	**0.037**	**−0.059**
(.06)	**(.08)**	**(.07)**	**(.05)**	**(.071)**
Invade Iran	Bomb Iran's nuclear development sites	Support for offshore drilling	Global warming is bad	Environment/ Job trade off
−0.083	**−0.083**	**0.067**	**−0.085**	**0.024**
(.060)	**(.060)**	**(.052)**	**(.064)**	**(.040)**
Federal spending on the environment	Investing social security in the stock market	Federal govt. should make it more difficult to buy a gun	Abortion	Support for nuclear power plants
−.063	**−.018**	**−0.045**	−.031	−0.06
(.052)	**(.055)**	**(.042)**	(.049)	(.055)

Source: 2012 ANES.
Includes controls for party, income, age, education, gender, region, church attendance, limited government, and racial resentment. The analysis on the question about immigrants is restricted to non-Hispanic whites, and the questions about gay issues are restricted to those who self-identify as straight. Areas that are bolded are significantly predicted by racial resentment.

APPENDIX TABLE 4.2 **Discriminant Validity Analysis of the Racial Sympathy Index**

	Environment/Job Trade Off (1 = Protect Environment)	Keystone Pipeline (1 = Support)	Increase Border Patrols (1 = Increase)	Deny Automatic Citizenship to US-Born Children (1 = Deny)	Ban Assault Rifles (1 = For Ban)
Racial Sympathy	0.08	-0.08	-0.05	-0.10	0.03
	(0.068)	(0.111)	(0.116)	(0.115)	(0.116)
Racial Resentment	-0.13**	0.30***	0.41***	0.62***	-0.13
	(0.061)	(0.107)	(0.116)	(0.104)	(0.114)
Party ID (1 = Republican)	-0.13**	-0.03	0.18*	0.01	-0.27***
	(0.052)	(0.081)	(0.094)	(0.091)	(0.090)
Limited Government	-0.12***	0.35***	0.14*	0.23***	-0.26***
	(0.040)	(0.065)	(0.071)	(0.070)	(0.068)
Constant	0.48***	0.72***	0.70***	0.56***	0.56***
	(0.073)	(0.145)	(0.140)	(0.145)	(0.142)
Observations	571	554	571	571	564

Source: 2013 CCES

*** $p < 0.01$; ** $p < 0.05$; * $p < 0.10$

Cell entries are ordinary least squares regression coefficients (standard errors in parentheses). Full model is specified in table 5.1. Here, for space considerations, I show the most relevant and powerful controls. Data are weighted for national representativeness. All variables are coded from 0 to 1.

The Correlates of Racial Sympathy and Self-Monitoring

Variables	Racial Sympathy	Self-Monitoring
Age	0.03	−0.25***
	(0.050)	(0.040)
Female	0.10***	−0.06***
	(0.023)	(0.018)
Education	0.04	0.05
	(0.043)	(0.033)
Income	0.02	−0.02
	(0.055)	(0.041)
Region	−0.02	−0.02
	(0.025)	(0.019)
Party	−0.19***	−0.04
	(0.051)	(0.036)
Ideology	−0.17**	−0.07
	(0.068)	(0.046)
Church Attendance	0.05	0.06**
	(0.039)	(0.027)
Constant	0.79***	0.44***
	(0.052)	(0.039)
Observations	503	503
R-squared	0.280	0.195

Source: 2020 YouGov, Wave 1
Cell entries are ordinary least squares regression coefficients (standard errors in parentheses). Data are weighted for national representativeness. All variables are coded from 0 to 1.

APPENDIX TABLE 4.4 **Factor Analysis of Racial Sympathy and Guilt**

Variable	Factor 1: Guilt	Factor 2: Sympathy
Eigenvalues	2.82	2.7
(% of variance explained)	(0.40)	(0.38)
Vignette 1: Mrs. Lewis, Hiring	−0.08	**0.88**
Vignette 2: Hair Salon Applicants	−0.07	**0.91**
Vignette 3: Bus Depot	0.12	**0.63**
Vignette 4: Michael, Police	0.15	**0.60**
Guilt 1: Association with White Race	**0.92**	−0.07
Guilt 2: Privileges and Benefits of Being White	**0.92**	−0.05
Guilt 3: Social inequality between White and Black	**0.88**	−0.06

Source: 2016 YouGov

Chapter 5

APPENDIX TABLE 5.1 **Racial Sympathy, Stereotypes, and Support for Redistributive Public Policies**

	Government Aid to Blacks			Welfare			Affirmative Action		
	2012 ANES	2008 ANES	1994 GSS	2012 ANES	2008 ANES	1994 GSS	2012 ANES	2008 ANES	1994 GSS
Racial Sympathy	0.11***	0.17***	0.19***	0.05**	0.05	0.06	0.15***	0.15***	0.08**
	(0.027)	(0.038)	(0.059)	(0.026)	(0.032)	(0.057)	(0.034)	(0.040)	(0.041)
Stereotypes	-0.11***	-0.06	-0.46***	-0.04	-0.09	0.09	-0.01	0.09	-0.10
	(0.039)	(0.069)	(0.118)	(0.046)	(0.062)	(0.120)	(0.046)	(0.070)	(0.080)
Racial Resentment	-0.51***	-0.49***	-0.92***	-0.26***	-0.23***	-0.28***	-0.49***	-0.42***	-0.29***
	(0.026)	(0.039)	(0.089)	(0.027)	(0.040)	(0.084)	(0.035)	(0.044)	(0.060)
Party ID	-0.09***	-0.09***	-0.04	-0.10***	-0.07**	-0.20***	-0.01	-0.07**	-0.05
	(0.017)	(0.030)	(0.048)	(0.018)	(0.027)	(0.049)	(0.023)	(0.030)	(0.034)
Limited Govt.	-0.08***	-0.06***	0.07	-0.14***	-0.09***	-0.06	-0.07***	-0.04*	-0.01
	(0.014)	(0.022)	(0.070)	(0.015)	(0.022)	(0.073)	(0.019)	(0.023)	(0.047)
Constant	0.79***	0.71***	0.51***	0.74***	0.90***	0.39***	0.62***	0.52***	0.28***
	(0.033)	(0.055)	(0.117)	(0.031)	(0.054)	(0.126)	(0.041)	(0.065)	(0.083)
Observations	5,132	1,988	409	5,393	2,138	494	5,349	2,080	615
R-squared	0.456	0.382	0.370	0.303	0.214	0.124	0.292	0.236	0.119

Sources: 2012 ANES, 2008 ANES, 1994 GSS

*** $p < 0.01$; ** $p < 0.05$; * $p < 0.10$

Cell entries are ordinary least squares regression coefficients (standard errors in parentheses). The top column headings display the dependent variables, which are questions about policy opinion. Below these headings, the results for each survey are presented. Coefficients on additional control variables are not shown for space considerations. These include income, age, education, gender, region (South), and church attendance. The 2012 ANES results include all self-identified white American respondents, regardless of survey mode. However, the results are similar when I restrict the analysis to face-to-face respondents alone. See Chudy 2021, Web Appendix. Where possible, data are weighted for national representativeness; the GSS did not include probability weights. All variables are coded from 0 to 1.

APPENDIX TABLE 5.2 **Racial Sympathy, Closeness, Implicit Attitudes, and Support for Racialized Public Policies**

	Government Aid to Blacks		Welfare		Affirmative Action	
	2012 ANES	2008 ANES	2012 ANES	2008 ANES	2012 ANES	2008 ANES
Racial Sympathy	0.11***	0.19***	0.05*	0.05	0.08**	0.15***
	(0.027)	(0.038)	(0.026)	(0.033)	(0.032)	(0.038)
Close to Blacks	0.03		0.02		0.07**	
	(0.024)		(0.027)		(0.029)	
Implicit Attitudes		−0.04		0.10*		−0.07
		(0.052)		(0.058)		(0.064)
Racial Resentment	−0.53***	−0.47***	−0.27***	−0.27***	−0.41***	−0.38***
	(0.025)	(0.040)	(0.026)	(0.042)	(0.031)	(0.044)
Party ID	−0.09***	−0.09***	−0.10***	−0.08***	−0.06***	−0.04
	(0.017)	(0.031)	(0.018)	(0.029)	(0.021)	(0.031)
Limited Govt.	−0.08***	−0.06***	−0.14***	−0.09***	−0.11***	−0.05**
	(0.014)	(0.023)	(0.015)	(0.023)	(0.017)	(0.023)
Constant	0.72***	0.69***	0.71***	0.80***	0.63***	0.57***
	(0.031)	(0.058)	(0.031)	(0.051)	(0.034)	(0.060)
Observations	5,128	1,933	5,384	2,074	5,380	2,023
R-squared	0.454	0.385	0.306	0.216	0.282	0.231

Sources: 2012 ANES, 2008 ANES
*** $p < 0.01$; ** $p < 0.05$; * $p < 0.10$
Cell entries are ordinary least squares regression coefficients (standard errors in parentheses). See note under appendix table 5.1. The Implicit Attitudes Measure refers to the AMP (see Kalmoe and Piston 2013 for a discussion of this measure). See note under appendix table 5.1. Data are weighted for national representativeness. All variables are coded from 0 to 1.

APPENDIX TABLE 5-3 **Racial Sympathy, Egalitarianism, and Support for Redistributive Public Policies**

	Government Aid to Blacks			Welfare			Affirmative Action		
	2012 ANES	2008 ANES	1994 GSS	2012 ANES	2008 ANES	1994 GSS	2012 ANES	2008 ANES	1994 GSS
Racial Sympathy	0.11***	0.16***	0.23***	0.04	0.04	0.09	0.15***	0.04	0.13***
	(0.027)	(0.038)	(0.061)	(0.026)	(0.033)	(0.060)	(0.034)	(0.033)	(0.042)
Egalitarianism	0.12***	0.10*	0.09	0.20***	0.20***	0.12**	0.07**	0.20***	0.13***
	(0.030)	(0.050)	(0.059)	(0.030)	(0.050)	(0.054)	(0.034)	(0.050)	(0.039)
Racial Resentment	-0.50***	-0.47***	-0.96***	-0.22***	-0.21***	-0.29***	-0.47***	-0.21***	-0.29***
	(0.026)	(0.040)	(0.091)	(0.028)	(0.040)	(0.087)	(0.035)	(0.040)	(0.060)
Party ID	-0.08***	-0.08***	-0.01	-0.08***	-0.05*	-0.16***	-0.01	-0.05*	-0.04
	(0.017)	(0.030)	(0.051)	(0.018)	(0.027)	(0.052)	(0.024)	(0.027)	(0.035)
Limited Govt.	-0.06***	-0.05**	0.07	-0.11***	-0.08***	-0.03	-0.06***	-0.08***	0.00
	(0.015)	(0.023)	(0.073)	(0.016)	(0.022)	(0.076)	(0.019)	(0.022)	(0.049)
Constant	0.63***	0.60***	0.21**	0.54***	0.69***	0.43***	0.56***	0.69***	0.25***
	(0.039)	(0.068)	(0.095)	(0.038)	(0.055)	(0.101)	(0.052)	(0.055)	(0.065)
Observations	3,495	2,013	382	3,495	2,169	455	3,495	2,169	567
R-squared	0.459	0.384	0.342	0.320	0.234	0.142	0.293	0.234	0.144

Sources: 2012 ANES, 2008 ANES, 1994 GSS

*** $p < 0.01$; ** $p < 0.05$; * $p < 0.10$

Cell entries are ordinary least squares regression coefficients (standard errors in parentheses). See note under appendix table 5.1. Data are weighted for national representativeness. All variables are coded from 0 to 1.

APPENDIX TABLE 5.4 **Racial Sympathy, Personality, and Support for Redistributive Public Policies**

	Government Aid to Blacks	Welfare	Affirmative Action in Hiring
Racial Sympathy	0.12***	0.06**	0.15***
	(0.028)	(0.027)	(0.036)
Agreeableness	−0.01	0.02	−0.06*
	(0.026)	(0.028)	(0.029)
Openness	0.02	−0.00	0.05*
	(0.021)	(0.024)	(0.026)
Racial Resentment	−0.53***	−0.26***	−0.50***
	(0.025)	(0.027)	(0.034)
Party ID	−0.08***	−0.10***	−0.01
	(0.017)	(0.019)	(0.024)
Limited Govt.	−0.08***	−0.14***	−0.08***
	(0.015)	(0.016)	(0.019)
Constant	0.72***	0.70***	0.63***
	(0.033)	(0.035)	(0.042)
Observations	3,495	3,495	3,495
R-squared	0.448	0.298	0.299

Source: 2012 ANES
*** $p < 0.01$; ** $p < 0.05$; * $p < 0.10$
Cell entries are ordinary least squares regression coefficients (standard errors in parentheses). See note under appendix table 5.1. Data are weighted for national representativeness. All variables are coded from 0 to 1.

APPENDIX TABLE 5.5 **Racial Sympathy, Contact, and Support for Redistributive Public Policies**

	Government Aid to Blacks	Welfare	Affirmative Action
Racial Sympathy	0.19***	0.05	0.15***
	(0.071)	(0.067)	(0.054)
Contact	−0.04	−0.02	−0.00
	(0.038)	(0.037)	(0.029)
Racial Resentment	−0.95***	−0.34***	−0.33***
	(0.105)	(0.096)	(0.074)
Party ID	−0.02	−0.21***	−0.07
	(0.061)	(0.058)	(0.046)
Ideology	0.04	0.03	−0.02
	(0.086)	(0.087)	(0.063)
Constant	1.23***	0.64***	0.54***
	(0.131)	(0.134)	(0.097)
Observations	283	349	319
R-squared	0.325	0.128	0.191

Source: 1994 GSS
*** $p < 0.01$; ** $p < 0.05$; * $p < 0.10$
Cell entries are ordinary least squares regression coefficients (standard errors in parentheses). See note under appendix table 5.1. All variables are coded from 0 to 1.

APPENDIX TABLE 5.6 **Racial Sympathy, Guilt, and Support for Racialized Public Policies**

Variables	Welfare	Police Force	Support for BLM
Racial Sympathy	0.16***	0.15***	0.18***
	(0.060)	(0.050)	(0.065)
Racial Resentment	−0.11	−0.19***	−0.54***
	(0.073)	(0.066)	(0.073)
Guilt	0.37***	0.18***	0.41***
	(0.079)	(0.053)	(0.066)
Ideology	−0.19***	−0.04	−0.12*
	(0.071)	(0.063)	(0.072)
Party	−0.07	−0.04	−0.08
	(0.045)	(0.038)	(0.052)
Income	−0.10	0.01	−0.19***
	(0.068)	(0.058)	(0.064)
Age	0.03	0.03	−0.00
	(0.055)	(0.048)	(0.049)
Education	0.03	−0.06	0.05
	(0.048)	(0.041)	(0.050)
Gender	−0.04	0.01	0.04
	(0.026)	(0.022)	(0.026)
Region	−0.01	0.02	0.03
	(0.026)	(0.023)	(0.027)
Church Attendance	−0.05	0.03	0.03
	(0.038)	(0.036)	(0.041)
Constant	0.59***	0.50***	0.58***
	(0.099)	(0.100)	(0.099)
Observations	513	512	511
R-squared	0.337	0.256	0.558

Source: 2016 YouGov
Note: Cell entries are ordinary least squares regression coefficients (standard errors in parentheses). Data are weighted for national representativeness. All variables are coded from 0 to 1.

APPENDIX TABLE 5.7 **Racial Sympathy, Empathy, and Support for Government Aid to Blacks**

Variables	Government Aid to Blacks
Racial Sympathy	0.20*
	(0.111)
Empathy	−0.09
	(0.142)
Party ID	−0.15*
	(0.086)
Education	0.14
	(0.091)
Female	−0.08
	(0.052)
Region (South = 1)	−0.02
	(0.049)
Limited Government	−0.18***
	(0.063)
Income	−0.02
	(0.089)
Constant	0.58***
	(0.123)
Observations	87
R-squared	0.326

Source: 2017 MTurk

Cell entries are ordinary least squares regression coefficients (standard errors in parentheses). Empathy is operationalized using the "Reading the Mind in the Eyes" index. Refer to chapter 3 for more details and consult the Web Appendix for item wording. All variables are coded from 0 to 1.

Racial Resentment and Policy Beneficiary, Experimental Results

	Black Businesses	Black Schools	Black Scholarships
Black Condition = 1	−0.34***	−0.14***	−0.31***
	(0.037)	(0.040)	(0.045)
Racial Resentment	−0.13*	−0.52***	−0.33***
	(0.065)	(0.059)	(0.070)
Black Condition × Racial Resentment	−0.47***	−0.13*	−0.32***
	(0.078)	(0.078)	(0.086)
Constant	0.55***	0.42***	0.56***
	(0.031)	(0.031)	(0.037)
Observations	569	570	571
R-squared	0.272	0.277	0.292

Source: 2013 CCES

*** $p < 0.01$; ** $p < 0.05$; * $p < 0.10$

Cell entries are ordinary least squares regression coefficients (standard errors in parentheses). These results are robust to models with control variables, including racial resentment, party identification, limited government, education, income, gender, region, and church attendance. However, since not all scholars agree this is an optimal approach, I present the bivariate results here (see Mutz 2011; and Morton and Williams 2010). See table 5.6 for analyses including racial resentment. Data are weighted for national representativeness. All variables are coded from 0 to 1.

Chapter 7

APPENDIX TABLE 7.1 **Opinion and Behavior Regressed on Racial Sympathy, by Levels of Self-Monitoring**
(Median Split on the Self-Monitoring Scale)

Variables	Educate about Racism	Confront Racist Others	Protest	Listen to POC	Vote in Elections	Campaign for Candidates
High Self-Monitors						
Racial Sympathy	0.35***	0.18*	0.17	0.26***	0.08	−0.31*
	(0.122)	(0.107)	(0.151)	(0.095)	(0.104)	(0.177)
Racial Resentment	−0.20	0.02	−0.35**	−0.30*	−0.04	−0.23
	(0.159)	(0.145)	(0.153)	(0.172)	(0.118)	(0.157)
Party ID	−0.11	−0.17**	−0.23	−0.08	−0.07	−0.15
	(0.076)	(0.077)	(0.14)	(0.068)	(0.064)	(0.118)
Observations	442	442	442	442	442	442
R-squared	0.336	0.363	0.433	0.351	0.212	0.154
Low Self-Monitors						
Racial Sympathy	0.43***	0.62***	0.31***	0.43***	0.15	−0.23
	(0.128)	(0.104)	(0.108)	(0.088)	(0.114)	(0.166)
Racial Resentment	−0.22***	−0.21*	−0.48***	−0.10	−0.00	−0.33*
	(0.084)	(0.106)	(0.106)	(0.071)	(0.098)	(0.173)
Party ID	−0.18**	−0.03	−0.13	−0.05	0.00	0.02
	(0.073)	(0.094)	(0.078)	(0.067)	(0.093)	(0.145)
Observations	442	442	442	442	442	442
R-squared	0.457	0.441	0.530	0.429	0.211	0.053

Source: 2020 YouGov
*** $p < 0.01$; ** $p < 0.05$; * $p < 0.10$
Cell entries are ordinary least squares regression coefficients (standard errors in parentheses). Column heading indicates the dependent variable, where higher values indicate that respondents place higher importance on pursuing a specific behavior. Coefficients on additional control variables included in the models here are not shown for space considerations; the following variables were also included in the models: income, age, education, gender, region (South), ideology, church attendance, political interest, party contact, and perceptions of a close election. Data are weighted for national representativeness. All variables are coded from 0 to 1.

APPENDIX TABLE 7.2 **Opinion and Behavior Regressed on Racial Sympathy, Self-Monitoring, and the Interaction between the Two**

Variables	Educate about Racism	Confront Racist Others	Protest	Listen to POC	Vote in Elections	Campaign for Candidates
Racial Sympathy	0.51***	0.65***	0.29**	0.33***	-0.03	-0.28
	(0.160)	(0.126)	(0.122)	(0.111)	(0.140)	(0.195)
Self-Monitoring	0.45	0.81***	0.26	-0.04	-0.28	-0.28
	(0.366)	(0.303)	(0.286)	(0.277)	(0.271)	(0.446)
Racial Sympathy × Self-Monitoring	-0.45	-0.85**	-0.09	-0.02	0.40	0.41
	(0.406)	(0.346)	(0.371)	(0.295)	(0.358)	(0.584)
Racial Resentment	-0.22***	-0.15*	-.42***	-0.22**	-0.05	-0.26**
	(0.084)	(0.089)	(0.090)	(0.086)	(0.081)	(0.124)
Observations	408	408	408	408	408	499
R-squared	0.412	0.405	0.493	0.361	0.192	0.060

Source: 2020 YouGov

*** $p < 0.01$; ** $p < 0.05$; * $p < 0.10$

Cell entries are ordinary least squares regression coefficients (standard errors in parentheses.) Column heading indicates the dependent variable, where higher values indicate that respondents place higher importance on pursuing a specific behavior. See note under appendix table 7.1. Data are weighted for national representativeness. All variables are coded from 0 to 1.

Chapter 8

APPENDIX TABLE 8.1 **Racial Sympathy and Support for Obama**

Variables	2008 ANES					2012 ANES	
	Obama Thermometer	Obama Makes R Proud	Comfortable with Black President	Black President Makes R Pleased	Hope for a Black President	Obama Thermometer	Obama Makes R Proud
Racial Sympathy	0.12**	0.24**	0.15**	0.15**	1.84***	-0.06	-0.06
	(0.056)	(0.119)	(0.056)	(0.073)	(0.647)	(0.058)	(0.087)
Racial Resentment	-0.39***	-0.57***	-0.10*	-0.26***	-2.42***	-0.22***	-0.11
	(0.056)	(0.136)	(0.060)	(0.081)	(0.801)	(0.060)	(0.075)
Party ID	-0.29***	-0.49***	0.09*	-0.11*	-0.39	-0.43***	-0.35***
	(0.053)	(0.092)	(0.055)	(0.058)	(0.575)	(0.040)	(0.055)
Ideology	-0.08**	0.05	-0.01	0.06	0.59	-0.14***	-0.03
	(0.036)	(0.074)	(0.033)	(0.046)	(0.478)	(0.040)	(0.049)
Political Interest	0.03	-0.03	0.06	0.16***	1.51***	-0.04	0.18***
	(0.050)	(0.089)	(0.053)	(0.059)	(0.559)	(0.050)	(0.062)
Party Contact	-0.01	-0.01	-0.02	-0.03	-0.79**	0.02	-0.00
	(0.025)	(0.052)	(0.028)	(0.035)	(0.352)	(0.025)	(0.036)
Perceptions of Close Election	-0.03	-0.05	0.03	-0.04	-0.07	-0.09**	-0.08*
	(0.029)	(0.062)	(0.037)	(0.038)	(0.376)	(0.036)	(0.043)
Constant	1.06***	1.23***	0.85***	0.56***	3.36***	1.16***	0.69***
	(0.061)	(0.173)	(0.063)	(0.093)	(1.122)	(0.070)	(0.095)
Observations	1,353	1,268	1,351	1,329	1,311	5,451	5,238
R-squared	0.513	0.395	0.165	0.237		0.517	0.369

Source: 2008 ANES, 2012 ANES

*** $p < 0.01$; ** $p < 0.05$; * $p < 0.10$

Cell entries are ordinary least squares regression coefficients (standard errors in parentheses). Other control variables in the model include income, age, education, gender, region (South), and church attendance. For the 2012 ANES, only face-to-face respondents are analyzed. Data are weighted for national representativeness. All variables are coded from 0 to 1.

APPENDIX F

Survey Items and Interview Script

2013 CCES Independent Variables

Racial Sympathy Index (UMI411, UMI415, UMI418, UMI421): See chapter 3 for text.

Gender Sympathy Index:

- **1B (UMI414):** Kate is looking to buy a co-op in an exclusive neighborhood of a big city. She submits an offer on a unit and it is accepted. The building co-op board sends her an extensive application to complete. The final step of the process requires an in-person interview, in which each member of the co-op board interviews Kate. Kate puts together an impressive application and also interviews well. Despite this, the board rejects her application, stating that it is not clear whether she has long-term financial stability and that she may not fit in with the other building residents. Kate is upset because she has an excellent, stable job. She thinks the real reason the co-op board rejected her is because she is a woman. Please indicate which statement best describes you. How much sympathy do you have for Kate? (A great deal of sympathy / A lot of sympathy / Some sympathy / A little sympathy / I do not feel any sympathy for her)

- **2A (UMI419):** Lisa Davis works for a construction company in Pennsylvania. She has worked as a flagger, alerting cars of construction projects on the highway, and has assisted the construction crew by performing laborer duties. Despite Lisa's good job performance, company supervisors have repeatedly rejected Lisa's attempts to apply for higher-paying positions. After Lisa complained about this treatment, the construction company reduced her work hours. Lisa is very upset by the company's actions. Please indicate which statement best describes you. How much sympathy do you feel for Lisa? (A great deal of sympathy / A lot of sympathy / Some sympathy / A little sympathy / I do not feel any sympathy for her)

Racial Resentment

- **UMI426:** Irish, Italians, Jewish, and many other minorities overcame prejudice and worked their way up. Blacks should do the same without any special favors. Do you (Agree strongly / Agree somewhat / Neither agree nor disagree / Disagree somewhat / Disagree strongly / Don't know) with this statement?

- **UMI428**: Over the past few years, blacks have gotten less than they deserve. Do you (Agree strongly / Agree somewhat / Neither agree nor disagree / Disagree somewhat / Disagree strongly / Don't know) with this statement?
- **CC352**: Generations of slavery and discrimination have created conditions that make it difficult for blacks to work their way out of the lower class. Do you (Agree strongly / Agree somewhat / Neither agree nor disagree / Disagree somewhat / Disagree strongly / Don't know) with this statement?
- **CC353**: It's really a matter of some people not trying hard enough; if blacks would only try harder they could be just as well off as whites. Do you (Agree strongly / Agree somewhat / Neither agree nor disagree / Disagree somewhat / Disagree strongly / Don't know) with this statement?

Party ID (pid7): Summary variable. (Strong Democrat / Not very strong Democrat / Lean Democrat / Independent / Lean Republican / Not very strong Republican / Strong Republican)

Limited government: Which of the two statements come closer to your view?

- **UMI423**: The main reason government has become bigger over the years is because it has gotten involved in things that people should do for themselves. / Government has become bigger because the problems we face have become bigger.
- **UMI424**: We need a strong government to handle today's complex economic problems. / The free market can handle these problems without government being involved.
- **UMI425**: The less government, the better. / There are more things that government should be doing.

Income (faminc): Thinking back over the past year, what was your family's annual income? (16-point scale ranging from less than $10,000 to $500,000 or more)

Age (birthyr): In what year were you born?

Education (educ): What is the highest level of education you have completed? (Did not graduate from high school / High school graduate / Some college, but no degree (yet) / 2-year college degree / 4-year college degree / Postgraduate degree (MA, MBA, MD, JD, PhD, etc.))

Gender (gender): Are you male or female? (Male / Female)

Region (inputstate): Please choose a state. (All states, territories, and Canadian provinces as options)

Church Attendance (pew_churatd): Aside from weddings and funerals, how often do you attend religious services? (More than once a week / Once a week / Once or twice a month / A few times a year / Seldom / Never / Don't know)

Ideology (ideo5): Thinking about politics these days, how would you describe your own political viewpoint? (Very liberal / Liberal / Moderate / Conservative / Very Conservative / Not sure)

2013 CCES Dependent Variables

Government Aid to Blacks (UMI433): Some people feel that the government in Washington should make every possible effort to improve the social and economic position of blacks. Others feel that the government should not make any special effort to help blacks because they should help themselves. Where would you place yourself on this scale, or haven't you thought much about this? (Government should help blacks / Blacks should help themselves)

Support for welfare (UMI430): In your opinion, should federal spending on welfare be increased, decreased, or kept about the same? (Greatly increased / Somewhat increased / Slightly increased / Neither increased nor decreased / Slightly decreased / Somewhat decreased / Greatly decreased)

Policy Questions: Here are several things that the government in Washington might do to deal with the problems of poverty and unemployment among black Americans. Please indicate whether you favor or oppose each.

- **Black business (UMI404)**: Government giving business and industry special tax breaks for locating in black neighborhoods (Strongly favor / Favor / Mixed / Opposed / Strongly opposed)
- **Black schools (UMI405)**: Spending more money on black schools (Strongly favor / Favor / Mixed / Opposed / Strongly opposed)
- **Black scholarship (UMI406)**: Providing scholarships for black students who maintain good grades (Strongly favor / Favor / Mixed / Opposed / Strongly opposed)

Affirmative Action (CC330): Affirmative action programs give preference to racial minorities in employment and college admissions in order to correct for past discrimination. Do you support or oppose affirmative action? (Strongly support / Somewhat support / Somewhat oppose / Strongly oppose)

2013 CCES Dependent Variables—Discriminant Validity Analysis

Government Assistance to Women (UMI434): Do you think the government should require companies to allow up to six months of unpaid leave for parents to spend time with their newborn or newly adopted children, or is this something that should be left up to the individual employer? (The government should require this / This should be left up to the individual employer)

Abortion (CC327): Which one of the opinions on this page best agrees with your view on abortion? (By law, abortion should never be permitted / The law should permit abortion only in case of rape, incest, or when the woman's life is in danger / The law should permit abortion for reasons other than rape, incest, or danger to the woman's life, but only after the need for the abortion has been clearly established / By law, a woman should always be able to obtain an abortion as a matter of personal choice)

Preferential Hiring for Women (UMI436): Because of past discrimination, women should be given preferential treatment when applying for jobs or promotions (Strongly in favor / In favor / Neither in favor nor against / Against / Strongly against)

2012 ANES Independent Variables

Sympathy for Blacks (racecasi_sympblacks): How often have you felt sympathy for blacks? (Always / Most of the time / About half the time / Some of the time / Never)

Negative Stereotypes (stype_hwkblack; stype_hwwhite): Respondents are presented with a scale numbered from 1 to 7, with 1 = lazy and 7 = hardworking. They are then asked: Where would you rate WHITES in general on this scale? Where would you rate BLACKS in general on this scale? To construct the measure of negative stereotypes, I construct a measure that reports the difference between respondents' ratings of whites and blacks. The stereotypes variable represents the extent to which the respondent rates Blacks as lazy relative to whites with a score of 1 = Blacks are lazier than whites and 0 = whites are lazier than blacks.

Acknowledge racial discrimination against Blacks (discrim_blacks): How much discrimination is there in the United States today against each of the following groups? The following groups were listed: Blacks, Hispanics, Whites, Gays and Lesbians, and Women. The variable listed here analyzes the responses to the "Blacks" category alone: (A great deal / A lot / A moderate amount / A little / None at all)

Close to Blacks (ftcasi_black): For this variable, I used a feeling thermometer. Using the same thermometer scale you used earlier in the survey, how would you rate Blacks? Please enter the rating number in the number box. Ratings between 50 degrees and 100 degrees mean that you feel favorable and warm toward the group. Ratings between 0 degrees and 50 degrees mean that you don't feel favorable toward the group and that you don't care too much for that group. You would rate the group at the 50 degree mark if you don't feel particularly warm or cold toward the group.

Party ID (pid_x): Summary variable. (Strong Democrat / Not very strong Democrat / Independent-Democrat / Independent / Independent-Republican / Not very strong Republican / Strong Republican)

Limited Government (govrole_big, govrole_market, govrole_lessmore): See 2013 CCES variables for text.

Egalitarianism: Respondents were presented with six statements and asked: Do you (Agree strongly / Agree somewhat / Neither agree nor disagree / Disagree somewhat / Disagree strongly) with this statement.

- **egal_equal**: Our society should do whatever is necessary to make sure that everyone has an equal opportunity to succeed.
- **egal_toofar**: We have gone too far in pushing equal rights in this country.
- **egal_bigprob**: One of the big problems in this country is that we don't give everyone an equal chance.
- **egal_worryless**: This country would be better off if we worried less about how equal people are.
- **egal_notbigprob**: It is not really that big a problem if some people have more of a chance in life than others.
- **egal_fewerprobs**: If people were treated more equally in this country, we would have many fewer problems.

Racial Resentment (resent_workway, resent_slavery, resent_deserve, resent_try): See 2013 CCES variables for text.

Income (incgroup_prepost): Information about income is very important to understand how people are doing financially these days. Your answers are confidential. Would you please give your best guess? Please mark the answer that includes the income of all members of your family living here in 2011 before taxes. (28-point scale ranging from under $5,000 to $250,000 or more)

Age (dem_agegrp_iwdate): Respondent age on interview date (13-point scale ranging from Age 17–20 to Age 75 or older)

Education (dem_edugroup): What is the highest level of school you have completed or the highest degree you have received? (Less than high school credential / High school credential / Some post-high-school, no bachelor's degree / Bachelor's degree / Graduate degree)

Region (sample_state): State of respondent's address.

Church attendance (relig_church and relig_churchoft): Lots of things come up that keep people from attending religious services even if they want to. Thinking about your life these days, do you ever attend religious services, apart from occasional weddings, baptisms, or funerals? (Yes / No). Do you go to religious services? (Every week / Almost every week / Once or twice a month / A few times a year / Never)

Years at current residence (dem3_lenaddr): How many years have you lived at this address?

Political interest (interest_attention): How often do you pay attention to what's going on in government and politics? (Always / Most of the time / About half the time / Some of the time / Never / Don't know)

Party contact (cses_contact): During the campaign, did a party or candidate contact you in person or by any other means? (Yes / No)

Perceptions of close election (preswin_close): Do you think the Presidential race will be CLOSE or will [candidate] WIN BY QUITE A BIT? (Will be close / Win by quite a bit)

Turnout (presvote2012_x): summary variable. For whom did R vote for President in 2012 (Barack Obama / Mitt Romney / Other / R did not vote or did not report voting)

Efficacy

- **effic_complicstd**: Sometimes, politics and government seem so complicated that a person like me can't really understand what's going on. Do you (agree strongly / agree somewhat / neither agree nor disagree / disagree somewhat / disagree strongly) with this statement?
- **effic_undstd**: I feel that I have a pretty good understanding of the important political issues facing our country. Do you (agree strongly / agree somewhat / neither agree nor disagree / disagree somewhat / disagree strongly) with this statement?

Personality Traits: Directions: We're interested in how you see yourself. Please mark how well the following pair of words describes you, even if one word describes you better than the other.

- **Agreeableness**: 'sympathetic, warm'
- **Open to new experiences**: 'open to new experiences, complex'

2012 ANES Dependent Variables

Welfare (cses_expwelf): Thinking about public expenditure on WELFARE BENEFITS, should there be: (much more than now / somewhat more than now / the same as now / somewhat less than now / much less than now)?

Aid to Blacks (aidblack_self): Where would you place YOURSELF on this scale, or haven't you thought much about this? (7-point scale, 1 = GOVERNMENT SHOULD HELP BLACKS, 7 = BLACKS SHOULD HELP THEMSELVES)

Affirmative action:

- **Universities (aa_uni_x)**: Do you favor, oppose, or neither favor nor oppose allowing universities to increase the number of black students studying at their schools by considering race along with other factors when choosing students? Respondents are then asked "Do you [favor/oppose] that a great deal, a moderate amount, or a little?" (Favor a great deal / Favor moderately / Favor a little / Neither favor nor oppose / Oppose a little / Oppose moderately / Oppose a great deal / Don't know)
- **Work (aa_work_x)**: Do you favor, oppose, or neither favor nor oppose allowing companies to increase the number of black workers by considering race along with other factors when choosing employees? Respondents are then asked "Do you [favor/oppose] that a great deal, a moderate amount, or a little?" (Favor a great deal / Favor moderately / Favor a little / Neither favor nor oppose / Oppose a little / Oppose moderately / Oppose a great deal / Don't know)
- **Hiring (aapost_hire_x)**: What about your opinion—are you FOR or AGAINST preferential hiring and promotion of blacks? Respondents are then asked "Do

you favor preference in hiring and promotion STRONGLY or NOT STRONGLY?" (Strongly for / Not strongly for / Not strongly against / Strongly against / Don't know)

Non-voting participation:

- **mobilpo_rmob**: We would like to find out about some of the things people do to help a party or a candidate win an election. During the campaign, did you talk to any people or try to show them why they should vote for or against one of the parties or candidates? (Yes / No)

- **mobilpo_rally**: Did you go to any political meetings, rallies, speeches, dinners, or things like that in support of a particular candidate? (Yes / No)

- **mobilpo_sign**: Did you wear a campaign button, put a campaign sticker on your car, or place a sign in your window or in front of your house? (Yes / No)

- **mobilpo_otherwork**: Did you do any (other) work for one of the parties or candidates? (Yes / No)

- **moblipo_ctbcand**: During an election year people are often asked to make a contribution to support campaigns. Did you give money to an INDIVIDUAL CANDIDATE running for public office? (Yes / No)

- **mobilpo_ctbpty**: Did you give money to a POLITICAL PARTY during this election year? (Yes / No)

- **mobilpo_ctboth**: Did you give any money to ANY OTHER GROUP that supported or opposed candidates? (Yes / No)

Civic engagement

- **hsinvolv_march**: During the past 4 years, have you joined in a protest march, rally, or demonstration, or have you not done this in the past 4 years? (Have done this / Have not done this)

- **dhsinvolv_board**: During the past 4 years, have you attended a meeting of a town or city government or school board, or have you not done this in the past 4 years? (Have done this / Have not done this)

- **dhsinvolv_netpetition**: During the past 4 years, have you signed a petition on the internet about a political or social issue, or have you not done this in the past 4 years? (Have done this / Have not done this)

- **dhsinvolv_petition**: During the past 4 years, have you signed a petition on paper about a political or social issue, or have you not done this in the past 4 years? (Have done this / Have not done this)

- **dhsinvolv_relig**: During the past 4 years, have you ever given money to a religious organization, or have you not done this in the past 4 years? (Have done this / Have not done this)

- **dhsinvolv_org**: Not counting a religious organization, during the past 4 years, have you given money to any other organization concerned with a political or social issue, or have you not done this in the past 4 years? (Have done this / Have not done this)

- **dhsinvolv_call**: During the past 4 years, have you called a radio or TV show

about a political issue, or have you not done this in the past 4 years? (Have
done this / Have not done this)

- **dhsinvolv_message**: During the past 4 years, have you ever posted a message
on Facebook or Twitter about a political issue, or have you never done this in
the past 4 years? (Have done this / Have not done this)
- **dhsinvolv_letter**: During the past 4 years, have you written a letter to a newspaper or magazine about a political issue, or have you not done this in the past
4 years? (Have done this / Have not done this)
- **dhsinvolv_contact1**: During the past 4 years, have you contacted or tried to
contact a member of the U.S. Senate or U.S. House of Representatives, or have
you not done this in the past 4 years? (Have done this / Have not done this)

2008 ANES Independent Variables

If wording is omitted, see 2012 ANES variables for phrasing.

Sympathy for Blacks (V085115)
Negative Stereotypes (V083207b; V083207a)
Close to Blacks (V085064y)
Party ID (V083098x)
Limited Government (V085105, V085106, V085107)
Ideology (V083069)
Egalitarianism (V085162, V085163, V085164, V085165, V085166, V085167)
Racial Resentment (V085143, V085144, V085145, V085146)
Income (V083248x): Household income (25-point scale ranging from None or less
than $2,999 to $150,000 and over)
Age (V081104): Respondent age on interview date.
Education (V083218x): Educational attainment. (0–8 grades—No HS diploma/
equivalency / 9–12 grades—No HS diploma/equivalency / 0–12 grades—HS di-
ploma/equivalency / 13+ grades, no degree / Junior or community college level
degree / BA level degree / Advanced degree or Less than high school creden-
tial / High school credential / Some post-high-school, no bachelor's degree /
Bachelor's degree / Graduate degree)
Region (V081201a): State of respondent's address.
Church attendance (V083186a and V083186)
Years at current residence (V083266A and V083266B): How long have you lived
in your present (city/town/township/county)?
Political interest (V085073B)
Party contact (V085025): As you know, the political parties try to talk to as many
people as they can to get them to vote for their candidate. Did anyone from
one of the political parties call you up or come around and talk to you about
the campaign this year? (Yes / No)

Perceptions of close election (V083074)
Turnout (V085195): summary variable. For whom did R vote for President in 2012 (Barack Obama / Mitt Romney / Other / R did not vote or did not report voting)
Efficacy (V085151A, V085151B)

2008 ANES Dependent Variables

Affirmative Action
- **Work (V085157a and V085157b)**: summary variable. Some people say that because of past discrimination, blacks should be given preference in hiring and promotion. Others say that such preference in hiring and promotion of blacks is wrong because it gives blacks advantages they haven't earned. What about your opinion—are you for or against preferential hiring and promotion of blacks? (For / Against / Other) Respondents are then asked: "Do you [favor/oppose] preference in hiring and promotion strongly or not strongly? (Strongly / Not strongly)"

Non-voting participation:
- **V085029**: We would like to find out about some of the things people do to help a party or a candidate win an election. During the campaign, did you talk to any people or try to show them why they should vote for or against one of the parties or candidates? (Yes / No)
- **V085030**: Did you go to any political meetings, rallies, speeches, dinners, or things like that in support of a particular candidate? (Yes / No)
- **V085031**: Did you wear a campaign button, put a campaign sticker on your car, or place a sign in your window or in front of your house? (Yes / No)
- **V085032**: Did you do any (other) work for one of the parties or candidates? (Yes / No)
- **V085033**: During an election year people are often asked to make a contribution to support campaigns. Did you give money to an individual candidate running for public office? (Yes / No)
- **V085034**: Did you give money to a political party during this election year? (Yes / No)
- **V085035**: Did you give any money to any other group that supported or opposed candidates? (Yes / No)

Civic engagement: Some other questions now. During the PAST 12 MONTHS, have you . . .
- **V085124**: Worked with other people to deal with some issues facing your community. (Yes / No)
- **V085125**: Telephoned, written a letter to, or visited a government official to express your views on a public issue? (Yes / No)
- **V085126**: Attend a meeting about an issue facing your community or school? (Yes / No)

- **Vo85128**: Many people say they have less time these days to do volunteer work. What about you, were you able to devote any time to volunteer work in the last 12 months or did you not do so? (Yes / No)
- **Vo85129**: Many people are finding it more difficult to make contributions to church or charity as much as they used to. How about you—were you able to contribute any money to church or charity in the last 12 months? (Yes / No)

Welfare (Vo83145x): What about welfare programs. Should federal spending be increased, decreased, or kept about the same? (Increased a great deal / Increased a moderate amount / Increased a little / Kept about the same / Decreased a little / Decreased a moderate amount / Decreased a great deal)

Government Aid to Blacks (Vo83137): The dependent variables from Appendix Table 8.1 appear in the Web Appendix.

1994 GSS Independent Variables

Sympathy for Blacks (symptblk): How often have you felt sympathy for Blacks? (Very often / Fairly often / Not too often / Never)

Racial Resentment: Regular 4-item scale not available.

- **immwrkup**: Do you agree strongly, agree somewhat, neither agree nor disagree, disagree somewhat, or disagree strongly with the following statement: Irish, Italians, Jewish and many other minorities overcame prejudice and worked their way up. Blacks should do the same without special favors.
- **blkgovt**: Do you think that Blacks get more attention from government than they deserve? (Much more / More / About right / Less / Much less)

Party ID (partyid): Generally speaking, do you usually think of yourself as a Republican, Democrat, Independent, or what? (Strongly Democrat / Not very strong Democrat / Independent, close to Democrat / Independent (neither/no response) / Independent, close to Republican / Not very strong Republican / Strong Republican)

Ideology (polviews): I'm going to show you a seven-point scale on which the political views that people might hold are arranged from extremely liberal to extremely conservative. Where would you place yourself on this scale? (Extremely liberal / Liberal / Slightly liberal / Moderate, middle of the road / Slightly conservative / Conservative / Extremely Conservative)

Income (INCOME91): In which of these groups did your total family income, from all sources, fall last year before taxes, that is? (21-point scale ranging from Under $1,000 to $75,000 and over)

Age (age): Respondent's age.

Education (degree): Highest educational degree earned by respondent. (Less than high school / High school / Associate/junior college / Bachelor's / Graduate)

Gender (I_GENDER): (Male / Female)

Region (region): Region of interview. South Atlantic, East South Central, and West South Central were coded as south.

Church Attendance (attend): How often do you attend religious services? (Never / Less than once a year / About once or twice a year / Several times a year / About once a month / Two to three times a month / Nearly every week / Every week / Several times a week)

Egalitarianism (eqincome): It is the responsibility of the government to reduce the differences in income between people with high incomes and those with low incomes. (Agree strongly / Agree / Neither agree nor disagree / Disagree / Disagree strongly)

Racial Contact (rachome): Finally, the question used to approximate interracial contact was: During the last few years, has anyone in your family brought a friend who was a [(Negro/ Black/ African-American)] home for dinner? (Yes / No)

Anti-Black Stereotype Index (workblks; workwhts): See 2012 ANES for text.

1994 GSS Dependent Variables

Government Aid to Blacks (natracey): We are faced with many problems in this country, none of which can be solved easily or inexpensively. I'm going to name some of these problems, and for each one I'd like you to tell me whether you think we're spending too much money on it, too little money, or about the right amount. Spending on assistance to Blacks. (Too little / About right / Too much)

Welfare (natfare): We are faced with many problems in this country, none of which can be solved easily or inexpensively. I'm going to name some of these problems, and for each one I'd like you to tell me whether you think we're spending too much money on it, too little money, or about the right amount. Welfare. (Too little / About right / Too much)

Affirmative Action (affrmact): Some people say that because of past discrimination, Blacks should be given preference in hiring and promotion. Others say that such preference in hiring and promotion of Blacks is wrong because it discriminates against others. What about your opinion—are you for or against preferential hiring and promotion of Blacks? (Strongly favor / Not strongly favor / Not strongly oppose / Strongly oppose)

2016 YouGov Independent Variables

Racial Sympathy (UMI403_w1, UMI409_w1, UMI413_w1, UMI418_w1): See chapter 3 for text.

Racial Resentment (UMI427_w1, UMI426_w1, UMI429_w1, UUMI428_w1): See 2013 CCES variables.

Anti-black stereotype (UMI433_w1): Now I have some questions about different groups in our society. I'm going to show you a seven-point scale on which the characteristics of the people in a group can be rated. In the first statement a score of 1 means that you think almost all of the people in that group tend to be hardworking. A score of 7 means that you think most people in the group are lazy. A score of 4 means that you think that most people in the group are not closer to one end or the other, and of course, you may choose any number in between. Where would you rate blacks in general on this scale? (7-point scale, 1 = Hardworking and 7 = Lazy)

Gender sympathy (UMI407_w1, UMI415_w1): See 2013 CCES variables.

Age (birthyr): In what year were you born?

Gender (gender): Please mark your gender. (Male / Female / Other)

Education (educ): What is the highest level of school you have completed or the highest degree you have received? (Grade School (Grades 1–8) or less / High School Diploma (including equivalency test) / Some College, no Bachelor's Degree / Bachelor's Degree / Graduate Degree)

Party ID (pid7): Now we want to get some information about your background. Generally speaking, do you usually think of yourself as a Democrat, a Republican, an Independent, or what? (Strong Democrat / Weak Democrat / Independent-Lean Democrat / Independent / Independent-Lean Republican / Weak Republican / Strong Republican)

Limited government (UMI420_w1, UMI421_w1, UMI425_w1): See 2013 CCES variables.

Church attendance (pew_churatd): Aside from weddings and funerals, how often do you attend religious services? (More than once a week / Once a week / Once or twice a month / A few times a year / Seldom / Never)

Region (inputstate): State in which the respondent lives.

Income (faminc): What is your combined annual household income? (9-point scale ranging from under $20,000 to $125,000+)

Collective guilt (UMI450_w2, UMI451_w2, UMI452_w2) 1) When you learn about racism, how much guilt do you feel due to your association with the white race? (A great deal / A lot / A moderate amount / A little / None). 2) How guilty do you feel about the privileges and benefits you receive as a white American? 3) How guilty do you feel about social inequality between white and black Americans? (Answer choices for 2 and 3: Extremely guilty / Very guilty / moderately guilty / a little guilty / not guilty at all)

2016 YouGov Dependent Variables

Welfare (UMI430_w2, UMI429_w2, UMI431_w2): Do you think federal spending on welfare should be (Increased / Kept about the same / Decreased)? If respondent answered "Increased" or "Decreased," they were then asked: By how much do you think federal spending on welfare should be [increased / decreased]? (Greatly increased / Moderately increased / Greatly decreased / Moderately decreased)

Police use more force than necessary (UMI439_w2): How often do you think the police use more force than is necessary when dealing with Black people? (Never / Rarely / Sometimes / Usually / Always)

Support for BLM (UMI441_w2): Do you support, oppose, or neither support nor oppose the Black Lives Matter movement? (Support strongly / Support somewhat / Support not very strongly / Neither support nor oppose / Oppose not very strongly / Oppose somewhat / Oppose strongly)

2020 YouGov Independent Variables

Racial Sympathy Wave 1 (wel002, wel004, wel005, wel007): See chapter 3 for text.

Racial Sympathy Wave 2: (wel002_w2, wel003_w2, wel004_w2, wel005_w2): See 2013 CCES variables.

Racial Resentment (wel060, wel059, wel062, wel061): See 2013 CCES variables.

Age (birthyr): Birth year of respondent.

Gender (gender): Gender of respondent.

Education (educ): Summary variable. (No HS / High school graduate / Some college / 2-year / 4-year / Post-grad)

Party ID (pid7): Summary variable. (Strong Democrat / Not very strong Democrat / Lean Democrat / Independent / Lean Republican / Not very strong Republican / Strong Republican)

- **Wave 2: pid7_w2**

Ideology (ideo5): Summary variable. (Very liberal / Liberal / Moderate / Conservative / Very conservative)

Church attendance (pew_churatd): Summary variable. (More than once a week / Once a week / Once or twice a month / A few times a year / Seldom / Never)

Region (inputstate): State of residence.

- **Wave 2: inputstate_w2**

Income (faminc_new): Family income (16-point scale ranging from Less than $10,000 to $500,000 or more)

- **Wave 2: faminc_new_w2**

Gender sympathy index (wel003, wel006): See 2013 CCES variables.

Political interest (newsint): Some people seem to follow what's going on in government and public affairs most of the time, whether there's an election going on or not. Others aren't that interested. Would you say you follow what's going on in government and public affairs (Most of the time / Some of the time / Only now and then / Hardly at all)

Self-monitoring items (wel063, wel064, wel065) 1) When you are with other people, how often do you put on a show to impress or entertain them? 2) When you are in a group of people, how often are you the center of attention? 3) How good or poor of an actor would you be? (Response options for first two questions:

Always, Most of the time, Some of the time, Once in a while, Never. Response option for third question: Excellent, Good, Fair, Poor, Very poor)

2020 YouGov Dependent Variables

Support for women's affirmative action (welo88): Because of past discrimination, women should be given preferential treatment when applying for jobs or promotions. (Strongly in favor / In favor / Neither in favor nor against / Against / Strongly Against)

Government aid to blacks (welo85_w2): See 2013 CCES variables.

Reparations (welo66): Would you support or oppose policies designed to reduce racial wealth gaps caused by slavery and Jim Crow, such as offering compensation or tax benefits to the descendants of slaves? (7-point scale where 1 = Extremely oppose and 7 = Extremely support)

- **Wave 2: welo31_w2**

Inequality actions: To address issues of race and racial inequality, how important is it for you personally to do the following?

- **Educate myself about racism (welo33_w2)**: Educate myself about the history of racial inequality in our country. (7-point scale where 1 is "Extremely important" and 7 is "Not at all important")
- **Confront other people being racist (welo34_w2)**: Confront other people when they say or do something racist. (7-point scale where 1 is "Extremely important" and 7 is "Not at all important")
- **Listen to POC (welo41_w2)**: Listen to people of color. (7-point scale where 1 is "Extremely important" and 7 is "Not at all important")
- **Attend protests (welo36_w2)**: Attend protests or rallies focused on issues related to racial equality. (7-point scale where 1 is "Extremely important" and 7 is "Not at all important")
- **Vote in elections (welo40_w2)**: Vote in elections. (7-point scale where 1 is "Extremely important" and 7 is "Not at all important")

Campaign for pro-Black candidates (welo51_w2): Among the two options listed below, please tell me which you think is more important to pursue: (Developing an understanding of the country's history of Black oppression / Campaigning in elections for political candidates who prioritize pro-Black policies)

Personal vs. political: Although there are a number of solutions we can pursue to address racial inequality, every person thinks that some solutions are more important than others. I am going to read you pairs of potential solutions. Among the two options, please tell me which you think is more important to pursue:

- **Address discriminatory laws or address white prejudice (welo48_w2)**: 1. Addressing white prejudice 2. Addressing discriminatory laws
- **Educate strangers vs. educate friends and family (welo49_w2)**: 1. Educating my

friends and family about racial inequality 2. Educating strangers in my community about racial inequality

- **Lobby officials vs. listen to young people (welo50_w2)**: 1. Lobbying electoral officials on racial issues 2. Listening to young people's plans for combatting racism

2020 CMPS Independent Variables

Party ID (Q23, Q21, Q22): Respondent's party ID. (Strong Democrat / Not strong Democrat / Independent / Not strong Republican / Strong Republican)

Ideology (Q43): When it comes to politics, do you think of yourself as liberal, moderate, or conservative? (Very Liberal / Somewhat Liberal / Moderate / Somewhat Conservative / Very Conservative)

Racial Sympathy (Q377, Q378, Q379, Q380): See chapter 3 for text.

Racial Resentment (Q213r1, Q213r3, Q213r2, Q213r4): See 2013 CCES variables.

Income (Q813): What was your total combined household income in 2020 before taxes? This question is completely confidential and just used to help classify the responses, but it is very important to the research. (12-point scale ranging from less than $20,000 to $200,000 or more)

Age (S5): In what year were you born?

Education (S13): What is the highest level of education you completed? (Grades 1–8 / Some high school, but did not graduate / High school graduate or GED / Some college / Associates, 2-year degree / Bachelors, 4-year degree / Post-graduate degree)

Gender (S3b): What is your gender? (Man / Woman / Non-binary / Something else)

Region (S4): Please select your current state of residence (50 states + DC).

Church attendance (Q59): Thinking back to before the coronavirus pandemic, generally speaking, about how often did you use to participate in worship services or religious rituals with others? (More than once per week / Once per week / A few times per month / About once per month / A few times per year / Never)

White identity (Q271): How important is being White to your identity? (Extremely important / Very important / Moderately important / Slightly important / Not at all important)

White linked fate (Q551_Q559r4): How much do you think what happens to the following groups here in the U.S. will have something to do with what happens in your life—What happens to White people will have (Nothing to do with what happens in my life, Only a little to do with what happens in my life, Something to do with what happens in my life, A lot to do with what happens in my life, A huge amount to do with what happens in my life)

Black linked fate (Q551_Q559r1): How much do you think what happens to the following groups here in the U.S. will have something to do with what happens in your life—What happens to Black people will have (Nothing to do with what happens in my life / Only a little to do with what happens in my life / Something to do with what happens in my life / A lot to do with what happens in my life / A huge amount to do with what happens in my life)

Racial discrimination against white people (Q619_Q6262r1): How much discrimination, if any, do you think exists against each of the following groups in the U.S. today? Whites (A lot, Some, A little, None at all)

Racial discrimination against Black people (Q619_Q6262r2): How much discrimination, if any, do you think exists against each of the following groups in the U.S. today? Blacks (A lot, Some, A little, None at all)

2020 CMPS Dependent Variables

Welfare (Q308r4): How would you rate your feelings toward each of the following groups on a scale from 0–100 where 0 means very cold, and 100 means very warm? Welfare recipients.

Reparations: To what degree would you support the following policies?

- **Generations of racism (Q417_Q24r1)**: Reparations to Black Americans to address inequities created by generations of racism. (Strongly support / Support / Somewhat support / Somewhat oppose / Oppose / Strongly oppose)
- **Role in slavery (Q417_Q424r2)**: Reparations to Black Americans to address America's role in slavery. (Strongly support / Support / Somewhat support / Somewhat oppose / Oppose / Strongly oppose)

Should addressing police brutality be a priority for whites (Q117r1): Please indicate if the following should be a high priority or low priority for the white community? Addressing police brutality. (Very low priority / Low priority / High priority / Very high priority)

Shifting funds from police to social service (Q417_Q424r3): To what degree would you support the following policies: Shifting some funds from local police departments to local social service agencies and urban community centers. (Strongly support / Support / Somewhat support / Somewhat oppose / Oppose / Strongly oppose)

Defunding the police (Q385): As you may have heard, in the wake of the murder of George Floyd and protests, there has been some talk of defunding the police. Some say that defunding the police is pushing things too far. Others feel that defunding the police is not going far enough. How about you—what do you think about defunding the police? (7-point scale where 1 = Defunding the police is pushing things too far and 7 = Defunding the police is not going far enough)

Support for BLM (Q358): Based on everything you have heard or seen, how much do you support or oppose the Black Lives Matter movement? (Strongly support / Somewhat support / Neither support nor oppose / Somewhat oppose / Strongly oppose)

Black Americans protest (Q359r4): When Black Americans speak up and protest injustice in the U.S., it always makes the country better. (Strongly agree / Somewhat agree / Neither agree nor disagree / Somewhat disagree / Strongly disagree)

BLM protest meaning (Q384r1): Some people say the Black Lives Matter protests in the Summer of 2020 were mainly a protest against unfair treatment of Black people. Others say they were mainly a way of vandalism and looting. Which of these statements seems more correct to you? In the first statement a score of "1" means that you think that the Black Lives Matter protests were only about protesting against unfair treatment of Black people. A score of "7" means that you think these protests were only about vandalism and looting. A score of "4" means that you think that the Black Lives Matter protests were about both of these aspects, equally and of course, you may choose any number in between.

Government Aid to Blacks (Q405): See 2013 CCES variables. The dependent variables from Table 8.2 appear in the Web Appendix.

2015 SSI Independent Variables

Racial Sympathy (racsymp1a, racsymp2a, racsymp3a, racsymp4a): See chapter 3 for text.

Racial Resentment (deserve, irish, tryharder, generation): See 2013 CCES variables.

Limited Government (lmtdgovt1, lmtdgovt2, lmtdgovt3): See 2013 CCES variables.

Party ID (fc, doyouthinkofyourselfasclose, wouldyoucallyourselfastrong): Summary variable. (Strong Democrat / Not very strong Democrat / Closer to Democratic Party / Independent / Closer to Republican Party / Not very strong Republican / Strong Republican)

Income (whatisyourcombinedannualhou): What is your combined annual household income? (9-point scale ranging from under $20,000 to $125,000+)

Age (whatisyourage): What is your age? (18–24 / 25–34 / 35–44 / 45–54 / 55–64 / 65+)

Education (whatisthehighestlevelofsch): What is the highest level of school you have completed or the highest degree you have received? (Less than high school / High school graduate / Some college / College degree / Post-graduate degree)

Gender (whatisyourgender): What is your gender? (Male / Female)

Region (inwhichpartofthecountrydo): In which part of the country do you live? (Northeast, Midwest, South, West)

Experimental Stimuli

2013 CCES: Social Policy Experiments

Here are several things that the government in Washington might do to deal with the problems of poverty and unemployment among black/poor Americans. Please indicate whether you favor or oppose each.

Government giving business and industry special tax breaks for locating in [black/
   poor] neighborhoods

Spending more money on [black/poor] schools

Providing scholarships for [black/poor] students who maintain good grades
   For answer choices, see 2013 CCES Policy Questions. The experimental stimuli
   for the other studies appear in the Web Appendix.

Interview Schedule

Introduction Script: *Thank you for agreeing to participate in this study. I am a professor in the Political Science Department at X and {} is an undergraduate research
assistant also at X. We are interested in learning more about your background and
how you became involved in social justice organizations and events. We are also
interested in learning about your political attitudes more generally.*

*We'll get started now. This interview should take about 60 minutes. I want to re-
mind you that your confidentiality is important to me. We will de-identify the data
collected today, and you will not be personally identified in any of the write-ups
and/or presentations related to this project. I am going to record our interview;
please let me know if you would prefer that I do not.*

*Throughout the course of our time together today, there may be occasions where
we ask you to return to something you mentioned earlier, or in other cases, ask you
new questions to move the conversation forward. We hope you do not take offense at
these suggestions, we are making them to ensure that we develop a full understanding
of your experiences while also staying mindful of your time. At the end of the interview,
we will provide time for you to share anything else you'd like with us, you can also
always follow up with us via email if you think of anything else you would like to say.*

Interview Questions: *Now I would like to ask you a few questions about your background and your experiences.*

OPENING QUESTIONS:
1. We want to spend the first five minutes getting to know you and hearing your
   life story. Some things you could share with us are: Where did you grow up?
   What was your home life like? Where did you go to school? Where did life take
   you after you left home?
   a. We'll get deep into emotions and your politics later, but for now, can you try
      to provide us with highlights of your biography? Please take about 5 minutes
      to share with us who you are.
2. You mentioned [x] school, what, if any, discussion of diversity or race did you
   have there? (ask for last school mentioned or for any school singled out as being
   formative in answer to #1)
3. (after they tell background) And that brings us to today. Where do you live
   now? How long have you lived there? Tell us a little bit about your community.
4. What is your current occupation? *(omit this if the answer is provided earlier)*

NATURE AND ORIGINS OF INVOLVEMENT IN RACE

5. As you know, we're interested in studying race in America. In thinking about your understanding of race in America, can you tell me a story about one memorable time or event that made you think about racial inequality among White and Black Americans?

    i. If they lead with personal experience, then press them on whether they learned about it at school (intellectual). Vice versa for if they lead with intellectual experience.

    ii. Note: omit this if the answer is provided earlier

6. When you think back to this memorable event, can you remember what sort of emotions you felt? Examples of emotions include: happy, sad, angry, ashamed, afraid.

7. Since this event, would you say your thinking about race and racial inequality has changed at all? How so?

8. Fast forward, nowadays, how do you primarily learn about race and racial issues? For example, news, word of mouth, books, literature.

Now to shift gears, we're going to ask you a little about your participation in events related to race—how much you participate, and how you learn about the organization's events. Note that we will not share any of your responses with any organizations—we are just interested in learning more about why you choose to or choose not to participate.

NATURE AND ORIGINS OF INVOLVEMENT IN ACTIVISM

9. How do you think about facilitating change when it comes to racial inequality?

10. When did you first decide to get involved in racial justice activism?

11. Did anyone recruit or encourage you to get involved? If so, who? Do you recruit or encourage people to get involved?

12. What is your sense of the people who participate in the organization?

    a. Where do they come from? City name? Region name?

    b. What are their backgrounds?

13. How often do you participate in events planned by the organization?

EXPERIENCES IN ACTIVISM

In the last section we were interested in learning about how you got started in activism. Now we want to ask you a little bit about your experiences in [X] organization.

14. Tell us how you learn [or communicate to others] about the organization's activities.

15. Before the coronavirus disruption, what was the most recent event you attended?

16. How did it make you feel?

17. *If they are facilitators, ask a bit about the content of the events and workshops. Questions like*: Can you tell me about some of the topics you cover in your workshops? What is the format? Do you have participants read or watch anything before they come in? If so, what are those materials?

a. In your experience, is there a topic or approach that gets your participants to that "ah- ha" moment? Can you tell us about when those moments typically happen?

   i. To what extent do participants' background histories come up?

b. What kinds of techniques do you teach in these events and workshops to get your participants to succeed in their education and actions?

c. In reflecting on these events you've been a part of, do you have any suggestions or critiques of the approach or format? For example, do you wish they would focus more on pressuring government or policymakers, ballot initiatives, or conducting more community outreach? Again, we won't share your responses with the organization's leaders, we just want to hear your thoughts on how effective these methods are.

GENERAL ATTITUDES AND OPINIONS

We're going to ask you about a few different policy areas and politicians. There are no right or wrong answers—we are just trying to get a sense of your opinions on some issues to understand more about how you think about politics. We want to hear about your views as an American citizen.

18. First, we would like to hear your thoughts about the national government's role in addressing racial inequality. Should the government be doing more? Less? About the same?

   a. How has the election of Donald Trump changed the way you think about the national government's role in addressing racial inequalities?

   b. Now moving on to your opinions on a few areas of public policy.

      What is the number one issue that the federal or even state governments should do to mitigate racial inequality?

19. What, if anything, should the national government do to address police brutality?

20. What, if anything, should the national government do to address the state of America's prisons?

21. What, if anything, should the national government do to address the role of race in higher education?

22. Now we're going to ask you about your opinion toward the major parties with respect to race. Tell me what you think about the Democrats and race. Do they do a good job on this topic?

23. How about Republicans?

CLOSING QUESTIONS: *NOW FOR SOME CLOSING QUESTIONS AS WE WRAP UP.*

24. Insofar as there has been any racial progress, how do you think that has been accomplished? For example, Is it the result of policy? (if so, which one?) Public opinion? Activism? Something else?

25. How do organizations like [x] fit into that picture (historically or now)?

26. What makes you pessimistic about where the country is headed with respect to race? What makes you optimistic? How do your optimism and pessimism inform your activism?

27. Finally, tell us a little bit about the process of answering these questions today. What has it been like for you?

Thank you so much for spending time with us today and sharing your experiences.

We are grateful for your honesty and want to let you know that what we've learned today will be a great help in our work to understand why and how White Americans mobilize for racial justice causes. Do you have any questions or feedback for us?

Notes

Chapter One

1. Throughout the book, I refer to these groups using the guidelines set forth in the *Associated Press Stylebook* as of August 2022. This includes uppercasing *Black* but not *white*. Many publications have made this modification. See, for example, Dean Baquet and Phil Corbett, "Uppercasing 'Black,'" *New York Times*, June 30, 2020, https://www.nytco.com/press/uppercasing-black/. On occasions where I am quoting directly from published material or a survey, I use the capitalization that appears in the original.

2. See, for example, Bynum 2023; Carter Jackson 2024; Hersey 2022; Carter Jackson 2021; Kelley 2003; Lewis-Giggetts 2022; Wanzo 2021.

3. I use the terms *Black* and *African American* interchangeably throughout the book.

4. Gordon Allport (1954) coined this term in reference to a form of prejudice in which negative verbal remarks against a person, group, or community are made but not addressed directly to the subject (Cousins 2014).

5. Toby Harnden, Hugo Gye, Lydia Warren, and Mark Duell, "US Election Day in Photos," *Daily Mail*, November 7, 2012, https://www.dailymail.co.uk/news/article-2228996/US-ELECTION-DAY-2012-IN-PICTURES-Obama-Romneys-final-campaign-hours.html.

6. Equal Justice Initiative, "White Minister Beaten Following Selma March, Dies from Injuries," *A History of Racial Injustice*, https://calendar.eji.org/racial-injustice/mar/11. See also Brown 2002.

7. Jennifer Medina, "Latinos Back Black Lives Matter Protests. They Want Change for Themselves, Too," *New York Times*, July 3, 2020, https://www.nytimes.com/2020/07/03/us/politics/latinos-police-racism-black-lives-matter.html; Zijia Eleanor Song and Noreen O'Donnell, "Black and Asian Americans Stand Together Against Hate Crimes," *NBC Philadelphia*, April 15, 2021, https://www.nbcphiladelphia.com/news/national-international/black-and-asian-americans-stand-together-against-hate-crimes/2780762/.

8. Erica Belfi, "Native Solidarity with Black Lives Matter as Both Communities Confront Centuries-Long State Violence," *Cultural Survival*, July 2, 2020, https://www.culturalsurvival.org/news/native-solidarity-black-lives-matter-both -communities-confront-centuries-long-state-violence.

9. About six million US adults identify as Afro-Latino. See Ana Gonzalez-Barrera, "About 6 Million U.S. Adults Identify as Afro-Latino," Pew Research Center, May 2, 2022, https://www.pewresearch.org/short-reads/2022/05/02/about -6-million-u-s-adults-identify-as-afro-latino/#:~:text=Afro%2DLatino%20identity %20is%20a,racial%20or%20national%20origin%20identities.

10. Center for Native American Youth, "What It Means to Be Both Black and Indigenous," Aspen Institute, February 18, 2021, https://www.aspeninstitute.org /blog-posts/what-it-means-to-be-both-black-and-indigenous/. See also public opinion studies of Indigenous populations (Clark 2005).

11. Nicholas Jones, Rachel Marks, Roberto Ramirez, and Merarys Ríos-Vargas, "2020 Census Illuminates Racial and Ethnic Composition of the Country," United States Census Bureau, August 12, 2021, https://www.census.gov/library/stories/2021 /08/improved-race-ethnicity-measures-reveal-united-states-population-much-more -multiracial.html.

12. Song and O'Donnell 2021.

13. On the specific topic of white men, the group represented at many of the upper echelons of political and social life; see Pugh 2015 and Silva 2013.

14. GBD 2019 Police Violence US Subnational Collaborators, "Fatal Police Violence by Race and State in the USA, 1980–2019: A Network Meta-Regression," *The Lancet* 398 (10307). On the other hand, some white people are the target of ethnoreligious attacks and incidents. For example, Ayal Feinberg noted that there had been over 850 anti-Semitic hate crimes since 2001 (Feinberg 2020).

15. For example, in "Racial Attitudes and the 'New South'" (Kuklinski, Cobb, and Gilens 1997), prejudice is the only racial attitude examined. Similarly, when Nicholas A. Valentino, Vincent L. Hutchings, and Ismail K. White (2002) examine "how political ads prime racial attitudes during campaigns," they are examining how ads prime three attitudes all related to animus: racial resentment, laissez-faire racism, and subscription to the notion that Black people have too much influence.

16. LaGina Gause's work (2020), for example, finds that upon observing protests, politicians are more likely to vote for legislation on civil rights, minority issues, and civil liberties or introduce their own measures.

17. Yair Ghitza and Jonathan Robinson, "What Happened in 2020," *Catalist*, accessed August 29, 2023, https://catalist.us/wh-national/#pp-toc-608eee40d2225-anchor-0.

Chapter Two

1. I do have one source from the 1990s: the 1994 General Social Survey (GSS). I describe this survey in more detail in chapter 3.

2. Reeb became quite well-known after his murder. There were thousands of vigils held in his honor, and President Johnson called Reeb's family to express his condolences, later invoking his memory when delivering a draft of the Voting Rights Act to Congress. In contrast, the national media did not draw attention to the death of local Black activist Jimmie Lee Jackson. Jackson was fatally shot while protesting in a peaceful voting rights march a few weeks earlier (Fiffer and Cohen 2015).

3. Sam Roberts, "Prof. Philip E. Converse, Expert on How Voters Decide, Dies at 86," *New York Times*, January 7, 2015, https://www.nytimes.com/2015/01/08/us /prof-philip-e-converse-86-expert-on-how-voters-decide.html.

4. David Remnick, "Going the Distance: On and Off the Road with Barack Obama," *New Yorker*, January 19, 2014, http://www.newyorker.com/magazine/2014 /01/27/going-the-distance-david-remnick.

5. Black representation carries many benefits. See Bobo and Gilliam 1990; Spence and McClerking 2010. But also see Gay 2001.

6. Somewhat surprisingly, scholars have found that *anti*-egalitarian whites— that is, those individuals who support "hierarchy-enhancing" outcomes—were especially inclined to *support* Obama (Knowles, Lowery, and Schaumerg 2009). Anti-egalitarians endorse the country's existing racial hierarchy and reject the notion that race plays an important role in stratifying American politics and society. They supported Obama, therefore, to demonstrate the *in*significance of his race.

7. Humanitarianism is studied less frequently than egalitarianism. Unfortunately, I could not identify any studies that evaluated the relationship between humanitarianism and support for Obama. Though given the relationship between the two measures, I expect it would be less influential than egalitarianism. Egalitarianism leads people to "embrace policies that mandate an extensive economic role for the government," while humanitarianism is "associated with more modest policies that seek to address the problems of the needy" (Feldman and Steenbergen 2001, 658). Although Obama did emphasize that the government might play an important role in the economy, especially with respect to stabilizing the financial crisis, he was not as attentive to addressing antipoverty. See Fording and Smith 2012.

8. According to John Sides and colleagues (2019), years later, when Hillary Clinton made racial issues a more central component of her 2016 candidacy, these white Democrats defected to the Republican Party.

9. I use the terms *racial resentment* and *symbolic racism* interchangeably throughout the book.

10. Other psychologists criticize emotional granularity (Barrett 2017), defined as the "ability to make fine-grained, nuanced distinctions between similar emotions" (Smidt and Suvak 2015, 48).

11. Not all scholars use *racial* in this way. For example, Claire Jean Kim's discussion of "racial ordering" and "racial scapegoating" reference other non-white groups (Kim 2000).

12. Ailsa Chang, Rachel Martin, and Eric Marrapodi, "Summer of Racial

Reckoning," *NPR*, August 16, 2020, https://www.npr.org/2020/08/16/902179773/sum
mer-of-racial-reckoning-the-match-lit.

13. Note that these studies often used a mediating concept—either Social Dominance Orientation or Right Wing Authoritarianism—to link personality to out-
group attitude (See Ekehammar et al. 2004).

14. I am not suggesting that sympathy is interchangeable with agreeableness or
openness to new experience. Indeed, in chapter 5, I take up this point empirically
through an analysis that considers the relative influence of personality traits and
racial sympathy on opinion and find that sympathy is independently associated
with policy opinion. That said, it is possible these personality traits are one of the
many sources that might contribute to a white person's level of racial sympathy.

15. Though see also Anoll, Engelhardt, and Israel-Trummel 2022.

16. In subsequent analyses, however, Sniderman and Carmines label those who
score below .5 on their racial stereotypes index as "tolerant" (1997, 79).

17. The term *Afro-Pessimism* refers to a stream of thought coming from African American or Black Studies that argues "Black people are integral to human
society but at all times and in all places excluded from it" (Cunningham 2020).

Chapter Three

1. That said, in chapters 5 and 6, I examine whether the *effects* of sympathy can
be activated or heightened.

2. For example, although Batson has employed these types of measures in his
research, he warns: "It seems likely that some subjects, even if they are experienc-
ing some distinct emotion such as empathy rather than distress, do not have the
language skills to interpret this experience accurately—at least not in the terms
provided on our rating scales" (1987, 357). Other psychologists see emotions as "a
tangled bank of poorly differentiated entities that are difficult to define and measure" (Sander and Scherer 2014, 162). I do not attempt to adjudicate this debate,
though based on the definitions I consult, my conceptualization of racial sympathy
best aligns with the definition of sympathy.

3. This analysis has found that the influence of implicit measures on political
outcomes is significantly reduced or eliminated altogether after controlling for explicit measures of prejudice. See Axt 2018 and Sears 2004.

4. Past theme semesters include Sport in the University (Fall 2014), Transla-
tion (Fall 2012), Water (Winter 2011), and 100 Years Beyond Einstein (Fall 2005).
More information about the LS&A theme semesters can be found at: "Theme Semester," U-M College of LSA, accessed September 21, 2023, http://www.lsa.umich
.edu/themesemester/.

5. Many of the students I interviewed had graduated from a two-credit course,
Training in Intergroup Dialogue Facilitation, cosponsored by the Sociology and

Psychology departments. In addition to weekly class meetings, students were required to participate in a three-day retreat. They were also expected to enroll in a second class after completing this one. In short, through these multiple requirements, these students demonstrated commitment to the program's mission.

6. See Walsh's discussion of "practical politics" (2007, 7–8).

7. Developmental psychologists have also employed similar approaches. "Picture-story" indices are "story narratives in which the characters are described and portrayed (by drawings, photos, slides, or more recently, by videotapes) in contexts likely to evoke sadness, fear, or other emotions" (Eisenberg and Strayer 1990, 350; Eisenberg and Strayer 1987). They have been used to study outcomes such as preschoolers' prosocial behavior (Lennon, Eisenberg, and Carroll 1986).

8. I refer to this question as *Question 1*. In an effort to reduce question error and increase response variation, I also fielded an additional question, *Question 2*. The content of Question 2 differed slightly among the four scenarios. For example, respondents were asked if they liked, or would be friends with, the target of discrimination or occasionally with the white perpetrator of discrimination (in this case, reverse coded). As a practical matter, I find that this eight-item index performed very similarly to a shortened, four-item index that only used the responses from Question 1 (correlation 0.95 among whites, using the 2013 CCES, sample properties described in the appendix). All of the analyses present here, therefore, use this four-item index (that is, an index that combines four responses to Question 1), though the results are robust across specifications that use the eight-item racial sympathy index.

9. Consistent with the 2013 CCES, which was also hosted by YouGov, the 2016 YouGov sample was selected through a two-stage sampling scheme. YouGov initially interviewed 730 respondents, who were matched down to a sample of 600 to produce the final dataset.

10. The principal investigators had intended to field the survey earlier; however, it was delayed in response to the unprecedented "post-election environment . . . including lawsuits and protests" (Lorrie Frasure, Janelle Wong, Edward Vargas, Matt Bareto, personal communication, January 25, 2021).

11. The studies conducted on convenience samples, the 2013 and 2015 MTurk studies, are excluded from the chart because they were primarily qualitative.

12. With gratitude to Ashley Jardina (2019) for inspiring this excellent idea.

13. Consult the appendix for the racial resentment items.

14. That said, I find similar patterns for the other studies as well.

15. See Inglehart 1985.

16. The break between waves occurred from late October 2020 to February 2021.

17. Maria Cramer, "Confederate Flag an Unnerving Sight in Capitol," *New York Times*, January 9, 2021, https://www.nytimes.com/2021/01/09/us/politics/con federate-flag-capitol.html.

18. For context, in a two-wave MTurk survey with six to twelve weeks between

the waves, Piston (2018) finds that the correlations of sympathy for the poor is .73 and resentment of the rich is .69, which he suggests "speaks to the test-retest reliability of the measure." He also notes that the correlation between limited government items in Wave 1 and Wave 2 is .73.

19. I devote special attention to exploring the relationship between racial sympathy and racial resentment for a few reasons. First, scholars have occasionally consulted the "low end" of racial resentment to approximate racial sympathy (Engelhardt 2021b; Tesler and Sears 2010). Thus, it serves as an appropriate starting point. Second, although the low end of the racial resentment scale has mostly been neglected, scholars have written about the high end at length (for just a sampling of this work, see Carmines, Sniderman, and Easter 2011; Cullen, Butler, and Graham 2021; Davis and Wilson 2022; Feldman and Huddy 2005). Some of this work has called into question whether the racial resentment items represent racial attitudes specifically or instead nonracial conservatism more generally. For this reason, if racial sympathy is significantly associated with political outcomes even while accounting for racial resentment, it clears a formidable hurdle. I explore this point at length in chapters 5 and 6. Here, by including racial resentment in my models that predict political opinions, I subject my measure of sympathy to a stringent empirical test. That said, racial resentment is not the only valid measure of prejudice. Thus, where possible, I consult alternative measures of prejudice, such as negative stereotypes.

20. Cronbach's alpha (expressed sometimes as α) is a measure of internal consistency—that is, how closely related a set of items are to each other. Generally considered to be a measure of scale reliability or consistency, it is expressed with a value from 0 to 1. If answers are highly interrelated, we would observe a high Cronbach's alpha (>.7).

Chapter Four

1. However, see work (Jardina 2019; Kinder and Kiewiet 1981) on the limited influence of economic self-interest in shaping political preferences.

2. The results are robust to other "cut points" for high racial sympathy, such as using the midpoint of the scale (.5) to determine who is "high," as well as looking at those whites who score above .75 on the 0–1 scale.

3. This number dropped to 44 percent in 2012 (Pew Research Center 2012).

4. During the 2016 election, political commentary often referenced this phenomenon by mentioning the role of "economic anxiety." See Sides, Tesler, and Vavreck 2019, 172.

5. I will occasionally refer to these respondents as *racially sympathetic* in shorthand.

6. The reader will recall that a correlation is a statistical measure of the strength

of the relationship between the relative movement of two variables. Refer to the discussion of correlations and correlation coefficients in chapter 3.

7. See Kim Parker, "What's Behind the Growing Gap Between Men and Women in College Completion?" Pew Research Center, November 8, 2021, https://www.pewresearch.org/fact-tank/2021/11/08/whats-behind-the-growing-gap-between-men-and-women-in-college-completion/.

8. Interestingly, there were a nontrivial number (roughly 18%) of highly racially sympathetic white people who declined to provide their partisanship.

9. This is similar but not exactly equivalent to a secular identity. See Campell, Layman, and Green 2020, 22.

10. Campbell and colleagues suggest that this may create a rift within the Democratic Party because grassroots activists within the Democratic Party are "highly secular (and predominantly white), [however] the party also has a large contingent of Religionist activists (who are far more likely to be African Americans and Latinos). Not only do these two groups of activists have different worldviews, they often disagree on both policy and strategy" (2020, 20).

11. That said, see Yancey 1999 on the effects of attending a racially integrated church.

12. Of course, this is just Whipple's characterization. Some denominations were concerned about the potentially disruptive effects of emancipation, and certainly not all white churches were supportive of such efforts (see McPherson 1995).

13. See research by Hahrie Han in which she examines how an evangelical megachurch in Cincinnati mobilized hundreds of volunteers from its "racial reconciliation" program to support a ballot initiative for universal pre-K, a policy initiative that disproportionately serves Black youth. Katie Pearce, "Cincinnati Megachurch Offers a Model of Collective Action in Divided Times," John Hopkins University: Hub, January 10, 2020, https://hub.jhu.edu/2020/01/10/agora-faith-race-politics-999-em1-art0-politics/.

14. These include Alabama, Arkansas, Florida, Georgia, Louisiana, Mississippi, North Carolina, South Carolina, Tennessee, Texas, and Virginia.

15. Ordinary least squares (OLS) is a common technique for estimating coefficients of linear regression equations. It is the technique I use most frequently throughout the book and has been described as "the workhorse" of applied econometrics (Kleiber and Zeileis 2008).

16. The correlation of the gender sympathy index and racial sympathy index was .3 for the entire sample ($n = 1000$) and .28 for whites alone ($n = 751$). The correlation of these two indices was .31 for white women and .3 for white men.

17. This is referred to as *Women's Affirmative Action* in table 4.6.

18. In a separate analysis, I use the ANES question to examine the relationship between racial sympathy and support for policies that benefit gays and lesbians. These appear in appendix table 4.1 and demonstrate that racial sympathy is not significantly related to policies concerning sexual minorities.

19. My surveys did not have sufficient space to measure sympathy toward every marginalized group in American society. However, they did include multiple questions on many other types of policies. Extending the logic of the preceding section, I continue the discriminant validity analysis by taking up a wide range of policy areas in appendix tables 4.1 and 4.2. Since the racial sympathy index collects distress over Black misfortune, it is possible that those who experience sympathy in response to the vignettes might experience sympathy in response to any instance of misfortune. Instead, I find that in most cases, racial sympathy does not align with a white person's support for environmental or gun policies. Similarly, on the 2012 ANES and 2013 CCES, I find racial sympathy does not influence opinion on many policies involving immigrants, who are often racialized as "low-skilled Hispanic laborers" (Brader, Valentino, and Suhay 2008, 961). On the other hand, in more recent studies, I have found that racial sympathy is associated with support for more liberal immigration policies. Overall, these discriminant validity tests suggest a present but inconsistent relationship between racial sympathy and support for policies that serve other non-white groups. I explore this topic further in chapter 9.

20. In the 2020 YouGov study, the scale's three questions hang together well ($\alpha = .67$) and load onto a single factor. The individual question items are listed in the appendix.

21. The self-monitoring scale is also limited insofar as it tracks respondents' tendency to monitor to conform to *others'* expectations. It does not reflect whether respondents may be lying to *themselves* about their own attitudes. Thank you to Drew Engelhardt for this important point.

22. See Chudy, Piston, and Shipper 2013.

23. Perry Bacon Jr., "How Lots of White Democrats Ended Up at the Protests," *FiveThirtyEight*, June 2, 2020, https://fivethirtyeight.com/features/how-lots-of-white -democrats-ended-up-protesting-the-death-of-george-floyd/.

Chapter Five

1. Rakesh Kochhar, "Unemployment Rose Higher in Three Months of COVID-19 Than It Did in Two Years of the Great Recession," Pew Research Center, June 11, 2020, https://www.pewresearch.org/fact-tank/2020/06/11/unemployment -rose-higher-in-three-months-of-covid-19-than-it-did-in-two-years-of-the-great -recession/. Lindsay M. Monte and Daniel J. Perez-Lopez, "COVID-19 Pandemic Hit Black Households Harder Than White Households, Even When Pre-Pandemic Socio-Economic Disparities Are Taken into Account," United States Census Bureau, July 21, 2021, https://www.census.gov/library/stories/2021/07/how-pandemic -affected-black-and-white-households.html.

2. The reality is more complicated. For example, some research finds that even

though Black women earn more college degrees, this does not translate into equivalent gains at the household level (Reeves and Guyot 2017).

3. Heather Hartline-Grafton and Ellen Vollinger, "New USDA Report Provides Picture of Who Participates in SNAP," Food Research and Action Center, accessed September 22, 2023, https://frac.org/blog/new-usda-report-provides-picture-of-who-participates-in-snap.

4. More explanation of this statistical technique is provided in chapter 4. This chapter also includes further explanation of the model's independent variables. For all regression analyses in the book, variables coded are from 0 to 1, and all analyses consider self-identified white respondents only.

5. Assessments of limited government (or government size) is another way to conceptualize ideology.

6. These results are robust to a specification that uses self-reported ideology in place of limited government.

7. Some scholars have argued that the relationship and boundaries between racial resentment and individualism are especially unclear (Sniderman and Tetlock 1986). Still, Sears and Henry (2003) find that racial resentment is most strongly correlated with those measures of individualism that make specific reference to African Americans, providing evidence that racial resentment, like sympathy, is rooted primarily in race.

8. Other analyses demonstrate that this result is robust to other conceptualizations of animus, like negative stereotypes. See appendix.

9. As a reminder, the 2012 ANES, 2008 ANES, and 1994 GSS do not include the racial sympathy index but instead have a question about how often a respondent experiences sympathy toward Blacks. See chapter 3.

10. Note the overall levels of support are much higher in the 2020 YouGov than in the 2020 ANES. This likely reflects the highly educated nature of the sample. We would expect that, on a nationally representative probability sample like the ANES, we would find far lower levels of support for reparations than uncovered in the YouGov study. Craemer notes that population estimates on reparations policy "fail to converge and vary over a range of 32 percentage points" (2009, 275). He attributes these stark differences to "random error by a public largely uninformed about the issue (e.g., Converse 1964)" or as reflecting "complex and meaningful considerations about 'who' should be compensated 'by whom' in 'what form' and 'for what' injustice" (2009, 276).

11. Though there are some differences depending on the type of reparation policy. On how framing and other factors can impact support on this policy area, see Craemer 2009.

12. See Darity Jr. and Mullen 2022 for a thorough discussion of reparations.

13. These experimental frames also appeared in the 1990 General Social Survey and have been used by Kinder and Sanders (1996) to examine the influence of negative racial stereotypes on policy opinion. It also resembles the experiment

conducted by Sidanius and colleagues, referenced in chapter 4 (Sidanius et al. 2000).

14. The results of these analyses are presented in appendix table 5.6.

15. NPR staff, "What Happens without Affirmative Action: The Story of UCLA," *NPR*, June 23, 2013, https://www.npr.org/2013/06/23/194656555/what -happens-without-affirmative-action-the-story-of-ucla.

16. For example, the child welfare system has separated many Black children from their families (Roberts 2022), and many of the "requirements" surrounding welfare eligibility, such as fingerprinting and drug testing, could be accurately described as "disciplining the poor" (Soss, Fording, and Schram 2011).

Chapter Six

1. Although police brutality against African Americans is not new, advances in cell phone technology have made it easier to document. I discuss technology more in the conclusion.

2. E. Ann Carson, "Prisoners in 2018," Bureau of Justice Statistics, accessed September 22, 2023, https://bjs.ojp.gov/content/pub/pdf/p18.pdf.

3. This effect was observed among "novices" but not those who had undergone training.

4. As with chapter 5, this result is robust to a model that includes collective guilt as a control measure.

5. Sean Illing, "The 'Abolish the Police' Movement, Explained by 7 Scholars and Activists," *Vox*, June 12, 2020, https://www.vox.com/policy-and-politics/2020 /6/12/21283813/george-floyd-blm-abolish-the-police-8cantwait-minneapolis.

6. This proposal failed in November 2021.

7. Hakeem Jefferson and I discuss this in a 2021 *New York Times* op-ed: "Support for Black Lives Matter Surged Last Year. Did It Last?" (Chudy and Jefferson 2021).

8. In chapter 5, I conduct robustness checks to ensure that the relationship between racial sympathy and public opinion endures in the presence of alternative hypotheses. I relied on the ANES and GSS for these analyses, as both surveys provide a host of important control variables. For the most part, however, they did not make queries about the criminal legal system in the years with the sympathy measure (1994 GSS, 2008 and 2012 ANES). In the two cases in which there were questions about decreasing police funding (1994 GSS and 2008 ANES), there was no relationship between racial sympathy and the policy item. It is possible that the relationship between racial sympathy and policing has intensified as high-profile police brutality cases have brought attention to the racial aspects of the criminal legal system. In the conclusion, I discuss how certain events may make sympathy more salient.

9. The experimental stimuli appear in the Web appendix.

10. These numbers roughly align with those reported in other national studies. A 2016 Pew study found that 45 percent of Americans thought the police did an "excellent" or "good" job in this domain. An additional 32 percent said the police were "only fair" at using the right amount of force for each situation (Pew Research Center 2020).

11. The profile format mirrored a manipulation that appeared in the 1986 GSS. For an example of this type of document, see "Neighborhoods: Mapping L.A.," *Los Angeles Times*, accessed September 22, 2023, http://maps.latimes.com/neighborhoods. The experimental stimulus appears in the Web Appendix.

Chapter Seven

1. Although there is no prescribed size for how many interviews a researcher should conduct for a project, the general approach is to reach a threshold of conceptual "saturation" (Glaser and Strauss 1967), the point at which new interviews do not reveal significantly new content. By the end of May 2020, we had conducted twenty interviews, and it did not seem like additional interviews were yielding new insight. Our research team therefore decided to wind down our study. Then, after George Floyd's murder on May 25, 2020, we decided to suspend our interviews, as the tenor of white attitudes and the focus on race had changed so dramatically in such a short period of time. Accordingly, we thought it might be difficult to compare those interviews we had conducted before Floyd's murder with those that were conducted after.

2. As a college professor, I have found this confession to be both frequent and depressing.

3. This is not to say that stronger government influence will always be beneficial, as the preceding chapter on the criminal legal system makes clear. Accordingly, some have advocated for approaches to racial equality that focus on community-based self-determination efforts, such as CopWatch. CopWatch is an autonomous activist organization that monitors police activity on the streets to prevent police brutality. I discuss political participation in greater detail in the following chapter.

4. Some scholars have pushed this further, calling into question the value of studying self-reported behavior at all. To take one paper as an example, Rogers and Aida (2011) title a paper on self-reported voting "Why Bother Asking? The Limited Value of Self-Reported Vote Intention."

5. I present the first self-monitoring analysis in table 7.3 and the other two in the appendix.

6. This is consistent with work by Anna Mikkelborg (2023), which has found that white Democrats support Black politicians out of genuine concerns related to racial injustice.

7. In contrast to earlier analyses, racial sympathy is not significantly associated with opinion on affirmative action under the second and third approach, although the coefficients are in the correct direction.

8. Unless they majored in political science or public policy!

9. LaGina Gause and Maneesh Arora, "Not All of Last Year's Black Lives Matter Protesters Supported Black Lives Matter," *Washington Post*, July 2, 2021, https://www.washingtonpost.com/politics/2021/07/01/not-all-last-years-black-lives -matter-protesters-supported-black-lives-matter/.

Chapter Eight

1. This research has explored social movements as a broad category but also devoted attention to variation among distinct causes, including subgroup support within these causes (Clendinen and Nagourney 2001; Cohen 2020; Heaney 2022; Lock and Kaufert 1998; Munson 2009). Much of this work considers the microlevel impact of social movements, exploring how individuals are affected by their participation in these movements, but there are important macrolevel consequences as well (Amenta and Polletta 2019; Burstein and Linton 2002; Rochon and Mazmanian 1993). Further, scholars do debate the effectiveness of social movements. See, for example, Giugni, McAdam, and Tilly 1999; Meyer 2004; Tilly, Castañeda, and Wood 2019. The broad scope of the social movement literature, which considers social movements all over the world throughout different historical periods, may contribute to this contestation; with so many iterations of social movements across time and place, it may be difficult to draw global conclusions on their effectiveness.

2. Throughout the years, scholars have introduced modifications to these questions on the ANES. In 2008, an alternate version of these questions (referred to as "Version D") included the following changes: "How often do politics and government seem so complicated, that you can't really understand what's going on? All the time, most of the time, about half the time, some of the time, or never?" and "How well do you understand the important political issues facing our country? Extremely well, very well, moderately well, slightly well, or not well at all?" When the two questions from Version C are combined into an additive index, the weighted mean among white Americans is .51. When the two questions from Version D are combined into an additive index, the weighted mean among white Americans is .50. Since these two averages are not significantly distinct from each other, they are combined into a single index of internal efficacy.

3. This reflects a broader dissatisfaction with the efficacy measures and their interpretation. Scholars of efficacy note that the concept is notoriously difficult to operationalize and "analysts have never been fully satisfied with its measurement" (Niemi, Craig, and Mattei 1991, 1407).

4. Here, racial sympathy scores are captured by the single-item ANES question. According to participation research, the traditional determinants of participation include demographics, years in residence, interest in politics, contact from one of the major parties, and perceptions of election closeness. The ANES analyses include all of these variables in the model.

5. For further precision, in 2008, I only consider activities that respondents undertook "in the last 12 months," confining the participation period to the election year. This option was not available in the 2012 ANES. However, here, subjects were asked if they participated in any of the activities "within the last four years," which would have extended throughout Obama's first term into his second election campaign.

6. These categories are frequently employed in participation research, but they may not be exhaustive, complete, or appropriately titled. See Ekman and Amnå 2012; Rosenstone and Hansen 1993; Teorell and Torcal 2007; and Verba, Schlozman, and Brady 1995 for thoughtful discussions of these analytic categories.

7. The Cronbach's alpha for the civic engagement index is .67 in the 2012 ANES and .78 in the 2008 ANES. The items differ slightly based on question availability. Refer to the appendix for full wording.

8. The alpha for this index is .66 in the 2008 ANES and .66 in the 2012 ANES.

9. To construct the charts, I use .375 as a cut point for "low efficacy" and .875 as a cut point for "high efficacy." These represented the twenty-fifth and seventy-fifth percentiles of efficacy on the 2008 ANES.

10. Almond and Verba, for instance, found the most frequent reason given for voting in the United States was that citizens received a sense of gratification from it (1963, 107–108).

11. See Remnick 2014.

12. Derrick Bryson Taylor, "George Floyd Protests: A Timeline," *New York Times*, November 5, 2021, https://www.nytimes.com/article/george-floyd-protests -timeline.html.

Chapter Nine

1. Rachel Treisman, "Darnella Frazier, Teen Who Filmed Floyd's Murder, Praised for Making Verdict Possible," *NPR*, April 21, 2021, https://www.npr.org /sections/trial-over-killing-of-george-floyd/2021/04/21/989480867/darnella-frazier -teen-who-filmed-floyds-murder-praised-for-making-verdict-possib.

2. For more information about Americans' cell phone usage, see "Mobile Fact Sheet," Pew Research Center, April 7, 2021, https://www.pewresearch.org/internet /fact-sheet/mobile/.

3. Allostatic load refers to the cumulative burden of chronic stress and life events. It involves the interaction of different physiological systems at varying

degrees of activity. When environmental challenges exceed the individual ability to cope, then allostatic overload ensues (Guidi et al. 2021).

4. These included voting, protesting, contacting elected officials, volunteering with organizations dedicated to Black equality, and supporting Black businesses. See Kiana Cox and Khadijah Edwards, "2. Black Americans' Views on Political Strategies, Leadership and Allyship for Achieving Equality," Pew Research Center, August 30, 2022, https://www.pewresearch.org/race-ethnicity/2022/08/30/black -americans-views-on-political-strategies-leadership-and-allyship-for-achieving-equality/.

5. Though see McGlone and colleagues' article "Stereotype Threat and the Gender Gap in Political Knowledge" (2006).

References

Aboud, Frances E., and Maria Amato. 2001. "Developmental and Socialization Influences on Intergroup Bias." In *Blackwell Handbook of Social Psychology: Intergroup Processes*, edited by Rupert Brown and Sam Gaertner. Hoboken, NJ: Wiley-Blackwell.

Aboud, Frances E., and Virginia Fenwick. 1999. "Exploring and Evaluating School-Based Interventions to Reduce Prejudice." *Journal of Social Issues* 55 (4): 767–785.

Abrajano, Marisa, and Zoltan L. Hajnal. 2015. "White Backlash." In *White Backlash: Immigration Race, and American Politics*. Princeton, NJ: Princeton University Press.

Abramson, Paul R. 1972. "Political Efficacy and Political Trust Among Black Schoolchildren: Two Explanations." *Journal of Politics* 34 (4): 1243–1275.

Abramson, Paul R., and John H. Aldrich. 1982. "The Decline of Electoral Participation in America." *American Political Science Review* 76 (3): 502–521.

Achen, Christopher, and André Blais. 2010. *Intention to Vote, Reported Vote, and Validated Vote*. American Political Science Association Annual Meeting Paper. Accessed November 22, 2021, https://papers.ssrn.com/abstract=1642497.

Adler, Jeffrey S. 2001. *African-American Mayors: Race, Politics, and the American City*. Champaign: University of Illinois Press.

Adorno, Theodor W., Elise Frankel-Brunswik, Daniel J. Levinson, and R. Nevitt Sanford. 1950. *The Authoritarian Personality*. New York: Harper and Row.

Agadjanian, Alexander, John Michael Carey, Yusaku Horiuchi, and Timothy J. Ryan. 2023. "Disfavor or Favor? Assessing the Valence of White Americans' Racial Attitudes." *Quarterly Journal of Political Science* 18 (1): 75–103.

Akesson, Jesper, Robert W. Hahn, Robert D. Metcalfe, and Itzhak Rasooly. 2022. "Race and Redistribution in the United States: An Experimental Analysis." *National Bureau of Economic Research* (working paper, September 5, 2022). https://www.nber.org/papers/w30426.

Alang, Sirry, Donna McAlpine, Ellen McCreedy, and Rachel Hardeman. 2017. "Police Brutality and Black Health: Setting the Agenda for Public Health

Scholars." *American Journal of Public Health* 107 (5): 662–665. https://doi.org/10.2105/AJPH.2017.303691.

Aldrich, John H., and Kathleen M. McGraw, eds. 2011. *Improving Public Opinion Surveys: Interdisciplinary Innovation and the American National Election Studies*. Princeton, NJ: Princeton University Press. Accessed May 17, 2022. https://princeton.universitypressscholarship.com/10.23943/princeton/9780691151458.001.0001/upso-9780691151458.

Alexander, Michelle. 2020. *The New Jim Crow: Mass Incarceration in the Age of Colorblindness*. New York: New Press.

Allard, Scott W. 2008. *Out of Reach: Place, Poverty, and the New American Welfare State*. New Haven, CT: Yale University Press.

Allport, Gordon. 1954. *The Nature of Prejudice*. Boston: Addison-Wesley.

Almond, Gabriel, and Sidney Verba. 1963. *The Civic Culture: Political Attitudes and Democracy in Five Countries*. Princeton, NJ: Princeton University Press.

Altemeyer, Bob. 1998. "The Other 'Authoritarian Personality.'" In *Advances in Experimental Social Psychology*, edited by L. Berkowitz, 47–92. Orlando, FL: Academic Press.

Amenta, Edwin, and Francesca Polletta. 2019. "The Cultural Impacts of Social Movements." *Annual Review of Sociology* 45: 279–299.

Anoll, Allison P., Andrew M. Engelhardt, and Mackenzie Israel-Trummel. 2022. "Black Lives, White Kids: White Parenting Practices Following Black-Led Protests." *Perspectives on Politics* 20 (4): 1–18. https://doi.org/10.1017/S153759272200105.0

Ansolabehere, Stephen, and Douglas Rivers. 2013. "Cooperative Survey Research." *Annual Review of Political Science* 16: 307–329.

Aoki, Keith. 1996. "Foreign-Ness and Asian American Identities: Yellowface, World War II Propaganda, and Bifurcated Racial Stereotypes." *UCLA Asian Pacific American Law Journal* 4: 1–72.

Apfelbaum, Evan P., Kristin Pauker, Nalini Ambady, Samuel R. Sommers, and Michael I. Norton. "Learning (Not) to Talk about Race: When Older Children Underperform in Social Categorization." *Developmental Psychology* 44 (5): 1513–1518. https://doi.org/10.1037/a0012835.

Aronson, Elliot, and Phoebe C. Ellsworth. 1990. *Methods of Research in Social Psychology*. New York: McGraw-Hill.

Aronson, Joshua, Michael J. Lustina, Catherine Godd, Kelli Keough, Claude M. Steele, and Joseph Brown. 1999. "When White Men Can't Do Math: Necessary and Sufficient Factors in Stereotype Threat." *Journal of Experimental Social Psychology* 35 (1): 29–46.

Arora, Maneesh. 2019. "Which Race Card? Understanding Racial Appeals in U.S. Politics." PhD diss., University of California, Irvine. ProQuest. Accessed November 22, 2021. https://www.proquest.com/docview/2302017929/abstract/808CC2D32A874F8DPQ/1.

Ashok, Vivekinan, Ilyana Kuziemko, and Ebonya Washington. 2015. "Support for Redistribution in an Age of Rising Inequality: New Stylized Facts and Some Tentative Explanations." Brookings Institution. Accessed August 16, 2022. https://www.brookings.edu/articles/support-for-redistribution-in-an-age-of-rising-inequality-new-stylized-facts-and-some-tentative-explanations/.

Axt, Jordan R. 2018. "The Best Way to Measure Explicit Racial Attitudes Is to Ask about Them." *Social Psychological and Personality Science* 9 (8): 896–906. https://doi.org/10.1177/1948550617728995.

Baker, Andy. 2015. "Race, Paternalism, and Foreign Aid: Evidence from U.S. Public Opinion." *American Political Science Review* 109 (1): 93–109.

Baker, Joseph O., and Buster G. Smith. 2009. "The Nones: Social Characteristics of the Religiously Unaffiliated." *Social Forces* 87 (3): 1251–1263.

Bandura, Albert. 1977. "Self-Efficacy: Toward a Unifying Theory of Behavioral Change." *Psychological Review* 84 (2): 191–215.

Banks, Antoine J. 2014. *Anger and Racial Politics: The Emotional Foundation of Racial Attitudes in America.* New York: Cambridge University Press.

Banks, Antoine J., and Nicholas A. Valentino. 2012. "Emotional Substrates of White Racial Attitudes." *American Journal of Political Science* 56 (2): 286–297.

Barber, Michael J., Brandice Canes-Wrone, and Sharece Thrower. 2017. "Ideologically Sophisticated Donors: Which Candidates Do Individual Contributors Finance?" *American Journal of Political Science* 61 (2): 271–288.

Baron-Cohen, Simon, Sally Wheelwright, Jacqueline Hill, Yogini Raste, and Ian Plumb. 2001. "The 'Reading the Mind in the Eyes' Test Revised Version: A Study with Normal Adults, and Adults with Asperger Syndrome or High-functioning Autism." *Journal of Child Psychology and Psychiatry and Allied Disciplines* 42 (2): 241–251.

Barrett, Lisa Feldman. 2006. "Solving the Emotion Paradox: Categorization and the Experience of Emotion." *Personality and Social Psychology Review* 10 (1): 20–46.

———. 2017. *How Emotions Are Made: The Secret Life of the Brain.* New York: HarperCollins.

Barry, Brian. 2010. *Political Argument (Routledge Revivals).* London, UK: Routledge.

Batson, C. Daniel. 1987. "Prosocial Motivation: Is It Ever Truly Altruistic?" In *Advances in Experimental Social Psychology*, edited by L. Berkowitz, 65–122. New York: Academic Press.

———. 2011. *Altruism in Humans.* New York: Cambridge University Press.

Benford, Robert D., and David A. Snow. 2000. "Framing Processes and Social Movements: An Overview and Assessment." *Annual Review of Sociology* 26 (1): 611–639.

Bergeman, Cindy S., Heather M. Chlpuer, Robert Plomin, Nancy L. Pedersen, Gerald E. McClearn, John R. Nesselroade, Paul T. Costa, and Robert R. McCrae. 1993. "Genetic and Environmental Effects on Openness to Experience,

Agreeableness, and Conscientiousness: An Adoption/Twin Study." *Journal of Personality* 61 (2): 159–179. https://doi.org/10.1111/j.1467-6494.1993.tb01030.x.

Berinsky, Adam J., Gregory A. Huber, and Gabriel S. Lenz. 2012. "Evaluating Online Labor Markets for Experimental Research: Amazon.com's Mechanical Turk." *Political Analysis* 20 (3): 351–368.

Berinsky, Adam J., and Howard Lavine. 2012. "Self-Monitoring and Political Attitudes." In *Improving Public Opinion Surveys*, edited by John Aldrich and Kathleen M. McGraw, 27–45. Princeton, NJ: Princeton University Press.

Berinsky, Adam J., and Gabriel S. Lenz. 2011. "Education and Political Participation: Exploring the Causal Link." *Political Behavior* 33 (3): 357–373.

Bigler, Rebecca S. 1999. "The Use of Multicultural Curricula and Materials to Counter Racism in Children." *Social Issues* 55 (4): 687–705.

Black Lives Matter. n.d. "About." Accessed February 3, 2023. https://blacklivesmatter.com/about/.

Blank, Rebecca M., Constance F. Citro, and Marilyn Dabady. 2004. *Measuring Racial Discrimination.* Washington, DC: National Academies.

Bleemer, Zachary. 2022. "Affirmative Action, Mismatch, and Economic Mobility after California's Proposition 209." *Quarterly Journal of Economics* 137 (1): 115–160.

Blumer, Herbert. 1958. "Race Prejudice as a Sense of Group Position." *Pacific Sociological Review* 1 (1): 3–7.

Bobo, Lawrence. 1991. "Social Responsibility, Individualism, and Redistributive Policies." *Sociological Forum* 6 (1): 71–92.

Bobo, Lawrence, and Franklin D. Gilliam. 1990. "Race, Sociopolitical Participation, and Black Empowerment." *American Political Science Review* 84 (2): 377–393.

Bobo, Lawrence, and Vincent L. Hutchings. 1996. "Perceptions of Racial Group Competition: Extending Blumer's Theory of Group Position to a Multiracial Social Context." *American Sociological Review* 61 (6): 951–972.

Bobo, Lawrence, and Frederick C. Licari. 1989. "Education and Political Tolerance: Testing the Effects of Cognitive Sophistication and Target Group Affect." *The Public Opinion Quarterly* 53 (3): 285–308.

Boden, Matthew Tyler, and Renee J. Thompson. 2015. "Facets of Emotional Awareness and Associations with Emotion Regulation and Depression." *Emotion* 15 (1): 399–410.

Bonilla, Tabitha, and Alvin B. Tillery. 2020. "Which Identity Frames Boost Support for and Mobilization in the #BlackLivesMatter Movement? An Experimental Test." *American Political Science Review* 114 (4): 947–962.

Bonilla, Yarimar, and Jonathan Rosa. 2015. "#Ferguson: Digital Protest, Hashtag Ethnography, and the Racial Politics of Social Media in the United States." *American Ethnologist* 42 (1): 4–17.

Brader, Ted, Nicholas A. Valentino, and Elizabeth Suhay. 2008. "What Triggers

Public Opposition to Immigration? Anxiety, Group Cues, and Immigration Threat" *American Journal of Political Science* 52 (4): 959–978.

Brewer, Marilynn B. 1999. "The Psychology of Prejudice: In-Group Love or Out-Group Hate?" *Journal of Social Issues* 55 (3): 429–444.

Brown, Cynthia Stokes. 2002. *Refusing Racism: White Allies and the Struggle for Civil Rights*. New York: Teachers College Press.

Brunson, Rod K. 2007. "'Police Don't Like Black People': African-American Young Men's Accumulated Police Experiences." *Criminology and Public Policy* 6 (1): 71–101.

Burns, Nancy, Ashley E. Jardina, Donald Kinder, and Molly E. Reynolds. 2016. "The Politics of Gender." In *New Directions in Public Opinion*, 2nd ed., edited by Adam J. Berinsky, 231–258. New York: Routledge.

Burstein, Paul. 1994. *Equal Employment Opportunity: Labor Market Discrimination and Public Policy*. 1st ed. Sociology and Economics Series. Milton: Routledge.

Burstein, Paul, and April Linton. 2002. "The Impact of Political Parties, Interest Groups, and Social Movement Organizations on Public Policy: Some Recent Evidence and Theoretical Concerns." *Social Forces* 81 (2): 380–408.

Bynum, Tara A. 2023. *Reading Pleasures: Everyday Black Living in Early America*. The New Black Studies Series. Champaign: University of Illinois Press.

Campbell, Angus. 1971. *White Attitudes Toward Black People*. Ann Arbor, MI: ISR Press.

Campbell, Angus, and Philip E. Converse. 1972. *The Human Meaning of Social Change*. New York: Russell Sage Foundation.

Campbell, Angus, Philip E. Converse, Warren E. Miller, and Donald E. Stokes. 1960. *The American Voter*. New York: J. Wiley.

Campbell, Angus, Gerald Gurin, and W. E. Miller. 1954. *The Voter Decides*. Oxford: Row, Peterson.

Campbell, David E., and Geoffrey C. Layman. 2016. "A Jump to the Right, A Step to the Left: Religion and Public Opinion." In *New Directions in Public Opinion*, 2nd ed., edited by Adam J. Berinsky, 231–258. New York: Routledge.

Campbell, David E., Geoffrey C. Layman, and John C. Green. 2021. *Secular Surge: A New Fault Line in American Politics*. New York: Cambridge University Press.

Campbell, Donald, and Donald W. Fiske. 1959. "Convergent and Discriminant Validation by the Multitrait-Multimethod Matrix." *Psychological Bulletin* 56 (2): 81–105.

Caren, Neal, Raj Andrew Ghoshal, and Vanesa Ribas. 2011. "A Social Movement Generation: Cohort and Period Trends in Protest Attendance and Petition Signing." *American Sociological Review* 76 (1): 125–151.

Carmines, Edward G., Paul M. Sniderman, and Beth C. Easter. 2011. "On the Meaning, Measurement, and Implications of Racial Resentment." *Annals of the American Academy of Political and Social Science* 634 (1): 98–116.

Carmines, Edward G., and James A. Stimson. 1989. *Issue Evolution: Race and the Transformation of American Politics*. Princeton, NJ: Princeton University Press.

Carter Jackson, Kellie. 2021. "Hollywood Has Finally Deemed Black Women Worthy of Feel-Good TV." *New York Times*, May 16, 2021. https://www.nytimes.com/2021/05/16/opinion/culture/Run-the-World-Black-Women-TV.html.

———. 2024. *We Refuse: A Forceful History of Black Resistance*. New York: Basic Books.

Castano, Emanuele, and Roger Giner-Sorolla. 2006. "Not Quite Human: Infrahumanization in Response to Collective Responsibility for Intergroup Killing." *Journal of Personality and Social Psychology* 90 (5): 804–818.

Castiglia, Christopher. 2002. "Abolition's Racial Interiors and the Making of White Civic Depth." *American Literary History* 14 (1): 32–59.

Cepuran, Colin J. G., and Justin Berry. 2022. "Whites' Racial Resentment and Perceived Relative Discrimination Interactively Predict Participation." *Political Behavior*. Accessed March 25, 2022. https://doi.org/10.1007/s11109-022-09786-2.

Chamberlain, Adam. 2013. "The (Dis)Connection Between Political Culture and External Efficacy." *American Politics Research* 41 (5): 761–782.

Chudy, Jennifer. 2021. "Racial Sympathy and Its Political Consequences." *Journal of Politics* 83 (1): 122–136.

Chudy, Jennifer, and Hakeem Jefferson. 2021. "Support for Black Lives Matter Surged Last Year. Did It Last?" *New York Times*. May 22, 2021. https://www.nytimes.com/2021/05/22/opinion/blm-movement-protests-support.html.

Chudy, Jennifer, Spencer Piston, and Joshua Shipper. 2013. "The Political Consequences of Two Pro-Black Attitudes: Racial Sympathy and Guilt." Paper presented at the Midwest Political Science Association Annual Meeting, April 11–14, 2013.

———. 2019. "Guilt by Association: White Collective Guilt in American Politics." *Journal of Politics* 81 (3): 968–981.

Cillizza, Chris, and Aaron Blake. 2012. "President Obama and the Misunderstood Youth Vote." *Washington Post*, April 24, 2012. https://www.washingtonpost.com/blogs/the-fix/post/president-obama-and-the-misunderstood-youth-vote/2012/04/23/gIQAuGIQdT_blog.html.

Citrin, Jack, Donald P. Green, and David O. Sears. 1990. "White Reactions to Black Candidates: When Does Race Matter?" *Public Opinion Quarterly* 54 (1): 74–96.

Clark, Candace. 1997. *Misery and Company: Sympathy in Everyday Life*. Chicago: University of Chicago Press.

Clark, D. Anthony Tyeeme. 2005. "Indigenous Voice and Vision as Commodity in a Mass-Consumption Society: The Colonial Politics of Public Opinion Polling." *American Indian Quarterly* 29 (1/2): 228–238.

Clark, Kenneth B., and Mamie K. Clark. 1939. "The Development of Consciousness of Self and the Emergence of Racial Identification in Negro Preschool Children." *Journal of Social Psychology* 4 (1): 591–599.

Clendinen, Dudley, and Adam Nagourney. 2001. *Out For Good: The Struggle to Build a Gay Rights Movement in America*. New York: Simon and Schuster.

Cobb, Jelani. 2016. "The Matter of Black Lives." *New Yorker*, March 6, 2016. http://www.newyorker.com/magazine/2016/03/14/where-is-black-lives-matter-headed.

Cohen, Cathy J. 2010. *Democracy Remixed: Black Youth and the Future of American Politics*. New York: Oxford University Press.

———. 2020. "Punks, Bulldaggers, and Welfare Queens: The Radical Potential of Queer Politics?" In *Feminist Theory Reader*, edited by Carole McCann, Seung-kyung Kim, and Emek Ergun. 311–323. New York: Routledge.

Cole, Geneva. 2020. "Types of White Identification and Attitudes About Black Lives Matter." *Social Science Quarterly* 101 (4): 1627–1633.

Conover, Pamela Johnston. 1988. "The Role of Social Groups in Political Thinking." *British Journal of Political Science* 18 (1): 51–76.

Conover, Pamela Johnston, and Stanley Feldman. 1981. "The Origins and Meaning of Liberal/Conservative Self-Identifications." *American Journal of Political Science* 25 (4): 617–645.

Converse, Jean M., and Stanley Presser. 1986. *Survey Questions: Handcrafting the Standardized Questionnaire*. Beverly Hills, CA: SAGE.

Converse, Philip E. 1964. "The Nature of Belief Systems in Mass Publics." In *Ideology and Discontent*, edited by David E. Apter, 206–261. New York: Free Press.

Corral, Álvaro J. 2020. "Allies, Antagonists, or Ambivalent? Exploring Latino Attitudes about the Black Lives Matter Movement." *Hispanic Journal of Behavioral Sciences* 42 (4): 431–454.

Cousins, Linwood H. 2014. *Encyclopedia of Human Services and Diversity*. Thousand Oaks, CA: SAGE.

Craemer, Thomas. 2008. "Nonconscious Feelings of Closeness toward African Americans and Support for Pro-Black Policies." *Political Psychology* 29 (3): 407–436.

———. 2009. "Framing Reparations." *Policy Studies Journal* 37 (2): 275–298.

Craig, Stephen C., and Michael A. Maggiotto. 1982. "Measuring Political Efficacy." *Political Methodology* 8 (3): 85–109.

Cramer, Katherine J. 2021. "Deflecting from Racism: Local Talk Radio Conversations about the Murder of George Floyd." In *Unequal Democracies: Public Policy, Responsiveness, and Redistribution in an Era of Rising Economic Inequality*, edited by Noam Lupu. Princeton, NJ: Princeton University Press.

Cullen, Francis T., Leah C. Butler, and Amanda Graham. 2021. "Racial Attitudes and Criminal Justice Policy." *Crime and Justice* 50 (1): 163–245.

Cunningham, Vinson. 2020. "The Argument of 'AfroPessimism.'" *New Yorker*, July 13, 2020. https://www.newyorker.com/magazine/2020/07/20/the-argument-of-afropessimism.

Dahl, Robert A. 2003. *How Democratic Is the American Constitution?* 2nd ed. New Haven, CT: Yale University Press.

Darity Jr., William, and Dania Frank. 2003. "The Economics of Reparations." *American Economic Review* 93 (2): 326–329.

Darity Jr., William A., and A. Kirsten Mullen. 2022. *From Here to Equality: Reparations for Black Americans in the Twenty-First Century*. 2nd ed. Chapel Hill, NC: University of North Carolina Press.

Davenport, Christian. 2021. "A Call for Integral Violence Studies." *Annals of the American Academy of Political and Social Science* 694 (1): 32–38.

Davenport, Lauren D. 2018. *Politics beyond Black and White: Biracial Identity and Attitudes in America*. Cambridge: Cambridge University Press.

———. 2020. "The Fluidity of Racial Classifications." *Annual Review of Political Science* 23 (1): 221–240.

Davenport, Lauren, Annie Franco, and Shanto Iyengar. 2021. *Racial Resentment in the Political Mind*. Chicago: University of Chicago Press.

———. 2022. "Multiracial Identity and Political Preferences." *Journal of Politics* 84 (1): 620–624.

Davis, Darren W., and David C. Wilson. 2022. "The Prospect of Antiracism: Racial Resentment and Resistance to Change." *Public Opinion Quarterly* 86 (S1): 445–472.

Dawson, Michael C., and Rovana Popoff. 2004. "Reparations: Justice and Greed in Black and White." *Du Bois Review: Social Science Research on Race* 1 (1): 47–91.

DellaPosta, Daniel, Yongren Shi, and Michael Macy. 2015. "Why Do Liberals Drink Lattes?" *American Journal of Sociology* 120 (5): 1473–1511.

DeSante, Christopher D., and Candis Watts Smith. 2020. *Racial Stasis*. Chicago: University of Chicago Press.

Deterding, Nicole M., and Mary C. Waters. 2018. "Flexible Coding of In-Depth Interviews: A Twenty-First-Century Approach." *Sociological Methods and Research* 50 (2): 1–32.

Ditonto, Tessa M., Richard R. Lau, and David O. Sears. 2013. "AMPing Racial Attitudes: Comparing the Power of Explicit and Implicit Racism Measures in 2008." *Political Psychology* 34 (4): 487–510.

Doan, Long, and Natasha Quadlin. 2019. "Partner Characteristics and Perceptions of Responsibility for Housework and Child Care." *Journal of Marriage and Family* 81 (1): 145–163.

Doble, John, and Andrew L. Yarrow. 2007. *Walking a Mile: A First Step Toward Mutual Understanding*. Washington, DC: Public Agenda.

Doosje, Bertjan, Nyla R. Branscombe, Russell Spears, and Antony S. R. Manstead. 1998. "Guilty by Association: When One's Group Has a Negative History." *Journal of Personality and Social Psychology* 75 (4): 872–886.

Dovidio, John F., Jennifer K. Smith, Amy Gershenfeld Donnella, and Samuel L. Gaertner. 1997. "Racial Attitudes and the Death Penalty." *Journal of Applied Social Psychology* 27 (16): 1468–1487.

Dunn, Judy, Inge Bretherton, and Penny Munn. 1987. "Conversations about Feeling States between Mothers and Their Young Children." *Developmental Psychology* 23 (1): 132–139.

Duru, O. Kenrik, Nina T. Harawa, Dulcie Kermah, and Keith C. Norris. 2012. "Allostatic Load Burden and Racial Disparities in Mortality." *Journal of the National Medical Association* 104 (1): 89–95.

Eagly, Alice H., and Shelly Chaiken. 1993. The Psychology of Attitudes. Fort Worth, TX: Harcourt Brace

Eagly, Alice H., Amanda B. Diekman, Mary C. Johannesen-Schmidt, and Anne M. Koenig. 2004. "Gender Gaps in Sociopolitical Attitudes: A Social Psychological Analysis." *Journal of Personality and Social Psychology* 87 (6): 796–816.

Edsall, Thomas B. 2018. "The Democrats' Left Turn Is Not an Illusion." *New York Times*, October 18, 2018. https://www.nytimes.com/2018/10/18/opinion/democrat-electorate-left-turn.html.

———. 2021. "One Thing We Can Agree On Is That We're Becoming a Different Country." *New York Times*, September 8, 2021. https://www.nytimes.com/2021/09/08/opinion/us-elites-populism.html.

Eisenberg, Nancy, Richard A. Fabes, Mark Schaller, and Paul A. Miller. 1989. "Sympathy and Personal Distress: Development, Gender Differences, and Interrelations of Indexes." *New Directions for Child and Adolescent Development* 1989 (44): 107–126.

Eisenberg, Nancy, and Janet Strayer. 1990. *Empathy and Its Development*. New York: Cambridge University Press.

Ekehammar, Bo, Nazar Akrami, Magnus Gylije, and Ingrid Zakrisson. 2004. "What Matters Most to Prejudice: Big Five Personality, Social Dominance Orientation, or Right-Wing Authoritarianism?" *European Journal of Personality* 18 (6): 463–482.

Ekman, Joakim, and Erik Amnå. 2012. "Political Participation and Civic Engagement: Towards a New Typology." *Human Affairs* 22 (3): 283–300.

Elbeshbishi, Sarah, and Mabinty Quarshie. 2021. "Fewer Than 1 in 5 Support 'Defund the Police' Movement, USA TODAY/Ipsos Poll Finds." *USA Today*, March 7, 2021. https://www.usatoday.com/story/news/politics/2021/03/07/usa-today-ipsos-poll-just-18-support-defund-police-movement/4599232001/.

Engelhardt, Andrew M. 2019. "Trumped by Race: Explanations for Race's Influence on Whites' Votes in 2016." *Quarterly Journal of Political Science* 14 (3): 313–328.

———. 2021a. "Generational Persistence in the Nature of White Racial Attitudes." *Public Opinion Quarterly* 85 (3): 887–899.

———. 2021b. "Observational Equivalence in Explaining Attitude Change: Have White Racial Attitudes Genuinely Changed?" *American Journal of Political Science* 67 (2). Accessed January 27, 2022. https://onlinelibrary.wiley.com/doi/abs/10.1111/ajps.12665.

———. 2021c. "The Content of Their Coverage: Contrasting Racially Conservative and Liberal Elite Rhetoric." *Politics, Groups, and Identities* 9 (5): 935–954.

Epp, Charles R., Steven Maynard-Moody, and Donald P. Haider-Markel. 2016. "Building the Policing State." Presented at the Conference on Police Actions and Citizen Mobilization in Democratic Societies, Yale University, New Haven, CT, April 22.

Erikson, Robert S., Michael B. MacKuen, and James A. Stimson. 2002. *The Macro Polity*. New York: Cambridge University Press.

Erikson, Robert S., and Kent L. Tedin. 2004. *American Public Opinion: Its Origin, Contents, and Impact*. 7th ed., update. New York: Pearson Longman.

Fagan, Jeffrey, Valerie West, and Jan Holland. 2004. "Neighborhood, Crime, and Incarceration in New York City." *Columbia Human Rights Law Review* 36 (1): 72–106.

Fägersten, Kristy Beers. 2012. *Who's Swearing Now? The Social Aspects of Conversational Swearing*. Newcastle upon Tyne, UK: Cambridge Scholars Publishing.

Fazio, Russell H., and Mark P. Zanna. 1981. "Direct Experience and Attitude-Behavior Consistency." In *Advances in Experimental Social Psychology*, edited by Leonard Berkowitz, 161–202. Cambridge, MA: Academic Press. Accessed August 29, 2022. https://www.sciencedirect.com/science/article/pii/S00 6526010860372X.

Feagin, Joe R., ed. 2013. *Systemic Racism: A Theory of Oppression*. New York: Routledge.

Feinberg, Ayal. 2020. "Explaining Ethnoreligious Minority Targeting: Variation in U.S. Anti-Semitic Incidents." *Perspective on Politics* 18 (3): 770–787.

Feldman, Stanley. 1988. "Structure and Consistency in Public Opinion: The Role of Core Beliefs and Values." *American Journal of Political Science* 32 (2): 416–440.

Feldman, Stanley, and Leonie Huddy. 2005. "Racial Resentment and White Opposition to Race-Conscious Programs: Principles or Prejudice?" *American Journal of Political Science* 49 (1): 168–183.

Feldman, Stanley, Leonie Huddy, Julie Wronski, and Patrick Lown. 2020. "The Interplay of Empathy and Individualism in Support for Social Welfare Policies." *Political Psychology* 41 (2): 343–362.

Feldman, Stanley, and Marco R. Steenbergen. 2001. "The Humanitarian Foundation of Public Support for Social Welfare." *American Journal of Political Science* 45 (3): 658–677.

Fiffer, Steve, and Adar Cohen. 2015. *Jimmie Lee & James: Two Lives, Two Deaths, and the Movement that Changed America*. New York: Simon and Schuster.

Finkel, Steven E. 1985. "Reciprocal Effects of Participation and Political Efficacy: A Panel Analysis." *American Journal of Political Science* 29 (4): 891–913.

Fording, Richard C., and Joseph L. Smith. 2012. "Barack Obama's 'Fight' to End Poverty: Rhetoric and Reality." *Social Science Quarterly* 95 (3): 1161–1184.

Forman, James, Jr. 2004. "Community Policing and Youth as Assets." *Journal of Criminal Law and Criminology* 95 (1): 1–48.

———. 2012. "Racial Critiques of Mass Incarceration: Beyond the New Jim Crow." *New York University Law Review* 87 (1): 21–69.

Forman, Tyrone A., and Amanda E. Lewis. 2006. "Racial Apathy and Hurricane Katrina: The Social Anatomy of Prejudice in the Post-Civil Rights Era." *Du Bois Review* 3 (1): 175–202.

Fowler, James H., and Christopher T. Dawes. 2008. "Two Genes Predict Voter Turnout." *Journal of Politics* 70 (3): 579–594.

Fraga, Bernard L. 2018. *The Turnout Gap: Race, Ethnicity, and Political Inequality in a Diversifying America*. New York: Cambridge University Press.

Framke, Caroline. 2020. "Why Posting Black Boxes for #BlackoutTuesday, or Hashtags Without Action, Is Useless." *Variety*, June 2, 2020. https://variety.com /2020/tv/columns/blackout-tuesday-instagram-blacklivesmatter-1234623358/.

Franzese, Robert, and Cindy Kam. 2009. *Modeling and Interpreting Interactive Hypotheses in Regression Analysis*. Ann Arbor: University of Michigan Press.

Frasure, Lorrie, Janelle Wong, and Edward D. Vargas. 2021. *The 2020 Collaborative Multiracial Post-election Survey (CMPS)*. Ann Arbor, MI: Inter-university Consortium for Political and Social Research.

Freedman, Paul, Michael Franz, and Kenneth Goldstein. 2004. "Campaign Advertising and Democratic Citizenship." *American Journal of Political Science* 48 (4): 723–741.

Funk, Carolyn L. 2000. "The Dual Influence of Self-Interest and Societal Interest in Public Opinion." *Political Research Quarterly* 53 (1): 37–62.

Furoto, Sharlene B. C. L., and David M. Furoto. 1983. "The Effects of Affective and Cognitive Treatment on Attitude Change toward Ethnic Minority Groups." *International Journal of Intercultural Relations* 7 (2): 149–165.

Gamson, William A. 1975. *The Strategy of Social Protest*. Homewood, IL: Dorsey Press.

Gamson, William A., and Andre Modigliani. 1987. "The Changing Culture of Affirmative Action." *Research in Political Sociology* 3 (1): 137–177.

Gangestad, Steven W., and Mark Snyder. 2000. "Self-Monitoring: Appraisal and Reappraisal." *Psychological Bulletin* 126 (4): 530–555.

Garland, David. 2001. "Introduction: The Meaning of Mass Imprisonment." *Punishment and Society* 3 (1): 5–7.

Gause, LaGina. 2020. "Revealing Issue Salience via Costly Protest: How Legislative Behavior Following Protest Advantages Low-Resource Groups." *British Journal of Political Science* 52 (1): 1–21.

Gay, Claudine. 2001. "The Effect of Black Congressional Representation on Political Participation." *American Political Science Review* 95 (3): 589–602.

Gibson, James L., and Amanda Gouws. 1999. "Social Identities and Political Intolerance: Linkages within the South African Mass Public." *American Journal of Political Science* 44 (2): 278–292.

Gilens, Martin. 1999. *Why Americans Hate Welfare*. Chicago: University of Chicago Press.

Gilliam, Franklin D., and Shanto Iyengaro. 2000. "Prime Suspects: The Influence of Local Television News on the Viewing Public." *American Journal of Political Science* 44 (3): 560–573.

Gilligan, Carol, and Jane Attanucci. 1988. "Two Moral Orientations: Gender Differences and Similarities." *Merrill-Palmer Quarterly* 34 (3): 223–237.

Giugni, Marco, Doug McAdam, and Charles Tilly. 1999. *How Social Movements Matter*. Minneapolis: University of Minnesota Press.

Glaser, Barney G., and Anselm L. Strauss. 1967. *The Discovery of Grounded Theory*. Chicago: Aldine Publishing.

Glasford, Demis E., Felicia Pratto, and John F. Dovidio. 2014. "When Extraordinary Injustice Leads to Ordinary Response: How Perpetrator Power and Size of an Injustice Event Affect Bystander Efficacy and Collective Action." *European Journal of Social Psychology* 44 (6): 590–601.

Glick, Peter, and Susan T. Fiske. 1996. "The Ambivalent Sexism Inventory: Differentiating Hostile and Benevolent Sexism." *Journal of Personality and Social Psychology* 70 (3): 491–512.

Goldberg, Lewis R. 1999. "A Broad-Bandwidth, Public Domain, Personality Inventory Measuring the Lower-Level Facets of Several Five-Factor Models." *Personality Psychology in Europe* 7: 7–28.

Goldin, Claudia. 2006. "The Quiet Revolution That Transformed Women's Employment, Education, and Family." *American Economic Review* 96 (2): 1–21.

Goldstein, Carole G., Elizabeth J. Koopman, and Harold H. Goldstein. 1979. "Racial Attitudes in Young Children as a Function of Interracial Contact in the Public Schools." *American Journal of Orthopsychiatry* 49 (1): 89–99.

Grant, Keneshia N. 2020. *The Great Migration and the Democratic Party*. Philadelphia, PA: Temple University Press.

Green, Donald P., Bradley Palmquist, and Eric Schickler. 2004. *Partisan Hearts and Minds: Political Parties and the Social Identities of Voters*. New Haven, CT: Yale University Press.

Griffin, Christine. 1992. "Fear of a Black (and Working-Class) Planet: Young Women and the Racialization of Reproductive Politics." *Feminism and Psychology* 2 (3): 491–494.

Guidi, Jenny, Marcella Lucente, Nicoletta Sonino, and Giovanni Fava. 2021. "Allostatic Load and Its Impact on Health: A Systematic Review." *Psychotherapy and Psychosomatics* 90 (1): 11–27.

Hajnal, Zoltan L. 2007. *Changing White Attitudes toward Black Political Leadership*. New York: Cambridge University Press.

Hamm, Jill V. 2001. "Barriers and Bridges to Positive Cross-Ethnic Relations: African American and White Parent Socialization Beliefs and Practices." *Youth and Society* 33 (1): 62–98.

Han, Hahrie. 2014. *How Organizations Develop Activists: Civic Associations and Leadership in the 21st Century*. New York: Oxford University Press.

Han, Hahrie, Elizabeth McKenna, and Michelle Oyakawa. 2021. *Prisms of the People: Power and Organizing in Twenty-First-Century America*. Chicago: University of Chicago Press.

Hannan, Kellie R., Francis T. Cullen, Leah C. Butler, Amanda Graham, Alexander L. Burton, and Velmer S. Burton Jr. 2021. "Racial Sympathy and Support for Capital Punishment: A Case Study in Concept Transfer." *Deviant Behavior* 43 (7): 780–803.

Hareli, Shiomo, and Bernard Weiner. 2002. "Dislike and Envy as Antecedents of Pleasure at Another's Misfortune." *Motivation and Emotion* 26 (4): 257–277.

Harmon, Amy, and Sabrina Tavernise. 2020. "One Big Difference About George Floyd Protests: Many White Faces." *New York Times*, June 12, 2020. https://www.nytimes.com/2020/06/12/us/hilan-floyd-white-protesters.html.

Harris, Allison P., Hannah L. Walker, and Laurel Eckhouse. 2020. "No Justice, No Peace: Political Science Perspectives on the American Carceral State." *Journal of Race, Ethnicity, and Politics* 5 (3): 427–449.

Hartman, Saidiya. 2022. *Scenes of Subjection: Terror, Slavery, and Self-Making in Nineteenth-Century America*. New York: WW Norton & Company.

Harvey, Richard D., and Debra L. Oswald. 2000. "Collective Guilt and Shame as Motivation for White Support of Black Programs." *Journal of Applied Social Psychology* 30 (9): 1790–1811. https://doi.org/10.1111/j.1559-1816.2000.tb02468.x.

Hatfield, Elaine, Richard L. Rapson, and Yen-Chi L. Le. 2009. "Emotional Contagion and Empathy." In *The Social Neuroscience of Empathy*, edited by Jean Decety and William Ickes, 19–30. Cambridge, MA: MIT Press.

Hawkins, Deion S. 2021. "'After Philando, I Had to Take a Sick Day to Recover': Psychological Distress, Trauma and Police Brutality in the Black Community." *Health Communication* 37 (9): 1113–1122.

Heaney, Michael T. 2022. "Who Are Black Lives Matter Activists? Niche Realization in a Multimovement Environment." *Perspectives on Politics* 20 (4): 1362–1385. https://doi.org/10.1017/s1537592722001281.

Helsel, Phil, Shamar Walters, and Alastair Jamieson. 2016. "Philando Castile Shooting in Falcon Heights, Minnesota, Sparks Protests." NBCNews.Com, July 7, 2016. https://www.nbcnews.com/news/us-news/hilando-castile-shooting-falcon-heights-minnesota-sparks-protests-n605051.

Henderson, Lenneal J. 2004. "Brown v. Board of Education at 50: The Multiple Legacies for Policy and Administration." *Public Administration Review* 64 (3): 270–274.

Henry, P. J., and David O. Sears. 2009. "The Crystallization of Contemporary Racial Prejudice across the Lifespan." *Political Psychology* 30 (4): 569–590.

Hersey, Tricia. 2022. *Rest Is Resistance: A Manifesto*. New York: Little, Brown Spark.

Hershey, Marjorie Randon, and John H. Aldrich. 2017. *Party Politics in America*. 17th ed. New York: Routledge.

Hertel, Shareen, Matthew M. Singer, and Donna Lee Van Cott. 2009. "Field Research in Developing Countries: Hitting the Road Running." *PS: Political Science and Politics* 42 (2): 305–309.

Hetey, Rebecca C., and Jennifer L. Eberhardt. 2014. "Racial Disparities in Incarceration Increase Acceptance of Punitive Policies." *Psychological Science* 25 (10): 1949–1954. https://doi.org/10.1177/0956797614540307.

Hiaeshutter-Rice, Dan, Fabian G. Neuner, and Stuart Soroka. 2023. "Cued by Culture: Political Imagery and Partisan Evaluations." *Political Behavior* 45 (2): 741–759.

Highton, Benjamin. 2004. "White Voters and African American Candidates for Congress." *Political Behavior* 26 (1): 1–25.

———. 2017. "Voter Identification Laws and Turnout in the United States." *Annual Review of Political Science* 20 (1): 149–167.

Himmelstein, Jerome L. 1986. "The Social Basis of Antifeminism: Religious Networks and Culture." *Journal for the Scientific Study of Religion* 25 (1): 1–15.

Hinton, Elizabeth. 2021. *America on Fire: the Untold History of Police Violence and Black Rebellion Since the 1960s*. New York: WW Norton.

Hogg, Michael A., and Dominic Abrams. 1988. *Social Identifications: Social Psychological Perspectives*. London: Routledge.

Hooker, Juliet. 2016. "Black Lives Matter and the Paradoxes of U.S. Black Politics: From Democratic Sacrifice to Democratic Repair." *Political Theory* 44 (4): 448–469.

Hopkins, Daniel J., and Samantha Washington. 2020. "The Rise of Trump, The Fall of Prejudice? Tracking White Americans' Racial Attitudes Via A Panel Survey, 2008–2018." *Public Opinion Quarterly* 84 (1): 119–140.

Hraba, Joseph, and Geoffrey Grant. 1970. "Black Is Beautiful: A Re-examination of Racial Preference and Identification." *Journal of Personality and Social Psychology* 16 (3): 398–402.

Huddy, Leonie, and Stanley Feldman. 2009. "On Assessing the Political Effects of Racial Prejudice." *Annual Review of Political Science* 12 (1): 423–447.

Hutchings, Vincent L. 2009. "Change or More of the Same? Evaluating Racial Attitudes in the Obama Era." *Public Opinion Quarterly* 73 (5): 917–942.

Hutchings, Vincent L., and Nicholas A. Valentino. 2004. "The Centrality of Race in American Politics." *Annual Review of Political Science* 7: 383–408.

Hutchings, Vincent L., Nicholas A. Valentino, Tasha S. Philpot, and Ismail K. White. 2004. "The Compassion Strategy: Race and the Gender Gap in Campaign 2000." *Public Opinion Quarterly* 68 (4): 512–541.

Hutchings, Vincent L., Hanes Walton, and Andrea Benjamin. 2010. "The Impact of Explicit Racial Cues on Gender Differences in Support for Confederate Symbols and Partisanship." *Journal of Politics* 72 (4): 1175–1188.

Inglehart, Ronald. 1985. "Aggregate Stability and Individual-Level Flux in Mass Belief Systems: The Level of Analysis Paradox." *American Political Science Review* 79 (1): 97–116.

Iyengar, Shanto. 1990. "Framing Responsibility for Political Issues: The Case of Poverty." *Political Behavior* 12 (1): 19–40.

Iyengar, Shanto, Tobias Konitzer, and Kent Tedin. 2018. "The Home as a Political Fortress: Family Agreement in an Era of Polarization." *Journal of Politics* 80 (4): 1326–1338.

Iyer, Aarti, Colin Wayne Leach, and Faye J. Crosby. 2003. "White Guilt and Racial Compensation: The Benefits and Limits of Self-Focus." *Personality and Social Psychology Bulletin* 29: 117–129.

Iyer, Aarti, Toni Schmader, and Brian Lickel. 2007. "Why Individuals Protest the Perceived Transgressions of Their Country: The Role of Anger, Shame, and Guilt." *Personality and Social Psychology Bulletin* 33 (4): 572–587.

Jardina, Ashley. 2019. *White Identity Politics*. New York: Cambridge University Press.

Jardina, Ashley, and Trent Ollerenshaw. 2022. "The Polarization of White Racial Attitudes and Support for Racial Equality in the US." Special issue, *Public Opinion Quarterly* 86: 576–587.

Jefferson, Hakeem, Fabian G. Neuner, and Josh Pasek. 2021. "Seeing Blue in Black and White: Race and Perceptions of Officer-Involved Shootings." *Perspectives on Politics* 19 (4): 1165–1183.

Jennings, Carly. 2020. "The Love Note That Launched a Movement." Special issue: Race, Police Violence, and Justice, *American Sociological Association* 48 (4): 15–16.

John, Oliver P., and Sanjay Srivastava. 1999. "The Big Five Trait Taxonomy: History, Measurement." In *Handbook of Personality: Theory and Research*, edited by Lawrence Pervin, 102–138. New York: Guilford.

Jones, Jeffrey M. 2020. "Black, White Adults' Confidence Diverges Most on Police." Gallup, August 12, 2022. https://news.gallup.com/poll/317114/black-white-adults-confidence-diverges-police.aspx.

Joyner, Kara, and Grace Kao. 2000. "School Racial Composition and Adolescent Racial Homophily." *Social Science Quarterly* 81 (3): 810–825.

Judd, Charles M., Bernadette Park, Carey S. Ryan, Markus Brauer, and Susan Kraus. 1995. "Stereotypes and Ethnocentrism: Diverging Interethnic Perceptions of African American and White American Youth." *Journal of Personality and Social Psychology* 69 (3): 460–481.

Kalmoe, Nathan P., and Lilliana Mason. 2022. *Radical American Partisanship: Mapping Violent Hostility, Its Causes, and the Consequences for Democracy*. Chicago: University of Chicago Press.

Kalmoe, Nathan P., and Spencer Piston. 2013. "Is Implicit Prejudice Against Blacks Politically Consequential? Evidence from the AMP." *Public Opinion Quarterly* 77 (1): 305–322.

Kam, Cindy D., and Donald Kinder. 2012. "Ethnocentrism as a Short-Term Force in the 2008 Presidential Election." *American Journal of Political Science* 56 (2): 326–340.

Kam, Cindy D., and Carl L. Palmer. 2008. "Reconsidering the Effects of Education on Political Participation." *Journal of Politics* 70 (3): 612–631.

Kantor, Jodi. 2008. "Obama Supporters Take His Name as Their Own." *New York Times*, June 29, 2008. https://www.nytimes.com/2008/06/29/us/politics/29hussein.html.

Kao, Grace, Kara Joyner, and Kelly Stamper Balistreri. 2019. *The Company We Keep: Interracial Friendships and Romantic Relationships from Adolescence to Adulthood*. New York: Russell Sage Foundation.

Karp, Jeffrey A., and Susan A. Banducci. 2008. "Political Efficacy and Participation in Twenty-Seven Democracies: How Electoral Systems Shape Political Behaviour." *British Journal of Political Science* 38 (2): 311–334.

Katz, Irwin, and R. Glen Hass. 1988. "Racial Ambivalence and American Value Conflict: Correlational and Priming Studies of Dual Cognitive Structures." *Journal of Personality and Social Psychology* 55 (6): 893–905.

Katz, Richard S., and Peter Mair. 1993. "The Evolution of Party Organizations in Europe: The Three Faces of Party Organization." *American Review of Politics* 14: 593–617.

Kelley, Robin D. G. 2003. *Freedom Dreams: The Black Radical Imagination*. Boston: Beacon Press.

Kerner Commission. 1968. *Report of the National Advisory Commission on Civil Disorders*. Washington, DC: Government Printing Office.

Key, V. O., Jr. 1961. *Public Opinion and American Democracy*. New York: Knopf.

Kiley, Kevin, and Stephen Vaisey. 2020. "Measuring Stability and Change in Personal Culture Using Panel Data." *American Sociological Review* 85 (3): 477–506.

Kim, Claire Jean. 2000. *Bitter Fruit: The Politics of Black-Korean Conflict in New York City*. New Haven, CT: Yale University Press.

Kim, JongHan, Scott T. Allison, Dafna Eylon, George R. Goethals, Michael J. Markus, Sheila M. Hindle, and Heather A. McGuire. 2008. "Rooting for (and Then Abandoning) the Underdog." *Journal of Applied Social Psychology* 38 (10): 2550–2573.

Kinder, Donald R. 1986. "The Continuing American Dilemma: White Resistance to Racial Change 40 Years After Myrdal." *Journal of Social Issues* 42 (2): 151–171.

———. 2013. "Prejudice and Politics.'" In *Handbook of Political Psychology*, edited by David O. Sears and Leonie Huddy, 812–851. New York: Oxford University Press.

Kinder, Donald R., and Allison Dale-Riddle. 2012. *The End of Race?* New Haven, CT: Yale University Press.

Kinder, Donald R., and Katherine W. Drake. 2009. "Myrdal's Prediction." *Political Psychology* 30 (4): 539–568.

Kinder, Donald R., and Nathan P. Kalmoe. 2017. *Neither Liberal nor Conservative: Ideological Innocence in the American Public*. Chicago: University of Chicago Press.

Kinder, Donald R., and Cindy D. Kam. 2009. *Us Against Them: Ethnocentric Foundations of American Opinion*. Chicago: University of Chicago Press.

Kinder, Donald R., and D. Roderick Kiewiet. 1981. "Sociotropic Politics: The American Case." *British Journal of Political Science* 11 (2): 129–161.

Kinder, Donald R., and Corrine M. McConnaughy. 2006. "Military Triumph, Racial Transcendence, and Colin Powell." *Public Opinion Quarterly* 70 (2): 139–165.

Kinder, Donald R., and Tali Mendelberg. 1995. "Cracks in American Apartheid: The Political Impact of Prejudice among Desegregated Whites." *Journal of Politics* 57 (2): 402–424.

Kinder, Donald R., and Timothy J. Ryan. 2015. "Prejudice and Politics Re-Examined: The Political Significance of Implicit Racial Bias." *Political Science Research and Methods* 5 (2): 1–9.

Kinder, Donald R., and Lynn M. Sanders. 1990. "Mimicking Political Debate with Survey Questions: The Case of White Opinion on Affirmative Action for Blacks." *Social Cognition* 8 (1): 73–103.

———. 1996 *Divided by Color: Racial Politics and Democratic Ideals*. Chicago: University of Chicago Press.

Kinder, Donald R., and David O. Sears. 1981. "Prejudice and Politics: Symbolic Racism Versus Racial Threats to the Good Life." *Journal of Personality and Social Psychology* 40 (3): 414–431.

Klandermans, Bert. 1984. "Mobilization and Participation: Social-Psychological Expansions of Resource Mobilization Theory." *American Sociological Review* 49 (5): 583–600.

Klandermans, Bert, and Dirk Oegema. 1987. "Potentials, Networks, Motivations, and Barriers: Steps Towards Participation in Social Movements." *American Sociological Review* 52 (4): 519–531.

Kleiber, Christian, and Achim Zeileis. 2008. *Applied Econometrics with R*. New York: Springer.

Klein, Kristi J. K., and Sara D. Hodges. 2001. "Gender Differences, Motivation, and Empathic Accuracy: When It Pays to Understand." *Personality and Social Psychology Bulletin* 27 (6): 720–730.

Knowles, Eric D., Brian S. Lowery, and Rebecca L. Schaumberg. 2009. "Anti-Egalitarians for Obama? Group-Dominance Motivation and the Obama Vote." *Journal of Experimental Social Psychology* 45 (4): 965–969.

Kofkin, Jennifer A., Phyllis A. Katz, and E. P. Downey. 1995. "Family Discourse about Race and the Development of Children's Racial Attitudes." Biennial Meeting of the Society for Research in Child Development, Indianapolis, IN.

Krebs, Dennis L., and Dale T. Miller. 1985. "Altruism and Aggression." *The Handbook of Social Psychology* 2: 1–71.

Krupnikov, Yanna, and Spencer Piston. 2015. "Racial Prejudice, Partisanship, and White Turnout in Elections with Black Candidates." *Political Behavior* 37 (2): 397–418.

Kuebli, Janet, Susan Butler, and Robyn Fivush. 1995. "Mother-Child Talk about Past Emotions: Relations of Maternal Language and Child Gender over Time." *Cognition and Emotion* 9 (2–3): 265–283.

Kuklinski, James H., Michael D. Cobb, and Martin Gilens. 1997. "Racial Attitudes and the 'New South.'" *Journal of Politics* 59 (2): 323–349.

Kuziemko, Ilyana, and Ebonya Washington. 2018. "Why Did the Democrats Lose the South? Bringing New Data to an Old Debate." *American Economic Review* 108 (10): 2830–2867.

Ladd, Helen F. 2012. "Education and Poverty: Confronting the Evidence." *Journal of Policy Analysis and Management* 31 (2): 203–227.

Lane, Robert E. 1962. *Political Ideology: Why the American Common Man Believes What He Does.* Glencoe, IL: Free Press of Glencoe.

Larsen, James E., and John P. Blair 2009. "The Importance of Police Performance as a Determinant of Satisfaction with Police." *American Journal of Economics and Business Administration* 1 (1): 1–10.

Lasswell, Harold D. 2018. *Politics: Who Gets What, When, How.* Potomac, MD: Pickle Partners.

Leach, Colin Wayne, and Aerielle M. Allen. 2017. "The Social Psychology of the Black Lives Matter Meme and Movement." *Current Directions in Psychological Science* 26 (6): 543–547.

Leighley, Jan E., and Jonathan Nagler. 1992. "Individual and Systemic Influences on Turnout: Who Votes? 1984." *Journal of Politics* 54 (3): 718–740.

Lench, Heather C., Thomas P. Tibbett, and Shane W. Bench. 2016. "Exploring the Toolkit of Emotion: What Do Sadness and Anger Do for Us?" *Social and Personality Psychology Compass* 10 (1): 11–25.

Lennon, Randy, Nancy Eisenberg, and James Carroll. 1986. "The Relation between Nonverbal Indices of Empathy and Preschoolers' Prosocial Behavior." *Journal of Applied Developmental Psychology* 7 (3): 219–224.

Lenz, Gabriel S. 2012. *Follow the Leader? How Voters Respond to Politicians' Policies and Performance.* Chicago: University of Chicago Press.

Lewis-Giggetts, Tracey M. 2022. *Black Joy: Stories of Resistance, Resilience, and Restoration.* New York: Simon and Schuster.

Lienesch, Rachel. 2023. "Racial Politics of the White Left and Beyond" Doctoral diss., Stanford University.

Lizotte, Mary Kate. 2016. "The Gender Gap in Public Opinion: Exploring Social Role Theory as an Explanation." In *The Political Psychology of Women in U.S. Politics*, edited by Angela L. Bos and Monica C. Schneider, 51–69. New York: Taylor and Francis. Accessed June 13, 2023. http://www.scopus.com/inward/record.url?scp=85027271967&partnerID=8YFLogxK.

Lock, Margaret, and Patricia Alice Kaufert. 1998. *Pragmatic Women and Body Politics.* Cambridge: Cambridge University Press.

Loewen, P., Christopher Cochrane, and Gabriel Arsenault. 2017. "Empathy and Political Preferences." Unpublished manuscript, University of Toronto.

Luker, Kristin. 2008. *Salsa Dancing into the Social Sciences*. Cambridge, MA: Harvard University Press.

Lurie, Julia. 2014. "10 Hours in Ferguson: A Visual Timeline of Michael Brown's Death and Its Aftermath." *Mother Jones*, August 27, 2014. https://www.mother jones.com/politics/2014/08/timeline-michael-brown-shooting-ferguson/.

Lynch, Julia F. 2013. "Aligning Sampling Strategies with Analytic Goals." In *Interview Research in Political Science*, edited by Layna Mosley, 31–44. Ithaca, NY: Cornell University Press.

Ma, Debbie S., Danita Hohl, and Justin Kantner. 2021. "The Politics of Identity: The Unexpected Role of Political Orientation on Racial Categorizations of Kamala Harris." *Analyses of Social Issues and Public Policy* 21 (1): 99–120.

Makhalemele, Oupa. 2004. *Still Not Talking: Government's Exclusive Reparations Policy and the Impact of the 30,000 Financial Reparations on Survivors*. Johannesburg, ZA: Centre for the Study of Violence and Reconciliation.

Malhotra, Neil, and Jon A. Krosnick. 2007. "The Effect of Survey Mode and Sampling on Inferences about Political Attitudes and Behavior: Comparing the 2000 and 2004 ANES to Internet Surveys with Nonprobability Samples." *Political Analysis* 15: 286–323.

Margolis, Michele F. 2018. *From Politics to the Pews: How Partisanship and the Political Environment Shape Religious Identity*. Chicago: University of Chicago Press.

Mason, Lilliana. 2018. *Uncivil Agreement: How Politics Became Our Identity*. Chicago: University of Chicago Press.

Massey, Douglas S. 1990. "American Apartheid: Segregation and the Making of the Underclass." *American Journal of Sociology* 96 (2): 329–357.

Masuoka, Natalie. 2008. "Political Attitudes and Ideologies of Multiracial Americans: The Implications of Mixed Race in the United States." *Political Research Quarterly* 61 (2): 253–267.

McAdam, Doug. 1990. *Freedom Summer*. New York: Oxford University Press.

———. 1999. *Political Process and the Development of Black Insurgency, 1930–1970*. Chicago: University of Chicago Press.

———. 2003. "Recruits to Civil Rights Activism." *The Social Movements Reader: Cases and Concepts* 2: 66–74.

McCalmont, Lucy. 2014. "Paul Cites High Cigarette Taxes in Death." Politico, December 4, 2014. https://www.politico.com/story/2014/12/rand-paul-eric-garner -death-reaction-113318.

McConnaughy, Corrine M., and Ismail K. White. 2011. "Racial Politics Complicated: The Work of Gendered Race Cues in American Politics." In an unpublished manuscript, New Research on Gender in Political Psychology Conference. New Brunswick, NJ: Rutgers University.

McConnell, Allen R., and Jill M. Leibold. 2001. "Relations Among the Implicit Attitude Test, Discriminatory Behavior, and Explicit Measures of Racial Attitudes." *Journal of Experimental Social Psychology* 37 (5): 435–442.

McCrae, Robert R., and Paul T. Costa. 2003. *Personality in Adulthood: A Five-Factor Theory Perspective.* New York: Guilford Press.

McGlone, Matthew S., Joshua Aronson, and Diane Kobrynowicz. 2006. "Stereotype Threat and the Gender Gap in Political Knowledge." *Psychology of Women Quarterly* 30 (4): 392–398.

McKenna, Elizabeth, and Hahrie Han. 2014. *Groundbreakers: How Obama's 2.2 Million Volunteers Transformed Campaigning in America.* New York: Oxford University Press.

McKivigan, John R. 1984. *The War against Proslavery Religion: Abolitionism and the Northern Churches, 1830–1865.* Ithaca, NY: Cornell University Press.

McPherson, James M. 1995. *The Abolitionist Legacy: From Reconstruction to the NAACP.* Princeton, NJ: Princeton University Press.

Mendelberg, Tali. 2001. *The Race Card: Campaign Strategy, Implicit Messages, and the Norm of Equality.* Princeton, NJ: Princeton University Press.

Merseth, Julie Lee. 2020. "Race-Ing Solidarity: Asian Americans and Support for Black Lives Matter." In *Asian Pacific American Politics: Celebrating the Scholarly Legacy of Don T. Nakanishi,* edited by Andrew Aoki and Pei-te Lien, 9–28. New York, NY: Routledge.

Mettler, Suzanne. 2018. *The Government-Citizen Disconnect.* New York: Russell Sage Foundation.

Meyer, David S. 2004. "Protest and Political Opportunities." *Annual Review of Sociology* 30:125–145.

Meyer, David S., and Sidney Tarrow. 1997. *The Social Movement Society: Contentious Politics for a New Century.* Lanham, MD: Rowman and Littlefield.

Michener, Jamila. 2018. *Fragmented Democracy: Medicaid, Federalism, and Unequal Politics.* New York: Cambridge University Press.

Mickey, Robert. 2022. "Challenges to Subnational Democracy in the United States, Past and Present." *Annals of the American Academy of Political and Social Science* 699 (1): 118–129.

Mikkelborg, Anna. 2023. "White Democrats' Growing Support for Black Politicians in the Era of the 'Great Awokening.'" American Political Science Association Annual Meeting Paper.

Moore, Steven T. 2020. "The Road to Hell: How Race Paternalism Shapes Political Behavior." Doctoral diss., University of Michigan. http://deepblue.lib.umich.edu/handle/2027.42/163012.

Morrison, Minion K. C. 1987. *Black Political Mobilization, Leadership, Power and Mass Behavior.* Albany, NY: SUNY Press.

Morton, Rebecca, and Charles Cameron. 1992. "Elections and the Theory of Campaign Contributions: A Survey and Critical Analysis." *Economics and Politics* 4 (1): 79–108.

Morton, Rebecca, and Kenneth C. Williams. 2010. *Experimental Political Science and the Study of Causality.* New York: Cambridge University Press.

Mosley, Layna. 2013. *Interview Research in Political Science*. Ithaca, NY: Cornell University Press.

Muller, Judy. 2020. "My Tiny, White Town Just Held a Protest. We're Not Alone." *Washington Post*, June 5, 2020. https://www.washingtonpost.com/opinions/2020 /06/05/my-tiny-white-town-just-held-protest-were-not-alone/.

Munson, Ziad. 2009. *The Making of Pro-Life Activists*. Chicago: University of Chicago Press.

Mutz, Diana. 2011. *Population-Based Survey Experiments*. Princeton, NJ: Princeton University Press.

Myrdal, Gunnar. 1944. *An American Dilemma: The Negro Problem and Modern Democracy*. New York: Harper & Row.

Nelson, Thomas, and Donald R. Kinder. 1996. "Issue Frames and Group-Centrism in American." *Journal of Politics* 58 (4): 1055–1078.

Neuman, W. Russell, George E. Marcus, and Michael B. MacKuen. 2018. "Hardwired for News: Affective Intelligence and Political Attention." *Journal of Broadcasting and Electric Media* 62 (4): 614–635.

Newcomb, T. M. 1943. *Personality and Social Change; Attitude Formation in a Student Community*. Fort Worth, TX: Dryden.

Newman, Benjamin, Jennifer L. Merolla, Sono Shah, Danielle Casarez Lemi, Loren Collingwood, and S. Karthick Ramakrishnan. 2021. "The Trump Effect: An Experimental Investigation of the Emboldening Effect of Racially Inflammatory Elite Communication." *British Journal of Political Science* 51 (3): 1138–1159.

Niemi, Richard G., Stephen C. Craig, and Franco Mattei. 1991. "Measuring Internal Political Efficacy in the 1988 National Election Study." *American Political Science Review* 85 (4): 1407–1413.

NORC at the University of Chicago. N.d. "About the GSS." Accessed June 28, 2023. https://gss.norc.org/About-The-GSS.

Nunnally, Jum C., and I. H. Bernstein. 1994. "The Assessment of Reliability." *Psychometric Theory* 3 (1): 248–292.

Olick, Jeffrey K., and Daniel Levy. 1997. "Collective Memory and Cultural Constraint: Holocaust Myth and Rationality in German Politics." *American Sociological Review* 62 (6): 921–936.

Oliver, J. Eric, and Tali Mendelberg. 2000. "Reconsidering the Environmental Determinants of White Racial Attitudes." *American Journal of Political Science* 44 (3): 574–589.

Olson, Laura R., and John C. Green. 2006. "The Religion Gap." *PS: Political Science and Politics* 39 (3): 455–459.

Olson, Laura R., and Adam L. Warber. 2008. "Belonging, Behaving, and Believing: Assessing the Role of Religion on Presidential Approval." *Political Research Quarterly* 61 (2): 192–204.

Olson, Michael A., and Russell H. Fazio. 2004. "Reducing the Influence of Extrapersonal Associations on the Implicit Association Test: Personalizing the IAT." *Journal of Personality and Social Psychology* 86 (5): 653–667.

Otis, Randall, and Josh Johnson. 2020. "A Day at the Church of White Guilt."
    New Yorker, June 25, 2020. https://www.newyorker.com/humor/daily-shouts/a
    -day-at-the-church-of-white-guilt.
Paluck, Elizabeth Levy, Roni Porat, Chelsey S. Clark, and Donald P. Green. 2021.
    "Prejudice Reduction: Progress and Challenges." *Annual Review of Psychol-
    ogy* 72 (1): 533–560.
Pasek, Josh, Lauren Feldman, Daniel Romer, and Kathleen Hall Jamieson. 2008.
    "Schools as Incubators of Democratic Participation: Building Long-Term Po-
    litical Efficacy with Civic Education." *Applied Developmental Science* 12 (1):
    26–37.
Pate, Glenn S. 1988. "Research on Reducing Prejudice." *Social Education* 52 (4):
    287–289.
Patton, Stacey. 2020. "White People Are Speaking Up at Protests: How Do
    We Know They Mean What They Say?" *Washington Post*, June 2, 2020.
    https://www.washingtonpost.com/outlook/2020/06/02/white-people-black
    -protests/.
Peele, Gillian. 2005. "Leadership and Politics: A Case for a Closer Relationship?"
    Leadership 1 (2): 187–204.
Peffley, Mark, and Jon Hurwitz. 2002. "The Racial Components of 'Race-Neutral'
    Crime Policy Attitudes." *Political Psychology* 23 (1): 59–75.
Percy, William Alexander. 2006. *Lanterns on the Levee: Recollections of a Planter's
    Son*. Baton Rouge, LA: LSU Press.
Perry, Brea L., Brian Aronson, and Bernice A. Pescosolido. 2021. "Pandemic Pre-
    carity: COVID-19 Is Exposing and Exacerbating Inequalities in the Ameri-
    can Heartland." *Proceedings of the National Academy of Sciences* 118 (8):
    e2020685118.
Petrow, Gregory A. 2010. "The Minimal Cue Hypothesis: How Black Candidates
    Cue Race to Increase White Voting Participation." *Political Psychology* 31 (6):
    915–950.
Pettigrew, Thomas F. 1959. "Regional Difference in Anti-Negro Prejudice." *Jour-
    nal of Abnormal and Social Psychology* 59 (1): 28–36.
———. 1982. *Prejudice*. Cambridge, MA: Harvard University Press.
———. 1997. "Generalized Intergroup Contact Effects on Prejudice." *Personality
    and Social Psychology Bulletin* 23: 173–185.
Pew Research Center. 2012. "Young Voters Supported Obama Less, But May
    Have Mattered More." November 26, 2012. https://www.pewresearch.org/poli-
    tics/2012/11/26/young-voters-supported-obama-less-but-may-have-mattered
    -more/.
———. 2020. "Majority of Public Favors Giving Civilians the Power to Sue Police
    Officers for Misconduct." July 9, 2020. https://www.pewresearch.org/politics
    /2020/07/09/majority-of-public-favors-giving-civilians-the-power-to-sue-police
    -officers-for-misconduct/.

————. 2021. "Demographics of Mobile Device Ownership and Adoption in the United States." April 7, 2021. https://www.pewresearch.org/internet/fact-sheet /mobile/.

Phoenix, Davin L. 2019. *The Anger Gap: How Race Shapes Emotion.* New York: Cambridge University Press.

Phoenix, Davin L., and Nathan Chan. 2023. "Clarifying the 'People Like Me': Racial Efficacy and Political Behavior." *Perspectives on Politics*: 1–18.

Pineda, Erin R. 2021. *Seeing Like an Activist: Civil Disobedience and the Civil Rights Movement.* New York: Oxford University Press.

Piston, Spencer. 2010. "How Explicit Racial Prejudice Hurt Obama in the 2008 Election." *Political Behavior* 32: 431–451.

————. 2014. "Sympathy for the Poor, Resentment of the Rich, and Their Political Consequences." Doctoral diss., University of Michigan.

————. 2018. *Class Attitudes in America: Sympathy for the Poor, Resentment of the Rich, and Political Implications.* New York: Cambridge University Press.

————. 2023. "Revisiting the Theory of Broken Windows Policing." *International Journal of Criminology and Sociology* 12: 141–150.

Prewitt, Kenneth. 2005. "Racial Classification in America: Where Do We Go from Here?" *Daedalus* 134 (1): 5–17.

Pugh, Allison J. 2013. "What Good Are Interviews for Thinking About Culture? Demystifying Interpretive Analysis." *American Journal of Cultural Sociology* 1 (1): 42–68.

————. 2015. *The Tumbleweed Society: Working and Caring in an Age of Insecurity.* New York: Oxford University Press.

Putnam, Robert D. 2000. *Bowling Alone: The Collapse and Revival of American Community.* New York: Simon and Schuster.

Putnam, Robert D., Robert Leonardi, and Raffaella Y. Nanetti. 1994. *Making Democracy Work: Civic Traditions in Modern Italy.* Princeton, NJ: Princeton University Press.

Quintana, Stephen M., Frances E. Aboud, Ruth K. Chao, Josefina Contreras-Grau, William E. Cross, Cynthia Hudley, Diane Hughes, Lynn S. Liben, Sharon Nelson-Le Gall, and Deborah L. Vietze. 2006. "Race, Ethnicity, and Culture in Child Development: Contemporary Research and Future Directions." *Child Development* 77 (5): 1129–1141.

Ray, Rashawn. 2020. "What Does 'Defund the Police' Mean and Does It Have Merit?" Brookings Institute. Accessed January 31, 2022. https://www.brookings .edu/blog/fixgov/2020/06/19/what-does-defund-the-police-mean-and-does-it -have-merit/.

Ray, Rashawn, and Andre Perry. 2020. "Why We Need Reparations for Black Americans." Brookings Institute. Accessed January 31, 2022. https://www.brook ings.edu/articles/why-we-need-reparations-for-black-americans/.

Ray, Victor Erik, Antonia Randolph, Megan Underhill, and David Luke. 2017.

"Critical Race Theory, Afro-Pessimism, and Racial Progress Narratives." *Sociology of Race and Ethnicity* 3 (2): 147–158.

Redbird, Beth, and Kat Albrecht. 2020. "Racial Disparity in Arrests Increased as Crime Rates Declined." Institute for Policy Research, Northwestern University. Accessed September 21, 2023. https://www.ipr.northwestern.edu/our-work /working-papers/2020/wp-20-28.html.

Reeves, Keith. 1997. *Voting Hopes or Fears?: White Voters, Black Candidates, and Racial Politics in America*. New York: Oxford University Press.

Reeves, Richard V., and Katherine Guyot. 2017. "Black Women Are Earning More College Degrees, but That Alone Won't Close Race Gaps." Brookings Institution. Accessed August 16, 2022. https://www.brookings.edu/blog/social -mobility-memos/2017/12/04/black-women-are-earning-more-college-degrees -but-that-alone-wont-close-race-gaps/.

Reichelmann, Ashley V., and Matthew O. Hunt. 2021a. "How We Repair It: White Americans' Attitudes toward Reparations." Brookings Institute. Accessed July 11, 2022. https://www.brookings.edu/blog/how-we-rise/2021/12/08/how-we -repair-it-white-americans-attitudes-toward-reparations/.

———. 2021b. "White Americans' Attitudes Toward Reparations for Slavery: Definitions and Determinants." *Race and Social Problems* 14: 269–281. Accessed September 21, 2023. https://link.springer.com/article/10.1007/s12552-021-09348-x.

Reid, Jonathan C., and Miltonette O. Craig. 2021. "Is It a Rally or a Riot? Racialized Media Framing of 2020 Protests in the United States." *Journal of Ethnicity in Criminal Justice* 19 (3–4): 291–310.

Reny, Tyler T., and Benjamin J. Newman. 2021. "The Opinion-Mobilizing Effect of Social Protest against Police Violence: Evidence from the 2020 George Floyd Protests." *American Political Science Review* 115 (4): 1499–1507.

Reny, Tyler T., Ali A. Valenzuela, and Loren Collingwood. 2020. "'No, You're Playing the Race Card': Testing the Effects of Anti-Black, Anti-Latino, and Anti-Immigrant Appeals in the Post-Obama Era." *Political Psychology* 41 (2): 283–302. https://doi.org/10.1111/pops.12614.

Reynolds, Katherine J., John C. Turner, S. Alexander Haslam, and Michelle K. Ryan. 2001. "Role of Personality and Group Factors in Explaining Prejudice." *Journal of Experimental Social Psychology* 37 (5): 427–434.

Riley, Emmitt Y., and Clarissa Peterson. 2020. "I Can't Breathe: Assessing the Role of Racial Resentment and Racial Prejudice in Whites' Feelings toward Black Lives Matter." *National Review of Black Politics* 1 (4): 496–515.

Roberts, Dorothy. 2022. *Torn Apart: How the Child Welfare System Destroys Black Families—and How Abolition Can Build a Safer World*. New York: Basic Books.

Rochon, Thomas R., and Daniel A. Mazmanian. 1993. "Social Movements and the Policy Process." *Annals of the American Academy of Political and Social Science* 528 (1): 75–87.

Rogers, Todd, and Masa Aida. 2011. *Why Bother Asking? The Limited Value of*

Self-Reported Vote Intention. SSRN scholarly paper. Rochester, NY: Social Science Research Network. Accessed November 22, 2021. https://papers.ssrn.com /abstract=1971312.

Rolfe, Meredith. 2012. *Voter Turnout: A Social Theory of Political Participation*. New York: Cambridge University Press.

Rosenstone, Steven J., and John Mark Hansen. 1993. *Mobilization, Participation, and Democracy in America*. Macmillan. Accessed March 25, 2022. https://www .pearson.com/content/one-dot-com/one-dot-com/us/en/higher-education/pro gram.html.

Ross, Catherine E., and Chia-ling Wu. 1995. "The Links Between Education and Health." *American Sociological Review* 60 (5): 719–745.

Rudolph, Thomas J., Amy Gangl, and Dan Stevens. 2000. "The Effects of Efficacy and Emotions on Campaign Involvement." *Journal of Politics* 62 (4): 1189–1197.

Salovey, Peter, and John D. Mayer. 1990. "Emotional Intelligence." *Imagination, Cognition and Personality* 9 (3): 185–211.

Sander, David, and Klaus Scherer. 2014. *Oxford Companion to Emotion and the Affective Sciences*. New York: Oxford University Press.

Sass, Tim R., and Bobby J. Pittman Jr. 2000. "The Changing Impact of Electoral Structure on Black Representation in the South, 1970–1996." *Public Choice* 104 (3): 369–388.

Schickler, Eric. 2016. *Racial Realignment: The Transformation of American Liberalism, 1932–1965*. Princeton, NJ: Princeton University Press.

Schuman, Howard, and Lawrence Bobo. 1988. "Survey-Based Experiments on White Racial Attitudes toward Residential Integration." *American Journal of Sociology* 94 (2): 273–299.

Schuman, Howard, and John Harding. 1963. "Sympathetic Identification with the Underdog." *Public Opinion Quarterly* 27 (2): 230–241.

Schwarz, Norbert. 1994. "Judgment in a Social Context: Biases, Shortcomings, and the Logic of Conversation." *Advances in Experimental Social Psychology* 26 (1): 123–162.

Schwartz, Shalom. 1975. "The Justice of Need and the Activation of Humanitarian Norms." *Journal of Social Issues* 31 (3): 111–136.

Sears, David O. 1983. "The Person-Positivity Bias." *Journal of Personality and Social Psychology* 44 (2): 230–250.

———. 2001. *The Role of Affect in Symbolic Politics*, edited by James H. Kuklinski. New York: Cambridge University Press.

———. 2004. "A Perspective on Implicit Prejudice from Survey Research." *Psychological Inquiry* 15 (4): 293–297.

———. 2008. "The American Color Line 50 Years after Brown v. Board: Many 'Peoples of Color' or Black Exceptionalism?" In *Decade of Behavior: Commemorating Brown; the Social Psychology of Racism and Discrimination*, edited by G. Adams, M. Biernat, N. R. Branscombe, C. S. Crandall, and L. S. Wrights-man, 133–152. Washington, DC: American Psychological Association.

Sears, David O., and Carolyn L. Funk. 1999. "Evidence of the Long-Term Persis-tence of Adults' Political Predispositions." *Journal of Politics* 61 (1): 1–28.

Sears, David O., and P. J. Henry. 2003. "The Origins of Symbolic Racism." *Journal of Personality and Social Psychology* 85 (2): 259–275.

Sears, David O., Carl P. Hensler, and Leslie K. Speer. 1979. "Whites' Opposition to 'Busing': Self-Interest or Symbolic Politics?" *American Political Science Review* 73 (2): 369–384.

Sears, David O., and Victoria Savalei. 2006. "The Political Color Line in America: Many 'Peoples of Color' or Black Exceptionalism?" *Political Psychology* 27 (6): 895–924.

Sears, David O., Colette Van Laar, Mary Carrillo, and Rick Kosterman. 1997. "Is It Really Racism? The Origins of White Americans' Opposition to Race-Targeted Policies." *Public Opinion Quarterly* 61 (1): 16–53.

Seawright, Jason, and John Gerring. 2008. "Case Selection Techniques in Case Study Research: A Menu of Qualitative and Quantitative Options." *Political Research Quarterly* 61 (2): 294–308.

Shafer, Byron E. 1983. *Quiet Revolution: Struggle for the Democratic Party and the Shaping of Post-Reform Politics*. New York: Russell Sage Foundation.

Sherif, Muzafer. 2012. *The Robbers Cave Experiment: Intergroup Conflict and Co-operation*. [orig. pub. as *Intergroup Conflict and Group Relations*]. Middletown, CT: Wesleyan University Press.

Sibley, Chris G., and John Duckitt. 2008. "Personality and Prejudice: A Meta-Analysis and Theoretical Review." *Personality and Social Psychology Review* 12 (3): 248–279.

Sidanius, Jim, and Felicia Pratto. 1999. *Social Dominance: An Intergroup Theory of Social Hierarchy and Oppression*. New York: Cambridge University Press.

Sidanius, Jim, Pam Singh, John J. Hetts, and Chris Federico. 2000. "It's Not Af-firmative Action, It's the Blacks: The Continuing Relevance of Race in Ameri-can Politics." *Racialized Politics: The Debate about Racism in America*: 191–235.

Sides, John, and Kimberly Gross. 2013. "Stereotypes of Muslims and Support for the War on Terror." *Journal of Politics* 75 (3): 583–598.

Sides, John, Michael Tesler, and Lynn Vavreck. 2019. *Identity Crisis: The 2016 Pres-idential Campaign and the Battle for the Meaning of America*. Princeton, NJ: Princeton University Press.

Sigelman, Carol K., Lee Sigelman, Barbara J. Walkosz, and Michael Nitz. 1995. "Black Candidates, White Voters: Understanding Racial Bias in Political Per-ceptions." *American Journal of Political Science* 39 (1): 243–265.

Sigelman, Lee, Timothy Bledsoe, Susan Welch, and Michael W. Combs. 1996. "Making Contact? Black-White Social Interaction in an Urban Setting." *Amer-ican Journal of Sociology* 101 (5): 1306–1332.

Silva, Jennifer M. 2013. *Coming Up Short: Working-Class Adulthood in an Age of Uncertainty*. Oxford: Oxford University Press

Sim, Jessica J., Joshua Correll, and Melody S. Sadler. 2013. "Understanding Police and Expert Performance: When Training Attenuates (vs. Exacerbates) Stereotypic Bias in the Decision to Shoot." *Personality and Social Psychology Bulletin* 39 (3): 291–304.

Simon, Bernd, and Bert Klandermans. 2001. "Politicized Collective Identity: A Social Psychological Analysis." *American Psychologist* 56 (4): 319–331.

Sirin, Cigdem V., Nicholas A. Valentino, and José D. Villalobos. 2021. *Seeing Us in Them: Social Divisions and the Politics of Group*. New York: Cambridge University Press.

Skocpol, Theda, and Morris P. Fiorina. 2004. *Civic Engagement in American Democracy*. Washington, DC: Brookings Institution Press.

Smidt, Katharine E., and Michael K. Suvak. 2015. "A Brief, But Nuanced, Review of Emotional Granularity and Emotion Differentiation Research." *Current Opinion in Psychology* (3): 48–51.

Smith, Adam. 1976. *Theory of Moral Sentiments*. Indianapolis, IN: Liberty Classics.

Smith, Rogers M. 1993. "Beyond Tocqueville, Myrdal, and Hartz: The Multiple Traditions in America." *American Political Science Review* 87 (3): 549–566.

Sniderman, Paul M. 2008. "Democracy, Diversity, and Leadership." *Domestic Perspectives on Contemporary Democracy*: 51–70.

Sniderman, Paul M., and Edward G. Carmines. 1997. *Reaching Beyond Race*. Cambridge, MA: Harvard University Press.

Sniderman, Paul M., Edward G. Carmines, Geoffrey C. Layman, and Michael Carter. 1996. "Beyond Race: Social Justice as a Race Neutral Ideal." *American Journal of Political Science* 40 (1): 33–55.

Sniderman, Paul M., and Thomas Piazza. 1993. *The Scar of Race*. Princeton, NJ: Princeton University Press.

Sniderman, Paul M., and Edward H. Stiglitz. 2009. "Race and the Moral Character of the Modern American Experience." *The Forum* 6 (4): 1540.

Sniderman, Paul M., and Philip E. Tetlock. 1986. "Symbolic Racism: Problems of Motive Attribution in Political Analysis." *Journal of Social Issues* 42 (2): 129–150.

Sokol, Jason. 2008. *There Goes My Everything: White Southerners in the Age of Civil Rights, 1945–1975*. New York: Knopf Doubleday.

Sommers, Samuel R., and Phoebe C. Ellsworth. 2003. "How Much Do We Really Know about Race and Juries — A Review of Social Science Theory and Research Symposium: The Jury at a Crossroad: The American Experience: II. The Jury and Race." *Chicago-Kent Law Review* 78 (3): 997–1032.

Sonenshein, Raphael. 1993. *Politics in Black and White: Race and Power in Los Angeles*. Princeton, NJ: Princeton University Press.

Soss, Joe, Richard C. Fording, and Sanford F. Schram. 2011. *Disciplining the Poor:*

Neoliberal Paternalism and the Persistent Power of Race. Chicago: University of Chicago Press.

Soss, Joe, and Vesla Weaver. 2017. "Police Are Our Government: Politics, Political Science, and the Policing of Race–Class Subjugated Communities." *Annual Review of Political Science* 20 (1): 565–591.

Spence, Lester K., and Harwood McClerking. 2010. "Context, Black Empowerment, and African American Political Participation." *American Politics Research* 38 (5): 909–930.

Stanford University. n.d. "Reeb, James." Martin Luther King Jr. Research and Education Institute. Accessed 27, 2023. https://kinginstitute.stanford.edu/encyclopedia /reeb-james.

Steele, Claude M. 1997. "A Threat in the Air: How Stereotypes Shape Intellectual Identity and Performance." *American Psychologist* 52 (6): 613–629.

Stephens-Davidowitz, Seth. 2014. "The Cost of Racial Animus on a Black Candidate: Evidence Using Google Search Data." *Journal of Public Economics* 118: 26–40.

Stephens-Dougan, LaFleur. 2016. "Priming Racial Resentment without Stereotypic Cues." *Journal of Politics* 78 (3): 687–704.

———. 2020. *Race to the Bottom.* Chicago: University of Chicago Press.

Stewart, Tracie L., Ioana M. Latu, Nyla R. Branscombe, and H. Ted Denney. 2010. "Yes We Can!: Prejudice Reduction Through Seeing (Inequality) and Believing (in Social Change)." *Psychological Science* 21 (11): 1557–1562.

Stimson, James A., Michael B. MacKuen, and Robert S. Erikson. 1995. "Dynamic Representation." *American Political Science Review* 89 (3): 543–565.

Stokes, Curtis. 1990. "Tocqueville and the Problem of Racial Inequality." *Journal of Negro History* 75 (1/2): 1–15.

Stone, Jeff, Christian I. Lynch, Mike Sjomeling, and John M. Darley. 1999. "Stereotype Threat Effects on Black and White Athletic Performance." *Journal of Personality and Social Psychology* 77 (6): 1213–1227.

Sullivan, Jessica, Leigh Wilton, and Evan P. Apfelbaum. 2021. "Adults Delay Conversations about Race Because They Underestimate Children's Processing of Race." *Journal of Experimental Psychology: General* 150 (2): 395–400.

Sullivan, John L., George E. Marcus, Stanley Feldman, and James E. Piereson. 1981. "The Sources of Political Tolerance: A Multivariate Analysis." *American Political Science Review* 75 (1): 92–106.

Tajfel, Henri, and John C. Turner. 1986. "The Social Identity Theory of Intergroup Behavior." *Psychology of Intergroup Relations* 81 (1): 7–24.

Tate, Katherine. 1991. "Black Political Participation in the 1984 and 1988 Presidential Elections." *American Political Science Review* 85 (4): 1159–1176.

Teixeira, Cátia P., Colin Wayne Leach, and Russell Spears. 2022. "White Americans' Belief in Systemic Racial Injustice and in-Group Identification Affect Reactions to (Peaceful vs. Destructive) 'Black Lives Matter' Protest." *Psychology of Violence* 12 (4): 280–292.

Teixeira, Ruy A. 1987. *Why Americans Don't Vote: Turnout Decline in the United States, 1960–1984.* Westport, CT: Greenwood.

Teorell, Jan, and Mariano Torcal. 2007. "Political Participation: Mapping the Terrain." In *Citizenship and Involvement in European Democracies: A Comparative Analysis,* edited by José Ramón Montero, 334–357. London: Routledge.

Terkildsen, Nayda. 1993. "When White Voters Evaluate Black Candidates: The Processing Implications of Candidate Skin Color, Prejudice, and Self-Monitoring." *American Journal of Political Science* 37 (4): 1032–1053.

Tesler, Michael. 2012. "The Spillover of Racialization into Health Care: How President Obama Polarized Public Opinion by Racial Attitudes and Race." *American Journal of Political Science* 56 (3): 690–704.

Tesler, Michael. 2016. *Post-Racial or Most-Racial?: Race and Politics in the Obama Era.* Chicago: University of Chicago Press.

Tesler, Michael, and David O. Sears. 2010. *Obama's Race: The 2008 Election and the Dream of a Post-Racial America.* Chicago: University of Chicago Press.

Theiss-Morse, Elizabeth, and John R. Hibbing. 2005. "Citizenship and Civic Engagement." *Annual Review of Political Science* 8 (1): 227–249. https://doi.org/10.1146/annurev.polisci.8.082103.104829.

Tilly, Charles, Ernesto Castañeda, Lesley J. Wood. 2019. *Social Movements, 1768–2018.* New York: Routledge.

Tocqueville, Alexis de. 2000. *Democracy in America.* Trans. and ed. Harvey C. Mansfield and Delba Winthrop. Chicago: University of Chicago Press.

Torr, Berna M. 2011. "The Changing Relationship between Education and Marriage in the United States, 1940–2000." *Journal of Family History* 36 (4): 483–503.

Turner, John C., and Katherine J. Reynolds. 2003. "Why Social Dominance Theory Has Been Falsified." *British Journal of Social Psychology* 42 (2): 199–206.

Turner, John C., R. K. Brown, and H. Tajfel. 1979. "Social Comparison and Group Interest in In-Group Favouritism." *European Journal of Social Psychology* 9 (2): 187–204.

Tyler, Tom R., and Robert J. Boeckmann. 1997. "Three Strikes and You Are Out, But Why? The Psychology of Public Support for Punishing Rule Breakers." *Law and Society Review* 31 (2): 237–266.

Valentino, Nicholas A., and Ted Brader. 2011. "The Sword's Other Edge: Perceptions of Discrimination and Racial Policy Opinion after Obama." *Public Opinion Quarterly* 75 (2): 201–226.

Valentino, Nicholas A., Krysha Gregorowicz, and Eric W. Groenendyk. 2009. "Efficacy, Emotions and the Habit of Participation." *Political Behavior* 31 (3): 307–330.

Valentino, Nicholas A., Vincent L. Hutchings, and Ismail K. White. 2002. "Cues That Matter: How Political Ads Prime Racial Attitudes during Campaigns." *American Political Science Review* 96 (1): 75–90.

Valentino, Nicholas A., Fabian G. Neuner, and L. Matthew Vandenbroek. 2018.

"The Changing Norms of Racial Political Rhetoric and the End of Racial Priming." *Journal of Politics* 80 (3): 757–771.

Valentino, Nicholas A., and David O. Sears. 2005. "Old Times There Are Not Forgotten: Race and Partisan Realignment in the Contemporary South." *American Journal of Political Science* 49 (3): 672–688.

Van Zomeren, Martijn, Russell Spears, Agneta H. Fischer, and Colin Wayne Leach. 2004. "Put Your Money Where Your Mouth Is! Explaining Collective Action Tendencies Through Group-Based Anger and Group Efficacy." *Journal of Personality and Social Psychology* 87: 649–664.

Vavrek, Lynn, and Douglas Rivers. 2008. "The 2006 Cooperative Congressional Election Study." *Journal of Elections, Public Opinion and Parties* 18 (4): 355–366.

Verba, Sidney, Kay Lehman Schlozman, and Henry E. Brady. 1995. *Voice and Equality: Civic Voluntarism in American Politics*. Cambridge, MA: Harvard University Press.

Verba, Sidney, and Norman H. Nie. 1987. *Participation in America: Political Democracy and Social Equality*. Chicago: University of Chicago Press.

Verba, Sidney, Norman H. Nie, and Jae-on Kim. 1978. *Participation and Political Equality: A Seven-Nation Comparison*. New York: Cambridge University Press.

Walker, Samuel. 1980. *Popular Justice: A History of American Criminal Justice*. New York: Oxford University Press.

Walsh, Katherine Cramer. 2007. *Talking about Race: Community Dialogues and the Politics of Difference*. Chicago: University of Chicago Press.

Wanzo, Rebecca. 2021. "How Long, Not Long: A Take on Black Joy." *Film Quarterly* 74 (4): 51–55.

Ward, Ian. 2021. "The Democrats' Privileged College-Kid Problem." Politico, October 9, 2021. https://www.politico.com/news/magazine/2021/10/09/david-shor-democrats-privileged-college-kid-problem-514992.

Warren, Mark. 2010. *Fire in the Heart: How White Activists Embrace Racial Justice*. New York: Oxford University Press.

Wasow, Omar. 2020. "Agenda Seeding: How 1960s Black Protests Moved Elites, Public Opinion and Voting." *American Political Science Review* 114 (3): 638–659.

Weaver, Vesla M. 2012. "The Significance of Policy Failures in Political Development: The Law Enforcement Assistance Administration and the Growth of the Carceral State." *Living Legislation: Durability, Change, and the Politics of American Lawmaking*: 221–254.

Weaver, Vesla M., and Amy E. Lerman. 2010. "Political Consequences of the Carceral State." *American Political Science Review* 104 (4): 817–833.

Weaver, Vesla, Gwen Prowse, and Spencer Piston. 2020. "Withdrawing and Drawing In: Political Discourse in Policed Communities." *Journal of Race, Ethnicity, and Politics* 5 (3): 604–647.

Weber, Christopher R., Howard Lavine, Leonie Huddy, and Christopher M. Federico. 2014. "Placing Racial Stereotypes in Context: Social Desirability and the Politics of Racial Hostility." *American Journal of Political Science* 58 (1): 63–78.

Westwood, Sean J., and Erik Peterson. 2020. "The Inseparability of Race and Partisanship in the United States." *Political Behavior*. Accessed June 16, 2022. https://doi.org/10.1007/s11109-020-09648-9.

White, Ismail K. 2007. "When Race Matters and When It Doesn't: Racial Group Differences in Response to Racial Cues." *American Political Science Review* 101 (2): 339–354.

White, Ismail K., and Chryl N. Laird. 2021. *Steadfast Democrats: How Social Forces Shape Black Political Behavior*. Princeton, NJ: Princeton University Press.

Wilcox, Clyde. 1990. "Religion and Politics among White Evangelicals: The Impact of Religious Variables on Political Attitudes." *Review of Religious Research* 32 (1): 27–42.

Williams, Princess. 2021. "The Politics of Place: How Southern Identity Shapes Americans' Political Beliefs." Doctoral diss, University of Michigan. http://deepblue.lib.umich.edu/handle/2027.42/171439.

Wilson, James Q., and George Kelling. 1982. "Broken Windows: The Police and Neighborhood Safety." *Atlantic Monthly* 249 (3): 29.

Wispé, Lauren. 1986. "The Distinction between Sympathy and Empathy: To Call Forth a Concept, a Word Is Needed." *Journal of Personality and Social Psychology* 50 (2): 314–321.

Wolak, Jennifer. 2018. "Feelings of Political Efficacy in the Fifty States." *Political Behavior* 40 (3): 763–784.

Wolfinger, Raymond E., and Steven J. Rosenstone. 1980. *Who Votes?* New Haven, CT: Yale University Press.

Woodly, Deva R. 2021. *Reckoning: Black Lives Matter and the Democratic Necessity of Social Movements*. New York: Oxford University Press.

Woodward, C. Vann. 1938. *Tom Watson: Agrarian Rebel*. Reprint. Eastford, CT: Martino Fine Books.

Yellow Horse, Aggie J., Karen Kuo, Eleanor K. Seaton, and Edward D. Vargas. 2021. "Asian Americans' Indifference to Black Lives Matter: The Role of Nativity, Belonging and Acknowledgment of Anti-Black Racism." *Social Sciences* 10 (5): 168.

Young, Michele D., and Julie Laible. 2000. "White Racism, Antiracism, and School Leadership Preparation." *Journal of School Leadership* 10 (5): 374–415.

Zhang, Yan, Lening Zhang, and Francis Benton. 2022. "Hate Crimes against Asian Americans." *American Journal of Criminal Justice* 47 (3): 441–461.

Zizzo, Daniel John. 2010. "Experimenter Demand Effects in Economic Experiments." *Experimental Economics* 13 (1): 75–98.

Index

Page numbers in italics refer to figures and tables. Where there is a range of italicized numbers, each number within the range points to a figure or table.

imprisonment: American rate of, 122–23;
American rate of vs. other Western
countries, 121; rehabilitation as goal
of, 123. *See also* criminal legal system;
police, attitudes toward
Independent party, and racial sympathy, 79
inequality, racial, 1–2, 150
insurrection, 2020 election and racial sympathy rates, 58–59
interviews: of racial justice activists, 145–51,
149, 160–61, 240–43; on racial sympathy,
45–47, 154–59, *157*; as research tool, 142–
44; skepticism expressed in, 140, 142,
151, 161, 186. *See also* racial sympathy
index; surveys; vignettes
Iyer, Aarti, 40

Jackson, Jimmie Lee, 247n2
Jardina, Ashley, 66, 185
Jim Crow segregation, attitudes toward,
47–48
Johnson, Josh, 69, 71
Johnson, Lyndon B., 107, 139

Katz, Irwin, 33
Kerner Commission, 139
Kinder, Donald, 19, 23, 24, 107, 110
King, Martin Luther, Jr., 46
Kofkin, Jennifer A., 30
Kondrich, Michelle, 69

Latino Americans, 6, 190–91
Lavine, Howard, 141
Lenz, Gabriel, 194–95
Lewis, Amanda E., 32
Lewis, John, 18
liberalism: parodied, 69–70; and racial sympathy, 78–80, *79*, 86–89, *88*, 97, 185. *See
also* Democratic Party
limited government index, and redistribution, 102
Los Angeles (CA), 3

MacKuen, Michael, 48
March on Washington, 17
Marcus, George E., 48
Martin, Trayvon, murder of, 127
mass incarceration (term), 121. *See also*
criminal legal system
McCain, John, 51

McConnaughy, Corrine M., 87, 189
measurement, of racial sympathy, 36–38;
arguments over, 38; data comprising,
53–67, *54*, *56*, *59–60*, *63–64*; development
of new, 42–47; via in-depth interviews,
43–44; via listening, 42–44; previous efforts in, 38–42; self-reporting vs. implicit,
39–40; sources for, 50–53; via surveys,
45–46, 50–53; vignettes (fictional) com-
prise, 47–50. *See also* interviews; racial
sympathy (of whites toward Blacks);
surveys; vignettes
Mechanical Turk (MTurk) surveys: 2013, 44,
45–46, 53; 2015, 52–53; 2017, 53
media, prejudice in crime coverage, 123
Mendelberg, Tali, 90, 93, 136
Michener, Jamila, 118–19
Miller, Orloff, 3
Minneapolis (MN), police issues and Floyd
murder, 126. *See also* Floyd, George,
murder of
mobilization: Black/white leadership and,
194–95; during BLM, 175–78, *177*; and
racial sympathy, 164–65. *See also* activism; demonstrations; political efficacy
Moore, Steven T., 189
Morrison, Toni, 147
multiracial Americans: "one-drop rule," 26;
self-identification of, 6–7
Myrdal, Gunnar, on "Negro problem," 14

National Research Council, 48
Native Americans, 6, 111, 191
"Negro problem," 14–15
Nelson, Thomas, 19
Neuman, W. Russell, 48
Newcomb, Theodore, 73
New Jersey, 110
New Yorker, 69
New York Times, 130; columns on white
Democrats, 69–70
1960s, 17, 151

Obama, Barack Hussein, 2–3, 15–16, 55;
attitudes and activism under, 165–67,
174, 191; and racial sympathy, 161, 170,
171, *222*; survey question(s) on, 46, 51;
victory of (2008), 20–24, 71; and voting,
171–74, *173*
Ollerenshaw, Trent, 185

Chicago Studies in American Politics

A SERIES EDITED BY SUSAN HERBST, LAWRENCE R. JACOBS, ADAM J. BERINSKY, AND FRANCES LEE;

BENJAMIN I. PAGE, EDITOR EMERITUS

Series titles, continued from front matter:

AMERICA'S INEQUALITY TRAP *by Nathan J. Kelly*

GOOD ENOUGH FOR GOVERNMENT WORK: THE PUBLIC REPUTATION CRISIS IN AMERICA (AND WHAT WE CAN DO TO FIX IT) *by Amy E. Lerman*

WHO WANTS TO RUN? HOW THE DEVALUING OF POLITICAL OFFICE DRIVES POLARIZATION *by Andrew B. Hall*

FROM POLITICS TO THE PEWS: HOW PARTISANSHIP AND THE POLITICAL ENVIRONMENT SHAPE RELIGIOUS IDENTITY *by Michele F. Margolis*

THE INCREASINGLY UNITED STATES: HOW AND WHY AMERICAN POLITICAL BEHAVIOR NATIONALIZED *by Daniel J. Hopkins*

LEGACIES OF LOSING IN AMERICAN POLITICS *by Jeffrey K. Tulis and Nicole Mellow*

LEGISLATIVE STYLE *by William Bernhard and Tracy Sulkin*

WHY PARTIES MATTER: POLITICAL COMPETITION AND DEMOCRACY IN THE AMERICAN SOUTH *by John H. Aldrich and John D. Griffin*

NEITHER LIBERAL NOR CONSERVATIVE: IDEOLOGICAL INNOCENCE IN THE AMERICAN PUBLIC *by Donald R. Kinder and Nathan P. Kalmoe*

STRATEGIC PARTY GOVERNMENT: WHY WINNING TRUMPS IDEOLOGY *by Gregory Koger and Matthew J. Lebo*

POST-RACIAL OR MOST-RACIAL? RACE AND POLITICS IN THE OBAMA ERA *by Michael Tesler*

THE POLITICS OF RESENTMENT: RURAL CONSCIOUSNESS IN WISCONSIN AND THE RISE OF SCOTT WALKER *by Katherine J. Cramer*

LEGISLATING IN THE DARK: INFORMATION AND POWER IN THE HOUSE OF REPRESENTATIVES *by James M. Curry*

WHY WASHINGTON WON'T WORK: POLARIZATION, POLITICAL TRUST, AND THE GOVERNING CRISIS *by Marc J. Hetherington and Thomas J. Rudolph*

WHO GOVERNS? PRESIDENTS, PUBLIC OPINION, AND MANIPULATION *by James N. Druckman and Lawrence R. Jacobs*

TRAPPED IN AMERICA'S SAFETY NET: ONE FAMILY'S STRUGGLE *by Andrea Louise Campbell*

ARRESTING CITIZENSHIP: THE DEMOCRATIC CONSEQUENCES OF AMERICAN CRIME CONTROL *by Amy E. Lerman and Vesla M. Weaver*

HOW THE STATES SHAPED THE NATION: AMERICAN ELECTORAL INSTITUTIONS AND VOTER TURNOUT, *1920–2000 by Melanie Jean Springer*

WHITE-COLLAR GOVERNMENT: THE HIDDEN ROLE OF CLASS IN ECONOMIC POLICY MAKING *by Nicholas Carnes*

HOW PARTISAN MEDIA POLARIZE AMERICA *by Matthew Levendusky*

CHANGING MINDS OR CHANGING CHANNELS? PARTISAN NEWS IN AN AGE OF CHOICE *by Kevin Arceneaux and Martin Johnson*

THE POLITICS OF BELONGING: RACE, PUBLIC OPINION, AND IMMIGRATION *by Natalie Masuoka and Jane Junn*

TRADING DEMOCRACY FOR JUSTICE: CRIMINAL CONVICTIONS AND THE DECLINE OF NEIGHBORHOOD POLITICAL PARTICIPATION *by Traci Burch*

POLITICAL TONE: HOW LEADERS TALK AND WHY *by Roderick P. Hart, Jay P. Childers, and Colene J. Lind*

LEARNING WHILE GOVERNING: EXPERTISE AND ACCOUNTABILITY IN THE EXECUTIVE BRANCH *by Sean Gailmard and John W. Patty*